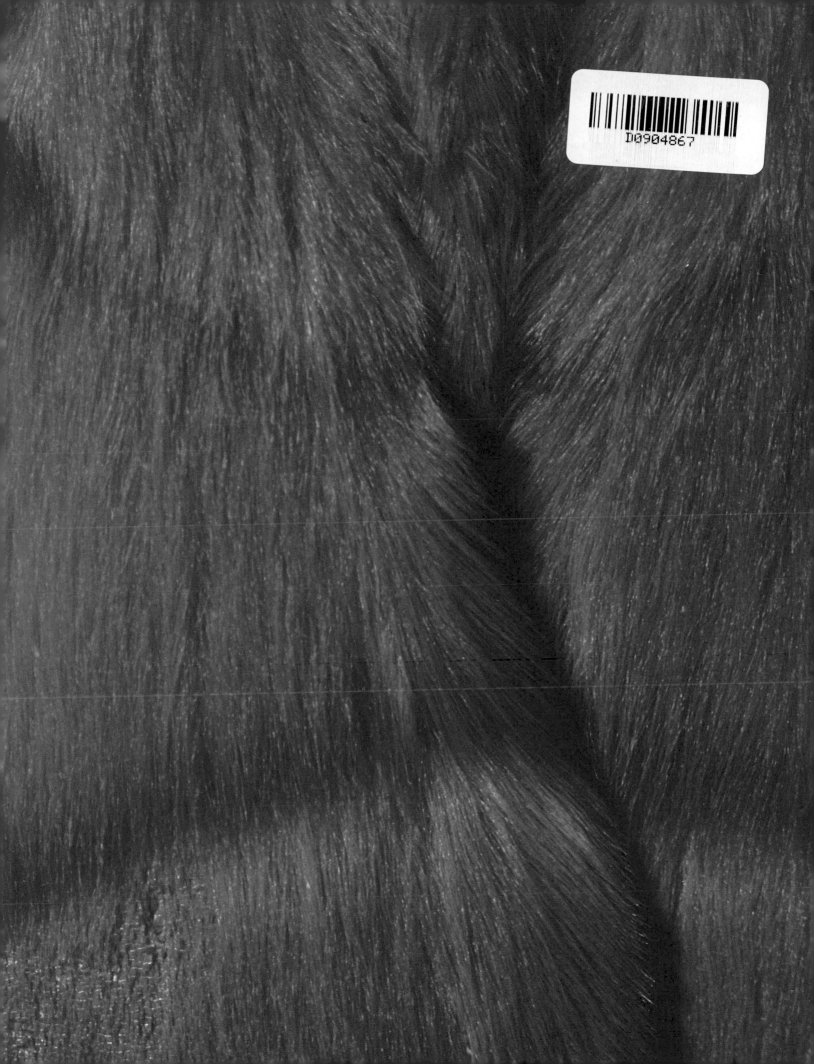

AUSTRALIAN
INSECTS

A NATURAL HISTORY

AUSTRALIAN
INSECTS
A NATURAL HISTORY

BERT BRUNET

This book is dedicated to my soulmate, Venus.

Published in Australia in 2000 by Reed New Holland
an imprint of New Holland Publishers (Australia) Pty Ltd
Sydney • Auckland • London • Cape Town
14 Aquatic Drive Frenchs Forest NSW 2086 Australia
218 Lake Road Northcote Auckland New Zealand
24 Nutford Place London W1H 6DQ United Kingdom
80 McKenzie Street Cape Town 8001 South Africa

National Library of Australia Cataloguing-in-Publication Data:

Brunet, Bert
Australian insects: a natural history
Bibliography.
Includes index.
ISBN 1 876334 43 6
1. Insects – Australia. 2. Insects – Australia – Anatomy.
I. Title.
595.70994

PROJECT EDITOR Fiona Doig
EDITORS Roderic Campbell, Fiona Doig
DESIGNER Avril Makula
REPRODUCTION Colour Symphony, Singapore
PRINTER Kyodo, Singapore

PHOTOGRAPHS
OPPOSITE Robber fly (*Asilus* species), alert for winged prey.
PAGES 6–7 Cotton harlequin jewel bug (*Tectocoris* species).
PAGE 8 Emperor gum caterpillar (*Opodiphthera* species).
ENDPAPERS Emperor gum moth; wing eyespot close-up

The body copy is set to 10 pt Revival 555 BT

Contents

Preface

From an early age I was greatly encouraged by my parents, neighbours and teachers to pursue an interest in nature. Curiosity prompted me into asking many questions, but first-hand experiences in the garden proved to be the best teacher. One of my first memories, from when I was about four years old, is of my grandfather, with a deft sweep of a cobweb broom or rake, shaking greengrocer and yellow Monday cicadas out of fruit trees in the backyard. Before handing them to me, however, he would usually snip off half of one of their forewings with his nail scissors—an unhappy event for the cicadas, which desperately struggled to fly, but couldn't.

My interest in insects was greatly nurtured by my father who built me some observational breeding cages in which I kept crickets, katydids and locusts. One especially large enclosure housed cicadas during summer. My mother was a talented artist who always encouraged me to paint, draw and write about natural subjects, so I was lucky in being able to draw on the talents of both parents.

One particular incident fired my interest in nature. One mild, overcast Sunday afternoon I was helping my father sieve soil for the garden, anticipating exciting finds with every spade of soil turned over. A cocoon covered in earth suddenly caught our attention. Opening it revealed a large, brilliantly golden-coloured, male Christmas beetle (*Anoplognathus montanus*). I have never lost that sense of amazement with nature that I felt that day.

For my tenth birthday, on a visit to the Australian Museum, my parents bought me a natural history book entitled *Natural Wonders of the World*, filled with information and photographs on insects. I dreamed of creating a book on this fascinating subject. From then until I was in my late teens my father introduced me to many beautiful areas of New South Wales, where I made field observations and collected particular insects in order to identify and study them further.

I have travelled Australia to study, make observational notes, collect and photograph our marvellous insect and spider fauna. I also spent four weeks in New Guinea, at the Wau Ecology Institute, where the late Dr Linsley Gressitt made me feel most welcome. I was greatly assisted by his staff and their knowledge of the local insect fauna. Not long after this I decided to sell my insect collection, mainly because I wished to concentrate on the real-life stories of living insects in their natural habitats, to provide me with material for natural history books. Much of the work in this book is the result of years of observation, and a great deal of it has been scientifically recorded, but some insights, I fancy, are new.

For those who have not studied insects, it may be hard to have any real appreciation of just how varied in form and lifestyle they actually are. We largely owe what knowledge we do have of insects to the work of 'spare-time naturalists', amateurs, people of all ages who labour for love—their one aim being able to share nature's 'secrets' and increase our appreciation of the natural world, in which we and all other creatures are inextricably linked. By closely observing nature, we may come to understand its ways, and develop a love for its complexity and beauty.

Despite the technological advances we have made, we are still only on the threshold of the largely unexplored world of insects. My earlier book, *The Silken Web*, dealt with the ways in which spiders keep abreast of the ongoing development of their prey, the insects. This book, in contrast, focuses on how insects manage to remain one step ahead of their formidable predators, the spiders. In evolution-ary terms, it seems that the spiders will always be chasing the insects.

This book emphasises the ecological roles insects play in nature, and highlights those insects that are utilising—celebrating, even—the power of having evolved wings. Some insects, through some regression, may have reduced their wings or lost them, or else have returned to the water whence they came—although many aquatic insects have wings, too. But, for practical purposes, a single volume has to be selective so I have picked out insects that are most commonly encountered or are of particular interest.

OPPOSITE A ridgeback grasshopper (*Goniaea* species) in the wheel-web snare of a golden orb-weaving spider (*Nephila* species). Spiders have assured their place in nature by keeping pace with their insect prey. In evolutionary terms, it seems that spiders will always be chasing insects.

Acknowledgments

In a field like insects, the current state of information is constantly changing. Insects are being reclassified as new information comes to hand, and new discoveries are continually being made in this fascinating field of study.

I have consulted a wide range of sources, and this book has owed a great deal to the careful and systematic work of specialists, whose works are cited in the bibliography.

In some instances where conflict may occur between the various sources of available data, or there may have been differences in interpretation, the most plausible and reliably based information has been carefully selected. But my constant and final point of referral, particularly in relation to questions about the classification and number of species described for Australia, has been *The Insects of Australia*, published in 1991 by the Division of Entomology of the CSIRO.

To broadly cover the field, species and families representing the major orders have been selected on the basis of their being among the most interesting and most frequently seen, and of being 'typical' representatives that may hopefully illustrate our main theme. Most of the insects selected in this book are either commonly encountered in given habitats or are of economic interest. The more obscure groups are mentioned only briefly and minor families are omitted, as their existence rarely comes to the attention of most people.

Wherever possible, insects have been referred to by their common names, as these are the names with which most non-specialist readers are familiar. Scientific names have also been included, however, to assist those who wish to refer to more scholarly works dealing with taxonomy. In the appendices there is also a list of insect families, with the numbers found in Australia. There is also a common name index at the end of the book.

Measurements have been supplied for the body length and wingspan of most groups of insects represented in this work. These details have been included wherever practical in order to give a fair indication of the actual proportions of the insects.

Much of the information in this book, of course, comes from sources outside my own observations and studies and there is an enormous number of people who have quite generously contributed their time, energy and supportive interest in one way or another to the compiling of this book.

My thanks go to Derelie Evely, Kathy Metcalfe, Fiona Doig, Rosemary Milburn and Louise Egerton, who have been of great assistance in the preparation of this book; Roderic Campbell for his brilliant attention to detail; Avril Makula for her elegant book design; and to Ted Edwards, Division of Entomology, CSIRO, for his invaluable advice and constructive criticism.

My thanks also extend to the Australian Museum, in College Street, Sydney, as it has greatly influenced my learning since early childhood through its highly educational displays and presentations of natural history for public viewing. I thank my wonderful parents Herbert William Brunet and Lyla May Brunet, who made it possible for me to devote the many years of time required for the work involved; my beautiful sister Lyla Kimble and her family; and Beverly Ruth Gibbons and Rudy Mulder for helping steer me onwards in learning more about nature. Appreciation is also extended to many friends and entomological colleagues in the Society for Insect Studies for their helpful discussions over the years, particularly David Hain, Joseph Stivala and Graham Owen, whose companionship I have always found most congenial. I am appreciative of the spontaneous sharing experienced with my children Alice and Daniel, who have always shown a keen interest in learning from nature. I should also like to thank Lynn Brunet and Anthony Saunders for their companionship and supportive interest on a number of field trips over the years. Very special thanks go to Joseph and Yuri Apap for their love and supportive interest, demonstrated throughout the years. Finally, and most appreciatively, I thank my dearest friend and soulmate Venus for her unconditional love, invaluable suggestions and constructive criticism throughout the work.

OPPOSITE A bulldog ant (*Myrmecia* species). The large, ferocious ants of this genus are considered to be the prototype of the most primitive living ants, which are represented elsewhere in the world only by the extinct genera *Prionomyrmex* and *Ameghinoa*. Fossils have been found that date back to the Oligocene Epoch (around 40 million years ago).

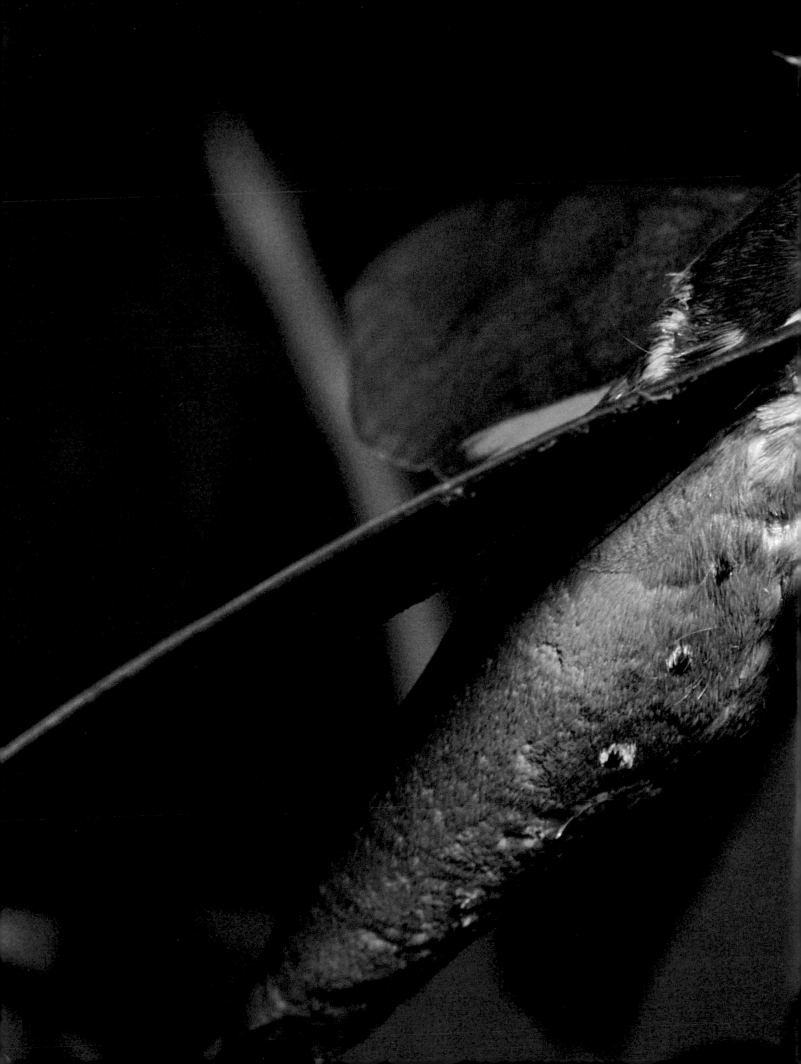

Introduction

Almost 900 years ago, a far-sighted woman named Hildegard of Bingen said: 'In the midst of all other creatures, humanity is the most significant and yet the most dependent upon other creatures'. Yet it has taken us humans too long to grasp the full extent of this dependency. We have only recently begun to understand how the importance of the larger animals goes beyond their value to us as providers of food. It has taken us this long to begin to understand their role as links in the chain of life—and in the meantime we have jeopardised so many of them that the preservation of the links in this ecological chain are weakening. It is even more difficult for us to grasp the even greater diversity and far stranger forms of these much smaller animals—the insects—and their ways of interacting with their environment. How significant, then, are these small creatures?

There are probably more insects than any other life form; certainly, they comprise more species than all other members of the animal kingdom combined. Insects fill every available terrestrial habitat and their lifestyles have become highly refined from intense competition for niches associated with procuring food, shelter and nesting sites.

Insects are unrivalled in their diversity of form and colour, yet our knowledge of them is still only partial. So many species, particularly those inhabiting the shrinking tropical rainforest regions, remain undiscovered; of those that have been discovered, many remain inadequately described—with the result that little is known of their lifestyles, habits and preferred habitats, and their ecological relevance for the complex environmental systems they inhabit.

Humans are all members of the same species (*Homo sapiens*) and we have only been on Earth for a relatively brief span of geological time. When humans appeared, insects were already very ancient.

Owing to the sheer numbers of insects and their enormous diversity, together with their powers of adaptability, insects have developed specialisations to a remarkable degree over their long evolutionary history—to an extent not seen in larger animals.

INSECTS' RELATIVES

The arthropods, the larger group to which insects belong, are thought to have arisen from early annelid-like stock of the phylum Annelida; present-day worms still resemble that group, having retained a clear segmentation in all their embryonic stages. From their earliest appearance, arthropods such as centipedes, millipedes, scorpions and spiders, all developed one pair of jointed appendages, which serve as 'jaws'. But the most important evolutionary change from annelids to arthropods was the development of the hard exoskeleton, or outer skeleton. The story of how arthropods have evolved is a long one, and fragments of their interesting history are still being uncovered in fossil finds throughout the world.

The superphylum Arthropoda contains the largest number of living invertebrate species and includes the class Insecta, or true insects. It also includes the following major, living classes: Malacostraca (for instance, crabs, crayfish, lobsters and slaters), Chilopoda and Diplopoda (for instance, centipedes and millipedes), and Arachnida (spiders and scorpions). The second-largest invertebrate phylum is the molluscs (Mollusca), with well over 80 000 described living species. As an aquatic group, molluscs have achieved the widest possible adaptive radiation, having mastered marine, freshwater, and terrestrial habitats.

ANCIENT CREATURES

Insects constitute an extraordinarily ancient group; they established themselves 100 million years before the dinosaurs—and the 'age of insects' continues to this day. They have survived catastrophic global changes—such as large-scale volcanic eruptions and massive upheavals of the Earth's crust, widespread changes in weather patterns and climatic conditions—and outlived the dinosaurs.

Fossil finds of insects show that insects existed at least as far back as the middle Devonian Period—some 370 million years ago.

PREVIOUS PAGES Yellow-winged hawk moth (*Gnathothlibus erotus eras*). Hawk moths have evolved a streamlined body, narrow pointed forewings, and an extremely long, coiled proboscis. They hover to feed on the nectar of deep-centred flowers.

OPPOSITE Leaf-roller caterpillars (*Cryptoptila* species). These aggregating caterpillars roll leaves and stems of their host plant, and bind them together with web-like silk. They feed, grow and pupate within this communal shelter.

OTHER ARTHROPOD GROUPS

CRUSTACEANS
phylum Crustacea
class Malacostraca

ABOVE A millipede (*Polydes-mido* species), belonging to the phylum Uniramia.

Crustaceans are readily distinguished by the presence of two pairs of antennae, behind which are the mandibles, followed by two pairs of ancillary mouthparts, the first and second maxillae.

The appendages of the main part of the body are much less uniform, and the enormous variation within the group—of body, limbs and functions—has resulted in around 35 000 species being described, including marine, freshwater and terrestrial forms. Crustaceans include the familiar crabs, lobsters, shrimps, sea slaters, land slaters (for instance, *Porcellio scaber*, which often may be found under stones in your garden) and sandhoppers.

Crustaceans vary in size, from the microscopic water flea (*Alonella* species) to the giant spider crab (*Macrocheira kaempferi*), 3.6 metres claw to claw.

CENTIPEDES AND MILLIPEDES
phylum Uniramia
class Chilopoda and class Diplopoda

ABOVE A jumping spider (*Cosmophasis bitaeniata*). Spiders and scorpions are placed in phylum Chelicerata.

These are elongated arthropods, with many leg-bearing segments: the centipedes (class Chilopoda) number 5000 species worldwide, and millipedes (class Diplopoda) number 6500 species worldwide.

Centipedes have flattened bodies, with one pair of antennae, three pairs of mandibles, and a pair of segmented appendages per body segment. The first pair of appendages, directly behind the mandibles, are modified into enlarged claws, which house poison glands. The large posterior pair of appendages are modified for pinning down prey, prior to biting it. Centipedes are widely distributed in tropical and temperate regions and live in soil, among leaf litter, and beneath decaying timber and stones, where they prey upon a large range of small creatures, including spiders and insect larvae.

Millipedes are cylindrical-shaped creatures with one pair of antennae and two pairs of mandibles; they have double segments (two body segments fused together), each bearing two pairs of legs. Being slow-moving animals, many millipedes have developed repellent secretions as a defensive strategy. Millipedes have 30 to over 200 legs, according to species, but never a thousand.

ABOVE Recent Australian research has disclosed 41 new species of velvet worms, making Australia the most velvet-worm rich region in the world.

ARACHNIDS—SPIDERS AND SCORPIONS
phylum Chelicerata
class Arachnida

Arachnids are readily distinguished from insects by having their head and thorax fused as a single body unit. The largest order of the Arachnida is the Araneae, the spiders, consisting of well over 35 000 described species. Scorpions are the oldest-known terrestrial arachnids, having been found in fossil records stretching back to the Silurian Period.

Spiders are distinctive from all other arthropods in having abdominal silk-making glands, spinnerets and poison fangs. They protect their eggs in silken sacs. Their first pair of appendages are pointed and fang-like, and provided with poison glands.

The pedipalps of the males are modified, forming the organs of copulation. However, many female spiders are known to devour the males of their species following copulation. So, in many species this has been overcome by developing males that are smaller than the size of the spider's normal prey, which means that the characteristic attacking action of the females is not triggered, and these males remain safe.

VELVET WORMS—THE ENIGMATIC ARTHROPOD
phylum Onychophora
class Onychophora

Early ancestors of terrestrial arthropods included creatures like the velvet worms, of the genera *Peripatus* and *Peripatopsis*, families Peripatidae and Peripatopsidae in the class Onychophora. Although these curious creatures are classed with the arthropods, much remains enigmatic about them, such as their 80 legs and velvet-like appearance. Velvet worms have a pair of ringed antennae, a pair of secretory lobes and a ventrally located mouth accompanied by chitinous mandibles acting as jaws. They live among the cool, damp conditions of moss-covered, decaying timber, feeding on vegetation, snails, worms and small insects such as termites.

A recent morphological analysis of specimens collected throughout Australia has revealed 41 new species of velvet worms. Australia thus has the greatest number of these creatures in the world.

In Australia over 400 fossil insect species—representing some 20 orders—have been described from deposits ranging in age from the Upper Carboniferous Period (280 million years old) to the Pliocene Epoch (5 million years old).

If we could trace back even further the ancestral form from which insects derived, its origin would most likely be found in the terrestrial branch of the arthropods, perhaps as far back as 500 million years ago. These early forms most likely lived along the shorelines, and later branched out in three directions: into water, onto land or into the air.

Evolutionary developments

The key to the staying power of insects was their development of wings. This development was preceded by, and probably arose out of, gliding flaps that evolved from the respiratory gills of aquatic ancestors. Unlike those of flying vertebrates, the wings of insects are not modifications of arms or legs, nor have they evolved from them.

The selection pressures towards flight steered wingless arthropods into a relatively fast transition towards wing development during the Carboniferous Period (300 million years ago). Thus flight was achieved by insects early in the history of life forms on Earth. In contrast, vertebrates postponed their full conquest of the air for more than 100 million years; by the time they achieved the power of flight—160 million years ago—the Mesozoic Era was well advanced.

It is their wings that set the insects apart from all other invertebrates and it is chiefly by their wings that they have been scientifically grouped into the orders by which we classify them. Beetles, for instance, have been grouped into the order Coleoptera, which means 'sheath-wings'; Lepidoptera, the order moths and butterflies are placed in, means 'scale-wings'. Another major feature used to classify insects into orders and families is the system of veins on their wings. Chapter Three in this book takes a closer look at the wings of insects.

Prior to the Permian Period—300 million years ago—all insect forms had essentially similar growth processes. They emerged from the egg as miniature look-alikes of their parents, with the same lifestyles and also resembling them in all but two respects—they lacked wings and were unable to reproduce. Their gradual

growth to maturity was in steps marked by a series of moults as they outgrew their old exoskeletons. In this process the body grows until it becomes too large for its outer casing (the exoskeleton), whereupon the insect sheds the outer casing and replaces it with a new, larger one. In the course of this process, wing buds appear on the outside of the insect's body and progressively develop with each moult. This growth process continues until the final moult, at which time the insect becomes an adult, developing mature sexual characteristics and complete wings, but their bodily structure changes very little throughout their life cycle.

However, during the Permian Period, changes began to take place in the way some insects developed. Many insect forms began to develop more complex life cycles after they emerged from the egg. The immature forms (or larvae) of these insects were very different in bodily structure to their parents and, generally, led quite different lives. Although each of these larvae underwent a series of moults as it grew, to attain maturity it also had to undergo an entirely new phase of change—as a pupa.

The pupal phase is like a secondary egg stage, an immobile process, during which their wings (which had been developing internally) become visible on the outside of the pupal case (often with no more than a line indicating where the wings are forming). On emerging from this pupal phase, the insect usually takes flight as an adult, which has a very different lifestyle to that of the insect's previous growth phases. Chapter Two looks more closely at insects' reproductive cycles and lifestyles.

This new development in the life cycle of insects meant that both adult and juvenile forms of the same creature would not have to compete with each other, as each could utilise two very different types of habitats and food sources during the course of its life. These more modern—or more evolved—insects were better adapted to take advantage of a greater range of ecological conditions.

This set the stage for the great increase and diversity of insect populations, and for insects to radiate their kind into virtually every available niche and habitat throughout the terrestrial landscape.

The winged insects that exist now, and are gathered and classified under the extensive class

INSECTS—SUPERCLASS HEXAPODA

PSEUDO INSECTS

CLASS ELLIPURA	CLASS DIPLURA
springtails order Collembola proturans order Protura	diplurans order Diplura

TRUE INSECTS—CLASS INSECTA

The orders of the true insects are arranged here
according to their lines of evolution, beginning with
the primitive wingless insects and moving on to the primitive
winged insects and then modern winged insects.

PRIMITIVE WINGLESS INSECTS—APTERYGOTES

Archaeognaths (bristletails)	order Archaeognatha
silverfish	order Thysanura

WINGED INSECTS—PTERYGOTES

Primitive Winged Insects—Exopterygotes

mayflies	order Ephemeroptera
damselflies and dragonflies	order Odonata
stoneflies	order Plecoptera
cockroaches	order Blattodea
termites	order Isoptera
praying mantids	order Mantodea
earwigs	order Dermaptera
katydids, true grasshoppers and crickets	order Orthoptera
stick and leaf insects	order Phasmatodea
web-spinners	order Embioptera
bark-lice	order Psocoptera
animal-lice	order Phthiraptera
aphids, mealy bugs, scale insects, gall-forming insects, cicadas, bugs, leaf-hoppers and allies	order Hemiptera
thrips	order Thysanoptera

Modern Winged Insects—Endopterygotes

alderflies and dobsonflies	order Megaloptera
lacewings	order Neuroptera
beetles and weevils	order Coleoptera
stylops	order Strepsiptera
scorpion-flies	order Mecoptera
fleas	order Siphonaptera
flies, mosquitoes and midges	order Diptera
caddis-flies	order Trichoptera
moths, skippers and butterflies	order Lepidoptera
sawflies, wasps, ants and bees	order Hymenoptera

Insecta, are divided into two groups reflecting their evolutionary development and the way their wings develop. Insects whose growth cycle still follows the more ancient pattern—as a series of moults with wing buds developing externally—are called exopterygotes. The more modern insects—whose growth cycle includes the pupal stage—are called endopterygotes.

ADAPTATION AND DIVERSITY

Natural selection has produced innumerable adaptations that help insects protect themselves and escape threatening situations, or conceal themselves to evade danger, and to hunt prey, find food, disperse and colonise unfavourable habitats. Every bristle, spine, joint and appendage of an insect serves its purpose precisely. Many species have, over time, developed complex survival strategies and behaviours; many others have evolved shapes or colourings that allow them to merge perfectly with their surroundings. Insects have also combined to form social groups working together for a common purpose, and have constructed shelters for their colonies, or for themselves to pupate in, for instance, or for their young. Their range of dispersal and their range of activities are indications of their powers of adaptation. Chapter Four looks at the various strategies, behaviours and adaptations different species have adopted for their survival.

In this long process of adaptation and survival, the fortunes of insects (with most other animals) have been closely linked with those of plants. Insects have been lured from a strictly ground-dwelling existence solely by plants. A symbiotic relationship has developed between plants and insects, based largely on the insects' need for food and the plants' need to propagate. The power of flight, apart from its other benefits, gives insects the ability to move easily from flower to flower in the search for nectar and also enables them to search more widely for food sources. Plants benefit in that crosspollination can take place effectively over greater distances.

Plants and insects have also influenced each other's form or appearance. Plants developed particular colours or shapes to attract the insects they need. Similarly, the shape, texture and colour of leaves, leaf veins, bark, flowers, hairs, spines and thorns of plants have all been significant influences on the body-shapes of insects and the colours they use for camouflage. Some of the implications of this special relationship between insects and plants are looked at in Chapters Four and Five.

Among such a widely diverse group, the external anatomy varies so greatly that it is difficult to consider any single insect as a 'typical' representative of its class. However, an orthopteroid insect such as the true grasshopper (locust) is a classic example, as its habits and features are not overspecialised. The word 'insect' refers to all those terrestrial animals with segmented, flexible joints and six legs, whose outer body surface is hardened to form an exoskeleton—something like a suit of armour. The body capsule is divided into a series of segments (or compartmented portions) that have specialised appendages such as antennae, genitalia, mandibles, rostrums, limbs, wings, cerci, and so on. Variations in anatomical details are dealt with extensively in Chapter One.

Of course, many of the anatomical variations between insects have to do with bodily features associated with their reproductive anatomy and courtship habits and requirements. For an adult insect, finding a mate and procreating is perhaps its most important activity—to ensure the species continues. Although some insects (for example, aphids) can reproduce without sex, most insects require sperm from the male to be combined with ova from the female for reproduction. Among some very primitive insects, the male and female do not even meet —the male simply leaves a packet of sperm in some place where a female will find it. Other insects either pass the sperm directly to the female or in a special casing (a spermatophore) as they couple. Most insects have specially interlocking genital parts, designed so that insects of different species cannot mate with each other.

Insects that do meet and couple need to be able to find each other and select partners. To this end, some insects have developed specialised attractants or behaviours or anatomical distinctions. Scent, sight, touch and sound play vital roles in bringing the sexes together. For example, the large, plumed antennae of male emperor moths (family Saturniidae) can pick up the scent emanating from females of their species from several kilometres away. The sounds some insects produce and their colouring have courtship functions, too. Their courtship ritual often includes intricate dance routines and related sexual behaviour before mating—like the mating wheel of the dragonfly or the way the males of butterflies, such as the wanderer butterfly (*Danaus plexippus plexippus*), brush the head and antennae of the female as the pair perform their upwardly spiralling courtship dance in the air.

The size, structure and number of eggs laid vary depending on the species and environmental factors such as food availability and climatic conditions. According to the species, a female may lay 1–20 eggs or (as some moths do) up to 18 000. Many species of female insects store sperm within their bodies, only releasing it as the eggs are passed into twin oviducts from ovaries. The shell of an insect's egg is not calcareous (like a bird's), but consists of a tough, horny, very durable substance, which is even capable of resisting fairly strong external pressure, and is formed around the yolk prior to fertilisation, with a tiny hole to receive the sperm as it is being laid. The eggshell is characteristic of each species. An egg can be identified chiefly by its size, shape and adornments, and also by how it has been laid.

The variations in courtship, reproduction patterns, growth and development, and metamorphosis are covered in greater detail in Chapter Two.

SHARING THE WORLD WITH INSECTS

The relationship between insects and humans has always been ambivalent. It may involve a fear of some insects, or distaste of others; or it might be a fascination for their lifestyles or admiration of their beauty. But often the human view is coloured by the ways insects directly affect our lives and activities.

Humans tend to regard many insects as pests because some of them are known to transmit diseases or interfere with our food in kitchens, gardens and plantations. However, of the myriad species of insects that exist in the world, relatively few cause serious harm to humans. The majority of insects play significant roles in the maintenance and wellbeing of the many ecosystems they inhabit.

GEOLOGICAL TIMELINE

	PALAEOZOIC ERA			MESOZOIC ERA			CAINOZOIC ERA						
								Tertiary				Quaternary	
Lines represent the extent of uncovered fossil records.	Devonian	Carboniferous	Permian	Triassic	Jurassic	Cretaceous	Palaeocene	Eocene	Oligocene	Miocene	Pliocene	Pleistocene	Recent
Approximate age in millions of years	408	360	286	245	208	144	66	60	40	25	5	1.6	0.01

PSEUDO INSECTS

springtails	Collembola
proturans	Protura
diplurans	Diplura

PRIMITIVE WINGLESS INSECTS

| archaeognaths | Archaeognatha |
| silverfish | Thysanura |

PRIMITIVE WINGED INSECTS

mayflies	Ephemeroptera
damselflies and dragonflies	Odonata
stoneflies	Plecoptera
cockroaches	Blattodea
termites	Isoptera
praying mantids	Mantodea
earwigs	Dermaptera
grasshoppers and crickets	Orthoptera
stick and leaf insects	Phasmatodea
web-spinners	Embioptera
bark-lice and allies	Psocoptera
animal-lice and allies	Phthiraptera
bugs, cicadas, allies	Hemiptera
thrips	Thysanoptera

MODERN WINGED INSECTS

alderflies, dobsonflies	Megaloptera
lacewings	Neuroptera
beetles and weevils	Coleoptera
stylops	Strepsiptera
scorpionflies	Mecoptera
fleas	Siphonaptera
true flies	Diptera
caddisflies	Trichoptera
moths and butterflies	Lepidoptera
sawflies, wasps, ants and bees	Hymenoptera

Either directly or indirectly, insects have a beneficial role in our planet's web of life.

It is as well to remember this when we feel motivated to employ insecticides to wipe out a local problem or infestation. These chemical solutions, being among the most dangerous substances known, will adversely affect many species other than those they were intended for. It is better to treat local imbalances by other means that take into account the overall wellbeing of the complete ecosystem, of which insects are one part only. Chapter Five offers some practical suggestions towards this end, and looks at the ecological interrelationships.

Despite our indiscriminate use of such substances, the insects have resisted eradication. This is just as well, as so much that we take for granted in the world around us would cease to exist without insects—including most animals and plants, the life forms higher up the food chain. Nevertheless, as part of the growing interest in the natural world around us more attention has been focused on the fascinating lives of the insects and the spiders. These terrestrial arthropods have much to teach us about adaptability and the need for diversity and acceptance of change. Some of the most amazing adaptations among insects, for instance, have evolved from their need to secure the nectar of flowers.

The world of insects is full of the most extraordinary diversity in lifestyles and shapes and behaviours—all of which are reflected in this book. Yet even a book like this cannot do justice to the full diversity that exists in the class Insecta, and there is much about them that remains enigmatic. As well, there are countless numbers of species that remain undescribed, or even undiscovered—and as their habitats come increasingly under threat from human activities, there may be many we never know at all.

Notwithstanding the relatively few pest species, the majority of insects are beneficial, enterprising, interesting and frequently beautiful creatures. And if we are to safeguard our own survival, we shall have to develop a greater understanding and acceptance of these small but crucial creatures.

From the humble scurrying silverfish to the highly evolved communities of ants and bees, this book explains many of the mysteries of nature's insect work force.

HOW TO USE THIS BOOK

Part 1 of this book concentrates on certain aspects of the life, habits and physical features of insects—the first five chapters cover their anatomy, life cycles, the development of wings and flight, and their patterns of behaviour, especially in respect of survival strategies. It also looks at the role insects play in ecological systems; in particular, it considers the interdependence of insects with other life forms. Chapter Six gives information on the study of insects and how to observe, record, photograph and collect them.

Each of the first five chapters is divided into two sections. The first sections take a broad overview of their subject; the second sections reveal more detailed descriptions of selected insect families or groups, specifically illustrating that chapter's subject. For example, in Chapter One, general anatomical features for all insects' bodies are described in the first section; in the second section, detailed anatomical descriptions are given for a number of specific insects.

Part 2 of this book provides a general listing of the main insect groups that occur in Australia, together with basic information about them, particularly for the purpose of identification. So, for example, to identify dragonflies and to be able to distinguish them from damselflies, you may prefer to go straight to the information in Part 2. This will usually provide a list of distinguishing features and summarise other aspects of the insect's life or behaviour that may be helpful in identifying it. But for a detailed anatomical description of a dragonfly's body, or for the full story of its interesting life cycle, you should look in the second section of chapters One or Two.

Not all insects are dealt with in every chapter of Part 1. For many insects, the available information is not as great; for these insects, all information may be contained in Part 2 alone. But some insects have an extraordinary range of features and habits; with such a diversity of facets to their activities, different aspects of their lives are described in different chapters, as well as summarised in Part 2.

How you use this book is a matter of personal choice. It gives you an opportunity to explore the various aspects of the lives and habits of many of our better-known insects in greater depth and in different contexts.

FOLLOWING PAGES A Broughton's snout-nosed katydid (*Euconocephalus broughtoni*). The mouth of an insect is closed by an upper lip (called the labrum), a lower lip (labium), and is flanked by two pairs of hinged jaws (mandibles and maxillae). These are remarkably modified in some orders such as flies, moths and butterflies.

1

THE LIVES
OF INSECTS

CHAPTER ONE

An Insect's Body

Insects vary greatly from one another in their bodily structure. Since leaving their restrictive aquatic environment hundreds of millions of years ago, they have evolved in many quite different ways. Insects belong to the superphylum Arthropoda, which includes all animals that have a hard or segmented outer skeleton (called an exoskeleton), such as crabs, lobsters, scorpions, spiders, millipedes and centipedes. All arthropods feature jointed limbs, but insects are identified by having only six. Individual insect species have evolved modifications to their exoskeletons according to their requirements, and they have developed a vast array of body shapes and patterns. This ranges from the long, thin stick insects that are barely distinguishable from the branch they live on to the delicate and colourful butterflies, and from squat bugs to gossamer damselflies with filamentous wings. This chapter explores the insects' body—both inside and out.

OPPOSITE It may look like a tiny teddy bear but the hardened outer skeleton and six jointed limbs of the emperor gum moth (*Opodiphthera eucalypti*) clearly classify it as an insect. The anatomical adaptions among insects are often astonishing. In this species, the male has huge multibranched antennae with thousands of olfactory sensilla that can detect odour molecules in very low concentrations. The female exudes these sexual scents, which are received by the males up to several kilometres away.

The body of an insect is divided into three distinct segments—the head, thorax, and abdomen. All are protected by an exoskeleton, which houses the internal organs and is also a multijointed framework providing the muscle attachment points for a highly efficient muscle operation. Each segment is bridged by muscles, allowing relatively free movement of all joints and moving parts of the body, such as the limbs, antennae, wings and mouthparts. The body wall of the insect exoskeleton has three distinct layers:
• cuticle (outer protective layer)
• hypodermis (intermediate cellular layer)
• base-membrane (inner membranous layer).

Growth is achieved by shedding each outgrown cuticle (a process called ecdysis), one after another until the insect attains its adult form.

Chitin, the basic material for the cuticle, is usually combined with sclerotin to make the outer layer tougher. However, sclerotin is never present in the cuticle of the numerous joints throughout the body. In some species a protein named resilin provides the particular flexibility and elasticity required for specialised feeding appendages (such as the tongues of moths and butterflies), for instance, or for jumping (as in the hindlimbs of fleas). Resilin stores energy and releases it when needed.

Water and unsaturated air are absorbed through the outer cuticle. Dehydration is prevented, as more than 50 per cent of the water taken in is retained. The main barrier preventing water evaporation is a waxy material covering the entire body—especially essential for all insect nymphs and larvae. This wax is protected by yet another layer—a varnish-like layer coating the entire area, including the numerous, tiny glands situated all over the body surface.

Soft-bodied insects—for instance, butterfly and moth caterpillars or beetle larvae—are those in which the external cuticular layer is unsclerotised, except for the head capsule and short thoracic legs (which are transformed into adult legs at final moult). The internal muscles of soft-bodied larvae maintain sufficient fluid pressure—rather like blood pressure—to keep the outer skin firm and taut. If the cuticle is punctured, the fluid (called haemolymph, the insect's blood) escapes, and the body collapses.

This pressure and the specialised muscles are also used for other purposes: to move the mouthparts (such as with cicadas, true bugs and true flies, moths and butterflies), and for the operation of the ovipositors of long-horned grasshoppers, crickets, cicadas and wasps. Fluid pressure is also used by an insect during its moulting process and for splitting its pupal case when it is ready to emerge as an adult, and for expanding its body and wings after emerging from its nymphal skin or pupal case.

HEAD

Head capsule

For all insects, the head is a capsule in which the sclerites of all its segments are fused together. It carries the feeding mechanism, principal sensory organs, eyes, antennae and the brain centre.

The original first segment of the head is formed by an upperlip (the labrum) hinged to a sclerotised flap (the clypeus). This protects and covers the mouth and the taste organs.

Much of the top of the head is generally occupied by two prominent, compound eyes, frequently accompanied by three (sometimes fewer) simple, single-lens light sensors known as ocelli. Situated between the compound eyes, the antennae (or feelers) are highly sensitive organs of smell. Up to 80 per cent of the information that an insect's brain processes is received from its eyes (compound and simple) and its specialised antennae.

Eyes

Insects have compound eyes comprising hundreds—or even thousands depending on the species—of hexagonally shaped lenses called ommatidia. Each lens has a narrow field of vision, and creates a separate image in the brain, which together produce a mosaic image. Many insects see colour, especially bees and butterflies. Bees see well at the blue end of the spectrum, including near ultraviolet light and this is exploited by flowering plants, which use such colours to lure bees. Apart from butterflies, most insects are insensitive to the red end of the spectrum.

The size of insects' eyes is directly related to lifestyle requirements. A mole cricket, which lives largely underground or in dark places, has small eyes compared to those of a dragonfly.

RIGHT The head capsule of the male Rosenberg longicorn beetle (*Rosenbergia megacephala*) houses the principal sensory organs, eyes, antennae, brain and feeding mechanism. Sporting two pairs of hinged 'jaws', its mouthparts are perfectly adapted for cutting timber.

BELOW The compound eyes of the floury-baker cicada (*Abricta curvicosta*) consist of large numbers of tightly packed light-sensitive units called ommatidia. These are separated by pigmented cells and are accompanied by three simple eyes called ocelli.

A dragonfly's eyes are larger as the adult spends most of its time on the wing, hawking insect prey. In addition to compound eyes, many insects have three ocelli. These are light detectors and they are ultrasensitive to the slightest change in light. They are set in a triangular formation on top of the head in front of, or between, the compound eyes. However, in some species ocelli may be reduced or entirely absent. Modern winged insects— the endopterygotes (for example, beetles and butterflies)—have simple eyes in their larval stage, only developing compound as pupae.

Mouthparts

The typical biting, chewing mouthparts occur in most insect larvae of endopterygotes and in both nymphs and adults of many of the primitive wingless insects—the exopterygotes. A large number of insects have a pair of toothed, horny mandibles serving as jaws. These occupy the fourth head-segment; their appearance and function vary greatly from species to species according to the specific requirements of each.

A pair of maxillae, with jointed sensory palps (which are taste receptors), occupy the fifth head-segment, and the lower lip (labium) occupies the sixth head-segment. Many groups—such as cicadas, plant-hoppers, true bugs, true flies, moths, butterflies, and bees— have modified mouthparts in the form of stout rostrums, beaks and tongues for drawing up liquid foods.

Sophisticated appendages

Many male beetles are well known for such features, with their strangely formed 'horns', 'jaws' and spines. Some use these appendages in wrestling matches as they rival for females, or as forceps capable of grasping a female beetle and carrying her off to where mating can take place without disturbance.

Such enormous appendages appear to be rather inconvenient, and at times it is hard to

ABOVE The mandibles of this male golden-green stag-beetle (*Lamprima aurata*) extend well beyond its head. Like many stag-beetles, these are used in 'wrestling matches' to stake territorial claims or in rivalry over females. It is the combination of chitin and sclerotin that gives them their incredible strength.

CHITIN—INSECT ARMOUR

An insect's tubular-shaped exoskeleton is a suit of armour enclosing all its vital organs. The development of this outer skeleton—which is far stronger than an internal skeleton comprised of small bones would be—has greatly contributed to the remarkable survival of insects generally and to their wide dispersal through every available terrestrial niche.

Chitin is the material out of which the exoskeleton of insects has been developed (just as keratin is the material for horns, beaks, hairs, nails and claws among vertebrates). When chitin is combined with sclerotin (a hardening agent), the resulting material is extremely tough but flexible, and light but strong.

The strength of this material is most apparent in the sclerotised wing-cases of some insects and the ovipositors, stings and mandibles of others. Some timber-boring species, for instance, are able to bite through sheet copper and silver. The forelimbs of certain insects (for example, mole crickets and cicada nymphs) are equipped to cut through plant roots, and for digging and tunnelling in hard soil.

The scales on the bodies and wings of butterflies and moths are formed from chitinous material, as are the furry coats of many bees, wasps, beetles and flies. The brilliant iridescence of many beetles is produced by an elaborate series of minute, six-sided pits covering the elytra—each pit reflecting light with changes in colour that occur as the beetle moves.

Chitin provides the material for the flying wings (which are stiffened by veins); for the elaborately shaped, interlocking mating organs occurring among many insects; for features designed to deter would-be predators, such as the stiff, spiny setae various moth larvae have, and the spines, spurs and barbs on the limbs and bodies of numerous insects. All these, and other anatomical features, are formed from this versatile material, which nature has moulded into some of the most amazing forms imaginable.

see what purpose they might serve. Indeed, many beetles are walking enigmas—especially certain weevils (superfamily Curculionoidea). In some weevil species, the head is drawn out into a preposterous rostrum or beak, which terminates in small mandibles. The antennae are hinged near the tip of these mandibles. Their small, compound eyes are situated well back on the head, near where the head region meets the thorax.

Some stag-beetles (family Lucanidae) have huge pseudo-jaws jutting forward from the front of their head, which can even impede their movement through thick vegetation. Yet, despite their formidable appearance, these grotesque appendages are never used for tearing or actual biting.

Antennae

A pair of antennae are located on the second head-segment, in front of and between the eyes. Antennae consist of three main regions. The basal segment (the scape) houses the controlling muscles. The second segment (the pedicel) houses the sense organ. The third region (the flagellum) is typically multisegmented. Antennae are many-jointed, with up to 100 segments, and they vary greatly in their structure and modifications according to the species.

Antennae of male insects are typically modified to increase their surface area, so as to detect the pheromones exuded by the female. Some beetles, for example, possess antennae that are much longer than their own body-length. Many beetles have antennae with fan-like parts that can be opened or closed—they are sensors that can detect airborne molecules, such as pheromones and other scents.

Taste

Taste sensors are typically found in the mouthparts but many species also have their sensory taste organs located on their tarsal segments or even on the tail of their abdomen near the ovipositor. A taste sensor is developed for sensing chemicals dissolved in solution instead of carried by air; otherwise, they work in much the same way as scent sensors.

THORAX

The thorax, like the head capsule, is a rigid framework, in this case typically consisting of three fused segments—prothorax, mesothorax, metathorax—with a pair of legs and, usually, wings, on each.

Limbs

Most insects, when in embryo, have potential legs on each of their abdominal segments. These 'legs' are generally lost prior to hatching, but they may become modified into other features. In all true insects, six of these legs are often retained (on the thoracic region) in the embryo, finally developing into the true legs when the insect reaches the adult stage of its life cycle.

Each limb is a series of sclerotised parts connected by joints. Progressing downwards from the ventral surface of the thoracic region, these basically consist of a coxa, trochanter, femur, tibia and tarsus. Limbs normally end in two curved claws, often with a fleshy pad between them. The legs themselves vary enormously among the insect orders, being modified according to the particular requirements of each different species.

Hearing

Over many millions of years, different insects have independently developed their own sensory hearing equipment, but for many it is in the form of a receptive organ, the tympanum. The location of this organ depends on the particular type of insect. For example, on a mole cricket or katydid, it is located on the front limbs; on a praying mantis, on the thorax between the hindlegs. In cicadas, it is situated ventrally on the first abdominal segment, but on lacewings and some moths and butterflies, it is found on their wings.

Wings

It seems likely that insects evolved their wings once only, given that there is a single basic design for the wing veins (with modifications due to insects' particular requirements). The role of the veins is to stiffen the membranes and carry oxygen, haemolymph and nerves.

Insects as a rule have two pairs of wings—the forewings (attached to the mesothorax) and the hindwings (attached to the metathorax). The wings are driven by the powerful muscles within the thoracic region. Although often both pairs are functional flying wings, for many insects, one pair may have become reduced or highly specialised and there is usually some degree of difference between each pair. With many insects, the wings are cryptically shaped and coloured to merge with their surroundings.

The forewings are often hardened, leathery, or specialised to produce sound. They serve to protect the membranous hindwings, the wings usually used for flying. In most insects, the thorax is partly covered by the flying wings.

INTERNAL ANATOMY OF AN INSECT

Circulatory System

The heart (dorsal vessel) of insects is a single closed vessel that carries the haemolymph (blood) located mid-dorsally in abdominal segments 2–9. It typically consists of eight chambers, with each opening into the one before it by a pair of valves; the last chamber is closed. Each chamber consists of a pair of openings, one either side, named ostia, through which haemolymph enters the body cavity; each ostium has a valve. The heart is elongated into a long narrow tube named the dorsal aorta, which passes through the thorax and into the head, opening in front of and above the brain (central nervous system).

Nervous System

This system includes the brain with a series of paired ganglia located in the thorax and abdomen connected by paired longitudinal nerves (short connectives) between which passes the esophagus. Typically, three pairs of ganglia occupy the thoracic region and eight pairs occupy the abdominal region (one pair per abdominal segment). From each ganglion of the central nervous system (brain), nerves connect to the muscles, the heart, and all other organs.

Digestive System

The salivary glands are situated in the prothorax and are connected to a pair of narrow salivary ducts that open into a common duct at the base of the hypopharynx. In insects that pulverise their food well, the digestive system has a strongly muscled chamber (gizzard) that often has an array of grinding ridges (internal teeth) opening up into a narrow duct. This foregut has a valve that opens into the midgut (stomach), the digestive region of the alimentary canal. Typically, it is an elongated sac lined with large cells that secrete digestive fluids, and is protected by a membrane that forms a sleeve around the food and passes it out with faeces.

Reproductive System

The essential parts of this system are the gonads, which produce reproductive cells. In females, these lead to the ovaries, which produce eggs. Those of the males lead to the testes, which produce spermatozoa. The gonads are located beneath the heart.

Excretory System

The junction of the midgut with the end of the hindgut is marked by the entry of the principal organs of excretion (Malpighian tubules). These tubules lie freely within the body cavity and extract uric acid from the haemolymph. In some larvae, they are specialised to produce silk, spun from the anus. The hindgut is separated into three parts: small intestine, large intestine (colon) and rectum—a large, swollen chamber equipped with strong bands of longitudinal muscle. It opens into the posterior opening of the alimentary canal (the anus).

Respiratory System

The respiratory system of insects consists of a series of tubes that carry air (tracheae) running throughout the body. Their openings are a series of valves (spiracles). Ten pairs typically exist: two pairs of thoracic spiracles and eight pairs of abdominal spiracles. In most insects, the main tracheae run the full length of the body.

LEFT The digestive and excretory systems of moth and butterfly larvae enable them to utilise their toxic waste products to produce pigments that create their bright and cryptic body colouring. These often serve as camouflage, as the colours match their host plants. Alternatively the colours may alert potential predators that the larvae are toxic. The colourful caterpillar of the peppered prominent moth (*Neola semiaurata*) bears no resemblance to its dark pupal form (below).

However, with shield-bugs and most beetles it is usually fully covered by a protective chitinous shield. Insects that use both pairs of wings directly for flight include dragonflies, damselflies, cicadas, moths, butterflies, wasps and bees. Flies evolved a flight action that is different to that of most other insects; their forewings are used for flying and their hind-wings as halteres.

Many insects have their wings coupled in flight for greater control. This is achieved by having either minute hooks or folds on the hind-wings. These grab and hook onto a membranous fold located on the forewings, locking both pairs of wings together, thus forming a single aerofoil.

ABDOMEN

The abdomen houses the heart and most other essential machinery for digestive and excretory functions. Abdominal segments 8 and 9 are typically modified to form the genitalia in both sexes. Primitive insects (such as cockroaches, grasshoppers, mantids and phasmatids) have retained a pair of 'abdominal antennae', called cerci, on the eleventh or posterior segment. The only other appendages that may be found on the posterior region are ovipositors and the organs of reproduction and mating. Stings, which are modified ovipositors, are typically found among the ants, wasps and bees.

Highly active insects require large amounts of oxygen to utilise the body's fats and sugars, producing the energy needed to operate their muscles. Insects obtain their oxygen through a series of breathing holes called spiracles, which are set along the walls of the abdomen and thorax on both sides of the body.

Water-frequenting insects, such as water bugs (several families), diving beetles and water beetles (families Dytiscidae and Hydrophilidae, for example) utilise their closely set leg and body hairs to trap and carry large amounts of air below the surface. Air is trapped beneath their body hairs and wing covers and, because these hairs often have bent ends, the surface tension of the water prevents the air escaping.

INTERNAL ANATOMY

Digestive system

The digestive system is a long tube with an opening at either end. It absorbs nutrients through the walls of the stomach and circulates them through the haemolymph. It also absorbs waste products in the haemolymph and expels these though the anus.

Most insects derive their nourishment from living plants—for most caterpillars, grass-hoppers or phasmatids, leaves provide the greatest proportion of their food. But some insects also consume a range of other materials.

For instance, yeasts, pollen, nectar, wood, sap flows, animal excreta, the horns of animals and their rotting carcasses, wax, wool, feathers or fungi. The oxidation of foods produces carbon dioxide and water. This water is utilised, being retained within the body to help combat dehydration. Water is also absorbed from waste materials, evident by examining the dry pellets of lepidopterous caterpillars.

Most insects have micro-organisms living within their gut, which help break down what has been eaten. This enables insects to consume a remarkable range of material that is otherwise unusable, and mostly unsuitable for other animals. Many insects can also store food for future use should food become unavailable.

Excretory system

Insects, like all life forms, must expel toxic wastes from their system and their excretory organs perform this function. In most insects, the muscle fibres that coil along the blind-ended Malpighian tubules contract and discharge 'waste' products into the rear of the midgut. Further along the Malpighian tubules, towards the hindgut, is where salts, sugar and water are stored.

Butterfly and moth larvae often use such toxic waste products to provide a chemical basis for their cryptic colouring, which perfectly matches their host plants. These toxins also make them highly distasteful to predators and the bold colours act as a clear warning.

Nervous system

Insect have a well-developed central nervous system, which consists of a double nerve cord branching into finer nerve cells that respond to stimuli. Tiny, erect hairs (setae) located all over an insect's body are ultrasensitive to vibrations. Each of these hairs, the length, shape and number of which vary from species to species, is equipped with a nerve cell attached to its base to record airwaves, sound, taste and smell.

The insect's brain controls the sensory organs of the head and receives survival information from the antennae, eyes and labrum; it serves the vital role of coordinating data required for finding food, finding and selecting members of the opposite sex, finding the required animal or plant host, and feeding.

Circulatory system

There are no arteries and veins like those in vertebrates. Instead, all internal organs and tissues of an insect's body are bathed in a haemolymph environment, which supplies them with nutrients, salts and hormones, and also moves waste products.

An insect's haemolymph circulation is achieved by means of a tubular-shaped heart (a dorsally located haemolymph vessel), which has diaphragms and a pumping mechanism. A number of small accessory hearts are also located at the base of each appendage to push the haemolymph into the antennae, palps, muscles, limbs, cerci, and so on.

Respiratory system

Respiration is achieved by taking in air through the spiracles. These are the breathing holes along the sides of the abdomen, and are readily seen in most lepidopterous larvae, but are often well hidden in the pleural membrane (located between the sternum and tergal plates). The spiracles are protected by external valves or covers, which regulate the flow of air by opening and closing. The spiracles' valves also prevent dust and contaminated air from entering, and assist in the reduction of moisture loss.

The air, as it is taken in, is piped along an internal network of branching tubes (called tracheae) to all parts of the body. The larger tracheae have a spiral ribbing in their walls to prevent collapsing, kinking or distortion. Carbon dioxide is expired by the reverse route and through the softer parts of the body surface.

BELOW The larvae of the leaf beetle (*Chrysophtharta* species) are poisonous, as the eucalypt leaves they digest produce toxins. They store these in their defence glands and secrete them as hydrogen cyanide when predators attack.

Fast-flying insects need a lot of oxygen in the flight muscles of the thorax—and the motion of the thorax in flight helps aerate these tissues. Some very active insects maintain a high thoracic temperature by restricting the haemolymph exchange between abdomen and thorax. It is interesting to observe an insect such as the cowboy beetle (*Diaphonia dorsalis*) warming its flight muscles with vigorous, concertina-like movements of its abdominal segments. If you closely observe bees, wasps, or true flies, you see their abdomens rising and falling at a regular pace to maintain circulation. Air entering the body travels mostly by diffusion, but the muscular pumping action improves its circulation.

Reproductive system

The essential parts of the reproductive system are the gonads, which are located beneath the heart. These are the organs that produce reproductive cells: a female's gonads lead to the ovaries, which produce eggs; a male's gonads lead to the testis, which produces the male's sex cells—the spermatozoa.

For most insects, the reproductive system is located within the rear part of the abdomen, but the particular anatomical details of the genitalia vary considerably from order to order, and even between species.

Insects reproduce in several different ways and the anatomy of their genitalia depends on which method is used. Mating between males and females usually involves some means of transferring sperm from one to the other (but not always: females of some species do not actually need males at all to reproduce). Males in several exopterygote orders transfer spermatophores—or, sperm capsules—to the female during copulation. In several endopterygote orders, such as Coleoptera, Trichoptera and Diptera, males typically inject sperm directly into the female's genital opening.

With many insects, after mating, the female will normally store the sperm for some period (which varies among species) in a sperm sac, called a spermatheca, only releasing it to fertilise the eggs as she lays them.

Most species recognise the opposite sex visually, chemically or auditorily long before they get into close contact. Insects are often confined to mating within their own species by a particular anatomical arrangement of their genitalia, through which the male and female parts will only engage with members of their own species—sometimes called a 'lock-and-key' arrangement. This ensures that any attempts by such insects to mate with different species would be unsuccessful.

ABOVE Mating yellow-bellied grasshoppers (*Praxibulus insolens*). The male transfers sperm by passing a sperm capsule into the female's genital opening. The female stores it in a sperm pouch and, when depositing the eggs, she fertilises them as they pass through the uterus.

DIVERSITY AMONG THE GROUPS

This section describes basic anatomical features for representatives of various orders, first looking at primitive winged insect groups (the exopterygotes), and then the modern winged insects (the endopterygotes). Owing to specialised modifications in insect anatomy, there is sometimes considerable variation within the orders, between families or even among species. For this reason, each description concentrates on the typical features characterising insects of the order described. Other, more unusual features are mentioned where appropriate.

MAYFLIES
order Ephemeroptera

Head capsule

The head capsule is short, transverse, and triangular-shaped, with short, thread-like antennae. The compound eyes are large and conspicuous—the male's are divided, typically meeting one another dorsally, with larger facets on the upper area. Three ocelli are usually present. The reduced mouthparts are shrunken together beneath the clypeus (adult mayflies do not feed).

Thorax

The thoracic region is well developed for flight: there is a reduced, shield-like prothorax, and a mesothorax and metathorax that are large, fused together and have spiracles. The mesothorax is more developed and strengthened, its notum being strongly convex, with longitudinal grooves. Wings have numerous cross-veins and are coupled in flight.

Limbs

The limbs are medium to long. The forelegs of the male are greatly elongated, being used to grasp the female during the mating flight over water. The male's middle and hindlegs and all the female's legs are weakly sclerotised and they terminate in paired, modified tarsal claws.

BELOW A damselfly (*Austro-argiolestes isabellae*). The compound eyes of damselflies are characteristically separated, while those of dragonflies typically meet. The spiny limbs are adapted for seizing and holding prey, climbing, and clinging to foliage. The short forelegs and long rear legs support the insect's long abdomen when it alights.

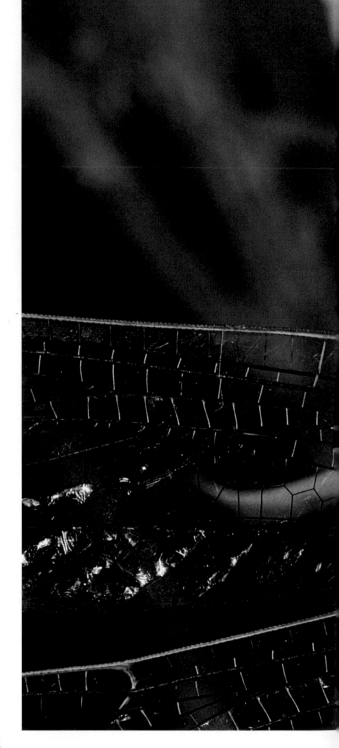

Abdomen

The long, cylindrical abdomen comprises 10 complete segments, the tenth terminating in three caudal filaments, and two cerci. Segments 1–8 have eight pairs of spiracles. The male has well-developed, external genitalia that vary in shape among species; the aedeagus is lobed or spined, or has other modifications associated with mating. In females, the rear of segment 9 varies: in some species, the oviducts open by a pair of gonophores; in others, they are fused with a common opening. They have no ovipositor but a genital opening lies between segments 7 and 8.

DAMSELFLIES AND DRAGONFLIES
order Odonata

Head capsule
The large, mobile head capsule (broad in damselflies, round in dragonflies), has fine, short antennae. In dragonflies, the head is connected to the prothorax by a highly flexible, slender neck. There are large, conspicuous, compound eyes. Three ocelli are also usually present, arranged in a triangular pattern on the front of the head capsule, but are reduced in some species to a small tubercle. Mouthparts are strongly mandibulate (that is, they have biting and chewing mandibles), with spiny maxillae that have unsegmented palps, and labial palps shaped into lateral lobes.

Thorax
These insects have a small, free-moving prothorax attached to a rigid synthorax composed of the fused mesothorax and metathorax. Female damselflies have an elongated thorax, with a modified pronotum to accommodate the male appendages.

ABOVE As many as 28 000 separate eye elements, called ommatidia, form the compound eyes of large dragonflies, such as this mosquito-hawk dragonfly (*Aeshna brevistyla*). Like most insects, dragonflies have a limited range of colour vision but they can see yellow, blue and ultra-violet. Other than butterflies, few insects can see red.

The highly specialised wings have an abundant network of veins, and are placed well back. The wings are powered by the great thoracic muscles.

Limbs

The short, spiny legs are situated well forward, close to the head, and are modified to form a basket that is used for holding prey in flight and for clinging to foliage when resting; they are not, however, adapted for walking. Three-segmented tarsi terminate in a pair of toothed claws, used for seizing and holding prey.

The legs are often progressively longer, with the hind pair being the longest. This type of arrangement helps support the extended body when the insect alights upon a branch or stem.

Abdomen

The abdomen consists of 10 segments. It is long, cylindrical, sometimes depressed and tapered, and distally clubbed, with short, unsegmented cerci. Segments 1–8 have eight pairs of spiracles.

In males, segments 2 and 3 are modified, forming secondary sexual organs. The transfer of sperm to the aedeagus vesicle, which is located on segment 3, is activated by the forward ventral bending of the abdominal segments. Segment 2 houses the aedeagus and the accompanying appendages for clasping the female genitalia during mating.

The female's gonophore is located behind the eighth sternal plate. It is accompanied by an ovipositor with cutting edges in damselflies, but in most dragonflies it is greatly reduced.

BELOW Freshly emerged from its outgrown exoskeleton at ecdysis, the cuticle of the red-brown wood-roach (*Panesthia laevicollis*) will darken and harden within a few hours. After the final moult, these cockroaches have the extraordinary habit of biting off one another's wings, as these are an encumbrance to its lifestyle among decaying timber.

STONEFLIES
order Plecoptera

Head capsule

The head capsule is broader than long, with well-developed, compound eyes, and three ocelli (two, in some species) and long, flexible, thread-like antennae. Mandibles are typically well formed, with well-developed maxillae, a complete labrum and, according to the species, three- to five-segmented palps.

Thorax

The thoracic segments are free-moving—the prothorax is large with a wide, flattened pronotum. The wings are very unequal, with abundant, supportive cross-veins, and are placed well back on the thorax.

Limbs

The long legs are placed well forward, and are adapted for walking. They have short coxae, long, stout, flattened femora, and slender tibiae without spurs. A three-segmented tarsus terminates in a pair of strong claws.

Abdomen

Cylindrical or compressed (according to the species), the soft abdomen consists of 10 distinct segments, with spiracles on segments 1–8. The female's gonophore opening is located on segments 7, 8 or 9 (depending on the species). In the male, the four posterior segments are modified as mating organs.

COCKROACHES
order Blattodea

Head capsule

Roundish or triangular in shape (according to the species), the head capsule has long, thread-like antennae. There are often well-developed compound eyes, which are reduced or lacking in some groups, and ocelli typically modified into two pale-coloured dots. Their biting mouthparts have five-segmented maxillary palps, and three-segmented labial palps.

Thorax

A protective, shield-like pronotum often overlaps the head capsule; the mesonotum and metanotum are rectangular and similar. Weakly sclerotised compressed pleura and sterna accommodate the coxae. The wings of most species are not well developed for long-distance flight.

Limbs

The stout, short-to-medium, flanged, spiny limbs have five-segmented tarsi, terminating in paired claws used for walking and running.

Abdomen

Wide and depressed, the abdomen consists of 10 overlapping segmental plates. Segments 1–8 have eight pairs of spiracles, those on segments 2–7 being located in the pleural membrane.

Sexual dimorphism occurs among several species. The male's sexual organs consist of asymmetrically shaped sclerotised phallomeres hidden in a genital pouch. A pair of styles usually accompanies the sub-genital plate. The female genitalia are reduced and internal. The female's ovipositor consists of three pairs of finger-like valves, located within the walls of the genital opening.

TERMITES
order Isoptera

Head capsule

The large head is round or oval, and somewhat flattened; it is greatly developed among soldier castes. There are reduced compound eyes, two ocelli (when present), and short, bead-like antennae. Termites have biting mouthparts (modified in certain castes), and the labium has large basal plates. The mandibles of workers and alates (winged forms) of the same genus are very similar in structure.

Thorax

The pronotum is well defined. The sub-equal metanotum and mesonotum lack distinctive features, the sterna being membranous.

Wings (when occurring) in most species have a specialised transverse suture at their base, which breaks easily when the wings are shed after mating.

Limbs

The slender legs are of medium length, and are all similar. They have four- to five-segmented tarsi (according to the species) terminating in paired claws.

Abdomen

The elongated, cylindrical abdomen consists of 10 segments. In all castes, the terminal segment bears a pair of short, one- to five-segmented cerci.

PRAYING MANTIDS
order Mantodea

Head capsule

The triangular-shaped, highly mobile and compressed head capsule is attached to its slender neck or, in some species, inserted into the thoracic region. It holds a pair of long, many-jointed, fine thread-like antennae, and the large, bulbous, compound eyes, which are either conical or pointed in shape but more often rounded (according to the species). All mantids have powerful chewing mouthparts.

Thorax

The narrow, elongated thorax is hinged from the mesothorax, with a transversely arched pronotum, and may, depending on the species, have shield-shaped, lateral expansions. The mesothorax and metathorax are similar and rigidly connected, with strongly sclerotised sterna. Wings are not adapted for long-distance flight.

Limbs

The long, slender middle and hindlegs are not specialised in any way other than for walking and running (although some can achieve

ABOVE The large praying mantis (*Archimantis latistyla*) varies in colour according to season, from summer-green to autumn-brown. Superbly camouflaged but slow on foot, mantids capture prey by stealth, moving into striking range where they can remain motionless for long periods. They then surprise-attack their prey, which is suddenly seized in the vice-like grip of their powerful raptorial forelimbs.

short leaps). The well-developed forelegs have been modified into a pair of raptorial, grasping hooks that close upon prey with a vice-like grip.

Abdomen

Typically telescopic, long and depressed, the abdomen consists of 11 segments (segment 1 is not obvious), terminating in segmented cerci. Spiracles are located in the pleural membrane of tergum 1, and on the ventral borders of terga 2–8.

The male genitalia are somewhat concealed beneath the sub-genital plate. The female genitalia are reduced and located internally. The ovipositor consists of three pairs of finger-like valves, which are located within the walls of the genital opening.

EARWIGS
order Dermaptera

Head capsule

Earwigs have a broad, flattened head capsule that has short, annulated antennae and is free-moving at the cylindrically shaped, unprotected neck. The large, compound eyes that are present in members of the suborder Forficulina (the giant earwig *Titanolabis colossea* being a typical representative) are lacking entirely, or very small, in some species; ocelli, too, are absent. Earwigs have biting mouthparts—mandibles with two apical teeth fitting into an incisor and molar region (in most species), much-divided maxillae, and a large labium.

Thorax

The thorax has free-moving segments, with the unequal prothorax and mesothorax being smaller than the metathorax. Two pairs of spiracles are set in the pleural membrane. Some wingless species have a large pronotum, and a smaller mesonotum and metanotum. The wings of earwigs are highly specialised, with the forewings modified as tegmina, protecting the flying wings when at rest.

Limbs

The legs are sub-equal and short- to medium-length, with short and widely placed coxae. They terminate in three-segmented tarsi bearing paired, long, pre-tarsal claws.

Abdomen

The long, depressed abdomen consists of free-moving segments (10 in males, eight in females), with the sternal and tergal plates both strongly overlapping. Eight pairs of spiracles are located in the pleural membrane. The forceps are larger and more curved in males.

The male's sexual organs are located within the body wall (genital chamber) just above the sub-genital plate. The female's ovipositor is reduced and hidden by the sub-genital plate in most families.

RIGHT A glossy mole cricket (*Gryllotalpa nitidula*). The forelimbs of mole crickets are used as 'shears' and 'picks' to excavate and shear grass roots. Their forewings are modified to produce sounds that attract the opposite sex. Eggs are laid in an underground nest and the female remains with them until they hatch, which may take up to two weeks.

KATYDIDS, CRICKETS AND SHORT-HORNED GRASSHOPPERS
order Orthoptera

The following anatomical information concerning orthopterans includes representatives of two suborders: the long-horned, primarily nocturnal ensiferans, such as katydids, bush crickets and true crickets; and the short-horned, primarily diurnal caeliferans, such as short-horned grasshoppers (also called locusts when they occur in plague proportions).

Head capsule
The head, which often has a conspicuous, conically shaped forehead, is usually inserted into the pronotum. Depending on the species, antennae can be short or several times the body-length. The compound eyes are medium to large (but reduced or absent among certain subterranean forms). There are large, biting chewing mandibles (modified according to lifestyle), with five- or six-segmented maxillary palps. The mandibles of males of some species, such as king crickets (family Stenopelmatidae), appear grossly over-large.

Thorax
While the large prothorax is not rigid, there is minimal movement at the mesothorax, which is rigidly connected to the metathorax. The pronotum, always larger than the mesonotum and metanotum, has large, descending, sub-vertical lobes forming its sides, with well-sclerotised sterna. Spiracles are located on the mesothorax and metathorax.

The wings of katydids and crickets are not particularly well developed for long-distance flight, although those of short-horned grasshoppers are.

Limbs
The forelegs and middle legs are usually similar. In some species, however, the forelegs are modified: in a number of predacious forms they have numerous spines running along the ventral sides of the femur and tibia; in certain burrowing forms they are greatly modified for digging among grass roots. Ears are present on the forelegs of many sound-producing species such as katydids and bush crickets (family Tettigoniidae). The larger hindlimbs are almost always modified for leaping.

ABOVE The cone-headed grasshopper (*Atractomorpha similis*) is active by day, feeding on low herbage along creeks and streams. Its resemblance to grass stems and its colour affords remarkable camouflage. Perched on the foliage, it remains hidden unless disturbed.

ABOVE The spiny back and forelimbs are characteristic of the stick insect *Cteno-morpha chronus*. These insects remain inconspicuous and, even when prodded, they are reluctant to move. Not strong flyers, their wings help break a fall.

RIGHT Seeing through their bulging compound eyes, cicadas such as this scissors-grinder cicada (*Henicopsaltria eydouxii*) can detect the slightest movement nearby. Its colouring and body pattern blend perfectly with the mottled bark of rainforest tree trunks.

Abdomen

The long, cylindrical, and sometimes tapering abdomen consists of 11 segments. Segments 1–8 have eight pairs of spiracles. In some groups, tergal plates have stridulatory ridges involved with sound production. In males of some groups, cerci are unsegmented and modified into clasping organs used during mating. The female's ovipositor (not present in some groups) consists of three pairs of valves in the body walls; in some species, such as the tree cricket *Paragryllacris combusta*, it may consist of a long, cylindrical tube exceeding the length of the body.

STICK INSECTS AND LEAF INSECTS (PHASMATIDS)
order Phasmatodea

Head capsule

In some species, the rectangular to oval-shaped head capsule is adorned with horns and spines. Antennae are short to very long, bead-like or thread-like. The small, compound eyes are situated well forward on the head and three ocelli are present in certain winged species, but only on males. Mouthparts consist of strong, cutting mandibles, with five-segmented maxillary palps and three-segmented labial palps.

Thorax

The prothorax is not rigid, and is the shortest thoracic segment. The pronotum is transversely arched, with no descending lateral lobes. The mesothorax extends well forward of the forewings' attachment points, being longer than other thoracic segments, and is often greatly elongated and spiny. Mesothoracic and metathoracic sterna are well sclerotised.

Wings are not well developed for long-distance flight, acting more as aids to gliding.

Limbs

Legs are long and slender with small, widely spaced coxae and often bear spines, lobes or broad expansions. The fore-femora typically are curved to accommodate the head capsule when the insect is at rest, forelegs extended straight ahead.

Abdomen

Long and cylindrical, sometimes depressed, slightly tapered, and often bearing spines, the abdomen consists of 11 movable segments.

Spiracles are located in the pleural membrane. The male genitalia consist of a cup-shaped lobe (the poculum). The female sexual organs consist of a keel-shaped structure (the operculum), which extends beyond the abdomen in some species.

APHIDS, CICADAS, TRUE BUGS, AND THEIR ALLIES
order Hemiptera

Head capsule

The head capsule varies enormously between members of the order. For example, it is triangular-shaped among cicadas and shield-bugs, and on some true bugs the head moves freely on the body. The antennae are short, with fewer than 10 segments, and the compound eyes range in size from very large to entirely lacking. Three ocelli are present among some (such as aphids, cicadas, plant-hoppers), while true bugs (such as shield-bugs and assassin bugs) typically have two; although ocelli are lacking among several families of the suborder Heteroptera, which includes many wingless forms.

All hemipterans have specialised mouth-parts, highly modified for such activities as piercing, stabbing and siphoning plant fluids, which evolved from chewing mouthparts. These mouthparts are called the rostrum. They consist of sharp, slender tubes fitted closely together within a sheath (quite visible in cicadas). They conspicuously extend ventrally from the very rear of the head. Housed within the rostrum, apically barbed stylets lie in an anterior groove.

The stylets, which may be one- to five-segmented (according to the species), are the parts that actually penetrate when feeding.

Thorax

The pronotum varies enormously in shape and size. Tegulae are present in most sternorrhynchans. The scutellum, typically large and triangular-shaped, covers the entire dorsal area of the abdomen, protecting the flying wings in some species. Apart from a few stronger flying forms, hemipterans' wings are not well developed for long-distance flight.

Limbs

Their short- to medium-length legs are generally similar except among predatory species—for example, assassin bugs and water bugs in which they are modified into highly efficient raptorial limbs used for seizing and holding prey.

Many hemipterans are equipped with adhesive footpads for climbing vertical surfaces. Aquatic species often have long, slender legs, for moving across the water surface, while others have modified limbs for swimming and paddling. The hindlegs of plant-hoppers are adapted for jumping, while in others (such as aphids) the forelegs are used for jumping. Cicada nymphs' forelimbs are highly modified digging and cutting tools, used for moving beneath the soil.

Abdomen

The abdomen, typically flattened, is tapered or shaped to accommodate folded wings, as in cicadas and plant-hoppers. There are eight pairs of spiracles (but in some species two or three pairs); aquatic bugs have spiracles modified to suit underwater habitats. Male genitalia are housed within a capsule-shaped protector (the

ABOVE A greengrocer cicada (*Cyclochila australasiae*) engrossed in feeding. The mouthparts of cicadas are modified for siphoning fluids. The nose-shaped mouth cavity and muscles of the sucking pump appear as an extension of the head. This narrows, forming a long rostrum, a sheath housing two pairs of slender stylets that penetrate plant tissue and channel the fluid into the mouth.

pygophore), and are often accompanied by a pair of clasping organs used during mating. The female's ovipositor is short (but absent among some species).

THRIPS
order Thysanoptera

Head capsule

The head capsules lack sutures. The small, compound eyes have only three facets in some forms, and are accompanied by three ocelli.

Thorax

The conspicuous pronotum has regular patterns of setae. Spiracles are located on the mesothorax and metathorax. The wings are not well developed for flight, and thrips depend more on the wind to transport them from one place to another.

Limbs

These insects have legs which terminate in one- to two-segmented tarsi, with eversible adhesive footpads. Typically slender, the forelegs are modified in some species with large tarsal teeth and swollen femora for gripping the surface of plants. To aid in jumping, the hindlimbs fold underneath the body.

Abdomen

The long, tapering abdomen consists of 11 segments, with segments 1–8 having two pairs of spiracles.

The male's sexual organs comprise a pair of fusiform testes, usually accompanied by one or two pairs of accessory glands. The female's ovipositor is reduced into an eversible structure.

ALDERFLIES AND DOBSONFLIES
order Megaloptera

Head capsule

The broad, flat head of alderflies and dobsonflies has long, thread-like antennae and protruding, compound eyes. Three ocelli are present in dobsonflies (family Corydalidae), but absent in alderflies (family Sialidae). Mandibles are adapted for biting and cutting, and have five-segmented maxillary palps and three- to four-segmented labial palps (according to the species).

Thorax

The mesothorax and metathorax are similarly shaped, the thoracic segments being mobile and well developed, with a large pronotum and normal spiracles. Wings are not well developed for long-distance flight.

Limbs

All pairs are strongly developed and similar. The coxae of the rear limbs are basally enlarged, terminating in five-segmented tarsi, each having a pair of simple claws used to move about foliage.

Abdomen

The soft, free-moving abdomen consists of 10 flexible segments, terminating with a pair of rear claspers used during mating. The dobsonfly *Archichauliodes guttiferus* is a typical representative. The male sexual organs are a pair of testes and an ejaculatory duct. In the female, segment 8 is highly modified to form the ovipositor.

LACEWINGS
order Neuroptera

Head capsule

The transverse head capsule has large, compound eyes. Ocelli are absent (except in the family Osmylidae). Antennae are long, thread-like and tapering (and club-tipped in the family Ascalaphidae). The mouthparts are modified for biting and cutting, with five-segmented maxillary palps and specialised labial palps. A conspicuous groove housing sensory equipment is located at the apical segment of the palps.

Thorax

The free-moving thorax is longer rather than broad, but very elongated in family Mantispidae. The mesothorax and metathorax are typically similar in size, but the metathorax is reduced in family Nemopteridae. Wings most of lacewings are not well developed for long-distance flight.

Limbs

The legs are simple and unspecialised (except for the forelimbs of family Mantispidae, which are raptorial for seizing and holding prey while feeding). In some species, the femora are sometimes expanded and flattened, each leg terminating in five-segmented tarsi, bearing a pair of claws (except among Mantispidae).

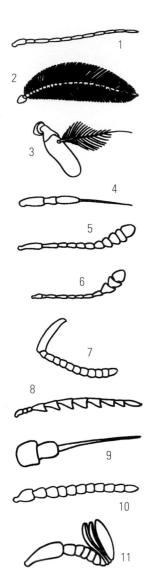

ABOVE Main antenna types:
1. Filiform: various orders.
2. Pectinate: many moths.
3. Aristate: many flies.
4. Stylate: dragonflies, cicadas, flies.
5. Clavate: beetles, some butterflies, sawflies.
6. Capitate: lacewings, beetles, butterflies, wasps.
7. Geniculate: wasps, ants and bees.
8. Serrate: many beetles.
9. Subulate: dragonflies, flies, various orders.
10. Moniliform: short-horned grasshoppers.
11. Lamellate: stag and scarab beetles.

Abdomen

The long, cylindrical abdomen consists of 10 segments. Among family Ascalaphidae, the males usually have a conspicuous dorsal process arising from segments 2 and 3 (differing in shape according to the species).

BEETLES
order Coleoptera

Head capsule

The rigid head capsule has compound eyes that greatly vary between families. In some aquatic species, the eye is divided into an upper and lower region. The compound eye lenses are small and flat in most species active by day, and large and convex in nocturnally active species. There are two or three ocelli (according to the species), and ocelli-associated eye-types,

including: a crystalline lens (the eucone eye), which is considered primitive, and a lens formed from the cornea (the exocone eye).

Antennae are typically 11-segmented (but sometimes reduced) and greatly vary in length—longicorn beetles (family Cerambycidae), for example, have antennae generally far longer than their body length. Some antennae are clubbed, lamellate and short (such as among most of the family Scarabaeidae). Antennae are basically chemosensory organs bearing sensory equipment. Males of many species use their antennae in courtship and even, in some groups, for combat with other males.

Mouthparts, which consist of biting and chewing mandibles, typically face forward, but in several groups are situated ventrally. The clypeus, which is extended on the front section of the head region between the compound eyes, and is attached to the flap of the labrum,

ABOVE Like many insects, figtree longicorn beetles (*Acalolepta vastator*) have antennae with segments of the flagellum greatly elongated. These serve as organs of feeling or touch and can also detect the pheromones emitted by the opposite sex.

RIGHT Scarabaeoid beetle larvae like this curl grub of *Rhyssonotus nebulosus* are remarkably adapted to digging into rotting timber and soil. They are typically C-shaped and have a hardened head capsule, powerful cutting mandibles, well-developed short antennae, six or fewer simple lenses and six short thoracic legs.

conceals and protects the transversely moving mouthparts. There are three- to five-segmented maxillary palps, accompanied by three- to five-segmented labial palps.

Thorax

The well-developed prothorax combines with the head capsule to form a rather conspicuous fore-body. This is clearly separated by an intersegmental membrane from the hindbody, which comprises the mesothorax, metathorax and abdomen. The pronotum of the prothorax is composed of a large, dorsal, sclerite plate extending ventrally. The mesothorax and metathorax are rigidly fused together, forming what is called the pterothorax, which bears the elytra and flying wings. Large metathoracic spiracles are located on each side of the thorax and sometimes in a membranous pocket concealed by the elytra.

Wings are generally well developed for long-distance flying. Many beetles, however, can only manage feeble efforts at flying, largely owing to the manner in which the elytra are held during flight. In flightless forms, elytra are often fused.

Limbs

The legs are modified for various activities. The forelegs, which are more often larger than the rear legs, are also modified in many families for digging, tunnelling, swimming and climbing. The rear edge of the hind coxa is typically excavated to receive the femur. Legs usually terminate in five-segmented tarsi (but vary in some groups

owing to enormously modified segments), with a pair of claws, also frequently modified.

Abdomen

Consisting of 10 free-moving segments in males, and nine in females, the abdomen is short, broad and tapered; sometimes it is elongated and compressed. Eight tergal plates are typical, but less conspicuous among flightless forms. The terga of those with short elytra, such as rove-beetles (family Staphylinidae), are more heavily sclerotised. Eight pairs of functional spiracles are located in the pleural membrane, and protected beneath the elytra.

Both sexes of these insects have capsule-like genitalia comprising a ring-like structure formed by terga 10 and segment 9. In the male, segments 10 and 9 are often fused, and the ejaculatory duct is modified to form mating organs (the aedeagus). The female's segment 9 is modified to form the genitalia.

STYLOPS
order Strepsiptera

Head capsule
The most obvious features of the head capsule of the male are the lamellate antennae and the unusually structured compound eyes, which consist of numerous lenses separated by setae. No ocelli are present. Mandibles, when present, are blade-shaped cutting tools.

Thorax
There is a tiny thoracic region, in which the mesothorax bears the anterior pair of wings. These have highly reduced venation with mostly radial veins. Forewings are reduced to halteres.

Limbs
The legs differ from most other insects in having no coxae on the hind legs and no trochanter on the pairs of the forelegs and middle legs. Five-segmented tarsi terminate in paired claws (reduced to a single claw in some families).

Abdomen
The abdomen is elongated and ends bluntly. Respiration is achieved through the cuticle wall itself. Segment 9 forms the sexual organs. The female is typically fertilised through the brood canal opening.

SCORPION-FLIES
order Mecoptera

Head capsule
There are large, compound eyes, and ocelli may or may not be present (depending on the species). The antennae are long and thread-like, distinctly tapering at the apex and, according to the species, have 14–60 flagellar segments with the scape and pedicel enlarged.

The modified clypeus and labrum form a rostrum. Mandibles typically are short, but certain families have longer mandibles—especially the Bittacidae, which have blade-shaped ones with a single apical tooth.

There are five-segmented maxillary palps (long and highly modified in some species) and two-segmented labial palps.

Thorax
The membranous cervix (neck) is elongated in some species. The saddle-shaped pronotum is wide rather than long, often bearing transverse ridges. The mesothorax and metathorax are about equal in size and shape, the metathorax being fused with the first abdominal segment. The sternum is infolded, touching the coxae at midpoint (but occasionally widely separated). Wings are not adapted for long-distance flight.

Limbs
In these insects the coxae, femora and tibiae are long and slender, and have five-segmented tarsi. Pretarsi terminate in paired claws, except in the family Bittacidae, in which a single large claw forms a raptorial structure. *Harpobittacus tillyardi* is a typical representative.

ABOVE A scorpion-fly (*Harpobittacus tillyardi*). Scorpion-flies frequent tall grasses and shrubs. They are often called hanging-flies owing to their habit of hanging onto a grass blade or leaf by their forelegs. Using the claws of its hindlegs, the male scorpion-fly seizes a fly, wasp or bee as it passes beneath. He then emits pheromones to attract a female. On her arrival, the freshly caught meal is offered to the female (pictured). After-wards they will mate.

RIGHT A cranefly (*Gynoplistia* species). Often called daddy-long-legs, craneflies are often taken for giant mosquitoes. However, their size distinguishes them. Adults have modified mouthparts that form a proboscis for sucking water and nectar.

1

2

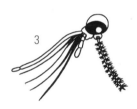

3

ABOVE Mouthparts of flies:
1. Dagger-shaped mandibles for penetrating and sucking: March flies.
2. Sponge-like mouthparts for mopping and absorbing: house flies.
3. Needle-like stylets for piercing and siphoning: mosquitoes.

RIGHT A female wattle goat moth (*Xyleutes encalypti*), emerges from its pupal case at the base of a black wattle (*Acacia decurrens*). As adults, these moths have non-functional mouthparts and live off their fat reserves, stored during larval growth (witchetty grub stage) when they feed on wattle tree roots.

Abdomen

Consisting of 11 segments, the abdomen in scorpion-flies is long, cylindrical and tapering, being broadest at mid-length. The female's external genitalia consist of a sub-genital plate located beneath the gonophore, typically accompanied by a sclerotised structure surrounding the spermathecal duct on segment 9.

FLIES
order Diptera

Head capsule

The compound eyes of male flies (and sometimes also of females), which almost entirely occupy the relatively large head

capsule, often meet dorsally in the centre. Among many flies, the eye lenses have rows of fine, erect setae protruding between them. Antennae vary greatly and are frequently distinctive according to sex, but they are typically fine and short (longer and branched in some groups).

Mouthparts are modified for sucking and siphoning fluids. Some groups—such as robber flies (family Asilidae) and march flies (family Tabanidae)—have primitive forms of mouthparts, however, which are long, beak-like and heavily sclerotised. Basal sclerites of maxillae are fused into the rostrum, the labium being the largest section of the mouthparts.

Thorax

The entire thoracic region is modified specifically to house and support the highly powerful flight muscles of the single pair of wings, the mesothorax being conspicuously enlarged for this reason. The prothorax and metathorax are greatly reduced.

Limbs

The legs vary enormously, being specialised according to the requirements and lifestyle of each species. The coxae are small and elongated (although they are swollen and enlarged among certain groups); the femur and tibia are the longest segments.

Notwithstanding modifications from species to species, five-segmented tarsi terminate in paired claws. Some species exude special adhesive fluids that allow them to negotiate smooth, vertical surfaces.

Abdomen

The abdomen is short and broad, although it is elongated in some groups, for example, robber flies, with 11 segments (segments 10 and 11 being fused in some groups). The spiracles are located within the lateral margins of the tergites.

The genitalia of male flies are typically located on segment 9 and closely associated with segments 7 and 8; they vary enormously, the aedeagus ranging from a sclerotised tube to very complex sexual organs. The female's tubular-shaped ovipositor is eversible and it is located on the reduced sixth and seventh segments. In some species, it is located on other posterior segments.

MOTHS AND BUTTERFLIES
order Lepidoptera

Head capsule

The rounded head capsule has antennae that
are three-segmented (the flagellum comprising
up to 60 units) and sparsely coated with scales.
The large, compound eyes often have fine,
erect setae between the lenses (similar to flies'
eyes). Two ocelli, when present, are located one
above each compound eye or, in some species,
adjacent to sensory organs (the chaetosemata).

The mouthparts vary among these
specialised nectar-feeders. The inner surfaces
of a butterfly's proboscis bear sclerotised
plates, joined together by a locking mechanism.
The proboscis is controlled by muscles that
coil it beneath the head capsule when the
insect is at rest. Most lepidopterans have five-
segmented maxillary palps (reduced or absent

in primitive families). The labial palps are
three-segmented and well developed, with the
apical segment bearing sensory equipment.

Thorax

There is a small prothorax, often with a pair of
dorsal processes (the patagia), and a large
mesothorax (smaller in primitive groups)
entirely covered by scales. Some moths
produce stridulatory sounds that range from
normal to ultrasonic frequencies. Clicking,
hissing or loud whistling sounds are used in
courtship behaviour. This confuses predators
and warns them of the moth's distastefulness.
Tympanal organs ('ears') located in the thorax
(or abdomen) help them avoid predators and
also to locate the opposite sex from 100 metres
or more. The wings of moths and butterflies
are especially developed for flight, this being
their most outstanding feature.

ABOVE A yellow-winged
hawk moth (*Gnathothlibus
erotus eras*). Hawk moths
are powerful fliers with
streamlined bodies and
narrow pointed forewings.
They hover at night, feeding
on nectar of deep bell-
shaped flowers, pollinating
as they move from flower to
flower. Their long uncoiled
'tongues' can determine
taste on contact and they
have minute organs called
chemoreceptors that 'taste
at a distance'. More
abundant on the softer
portions of mouthparts,
these are also present on
other parts of the body.

ABOVE A copper butterfly (*Paralucia* species). The underwings of butterflies often have sombre colours to enhance survival when at rest. The wings are folded above the body. Like most other members of its family (Lycaenidae), this species is intimately involved with ants, feeding on their larvae. The ants 'tolerate' the butterfly larvae's presence within their nest in exchange for the sweet exudations they offer.

Limbs

The three pairs of scale-covered legs are well developed for moving over the wide range of surfaces encountered in nectar-feeding. The forelimbs are reduced in some species. There are rigidly attached pterothoracic coxae, a small trochanter and a strong femur, bearing long hair-scales. Five-segmented tarsi terminate in a pair of curved, simple claws. An epiphysis on the fore-tibia serves to clean the antennae and proboscis of pollen dust. The hind tibiae of males of certain species have expandable tufts of scent-scales.

Abdomen

The abdomen is long, cylindrical and sometimes flattened and tapered, and it consists of 7–11 segments. In some groups, it is greatly modified by the sexual organs. There are seven pairs of spiracles (eight in some families) and there are no cerci.

The male genitalia constitute a complicated arrangement, which varies considerably between different families. Basically, there is a protective, hood-like tegumen, typically located on tergum 9 and parts of tergum 10; arising from this tegumen are paired processes, which are the genitalia. The testes are located beneath terga 5 and 6, the ejaculatory organ consisting of two sections.

The basic female genitalia consist of two openings, one ventrally located between segments 7 and 8 (used for mating) and the other opening, called an ovipore, which is typically located on fused segments 9–11 at the tip of the abdomen. It is often accompanied by a pair of lobe-like structures. These lobes are often modified for inserting eggs into plants, and the terminal segments are sometimes extensible to serve as an ovipositor, too. However, the basic genital arrangement is subject to various modifications or variations among different families.

WASPS, ANTS AND BEES
order Hymenoptera

Head capsule

On the mobile head capsule there are large, compound eyes, often with fine, erect setae between the lenses, and three ocelli (but reduced or absent in hymenopterans with wing reduction). Antennae vary considerably between groups; they often also differ distinctly by sex. They are often elbowed at the scape-pedical joint, and the flagellum in some species has ring-like segments that end in a distinct distal club.

The mouthparts of hymenopterans range from biting and cutting mandibles to the combined sucking and chewing types of advanced forms. The labrum is concealed by the clypeus in some groups. There are one- to seven-segmented maxillary palps and one- to four-segmented labial palps. The labium and maxillae are elongated in some groups, forming a retractable rostrum or proboscis used in nectar-feeding.

Thorax

The first abdominal segment is often merged with the metathorax, which is smaller than the other thoracic segments. The pronotum is large, with a loss of free movement on the mesothorax. Those with a more rigid pronotum generally have well-developed wing muscles. The meso-thorax is large and houses the flight muscles controlling the forewings. Metathoracic spiracles, located at the base of the hind wings, are sometimes visible in some species. Hymenopterans' wings are generally well developed for vigorous long-distance flight.

LEFT A golden-haired mortar bee (*Amegilla bombiformis*), the 'teddy bear bee'. This large bee excavates an underground nest, constructing a maze of tunnels within hard clay and soil. During daylight, the females come and go, collecting nectar and pollen for the larvae. Males remain alert for opportunities to mate with incoming females and at night they sleep nearby, firmly grasping onto twigs with their strong mandibles. Note the large pollen-carrying hairs, called scopa, on the hindlegs.

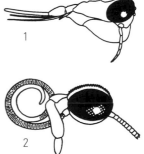

ABOVE Various mouthparts:
1. Spear-like rostrum for piercing and sucking: cicadas.
2. Long, slender coiled tube for probing and siphoning: butterflies and moths.
3. Tongue-like mandibles for chewing and lapping: bees.

Limbs

The legs vary greatly, being highly modified in some groups. The forelegs are used to clean the head, face and eyes. Many ants and bees have specialised spurs on all six legs, sometimes accompanied by preening brushes composed of thickly growing setae located on hind tibiae. These brushes are used to clean the wings, parts of the body and middle legs; the hindlegs are cleaned by being scraped against one another. Tarsi are five-segmented (four- or three-segmented in some groups) and terminate in paired claws, sometimes with lobe-shaped padding (the arolium) between them. Many bees have pollen-carrying scopa (hairs) on their hindlimbs.

Abdomen

Long, roundish, and tapered, the abdomen has 11 segments in primitive forms (suborder Symphyta). Segments 1–8 have eight pairs of spiracles (as with ichneumonoid wasps), but spiracles are reduced in many families. The cerci either consist of one segment or are reduced with sensory hairs (although they are absent in some forms, too). The tergal plates of some of the digging or burrowing species are modified by way of ridges or compressions, allowing free movement in the burrow or nest. For example, the bodies of hairy flower wasps (family Scoliidae) are greatly modified for digging into decaying timber in order to search for beetle larvae.

Male genitalia consist of a basal ring, with a sexual organ at the midpoint, accompanied by a pair of small, pincer-like structures used for mating. The female's ovipositor is located on segment 7 and consists of three valves and two basal sclerites. The valves, often bearing minute teeth, form the cutting or piercing structure. In some groups, the valves are elongated; in others, they form a stabbing instrument, like a hypodermic needle, used to inject paralysing chemicals into intended prey —these are connected to a poisonous gland that injects toxic fluid into the puncture.

CHAPTER TWO

Life Cycles

The way in which awkward, earth-bound, grub-like creatures transform themselves into brilliant winged jewels seems almost miraculous. The life cycles of insects have long attracted the human imagination—the 'lowly' caterpillar shrouds itself in a silken cocoon and, in this private chamber, recreates itself into a completely new creature, emerging exultant, perhaps as a beautiful butterfly. This dramatic change has, in many cultures, become symbolic of resurrection or trans-formation. All insects undergo this most fascinating process of change and growth called metamorphosis. Starting life as an egg, an insect may become a nymph, or a larva then a pupa. Finally, it reaches its adult stage, which is often strikingly different in body shape, size and form, as well as lifestyle, to that of its earlier incarnations. This chapter explores these numerous phases of insect metamorphosis, as well as courtship, mating and reproduction.

OPPOSITE A raspy cricket—also known as a tree cricket (*Paragryllacris* species) chirps to attract a female. Some male tree crickets have feeble voices and may resort to sneaky means to get a mate. Such a male will position himself near one that sings well, and often manages to mate with any females lured by the other cricket's song. However, if the singing male cricket notices the trespasser, he will give out an aggressive call. If the offender is not deterred, a fierce struggle may ensue.

An insect's life cycle normally divides into two distinct phases: first, a period from egg to final instar nymph or larva, during which the creature grows and develops but is unable to reproduce. Then, it is an adult, when it is sexually mature and has ceased growing.

After hatching, the stages of metamorphosis depend on whether the insect is an exopterygote or an endopterygote. An immature exopterygote is usually known as a nymph; it bears some resemblance to its adult form, but may live in water, as dragonfly or damselfly nymphs do, until its final moult when the wings develop and it takes to the air. As its body increases in size, the insect must moult its outer skin every so often (a process called ecdysis) and grow a new skin, the period between moults being known as an instar. All insects moult several times before attaining their adult form.

An immature endopterygote is known as a larva; it has no resemblance to its adult form, and its lifestyle is very different to the adult. A larva could be legless like fly larvae (maggots), or have six thoracic legs as do sawfly larvae (spitfires) and the majority of beetle larvae (for example, curl grubs and witchetty grubs). Moth and butterfly larvae (caterpillars) usually have leg-like appendages, called prolegs, on their abdominal segments. To become an adult, as well as a series of moults, the larva has to undergo what is

effectively a secondary egg stage—the pupal or chrysalid stage. When fully grown, the larva changes into a pupa, which does not feed. During this, its most vulnerable period, it is usually protected inside a silken cocoon or cell within soil or timber, although most butterflies have a naked chrysalis stage (that is, without a cocoon).

Once an insect has passed into the second phase of its life cycle and become an adult, its wings have developed and it is able to reproduce, but it cannot grow any larger. An adult insect's size is largely determined by the amount of food it consumes in its growth period as a larva or nymph. Many insects do not feed at as adults, deriving their energy from fat reserves stored as a larva. For some insects, the adult phase of the life cycle is extremely short, lasting only long enough to mate and lay eggs.

REPRODUCTION

While most insects reproduce sexually, parthenogenesis—where females develop ova (eggs) not requiring fertilisation by males—does occur, though rarely, as do some other rather unusual reproductive patterns. Reproduction generally, however, requires genetic material from both sexes, although the way the sperm and ovum are combined can vary greatly from species to

RIGHT Eggs of *Poecilometis armatus*, a species of cryptic shield-bug.

BELOW Eggs of the emperor gum moth (*Opodiphthera eucalypti*) are deposited singly or in batches adhered to the larvae's food source.

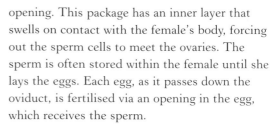

BELOW First instar nymphs of *Poecilometis armatus*, a cryptic shield-bug. The tiny nymph pushes against the egg wall to split it. Some baby insects bite their way out or break or split the shell-cap using sharp spiny blades or spikes.

species. In many cases, the mating and the fertilisation of the eggs are separate events, with the female carrying the sperm and using it at a later stage. For instance, numerous types of female insects have a special sac in which they store the sperm, until they lay their eggs. Males in some orders—such as Heteroptera, Coleoptera, Diptera and Hymenoptera—pass sperm as a fluid suspension directly into a female's brood canal. In yet other orders—such as Blattodea, Mantodea, Orthoptera and Lepidoptera—males transfer sperm contained in a special packet called a spermatophore. This is created when glands within the male's reproductive system produce protein that is poured around the sperm mass. During copulation, the spermatophore is transferred to the female and partially inserted into her genital

opening. This package has an inner layer that swells on contact with the female's body, forcing out the sperm cells to meet the ovaries. The sperm is often stored within the female until she lays the eggs. Each egg, as it passes down the oviduct, is fertilised via an opening in the egg, which receives the sperm.

Some primitive male arthropods (for instance, springtails and diplurans) do not actually mate with the female but instead produce a spermatophore, which they leave where the female will find it. She introduces it into her genital aperture and fertilisation takes place without any interaction with the male whatsoever.

In exceptional cases, reproduction may take place without any involvement by males—in other words, by parthenogenesis. This occurs among aphids and more rarely among insects such as short-horned grasshoppers, phasmatids, mantids, cockroaches, some wasps such as sawflies, and certain moths.

Among certain scale insects (family Coccidae) there are hermaphrodites—meaning each individual has both male and female sex glands. Other insects, such as the chalcidoid wasps (family Chalcididae), reproduce by a process known as 'budding', whereby a single fertilised egg divides itself into two; these two each divide themselves and the process thus continues, by which a long chain of embryos is formed until the energy required to continue this process is exhausted.

INSECT EGGS

The eggs of insects are extremely diverse in their form, size, shape and colour; many are exceptionally beautiful. Most eggs can be distinguished by the naked eye, and a pocket lens usually provides ample magnification for closer inspection, although for more detailed study, a microscope is indispensable.

The shell of an insect's egg is not calcareous like a bird's egg, but consists of a tough, horny substance, which is very durable, even capable of resisting fairly strong external pressure. It may be glossy or opaque, smooth or exquisitely sculptured. Each species has its characteristic eggshell and an entomologist—an insect scientist—can usually determine at a glance what kind of insect will emerge from it. Identification is made chiefly from the size,

shape and adornments of the eggs and also by the manner in which they have been laid.

Eggs are deposited in different ways by different insects—laid singly or in batches, in long rows or spiral patterns, usually glued to leaves or tree trunks. To securely fix the newly laid eggs in place, a tiny amount of adhesive material, which sets rapidly upon exposure to air, may be used. Some insects use this viscid cement in an unusual way: drawing it out to form a stem, they deposit an egg at its very tip. Sometimes 20 or more of these stems are laid in clusters.

This unusual method gives the eggs some protection from egg-eating insects such as ants; it also deters the cannibalistic tendency of the hatchlings to devour the unhatched eggs.

Another means of protecting eggs—practised by praying mantids and cockroaches—is by packing them into stoutly formed envelopes or capsules called oothecae, which contain anywhere from 20 to 200 eggs, depending on the species.

Insect eggs can resist extreme cold, and may even be frozen solid without their viability being reduced. At the appointed season, the eggshell opens to disclose a fully equipped individual with the potential to reproduce all of its parents' attributes. From the instant it hatches, the tiny creature already appears to be much too large to fit back into the protective confines of the eggshell from which it has just emerged.

Infant insects use a variety of methods to escape the confines of their eggs, including

ABOVE Dutifully protecting her eggs, a female cotton harlequin jewel bug · (*Tectocoris diophthalmus*) head-butts an amorous male, whose ardent advances are unwelcome during the incubation period.

ABOVE After leaving its burrow at dusk, a crawling floury-baker cicada (*Abricta curvicosta*) nymph headed for the nearest tree trunk where it is emerging. Highly vulnerable, it can fall prey to ravaging tree crickets, which tear into its cuticle with powerful mandibles, and devour its flesh. Although thousands of individuals may emerge simultaneously, each individual cicada has its own timing to undergo its final moult.

RIGHT Flower beetles undergo transformation a few centimetres below the ground, concealed within mud-frass cells formed by the fully-grown larvae. Their larvae, such as this curl grub of the cowboy beetle (*Diaphonia dorsalis*) seen with a pupa, feed on plant roots and decaying vegetation.

gnawing their way out or swelling and contorting themselves to split it open. In some species, the hatchling pushes away one end of the egg or pushes open a 'lid'. Many species are equipped with a specialised, spine-shaped 'egg-opener', formed as a set of teeth or sharp ridges on the top of the head, which creates an emergence slit. A newly hatched infant usually devours its entire eggshell as a first meal.

COURTSHIP AND MATING

Not all insects engage in courtship behaviour before mating. For some, mating is a somewhat perfunctory matter but for others, courtship may include intricate dance routines or other sexual behaviour. Various means exist for bringing males and females together: scent, sight, touch and sound—singly and combined—

all play vital roles in courtship preliminaries. The males of numerous species (certain wasps, for instance), are territorial. They claim a particular area through mating calls or by patrolling on the wing and will intercept females that enter their area.

Most butterflies recognise the opposite sex, usually at a distance, using colour as a means of identifying them. Among the emperor moths (family Saturniidae), females emit a pheromone, scent vapours, which a male of the same species can detect from several kilometres away.

Prior to courtship, a male butterfly such as the wanderer butterfly, *Danaus plexippus plexippus*, will brush the tip of his abdomen into its wing pockets to collect the sex-attracting pheromones. He then brushes the head and antennae of the female as the pair perform an upward-spiralling dance in the air.

TYPES OF METAMORPHOSIS

The total metamorphosis that occurs in the advanced insects—the endopterygotes—represents a special type of change. This is a complete change in form, one that also involves changes in biochemistry, in behavioural patterns, and in lifestyle: the caterpillar lives a completely different lifestyle to that of its metamorphosed form, the butterfly; each feeds on different foods and occupies different microhabitats.

Metamorphosis is a phenomenon widely found throughout nature, but it is not always, or necessarily so dramatic. Scientifically defined, the term signifies a particular degree of change of form occurring during the development from egg to adult, and insects have evolved various forms of metamorphosis. For scientific study, insects can be divided into the following four categories, based on the degree of change they undergo in their life cycles—in other words, the extent to which metamorphosis takes place:
• no marked metamorphosis occurs (apterygotes)
• partial metamorphosis (one group of exopterygotes—mayflies only)
• gradual metamorphosis (exopterygotes generally)
• complete metamorphosis (endopterygotes).

No marked metamorphosis

The first category includes pseudo insects such as springtails (order Collembola), proturans (order Protura), and diplurans (order Diplura). It also includes the very primitive insects stemming from wingless ancestors, archaeognaths (order Archaeognatha) and silverfish (order Thysanura). These insects do not undergo any distinct stage of meta-morphosis, being look-alikes of their parents from the moment of hatching. Growth is by a series of moults.

Partial metamorphosis

The second category comprises just one group of exopterygotes—the mayflies (order Ephem-eroptera). They are the only living insects to undergo partial metamorphosis, which consists of four marked stages in their life cycle: egg, nymph, subimago, adult.

Mayflies are the only winged insects to moult again after having emerged as a winged form (the subimago): they even have to moult their delicate wings before they reach maturity.

Gradual metamorphosis

Insects that have evolved this intermediary form of metamorphosis undergo three distinct stages in their life cycle: egg, nymph and adult.

Included here are endopterygote insects such as the damselflies and dragonflies (order Odonata), stoneflies (order Plecoptera), cockroaches (order Blattodea), mantids (order Mantodea), earwigs (order Dermaptera), katydids, crickets and short-horned grass-hoppers (order Orthoptera), phasmatids (order Phasmatodea), and true bugs, cicadas and their various allies (order Hemiptera).

Among exopterygotes, the nymphal or immature forms usually resemble their parents

ABOVE Mating meadow argus butterflies (*Precis villida calybe*); the female above. The genitalia of female butterflies have two openings. One is ventrally located between segments 7 and 8 (for mating); the other is at the apex of the abdomen (for egg-laying). Caterpillars of meadow argus butterflies feed on purple-top verbena, pigweed and convolvulus.

Complete metamorphosis

In this final category are the most advanced insects in terms of metamorphosis—the endopterygotes, which have a life cycle consisting of four distinct stages: egg, larval, pupal and adult. Included here are four major orders—the beetles (Coleoptera), flies (Diptera), moths and butterflies (Lepidoptera), and wasps, ants and bees (Hymenoptera), as well as others such as the lacewings (Neuroptera), alderflies and dobsonflies (Megaloptera), scorpion-flies (Mecoptera), caddis-flies (Trichoptera). In all these insects, during the larval stage (in which there are typically five larval instars), the wing buds grow larger internally with each moult; they only become everted and visible in the pupal (or chrysalid) stage. The pupal stage also provides a mould for the adult muscles to develop their appropriate form and length.

During the pupal stage of many modern winged insects (especially moths and butterflies) their appendages—rudimentary wings, legs, antennae and mouthparts—are fused together close to the body by a secretion produced during the larval phase. These appendages are normally well sclerotised and fit together in the pupal case as neatly as the pieces of a jigsaw puzzle, being visible in outline only, on the surface of the case. Many modern winged insects have their appendages free of the body in the pupal case. While they can wriggle their abdomens, their rudimentary appendages are incapable of movement.

The complete physical change that the endopterygotes undergo is the most remarkable of these metamorphoses. Upon hatching from an egg, most other animals look like their parents, or at least resemble them in some way. But the butterfly caterpillar, for example, in no way resembles the delicate, brightly winged, graceful, nectar-feeding adult it becomes.

The biochemical changes involved in this process are no less startling. Just as the juvenile caterpillar cells have been retained within butterflies to create new generations of caterpillars, so, too, do adult cells exist within caterpillars to create new generations of adult butterflies. These two, distinctly different, forms meet at a midway point—when the pupa is formed. During this immobile pupal stage, the organs of the caterpillar dissolve to rearrange into the organs of the adult butterfly. The insect's biological clock coordinates the entire biochemical and physiological process.

ABOVE Rearing offspring: a male cotton harlequin jewel bug (*Tectocoris diophthalmus*), with second and third instar nymphs. After hatching, the young bugs cluster together with the ongoing protection of the adults until they can fend for themselves.

in bodily structure, except for their size and in being wingless and sexually immature. As they grow, they undergo a series of moults (typically five instars). All their flight muscles are present, but in the form of wing buds that grow larger with each moult throughout the nymphal stage of development. Otherwise, there is little change at this stage. It is only at the final moult that they become equipped with fully developed membranous outgrowths (that is, their wing structures), and their contracted wing buds fully expand. Only then, too, do they become sexually mature insects, able to reproduce.

RIGHT A few days before emergence, the wing patterns and colouring of the pre-adult 'chrysalis' of the tailed emperor butterfly (*Polyura pyrrhus sempronius*) begins to show through the chrysalis case, deepening as pigments develop in the wing-scales.

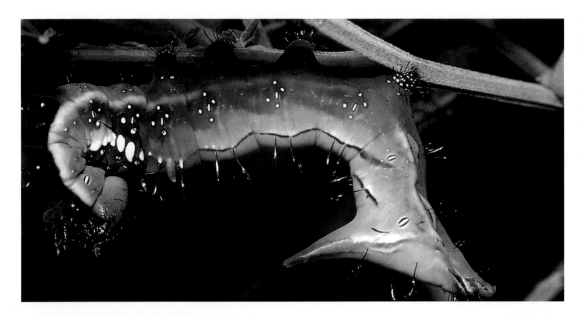

LEFT A caterpillar of the peppered prominent moth (*Neola semiaurata*). Older larvae are conspicuously coloured and have two large blue-ringed eyespots hidden within opening slits of a 'horn' stemming from their eighth abdominal segment. The female moth deposits her eggs singly on black wattle (*Acacia decurrens*).

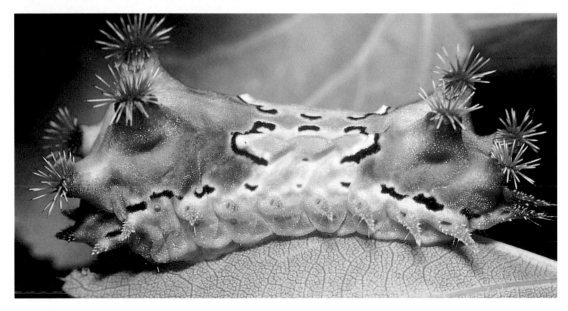

LEFT The brightly coloured sea anemone-like caterpillar of the mottled cup moth (*Doratifera vulnerans*) is armed with expansible tufts of sharp stinging spines (setae). These expanded spines retract when at rest. These caterpillars feed on the leaves of eucalypts and fruit trees.

LEFT A caterpillar of a tussock moth (family Lymantriidae). The stout setae are woven into the silken cocoon to deter predators during pupation. They can irritate the skin if handled. The hairy larvae feed on leaves of exotic shrubs and eucalypts.

DIVERSITY AMONG THE GROUPS

This part of the chapter explores many individual stories of the life change and reproduction processes that some insects undergo—the primitive winged insects (exopterygotes) are first, followed by the modern winged insects (endopterygotes).

Exopterygotes include insects with an immature or nymphal form that resembles, to a great degree, their mature or adult form: their wing buds develop externally and growth takes place through gradual (or, in the case of mayflies, partial) metamorphosis.

Endopterygotes include insects where their immature form, the larva, differs from the adult form—in appearance, lifestyle and microhabitat. The life cycle of these insects takes place in four distinct stages: egg, larval, pupal and adult.

MAYFLIES
order Ephemeroptera

Mayflies are among the most primitive survivors of winged insects and the only known group in which the adult form moults again.

Depending on the species, the life cycle of the mayfly can last from six months to three years, with overlapping generations.

Nymphal phase
A newly hatched nymph hastens to seek shelter beneath a stone or a crevice on the banks of a stream, or may burrow into the mud. The nymph has gills and well-developed mouthparts, and feeds on algae, plant tissue and decaying vegetation.

The various species of mayfly nymphs often distinctly differ from one another, unlike adult mayflies, mainly owing to differences in habitat and food source. One recent interesting discovery about mayfly nymphs is how they orientate themselves under water. It was formerly believed that their sense of balance was maintained by gravity, but it is now known that the light filtering through the water reaches their eyes and this keeps them on course.

Emergence
After undergoing a series of moults (up to 23 have been recorded), the fully grown mayfly nymph is ready to leave its water environment. It rises and floats, or crawls out of the water and clings to a nearby rock or plant stem. Its old nymphal shell splits open and it emerges and expands its wings.

The insect is at this stage called a subimago. It is not yet sexually mature but is fully winged, its new wings being a smoky colour. Shortly afterwards, when its wings have dried and hardened, the mayfly flies off seeking a place to rest for a couple of days, sometimes venturing far from water. Then it moults again, finally emerging as the perfect insect, its sole purpose being to mate. By now its flying power has markedly improved. In the adult stage it does not feed and its mouthparts are non-functional.

Reproduction
Adults normally frequent lakes, streams and ponds, resting during daylight on tree trunks and foliage. At dusk they take to the air and perform a brief, lively mating dance, swarming above the water. The females hover on the outskirts of the whirling mass of males and make sudden dashes into the swarm to be seized by waiting males. Mating pairs immediately leave the dance to alight on nearby leaves and branches. The population diminishes later in the evening as the females deposit their eggs.

Egg-laying
The female trails her egg masses in long ribbons from the tip of her abdomen. She dips this beneath the surface of running water to deposit them. Each egg, measuring around a millimetre long, is collected by the running water and quickly sinks to become attached to a submerged plant, rock or log. Parthenogenesis occurs among some species of mayflies.

DAMSELFLIES
order Odonata: suborder Zygoptera

Nymphal phase
Damselfly nymphs are thin, frail creatures. Their nymphal phase is normally completed within 12 months, during which time they live among aquatic plant life, preying upon smaller water creatures. Clinging to the stems of water

plants, and being cryptically coloured in greens and browns, the nymphs blend well with their surroundings. Their behaviour during the nymphal phase and emergence is essentially similar to that of dragonflies.

The nymphs of damselflies (like those of dragonflies) are equipped with gills that allow them to extract oxygen beneath the water. They have three long, plate-like tails, like mayfly nymphs, but in damselflies these serve as caudal, tracheal gills that trail from the tip of the abdomen. Lost or damaged gills are regenerated between moults. A nymph utilises these external gills to propel itself through the water by vigorously swishing its abdomen from side to side.

Reproduction and egg-laying

Visual courtship precedes mating. The two insects chase one another in the air until the male seizes the prothorax of the female. After mating, the male helps his mate by steadying her on a slippery reed stem as she lays her batches of eggs.

The female's ovipositor is modified to enable it to make slits in leaves, submerged vegetation or reed stems, into which the eggs are deposited. Females also crawl beneath the water with their wings tightly folded together above their body, to lay their eggs. Females of some larger species produce thousands of eggs but of these the proportion living long enough to complete the life cycle is only small.

DRAGONFLIES
order Odonata: suborder Anisoptera

Nymphal phase

Compared to damselfly nymphs, true dragonfly nymphs are much stouter, more robust and, because dragonflies are generally large, they naturally grow much larger, too. They are powerful enough to capture tadpoles, small fish and other prey that are often much larger than themselves, which they do with their unique mouthparts.

Unlike the damselfly nymph, a dragonfly nymph has no external gills for breathing in water. Instead, its breathing organs are greatly modified, consisting of a mesh of tracheal gills situated within the walls of the rectum. To obtain the required oxygen, it draws water into

its rectum, and expels it through the same anal opening. This respiratory system also provides the nymph's means of movement through the water: the forcible expulsion of water propels it forward in short bursts of speed.

Those species frequenting slow-moving water habitats crawl about the bottom among decaying debris, where they become coated with a slimy silt that clings to their body hairs. The cryptic colouring of the silt-covered nymph serves to camouflage it at the bottom of the creek bed. Some species burrow their way through the sandy bottom of a creek bed, using their blade-like forelimbs and a wedge-shaped head, to completely cover themselves.

After hatching, the nymph's tiny wing buds emerge, growing larger with each moult.

LEFT Typical of exopterygote insects, dragonflies undergo a gradual metamorphosis, which involves three distinct stages: egg, nymph and adult. At the top is a dragonfly nymph (*Noto-aeschna* species) in its final instar. Fully grown, the nymph becomes restless and climbs out of its water environment at dawn. Resting, it expands until the exuviae split and the pro-adult works itself free. In the centre, the exuviae of the large dragonfly (*N. sagittata*). The dried remains of trachaea (the air-tubes leading to spiracles) are conspicuously trailing out of the split exuviae. At the bottom is another *Notoaeschna* species dragonfly, which has twisted and turned like a tiny acrobat to free itself from its exuviae. Finally emerged, it pauses to rest, dry its expanded wings and gain pigmentation in the fresh air and sunshine.

The number of moults varies from 10–15 and (depending on the species, food supply and climatic conditions) the nymphal phase can take weeks, months or, for some of the larger true dragonflies, several years.

Emergence

When the nymph is fully grown, its wing buds are prominent and feeding ceases entirely. In preparation for its transition from an aquatic-breathing to an aerial-breathing animal, it moves to the edge of the stream. To avoid predators, the nymph leaves the water normally under cover of night (just before dawn) and then crawls up the nearest tree trunk, rock or reed-stem. It secures a firm grip, using its sharp tarsal claws to safeguard against falling.

Here it remains motionless, swelling its body until its old exoskeleton splits along the back of the thorax and head region when, with great persistence, it pulls itself free. It slowly inflates its new body and wing buds by pumping haemolymph through its veins until its magnificent wings are fully extended.

After drying in the sunshine, the now-adult dragonfly takes to the air on its shimmering wings. It can be as much as six days before its body and wings fully harden and its brilliant colours become apparent. During this time, it stays away from water, and glories in its power of flight. Under favourable conditions, some species take part in large-scale, long-distance migratory flights.

The empty shells from which they hatch can remain hanging intact, attached to reed stems at the water's edge, for some time after emergence. The shells are sometimes occupied by sac spiders, which use them as brood chambers.

Reproduction

Prior to mating and egg production, female dragonflies require a continual supply of food, which can only be accomplished by being free from interference from the amorous males. For this reason, recently emerged females make excursions far afield into forests and woodlands to dry and harden their new exoskeletons in preparation for the active life ahead of them.

Mating always takes place close to water. This is where the males wait patiently for the females to return to the area in which they first emerged. Sight is very important for dragonflies. Visual courtship always precedes mating and it

is by their brilliant colouring and specific signals, characteristic for each species, that the sexes recognise one another. Males that have alighted will, for instance, wave their abdomens to advertise themselves. As is common with damselflies, males and females of the same species of dragonfly are often markedly different in colour.

During the mating season, each male stakes out a territorial flightpath near the water and claims a vantage position on a particular branch or reed stem, on which he perches. From here he watches for other dragonflies entering 'his territory', with any trespasser being promptly chased. If the intruder is another male, a mid-air skirmish results with, normally, the intruder being driven away.

The male's immediate response is the same when a female, returning from her maiden flight, enters his territory. However, he will quickly recognise a female of his species and the two engage in a wild mid-air chase, the female leading the male wherever takes her fancy. Eventually, the male catches up and grasps her behind her head with his anal claspers located at the tip of his abdomen. They then fly together, in a tandem position, forming a typical 'mating wheel'.

Both dragonflies and damselflies have adopted a uniquely complex technique of mating and transference of sperm. Copulation normally continues in the air, but at times the pair alight on foliage to complete their union: the male, positioning himself above and ahead of her, grips hold of a leaf or twig with his spiny limbs and the female holds on tightly around his abdomen. Prior to mating, the male transfers the seminal fluid into his large sperm pouch, by bending the tip of his abdomen forward. The female curves her abdominal segments to meet his sperm pouch (ventrally located close to the thorax on the second abdominal segment, and not at the tip of the abdomen as in most other male insects). The mating organs of the male dragonfly are separated from the sperm duct opening (the vas deferens), which is located on the ninth abdominal segment.

Both sexes normally mate several times a day, each session extending an hour or more (depending on the individuals and the species involved). Adults are potentially long-lived, often surviving several weeks, with ample opportunities to meet one another.

OPPOSITE Mating mosquito hawk dragonflies (*Aeshna brevistyla*). When mating, the male situates himself above the female to clasp the back of her neck. She curls her abdomen to meet his sperm pouch, forming a 'mating wheel'. Nymphs spend several years in freshwater ponds before they reach maturity.

Egg-laying

The pair normally remain together after mating to carry out egg-laying. The male often assists by hovering with the female during the process, which enables her to dip her abdomen deeply into the water. Some species have specialised ovipositors that can make slits in vegetation such as plant-stems, for inserting their eggs; others lay their eggs on leaves that are submerged or growing out of the water.

STONEFLIES
order Plecoptera

Stonefly nymphs have an aquatic lifestyle and require well-aerated water. Growing to maturity may take from several months to years.

Reproduction and egg-laying

In some species the female deposits her eggs by dipping the tip of her abdomen into the water while in flight; the eggs then disperse in water as they are washed about. In other species the female crawls beneath the water and deposits her egg-mass beneath stones and fallen timber. Depending on the species, eggs may be laid singly or in masses numbering up to a thousand.

COCKROACHES
order Blattodea

Nymphal phase

On hatching, cockroach nymphs normally stay close together and may remain so during the first few moults. They are look-alikes of their parents, and live the same nocturnal, scavenging lifestyle. They may have 7–14 moults, depending on the species, and they take from four to 12 months before attaining sexual maturity and their wings.

Reproduction and egg-laying

Males and females find one another through body scents. Mating is preceded by a simple display of courtship, and the male cockroach (like the mantid) transfers a spermatophore to the female.

Eggs are enclosed within a highly protective capsule (called an ootheca). Inside the ootheca the eggs are laid in two rows of pockets, separated by partitions (the whole arrangement resembling certain seedpods). Normally, several of these capsules are produced in one season.

For several days the female carries around her egg capsule protruding from claspers at the tip of her abdomen before she releases it or attaches it to foliage, bark or rock. There are certain species that hold onto the capsule throughout the incubation period, while others incubate the eggs internally within a brood sac in the abdomen.

TERMITES
order Isoptera

Nymphal phase

On hatching, termite nymphs are look-alikes of adult workers and they undergo seven moults to reach maturity. However, stationary and irregular moulting occurs among some families.

Nymphs of the reproductive castes (which are winged as adult forms, and called alates) typically develop by moulting their old skins and forming wing buds during their third moult. The nymphs of non-reproductive castes (which become workers or soldiers as adults) undergo one or more nymphal stages. In a new colony only worker and soldier castes are produced.

Reproduction and egg-laying

To reproduce, male and female alates take flight to find suitable sites to start new colonies in which they become the new king and queen.

When the new queen is ready to lay eggs, her sausage-shaped body becomes enormous—up to 35 mm in length and 15 mm across (some African species swell to five times this size). The eggs are laid singly and collected by the workers who pile them into masses within allocated chambers in the nest. Queens of some species lay their eggs within ootheca-like egg capsules (closely resembling those of cockroaches, their close relatives).

RIGHT A late instar of the German cockroach (*Blatella germanica*), a widespread species well known as a prolific breeder. Shown here in the process of moulting, it will gain its colouring in a few hours. Although attaining wings at its final moult, this species does not fly.

PRAYING MANTIDS
order Mantodea

Nymphal phase

After hatching from its egg, but before actually emerging from the egg-capsule (or ootheca), each tiny mantid is covered with a membranous sac, which protects it from abrasion and from drying out. At this stage it is called a 'pro-nymph'. Blood pressure builds up inside its head to a point where it bursts the protective sac. Having broken through, the frail, slender nymphs form a festooning mass on the outside of their old home.

Except for wings and reproductive organs, the black-eyed nymphs look exactly like their parents and they have the same predatory lifestyle. At first they can only handle aphid-sized prey but, as they grow, they begin to take on bigger prey. Their cannibalistic tendencies are exhibited early on but normally they feed upon other insects their own size or smaller. After several moults, they cast off their final exoskeleton to become sexually mature. Many species have flying wings.

Reproduction

There are a few parthenogenetic species, but most mantis species mate. Courtship displays are extremely rare. The male, having located the female by the pheromones she emits, cautiously approaches her from behind. When he is within a few centimetres, he suddenly makes a flying leap onto her. If timed right, he lands on her back.

If he keeps his head down and closely clasps her, his chance of remaining intact increases. More frequently, however (especially among larger species), the female reaches around, grabs him in a deadly headlock and begins devouring his head and prothorax. Although decapitated, his nervous system is designed to continue mating, with his abdomen curled beneath hers, usually remaining in this position for hours.

Afterwards, the female devours him, which furnishes his offspring with the protein needed for healthy egg development. His decapitation is the female's guarantee against being eaten herself during mating.

Egg-laying

Like cockroaches, female mantids lay their eggs inside a protective, highly insulated 'purse' or egg-capsule, which she begins constructing some 48 hours after mating. The eggs are deposited amidst frothy material exuded from the tip of her abdomen. Once the laying is completed, the protein substance hardens to form a tough capsule housing 10–100 eggs. These capsules vary in shape and size from species to species—some larger species lay up to 400 eggs within a single capsule.

A healthy female can produce 10 or more capsules in a season. They are laid in a variety of microhabitats. Some survive winter in cold climates, thanks to their excellent insulative properties; others can withstand long, dry spells in arid regions, securely attached beneath rock ledges and branches. The females of certain species guard their brood until the young hatch, but most leave after depositing their eggs.

EARWIGS
order Dermaptera

Nymphal phase

After hatching, the nymphs remain with their mother, clustering beneath her body when threatened. Female earwigs demonstrate remarkable maternal care for their eggs and young, behaviour that is unusual among insects. She generally looks after the nymphs until they can fend for themselves—usually after their second moult. However, if the nymphs do not leave the nest then and disperse to go about their own lives, the mother will eat them.

Nymphs resemble the adults and grow by moulting several times and, in winged species, they develop wing buds in the second or third moult. An early source of food for the nymphs is their own moulted skins.

ABOVE A female praying mantis (*Archimantis latistyla*) with her ootheca attached to the leaves of a *Lobelia* plant. During her active life she may produce 20 of these egg cases. She exudes a special liquid stirred into a frothy mass by the tip of her abdomen and encloses in this are the 80–100 eggs, laid in rows. This liquid hardens, offering protection against harsh weather and birds but it does not prevent tree crickets or parasitic wasp larvae, the biggest enemies of mantids, from devouring the eggs.

Reproduction

During late summer, the male and female mate inside a chamber which is excavated some 25 cm below the surface of the soil or in crevices among decaying vegetation. This follows a short, ritual courtship display. They bring their genitalia into contact by facing opposite directions and they will normally remain together for some time.

After the female has laid her eggs, her strong maternal instinct leads her to drive the male away. She then cleans the eggs, keeps them neatly together and guards the hatchlings until they disperse.

Egg-laying

The smooth, cream-coloured eggs are oval-shaped, measuring up to 2 mm in length. The eggs, laid in batches of 20–80, are usually deposited in soil debris and rotting logs. They hatch within 2–4 weeks, depending upon climatic conditions, but they must be licked by the mother in order for them to hatch.

BELOW A nymph of the rainforest spiny katydid (*Phricta* species) clings to a lichen-covered tree trunk a couple of metres off the ground. Adults climb higher up tree trunks, with females descending only to oviposit late in the rainy season. When disturbed, its defensive ploy is to repeatedly kick its spiny hindlegs above its body.

RIGHT Both the nymphs (pictured) and adults of the tropical yellow tree cricket (*Craspedogryllacris* species) have pegs situated on the inner surface of their hind femurs. They rub these against abdominal tubercles to produce stridulating sounds to lure and locate one another.

KATYDIDS, CRICKETS AND SHORT-HORNED GRASSHOPPERS
order Orthoptera

This section includes representatives of both suborders: ensiferans, which are long-horned and primarily nocturnal, such as katydids, bush crickets and true crickets; and caeliferans, which are short-horned and primarily diurnal, such as short-horned grasshoppers (or locusts).

Nymphal phase

An orthopteran nymph looks like its parents, except that its head is large in proportion to its body. It also, of course, lacks wings and sexual development. Nymphs have the same lifestyle as their parents, whether herbivorous or carnivorous. They grow quickly, and all orthopterans undergo a gradual metamorphosis, with several instars.

The wing buds continue to enlarge with each moult (although there are many wingless forms). From hatching to maturity, katydids, crickets and short-horned grasshoppers undergo 5–6 moults, and require 2–3 months to acquire fully expanded flying wings, modified wings (used by many species for stridulating), and reproductive organs. At the final moult, the juvenile cuticle is shed and the soft, crumpled wings are pumped out to full size. After an hour or more of hardening, the adult insect is ready to pursue its new stage of life.

Reproduction

Among orthopterans, the sexual organs and abdominal appendages vary enormously; so, too, do the positions adopted during mating. Sound plays the key role in bringing the male and female ensiferans together.

The males of many orthopteran species stridulate by rubbing the wings and legs together. The females, on hearing this 'serenading', move about until they locate its source. Mating is then assured. Most short-horned grasshoppers (family Acrididae) mate on bare patches of ground, into which the eggs are also laid.

Grasshoppers and crickets, like many insects, have evolved a spermatophore, which is transferred to the female during copulation. After mating, the two insects rest together, and the female normally eats the empty spermatophore for its rich source of protein.

Egg-laying

Eggs vary in shape and size from species to species, and can be cylindrical, curved, flattened or oval. To protect them from adverse climatic conditions and predators, the female inserts the eggs into plant tissue or into soil by means of a long, stout ovipositor.

Many different species of crickets and short-horned grasshoppers have developed specialised ovipositors for laying eggs in a variety of situations. Most long-horned grasshoppers insert their eggs into the tissue of young stems or leaves of a wide range of plants. Some are equipped with remarkably long, sickle-shaped ovipositors capable of piercing tough plant tissue. Many tree-frequenting species have evolved a range of short to long ovipositors, with which they insert their eggs into leaf tissue or tree bark. Some species cement their eggs in rows on leaves or branches.

Short-horned grasshoppers mostly deposit their eggs in the soil, though some have ovipositors capable of drilling holes in logs and tree stumps. With the tip of her abdomen, a

ABOVE A nymph of the Sydney katydid (*Terpandrus horridus*) on a yellow drumstick (*Isopogon* species). Like many katydid nymphs, it grows by feeding on protein derived from flower petals and pollen-coated anthers. It is quick to hide among foliage if disturbed. Other insects are also included in its diet.

ABOVE Mating meadow katydids or 'bullyheads' (*Conocephalus semivittatus*). The male deposits his sperm in a sperm capsule into the female's genital opening. She then eats the protein-rich capsule; its nutrients are required to produce healthy eggs. The sperm itself is stored in her sperm pouch and the eggs are fertilised as they are laid.

female bores a deep hole into which she stretches her abdominal segments as deeply as she can before depositing the eggs. With some species, the abdominal segments have evolved to an amazing degree, enabling the female to penetrate deep into soil or rotting timber. Short-horned grasshoppers normally deposit their eggs in masses; they are fertilised as they are laid and then covered with a layer of tough, protective material, which is excreted by the female.

STICK INSECTS AND LEAF INSECTS (PHASMATIDS)
order Phasmatodea

Nymphal phase
Depending on the available leaf growth, phasmatid nymphs hatch during spring and summer. On hatching, they make the long climb to the top of the nearest shrubs and trees to reach the young tips, where they rest during the day and feed at night.

Phasmatids undergo gradual metamorphosis, typically moulting several times (fewer in males) before attaining adulthood, which can take up to three years for some species. During their nymphal period, they can (like many mantids) regenerate injured or lost appendages.

Reproduction
Courtship is minimal, and many species are parthenogenetic—males being unknown or rarely found in some species. The slightly built male mounts the larger female, curving his abdomen beneath hers to transfer a small spermatophore into her genital opening.

Egg-laying
The female drops her eggs singly to the forest floor while feeding high in the canopy—usually in late summer. Just as the adults mimic plant twigs and leaves, the eggs strongly resemble plant seeds and, typically, are ovoid, with hardened, sculptured or patterned shells. The

eggshell is supplied with a lid, which the tiny nymph pushes open from the inside.

Development of the embryo is variable, owing to numerous genetic and environmental pressures, and the eggs do not hatch until the following spring, or, if the conditions are unfavourable, the spring after that.

APHIDS, SCALE INSECTS, MEALY BUGS
order Hemiptera:
suborder Sternorrhyncha

Nymphal phase
On hatching, these insects' nymphs resemble their parents. Like other insects in this suborder, they undergo gradual metamorphosis, moulting 3–7 times (depending on the species) before reaching maturity.

Reproduction
The most interesting fact about aphids is that parthenogenesis plays a major role in reproduction. In most species, a wingless caste of 'stem-mothers' can produce many generations of living young without developing any males and without the intervention of, or insemination by, males. Seven or more generations can occur yearly, but this depends strongly on variables such as temperature changes and other environmental conditions, or available food sources, and so on.

Every few generations, winged migratory females are produced to form new colonies. When the conditions are favourable for migrating—and this is at temperatures reaching higher than 17°C—the tiny, winged females ride the air currents in their millions, sometimes covering considerable distances.

Both winged males and females are produced in autumn. They mate and then the winged females fly away to lay their eggs on herbaceous plants. The eggs overwinter there, producing the first brood of 'stem-mothers' the following spring.

From these wingless females, other females are produced by laying eggs that do not require fertilisation by a male—they are already complete embryos. Then, perhaps one or two generations later, winged females again develop, which in turn fly away, recommencing the cycle elsewhere.

CICADAS
order Hemiptera:
suborder Auchenorrhyncha

The cicada courts much publicity owing to its habit of leaving its old shell clinging to the trunk of a tree for all to see. Some cicadas emerge at night, such as the greengrocer (or yellow Monday) cicada, *Cyclochila australasiae*, which typically emerges before 11 pm. Other species, such as the double-drummer cicada *Thopha saccata*, can be observed shedding their shells at sunrise or later in the day, sometimes even during the afternoon.

Nymphal phase
Numbers of tiny white nymphs hatch and drop to the ground together; regardless of how far they fall, they do so without injury. Once landed, they actively work their way out of sight beneath the soil, where they construct small air-cells up against a tree root.

Throughout its long life underground, the cicada nymph subsists entirely on fresh, cool sap, which it draws up from the roots of trees and shrubs by embedding its rostrum deeply in the root of the host plant. The nymph normally burrows down to 20 cm–45 cm below the soil surface. However, depending on the terrain and species of the host plant, it may burrow as deeply as 3 metres.

The subterranean burrow has a distinct enlargement at its bottom end, and is seldom straight—its course being determined by obstructing rocks and tree roots. The upper

BELOW Mating *Pachymorpha squalida* stick insects. This short-antennaed species frequents foliage, twigs and tree branches of eucalypts in open woodlands and sclerophyll forest. Looking like a dead twig, these insects can easily defy detection, even at close range, its form becoming obvious only when it moves.

wall is closed at its top, separated from the ground surface by a layer of undisturbed soil, which is broken only when the nymph emerges. The burrow's interior is clear of all debris. Even though the largest chamber is several times bigger than its occupant, the excavated material is not brought to the surface but is tightly compacted and pushed back into the burrow walls. These walls are made smooth, and waste bodily fluids are used to cement and waterproof them.

The nymph may live underground for several months or even years, depending on the species. Observations in different localities show that temperature plays a large role in determining how long it spends underground. As it grows, it moults several times, with its wing buds progressively enlarging.

In spring, the fully grown nymph becomes restless and begins tunnelling upwards until it is just a few centimetres beneath the surface. Here it waits for favourable conditions for its emergence. Conditions are especially favourable after a day or two of heavy rain or steady showers.

Species such as the greengrocer cicada, *Cyclochila australasiae*, sometimes build a mud tower above the ground, in which they remain, testing the humidity to see if conditions are favourable for emergence. In certain situations, such as when the soil is unusually wet, numerous towers are constructed; they appear in dry conditions as well, but not in such great numbers. Some towers have measured as high as 18 cm, but they are usually much shorter.

If, after 'testing the air' in this way, the conditions are found to be favourable, the nymph emerges. When they are unfavourable for emergence, it re-descends and remains underground until the following season or even the season after that.

Emergence

Most species use the cover of darkness to emerge from the ground. It is extremely difficult to witness a nymph in the very act of exiting from the soil; even digging up numerous open burrows may not reveal a single nymph. After leaving its subterranean home, the mud-smeared nymph slowly ascends the nearest tree trunk or rock, normally coming to rest within a couple of metres off the ground.

The nymph normally maintains a position for itself by hooking its claws into the tree bark.

OPPOSITE A male greengrocer cicada (*Cyclochila australasiae*), stretches and expands his abdominal segments as he frees himself from his nymphal skin. Once out, he suspends himself head-down, then rights himself to gain the nearest foothold with the tarsal claws of his fore- and mid-legs, his hindlimbs trailing. The wings unfurl and finally hang flat to dry, ready to be operated by the cicada's powerful thoracic muscles.

ABOVE A female greengrocer cicada (*Cyclochila australasiae*) becomes restless and moves from her exuviae. She takes a firm hold some distance away in readiness for the climb up the tree trunk. Females are normally a little slower than males to ascend the tree because their abdomens are filled with reproductive organs, so their new exoskeletons require more time to dry and harden. Note how much larger the adult is compared with its nymphal shell.

To gain further security, it may enfold its limbs around a twig or branch, thereby extending the duration of the extraction process. It spends a good half-hour or more carefully positioning itself until it has gained a firm anchorage. Should it fall during the critical stage of emergence, its body and wings would be bruised and crippled, and it will not live long.

Once exposed to the warm air, its old shell begins to stiffen. The insect contracts its muscles in readiness—this forces body fluids into its thoracic region, which increases in size from the air taken in. The internal pressure finally splits the outer cuticle and a distinct line (a 'moulting suture') appears down the centre of the head and thorax. The cuticle is not sclerotised along this line and it quickly softens as the moulting fluids, which dissolve chitin, fill the spaces between the old and the new cuticle. This process occurs with all arthropods during ecdysis.

Slowly its head emerges, dragging its 'nose' from the old shell in a dented state, but this quickly expands to its proper shape once free of its encumbrances. Next to appear are the tiny, bunched-up wing buds. This is followed by the difficult process of freeing its legs, one pair at a time—if you imagine pulling your legs out of knee-high riding boots, it should give some idea of the problems involved, remembering that the cicada has six legs to extract.

At this point the vulnerable creature gently throws itself backwards to rest for a while. It is only held in this position by its abdominal tip wedged in the opened shell. The long, white fibres that trail out from the empty shell are the linings of the hindgut, foregut and the delicate membranes of the tracheae, which are slowly drawn out through the spiracles during the emergence process.

In this position its body is distended and the insect takes in a lot of air. Its muscles contract in rhythm as it pumps in air. This produces pressure, which causes the compressed body fluids to smooth out all the folds of its new outer skeleton and expand its soft, glistening new wings.

Each wing—at first a bag of veins and membranes—unfolds gradually while the cicada remains motionless. The veins are pumped up and the membranes expand and dry, after which both sides of the membrane adhere to form the clear, flat wing.

When its limbs become strong enough to support its weight, it then arches its body forwards to reach for a secure hold, often using its old nymphal shell for this purpose, and then it withdraws its abdomen from the shell. Finally, the new cicada flexes its limbs and wings, and crawls higher into the branches to merge with foliage, resting here for a time to successfully complete its transformation. During this vulnerable stage, marauding ants and prowling bush crickets often discover them and feed upon them.

The old, cast skin has served its purpose and remains clinging to the tree trunk. By the following morning, the cicada is ready to fly, and join the chorus in the treetops, although it takes a day or two before the male properly finds his voice amidst the competition.

Reproduction

The loud, continual waves of sound made by the singing males are responsible for bringing the sexes of a particular species together. Each type of cicada has its own particular love song and the female only responds to the song by a male of her own species. In addition, nature has designed the sexual organs of each species as a 'lock and key' system so that effective mating between different species is physically impossible.

When a female cicada responds favourably to the shrill note of a particular male, it sets her body vibrating; she encircles the tree or shrub the song is coming from and alights near the male making it. Immediately the male senses her presence, his singing changes to an excitable pitch and he quickly moves along a branch towards her.

On initial contact his singing becomes quieter but distinctly triumphant and the female further responds by flicking her wings as she sidles up to him. The two move close together, and, almost affectionately, they 'hug'. Then, positioned tail to tail (similar to true bugs), they settle on a selected branch, where mating may continue for an hour or more (with certain individuals).

Females normally mate several times, with intervals of a day or two in between, during which time the eggs are deposited.

Egg-layng

The elongated eggs are uniform throughout the different species, white to cream-coloured and measure up to 2 mm long (according to the species). They are passed down a tube between the cutting apparatus of the ovipositor into slits made in a wide range of plant tissue, including grass stems, tree trunks and branches.

The female's strong, spear-shaped ovipositor is located within a protective sheath, which is located ventrally at the abdominal tip. It has serrated teeth along its length, and serves as a saw-drill. She uses this to cut a series of slits into a branch. Some 20 eggs are deposited in each slit, then the female moves to another branch, repeating the process. In some species, a female will lay over 500 eggs during the season.

Females usually lay their eggs over a period of some days, mating several times in between. Depending on the species, up to three months may pass before the eggs hatch, and this usually occurs *en masse*.

TRUE BUGS
order Hemiptera: suborder Heteroptera

A heteropteran nymph typically undergoes 5–6 moults before attaining sexual maturity and also gaining its wings. When fully grown, it casts off its juvenile exoskeleton and, using its blood pressure, pumps up its soft, crumpled wings until they are fully expanded.

Reproduction
There is little courtship display among the majority of species—the female is simply approached by the male and mounted without any preliminaries. Once united, they position themselves tail-to-tail, facing away from one another, and then continue mating. The female often drags the male about as she continues feeding during the process.

Egg-laying
True bugs lay egg-clusters of up to 50 per batch, all neatly glued together on a plant stem or leaf. Certain species produce many clusters, each one numbering as many as 500 eggs.

The females often demonstrate a remarkable degree of maternal care, remaining with the eggs until they hatch, sometimes overwintering with the young. The attractively jewel-coloured harlequin bug *Tectocoris diophthalmus* is one that typically exhibits this behaviour.

ALDERFLIES AND DOBSONFLIES
order Megaloptera

Pre-adult stage
A megalopteran larva has seven pairs of five-segmented abdominal gills and one tail gill developed for breathing under water; these superficially resemble legs. Apart from having functional mouthparts, it resembles the pupal stage of certain coleopterans (beetles).

After hatching, the larvae crawl into the water, where they have an active, predatory lifestyle. The larvae spend two years growing and undergo 10–12 moults, varying according to the species.

In spring, they leave the water and crawl up the bank of a stream, coming to rest underneath a stone or log. Here, they construct an oval-shaped mud cell for their pupal stage, which usually requires three weeks or so before emerging as adults. Interestingly, unlike many endopterygotes, which develop antennae, limbs and wings fused to the pupal case, megalopterans form their appendages within special sheaths that grow free of the body, similar to that of some coleopterans. As well, even in their pupal stage, they are active, moving freely about beneath the water.

Reproduction and egg-laying
Mating always occurs near water. The female lays up to 2000 eggs in large clusters, depositing them on overhanging tree branches, logs, rocks or plants close to water. They are laid in such a way as to closely resemble lichen in both colour and form. It takes about 10–14 days before the eggs hatch and the young larvae crawl into the water.

LACEWINGS
order Neuroptera

Pre-adult stage
The life cycle of lacewings involves complete metamorphosis, with most families undergoing three larval moults. One of the largest lacewing groups is the family Myrmeleontidae, generally well known from its stout-bodied larvae, called ant-lions. Typically creatures with a flattened shape, ant-lions are equipped with extremely sharp-pointed jaws resembling calipers.

Depending on the species, lacewing larvae may live among leaf litter or beneath the bark of

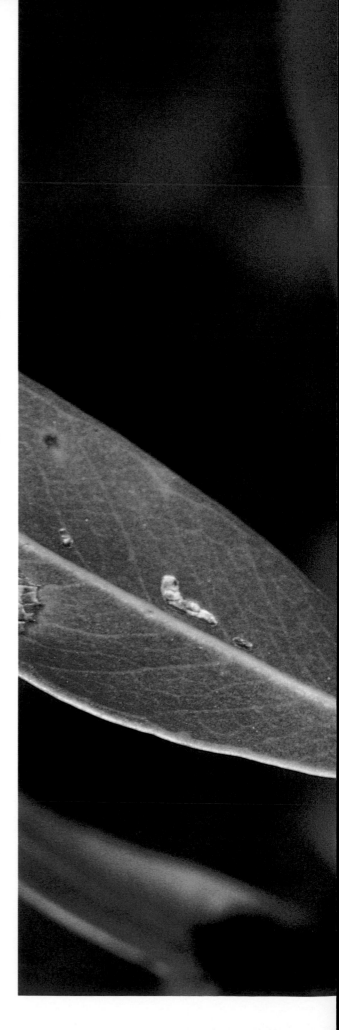

RIGHT Mating golden-bronze Christmas beetles (*Anoplognathus montanus*). These beetles cling to the eucalypt foliage on which they feed and mate, and during favourable seasons they congregate in large numbers. The eggs are laid in soil or under rotting logs. The curl grub larvae feed on decaying wood, roots of grasses and other plants and form mud-cells in which they undergo pupation.

trees or in sandy soil, and feed on a wide range of insect prey. When fully grown, the larva constructs a densely woven, silken cocoon, in which pupation takes place the following spring. The cocoon, rounded in form and often with a pearly sheen, is attached to leaves or beneath bark or in a crevice in the timber. Lacewings of the family Ascalaphidae camouflage their cocoon by securing leaves and twigs among the densely woven silken strands.

Egg-laying

The female has an unusual method of depositing her eggs: she lays them on slender stalks that she attaches to vegetation. This is believed to deter predators from devouring the eggs and to avoid potential cannibalism among the larvae upon hatching. She first dabs the surface of a leaf, tree trunk or rock with a drop of gummy liquid, which she draws out into a stalk by raising the tip of her abdomen. The stalk hardens in the air, and an egg is laid at its tip. Laid in batches, the eggs can resemble a tiny pincushion, or they are laid in rows. Eggs of the species *Nymphes myrmeleonoides* are laid in the form of a pearl necklace upon a tree branch or rockface.

BEETLES AND WEEVILS
order Coleoptera

Pre-adult stage

The typical early growing stage—the larval stage—of many beetles is the familiar curl grub larva of the family Scarabaeidae, found in the soil, or the witchetty grubs of the family Cerambycidae, found in timber. The white or cream-coloured beetle larva sheds its cuticle several times before reaching the pupal stage.

The length of time spent in the larval stage varies from species to species but more often is dependent on climatic conditions and available food sources: when food quality is poor, the larva may develop very slowly. An enormous amount of fibre has to be digested to extract any nourishment. Many beetle larvae can survive for lengthy periods on cellulose alone but they need organic nitrogen to actually grow. Countless micro-organisms and fungi growing within decaying plant material supply this requirement.

A beetle's pupal stage is relatively short, compared with its larval stage. In this stage, it completely reforms to develop into the adult. As

a pupa, the creature has external features similar to those of the adult, except that it is entirely immobile—unable to move its limbs. Slowly but surely the pupa darkens in colour until it is fully formed, ready to emerge as an adult. Then, its colouring and features can be seen through the cuticle of the pupal wrappings. When this occurs, the beetle will emerge from its pupal wrapping within days.

Once having shed its pupal wrappings and expanded its soft body and wings, the newly formed—or 'callow'—adult beetle usually spends several weeks to months within its earthen or timber cell. This is necessary for its cuticle to properly develop and harden before emerging into the outside world. The softening of the soil or timber by rain often triggers its emergence, whereupon the newly adult beetle digs its way out to explore its new surroundings.

Beetle larvae differ markedly from their adult forms—most obviously in their body form, choice of microhabitat and food source. There are four basic types of beetle larvae:

- limbless forms (called apodous) that spend their entire growing period within the food source itself—which includes seed capsules, plant stems, roots, and decaying wood. This form is typical of the longicorn beetles (family Cerambycidae) and the weevils or snout beetles (family Curculionidae).
- very active forms (called campodeiform) that have long limbs and often a pair of cerci at the tip of the abdomen. This is a predatory form of beetle, typical of the ground beetles (family Carabidae) and the rove-beetles (family Staphylinidae).

- stout, grub-like forms (called eruciform) that have short limbs, usually without tail appendages. This is typical of leaf beetles (family Chrysomelidae).
- curl grub larvae (called scarabeiform), which hold their body in a C-shape posture—a form typical of the cockchafers, Christmas beetles, flower beetles, and dung beetles (family Scarabaeidae). These larvae have head capsules with powerful mandibles and medium-sized mobile limbs that can pull them through the mulch and decaying timber.

Many larvae are relatively long-lived—especially those of wood-eating beetles, which may remain feeding within the timber for up to 10–20 years prior to pupation, or even longer, depending on the quality of their food and the level of humidity. Many adult coleopterans live for several weeks—also relatively long by comparison with other insects—and some live well beyond a single season, such as darkling beetles (family Tenebrionidae), ladybird beetles (family Coccinellidae) and ground weevils (family Curculionidae).

Reproduction

As adults, some beetles are highly active and spend a good portion of their life on the wing—especially the males, seeking mates—but patterns of courtship behaviour are rare. It is their sense of smell that plays the key role in bringing the sexes together during the mating season. When ready to mate, the female exudes an attractive scent, which varies according to the species. Males are able to pick up this scent and locate the female emitting it by means of their highly modified antennae. Antennae are often large and elaborate—like, for instance, those of the longicorns and the cockchafers.

Beetles congregate in large numbers around their particular food source—such as flowers, fruit, leaves, humus, decaying timber, or mulch—and this is also usually where they mate. Most beetles usually mate several times with a number of individuals—male beetles normally mate with several females in the course of a season.

It not unusual to find different species attempting to mate but the 'lock and key' system (by which only genitalia of the same species match) ensures that such attempts fail. Once fertilised, the female sets off to find the particular larval host plant or microhabitat in which to lay her eggs.

BELOW A curl grub larva of the colour-changing stag beetle (*Rhyssonotus nebulosus*). Remaining in close vicinity to the oviposition site, these larvae feed on decaying wood. Within its feeding tunnel, the larva—shown here nearing pupation—forms an oval-shaped cell, in which it will pupate.

Egg-laying

Most eggs are round or ovate, soft and simple in structure. Depending on the species, the number of eggs laid varies—from one to several thousand—being deposited singly or in batches. They may be laid in the soil, in decaying timber, fruit, leaf litter, animal dung, leaves, plant stems or beneath tree bark, logs or stones. Soon after being laid in the soil, the eggs of beetles of the family Scarabaeidae almost double in size through the absorption of water.

Because, generally, their life cycle is completed before the egg hatches, adult beetles do not, as a rule, associate with their young. However, instances of parental care of both eggs and larvae have been recorded in nine beetle families. Monogamy occurs among certain species, whereby the male and female live and work together, building a home for their offspring. For example, male and female bess beetles (family Passalidae) remain with their young throughout their growing period, and regurgitate digested wood fibre into the waiting mouths of the offspring.

Many dung beetles also live a monogamous existence and work in pairs collecting animal dung for their offspring. They select the softer portions of the dung as food for the young larva upon hatching. Other species of dung beetle construct their brood chambers directly below the dung—for instance, beneath a cow pat.

STYLOPS
order Strepsiptera

All stylops are parasitic. The wingless female lives her entire life cycle within the abdomen of the host insect—she even mates and gives birth there.

Pre-adult stage

The larvae hatch within the female's body, emerging in their thousands. They usually remain in the female's body until ready to disperse. Stylops larvae that are parasitic on hymenopterans, for example, normally disperse when the host wasp or bee is visiting flowers.

The tiny, active larva leaves its mother's brood canal when the host is at the flower and attaches itself to the next available flower-visiting wasp or bee that comes along. In this

way, the stylops larva is transported to the hymenopteran's nest. Once inside the nest, the stylops larva seeks out the first available wasp or bee larva. It burrows through the abdominal wall of its intended host and the cycle continues. Although the host's vital organs are left untouched by the growing parasitic stylops larva, they are pushed out of alignment as a result of its increasing size.

After entering the body of a wasp or bee larva, and following its second moult, the previously active stylops larva takes on another shape, becoming a maggot-like creature. It grows until finally pupating within the host—and the cycle continues.

Emergence

At its seventh moult, the stylops larva pushes its way through the abdominal wall of its host until it is protruding. In this position the male undergoes pupation within the cast-off skin (exuviae) of its old moult, finally emerging as a winged adult. The wingless female remains within her host's abdomen and retains her final larval skin.

Reproduction and egg-laying

During the mating season, the female makes herself available for the fertilisation of her eggs by protruding part of her body through the body-wall of the host. Mating occurs when the male, alighting on the host insect, inserts his genitalia into the opening of the female's brood canal. The female remains inside the body of the host insect—the eggs hatching out and the larvae remaining inside her until the opportunity to disperse arises.

ABOVE Dung beetle larva and pupa (*Onthophagus capella*), in cells formed from cattle dung. Dung beetles play a vital role in breaking down animal excreta and thus returning the nutrients it contains back to the soil.

FLIES
order Diptera

Pre-adult stage

Once hatched, the fly larvae (called maggots) grow quickly through continual feeding, developing rapidly compared to most other insect larvae. Larvae require brackish water, and they are particularly drawn to feeding on decaying matter, such as rotting fruit, rotting timber, vegetation in a decomposed state or decaying animal carcasses and animal excrement, and so on. They breathe through spiracles regularly dotted along the length of their abdominal segments.

Fly larvae vary in appearance and lifestyle between the different families more than in any other insect group, but they are always legless (no segmented limbs) and wriggle to move about. They generally go through four moults before they are fully grown—over a period of one to several weeks (depending on the species).

Once fully grown, the maggot prepares itself for the internal changes of the pupal stage. The pupae of flies may lie naked beneath the soil or within decaying timber, or may be enclosed in silken cocoons; or they may be enclosed within the final larval skin, which hardens around them, forming a tough, hardened, barrel-shaped casing known as a 'puparium'. Inside this brown to black puparium, the delicate, white pupa is unable to move about. Depending upon the humidity and temperature, it may spend an entire season—a dry season in tropical regions, or a cold winter in temperate regions—in its pupal stage within the puparium.

Emergence

When conditions are favourable, the new adult frees itself of its old wrappings. Some species are equipped with cocoon-cutters, but a puparium is designed to open by being pushed from within. The fly has a specialised sac located on its head which it fills with fluid; this forces the puparium lid open at one end.

Having achieved this, the fly has to emerge from the soil or rotting timber in which it originally buried itself as a maggot. To do this, it uses the same fluid-filled head-sac. By expanding and contracting the sac, debris is pushed aside as the fly forges its way to the surface. Once finally free of the soil, the fly retracts the sac into its head, and then inflates its body and wings.

Reproduction

Parthenogenesis is uncommon among flies; most species reproduce by the male and female uniting. Elaborate courtship rituals are performed by a number of species, with many females mating only once. Flies are generally sun-loving insects (there are exceptions, such as mosquitoes and craneflies) and require warm conditions before mating. In most species. the female also requires a protein meal prior to mating.

Egg-laying

After mating, the female fly stores the sperm in pouches located at the base of her oviduct. The eggs are fertilised as they pass through the oviduct prior to being laid, which the female does close to or directly upon the food source her offspring require. The number of eggs laid varies from species to species, and is affected by the particular individual and environmental factors, such as available food, recent bushfires, or rainfall.

MOTHS AND BUTTERFLIES
order Lepidoptera

Moths and butterflies undergo a complete metamorphosis, and have exploited the phenomenon of metamorphosis more fully than any other insect group.

Larval phase

All moth and butterfly larvae vary greatly in size, form and colouring but do not significantly vary in structure and in function. They are caterpillar-like (eruciform), and most are cylindrical, with six sclerotised thoracic legs and as many as 10 pro-legs. Several wood-boring and leaf-mining species of moth larvae (also known as witchetty grubs) have lost both pro-legs and thoracic legs.

All larvae take in a solid diet, thoroughly utilising all plant habitats—they feed on roots, trunks, bark, branches, twigs, leaves and galls, buds and flowers, fruits and seeds, pods and grains. Most caterpillars need to chew and swallow plant fibre. One particular feature developed by different species of lepidopterous larvae is a digestive system with specialised adaptations to specific plant chemicals. Many are so specialised that they will accept only one plant species, refusing all others to the point of starvation and death, even though the majority

OPPOSITE Large flesh flies (*Sarcorohdendorfia hardyi*) mating. Flesh-flies often have red compound eyes, plumed antennae (first half), sturdy limbs, a grey-ochre-coloured body and a striped thorax. Females bear live larvae on decomposing organic matter on which the larvae will feed. Some species parasitise other insect larvae.

of plants contain all their essential nutritional requirements.

As well, specific plants have chemicals that serve to protect the caterpillar from being eaten. This protection carries through to the adult—as occurs, for instance, with the wanderer butterflies (family Nymphalidae).

However, not all caterpillars are exclusively plant-eating: several species are carnivorous. Larvae of butterflies known as coppers and hairstreaks have cannibalistic tendencies. Other species of larvae feed on the eggs and larvae of various arthropods, including some (family Lycaenidae) that live within the ants' nest-site while feeding on ant eggs and larvae.

The caterpillar's only means of structural support is its tightly stretched outer cuticle. This taut skin supports its internal organs and prevents the body from collapsing, but it has to be replaced at regular intervals as the body grows, stretching and filling the skin to capacity. Like all other larval forms, caterpillars have to

BELOW AND RIGHT Irritative hairs on the white-stemmed gum moth larva (*Chelepteryx collesi*), below, are part of its defensive armory. Some of these hairs are modified as toxic spines to deter would-be predators. When it has nearly completed spinning its silk cocoon, the larva forces its spiny hairs through the walls, creating a prickly shelter. Emerging during the winter months, its pupa (right) is well insulated in its double-walled silk cocoon.

moult several times before reaching maturity. Each moult is controlled by juvenile hormones produced within the central nervous system, which are replaced by adult hormones in the pupal stage.

Pupation

When fully fed, and fully grown, the caterpillar empties its digestive tract and becomes very restless. It often leaves its food plant, travelling some distance away (often several metres) to select a secluded site for its pupal stage. Finally, it settles upon a plant, to which it firmly attaches itself with silk to begin the transformation process.

Many species construct a silken cocoon around themselves and locate it beneath a leaf or behind loose bark. Other species pupate naked, unprotected from the elements, and rely upon camouflage or leaf litter cover to protect them—their cryptic patterns, shapes and colours merging with their surroundings. Most pupae manage to remain invisible to most predators, except to the tiny parasitic wasps (such families as Ichneumonidae, Braconidae and Chalcididae).

A number of moth caterpillars, after leaving the food plant, descend into the ground and dig a cell beneath the soil to remain out of sight. Butterfly pupae usually have, at the tip of their abdomen, a specialised structure (the cremaster) with attachment hooks, used for firmly holding onto a leaf or tree branch. Thus, the vulnerable pupa either hangs head-down, or else it supports itself with a central girdle of silk in a head-up position for the entire pupal stage.

The old larval skin gradually starts to shrivel, finally splitting midway along the back of the thoracic region. Its major bodily features become externally visible, until the parts are finally fused together, fitting like a jigsaw puzzle; its mouth and anus, now non-functional, are sealed. Whether naked or cocooned, the creature may appear to be motionless but peak activity is taking place inside—all its tissues are 'liquefying', that is, biochemically rearranging themselves into its new form. During pupation, the tissues and organs—its body structure—are all broken down and reabsorbed by the changing pupa (in effect, it is feeding upon itself).

Remarkable and striking changes take place within this miniature, Egyptian-mummy-like pupal case. Simple eyes (ocelli)—represented by

six small 'dots', three either side of the caterpillar's head capsule, are replaced by compound eyes. Chewing mandibles are replaced by a long, coiled tongue with sensory palps on either side. Fleshy pro-legs completely withdraw into the abdominal region. Thoracic legs reform into long, graceful limbs equipped with taste organs on the feet. The caterpillar's 'feelers' and hairs fall away, and the characteristic thread-like (clubbed or plumed) antennae become the olfactory organs.

Although not visible in the caterpillar, its gender was predetermined genetically within the egg and the developing adult can be easily identified in the pupal case. The most dominant feature of the pupa is its large wing cases.

Emergence

Two to three days prior to emergence, when the bodily structure of the butterfly has fully formed within, the pupal case loses its opaqueness and the patterns and colours of the yet-to-emerge insect boldly show through the old cuticle.

Emergence often occurs early in the morning with butterflies, and in the evening with moths. After emerging, the insect spends some time expanding and drying its soft new wings, opening and closing them, and rests in preparation for its maiden flight and to visit flowers.

The length of time lepidopterans spend in the pupal stage is directly influenced by the hours of daylight, the temperature and humidity. During winter in cold climates and the dry season in tropical regions, the pupa goes into a limbo-like state of suspended growth (called diapause). This ensures that emergence will occur at a favourable season for food, mating, reproduction and egg-laying.

Reproduction

Most female lepidopterans need to mate only once, but many mate more frequently to fertilise the eggs. Males normally mate with several females and expend a lot of energy during their vigorous courtship displays. Often a male butterfly will follow a female for some distance (50 metres or more); female moths, on the other hand, generally remain close to the host plant (where the eggs will be laid), awaiting the arrival of males.

Males and females of numerous species are equipped with attractants that evoke a sexual response. Female moths have scent-producing

glands located at the tip of the abdomen. The males' attractants are produced by hair scales in pouches or folds located on their hindwings or as tensile brushes at the tip of the abdomen.

Most male and female moths find one another through the sense of smell during the evening or later at night. The powerfully attractive pheromones female moths emit are detected by the males with their elaborate antennae. Some female moths (such as those of the family Saturniidae) often attract vast numbers of suitors but only mate with one.

Male and female butterflies actively seek out each other visually based on a particular colour, wing pattern, flight or body movement. A courtship dance follows, during which the male may use his own scent. The female lets the male know if she is not interested in mating by curling the tip of her abdomen into the air.

If she is receptive, she signals this by alighting upon a leaf. The male gently alights upon her, grasping her with his anal claspers,

TOP A caterpillar of the pine beauty looper moth (*Chlenias auctaria*) clings to foliage with its six short segmented legs. To move forward, first it releases its hold with its anal claspers and brings them up to meet its forelegs, arching its body. It then stretches out to gain a new foothold and repeats the process.

ABOVE The peppered prominent moth (*Neola semiaurata*) pupates almost naked within soil in a flimsy silk wrapping. Like all primitive winged insects, it reverts to a near-embryonic condition during its transition from pupa to adult.

often lifting her into the air. They normally position themselves so that the male hangs beneath her, then settle in a secluded spot, often remaining united for an hour or more. During this time, the male transfers his sperm by way of a spermatophore, which is retained within the female and helps provide nutrients for her eggs.

Some species produce entirely wingless females (for example, families Lymantriidae and Psychidae), the latter never emerge from their silken cocoons. The males of these psychids are rapid fliers with abdomens that can be extended to an extraordinary length in order to reach inside the female's cocoon and mate with her there.

Egg-laying

Once mating has taken place, the female moth or butterfly locates the specific larval host plant by her acute sense of smell—detecting the essential oils of the plant where she lays her eggs. The number of eggs varies according to the species. A single female of the giant wood moths (family Cossidae) or swift moths (family Hepialidae) lays more than 18 000 eggs.

The eggs are normally laid underneath or on the leaves, or within the crevices on tree bark of the host plant. Some species lay their eggs singly or in clusters; others, such as the swift moths, scatter them while flying, letting them fall over the food plant to land where they will.

SAWFLIES, WASPS, ANTS AND BEES
order Hymenoptera

Hymenopterans undergo complete metamorphosis and, as a group, they are undoubtedly the most advanced insects, solving life's challenges with practical application. Providing nests for the young led these insects to evolve amazing social structures whereby a colony works together as a single organism, providing shelter, security and

BELOW Ready to pupate, the caterpillar of the orchard swallowtail butterfly (*Princeps aegeus*) attaches itself to a twig by inserting its anal hooks onto a silken pad it has woven into position, finally securing itself with a silken girdle.

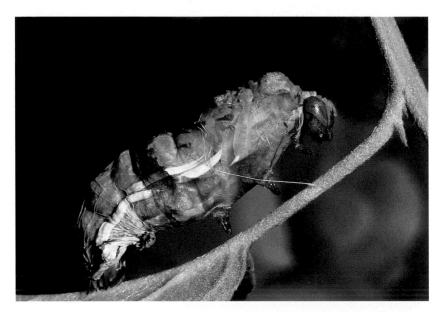

RIGHT Exposed pupae of the orchard swallowtail are cryptically sculptured and coloured to match their surroundings. Butterfly pupae that shelter among debris are brown and unsculptured.

FAR RIGHT Ready to emerge, an orchard swallowtail pushes its chrysalis case wide open, thrusts its thorax and head clear, withdraws its antennae, mouthparts, palpi, legs and wings from their sheaths and grasps the empty case to withdraw its abdomen.

food for all its occupants. However, many species of wasps and bees are solitary and provide food only for their own young. Upon hatching, larvae feed on the food provided by the females or, in some species, by both parents.

Larval phase

The larvae may be caterpillar-like (eruciform), as occurs with sawflies (suborder Symphyta). Most hymenopteran larvae, however, are white, legless, grub-like or maggot-like creatures, as with most of the suborder Apocrita. The typical hymenopterous larva has a sclerotised head capsule, a single, well-defined ocellus on either side of the head, mandibles and mouthparts, three thoracic segments and nine abdominal segments. As it grows it undergoes a number of moults that varies by species, but not exceeding six.

Ant larvae are also white, grub-like creatures and usually undergo three moults. They are all dependent for food on the female workers, who also transport them about the nest whenever the need arises, such as if the nest is flooded or disturbed. Different species of hymenopterous larvae feed in a variety of ways:

- feeding on paralysed insects or spiders provided by the adult female—for example, spider-hunting wasps, sand wasps and velvet ants (families Pompilidae, Sphecidae, Mutillidae).
- feeding on masticated insects or spiders provided by adults—for example, mason wasps and paper-nest wasps, and ants (families Vespidae, Formicidae).
- feeding on plant products, collected by adults and provided within closed cells—for example, bees (family Apidae).
- feeding on plants or gall-forming; these larvae are not fed by adults—for example, sawflies (families Tenthredinidae, Pergidae).
- as internal parasites (lodged inside the host) feeding off living hosts or insect eggs—for example, ichneumon, braconid and chalcidoid wasps (families Ichneumonidae, Braconidae and Chalcididae).
- as external parasites (lodged on the outer body of the host) feeding off living hemipteran hosts, for instance, plant bugs and cicadas—for example, subfamilies Driyininae and Gonatopodinae, where the eggs are laid on the host and the larvae start eating the host as soon as they hatch.
- as secondary parasites on other hymenopteran larvae—for example, cuckoo wasps and chalcidoid wasps (families Chrysididae and Chalcididae). In this case, eggs are laid on larvae inside wasp, bee and ant nests; the parasitic larvae then eat their hosts.

Pupation

After feeding for several weeks, the larva is fully grown and enters the typical 'resting' or pre-pupal phase common to endopterygotes.

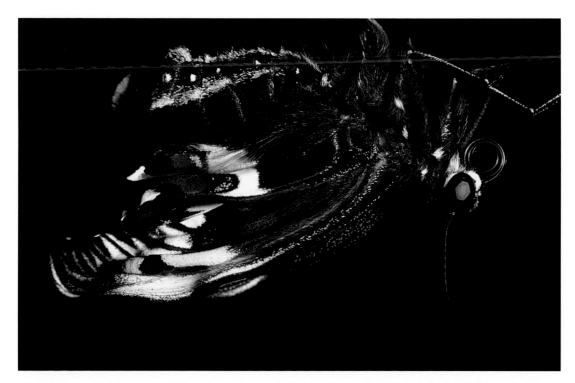

LEFT Entirely free of its restrictive chrysalis case, a male orchard swallowtail butterfly expands its wings. The butterfly then expels a considerable amount of milky-coloured liquid from its anus—metabolic waste products that accumulated during its larval and pupal stages of development—and is ready for its new life as an adult.

Social wasps and bees are among many species that spin a flimsy silken cocoon around themselves, really just lining their cells with silk; sometimes they also make a sealing cap. Most species overwinter in the pre-pupal stage, but it can last up to nine months or, in arid regions, several years.

The pupal stage itself is brought on by favourable conditions and is short—for most hymenopterans, it is only a couple of weeks.

Most wasps and bees pupate within cells beneath the soil or within timber. The pupa is often well protected from the elements within an oval-shaped cocoon, spun of coarse silk exuded from the larva's mouth. Many of the pompilid wasps (family Pompilidae) and sand wasps (family Sphecidae) incorporate grains of

sand into their silk cocoons, within which they normally spend the winter months unchanged until spring or summer. Many ant species spin silken cocoons when they are ready to pupate; some simply pupate naked.

When the appropriate season arrives, the old larval skin is moulted and the insect goes into its pupal stage, developing quickly within its pupal wrappings. The pupa has the general form of the adult but is white or cream in colour. Its limbs are free of the body and its wings packed within small wing cases. In the course of this stage, the pupal case deepens in colour until finally the insect within sheds its old skin, expands its new form and eats its way out of the cocoon, able to fly and begin its work.

Males normally emerge well before the females to ensure the females are fertilised soon after their emergence when they are in a healthy condition to begin the work of nest-building.

Reproduction

Parthenogenesis occurs among some sawfly species (for example, families Tenthredinidae and Pergidae), but reproduction among hymenopterans mostly occurs as a result of mating.

The males of solitary wasps are often territorial in their habits and can be seen cruising up and down over sandy patches of ground or along forest trails throughout the day, patiently waiting for the appearance of a freshly emerged female. As soon as a female emerges,

she is surrounded by eager males. She usually flies away, closely followed by one or more suitors. When she makes clear her intention of favouring a particular male, the two alight upon foliage or a tree branch, and mating takes place. The male has now completed his purpose in life. For females, however, this is only the beginning. Solitary female wasps or bees must then set to work preparing the nest-site for their young.

Egg-laying and nest-building

The vespid wasps, bees, and most ants stand apart from most other insects (termites excepted) in that reproduction in a particular colony is vested in the one fertile female (or queen) of that colony, which lays the eggs. Unlike bees or wasps, ants generally tolerate more than one queen in a single colony.

A queen bee or queen ant has initially mated several times, from which she has stored enough sperm to last throughout her egg-laying life. Egg production for ants and social bees reaches a peak in early summer, the queen laying as many as 1500 eggs a day.

A form of birth selection and control is practised by most hymenopterans. The ratio of males to females is regulated by the females to meet the population needs of a particular species in a given season and location. The fertilised female achieves this by releasing or withholding sperm stored within the sperma-theca inside her, as she actually lays the eggs—all males are produced from unfertilised eggs; all females, from fertilised eggs.

Males or drones are produced for one role only—fertilising the young, emerging queens—after which they die. Females guard the eggs. New queens are produced to replace either an exhausted queen or an old queen leaving the colony with a swarm of workers to begin a new nest. Among ants and bees, the different castes —workers, drones and soldiers—are produced as the colony requires them.

Unlike the social bees and ants, vespid wasps (superfamily Vespoideae) do not have different castes, and do not form colonies by swarming. The formation of a colony is an annual event, founded by fertilised females that survived the winter. Several females may participate in building the new nest in spring, but one always remains socially dominant and furnishes the cells with eggs. Should anything happen to remove her from the nest-site,

one of the other females takes over her role. This control of the nest is largely due to pheromones released from the queen wasp. These determine her dominance and simul-taneously inhibit the development of the other females present.

Food gathering for the future offspring requires much labour. Each cell has to be stocked with food such as pollen, nectar, insects or spiders. In general, hymenopteran males only exist to fertilise the females, though there are some exceptions. For example, male wasps of certain species, such as those of the genus *Trypoxylon*, participate in nest-building. Early in construction, they prepare and pack the cells with spiders brought by the females as future food for their offspring. Female parasitic wasps (family Ichneumonidae) are generally equipped with long ovipositors that function as drills as well as egg-depositors, which these wasps use to inject the living hosts with their eggs.

Upon hatching, the tiny larvae immediately begin feeding on the living tissue of the insect or spider they've been supplied with, and continue doing so until fully grown, at this stage killing their food source by finally eating its vital organs.

Some wasp species within the superfamilies Sphecoidea and Vespoidea continually feed their young until they are mature (called 'progressive provisioning'). Once emerged from their pupal stage, the offspring work for the colony in exchange for being raised. Bees also feed their young in this way, although members of the family Apidae also have a pronounced caste system. Workers perform different duties according to their age. When newly emerged, they clean, nurse, form honeycombs and stand guard. After three weeks, they collect nectar, pollen, resin and water.

BELOW Baby ants being reared in the nursery. The pupae of most ant species (subfamilies Dolichoderinae and Psuedomyrmecinae) lie naked among growing larvae. The final instar ant larvae of several species (subfamilies Ponerinae and Myrmicinae) enclose themselves in brown parchment-like silk cocoons or puparia.

BOTTOM Workers of the yellow field-ant (*Lasius* species), assisting the departure of reproductive ants after rain. During summer, winged male and female ants (alates) leave the nest and swarm in nuptial flights, after which they shed their wings and establish new colonies.

CHAPTER THREE

Wings and Flight

The wings of insects are unique among flying creatures. The function of all wings is, of course, flight, but in their design and in how they work, the wings of insects feature many superb innovations. There is extraordinary diversity in wing types, from the delicate clear, glass-like structures of lacewings, to the hard iridescent coverings of beetles and the vivid hues and patterns of butterflies. But the wing design is only one piece of the puzzle: it is in flight that insects are so fascinating. Observation of insects reveals much variety in their style of movements, flying agility and speed. Compare the gliding of a ladybug to the buzzing of a mosquito; the slow flapping of an emperor moth to the rapid motion of a hawk moth or the speedy manouevres of a dragonfly as it zips, darts and hovers, taking off with bullet-like speed. This chapter reveals the variations in wings and shows the means and methods by which insects take flight.

OPPOSITE A green golden-eyed lacewing (*Chrysopa ramburi*) is caught in the sticky wheel-web snare of an *Eriophora* spider. Lacewings of this family (Chrysopidae) are slender soft-bodied insects with beautiful delicate wings and are not strong fliers. The major function of their wings is to help them to disperse into suitable habitats, meet the opposite sex and reproduce.

Insect wings have almost nothing in common with those of flying vertebrates—the birds and bats, whose wings or gliders all derive from modified arms or legs. There is only one correspondence between the wings of insects and those of vertebrates—in both cases the wing is composed of an expanded surface of membrane, stretched upon a stiffened framework. With most flying insects, the frame is an extension of air tubes and vessels from within the body; it is the network of thickened veins that supports the membranes.

Insects have developed specialised wing structures to control flight that overcome the restrictions of living muscles. The basic wing action is hinge-like at the point where the wings attach to the thorax. Here the powerful flight muscles are housed. Of all the insects, the airborne skill of dragonflies is one of the best examples of flight-power used to out-manouevre prey and evade capture.

The primary purposes for which insects have evolved wings are:
- to move more efficiently from place to place
- to avoid predators by being able to make a quick exit from danger
- for wider dispersal and to locate food sources in different locations
- to migrate to more favourable sites during seasonal extremes of temperatures.

THE DEVELOPMENT OF WINGS

The best-known clue to the origin of insect wings are the winglet-gills. These are shaped as dorsal projections stemming from the abdominal gill-plates. They are found in the fossils of flying insects approximately 270 million years old. These fossils show a marked advance in body structure over simpler insect forms, suggesting that the first winged insects would have existed even earlier. These flap-like gill-plates, from which wings developed, were used for breathing when these older insect forms lived an aquatic existence.

Fossils also show that some of the very earliest, prehistoric insects were equipped with three pairs of lateral outgrowths or aerofoils stemming from each of the three thoracic segments (the pronotum, mesothorax and metathorax). The external flattened wing buds stemming from the second and third thoracic segments, which you can see in the immature (or nymphal) stages of exopterygotes (for example, cockroaches or grasshoppers), is typical of the lobe-like structures seen in fossil insects. These lobes helped not only to shield the insects' limbs but also to cushion them after long falls from tall plants. So, one theory is that, from their earliest development, insects used wings for aerial movement—that these

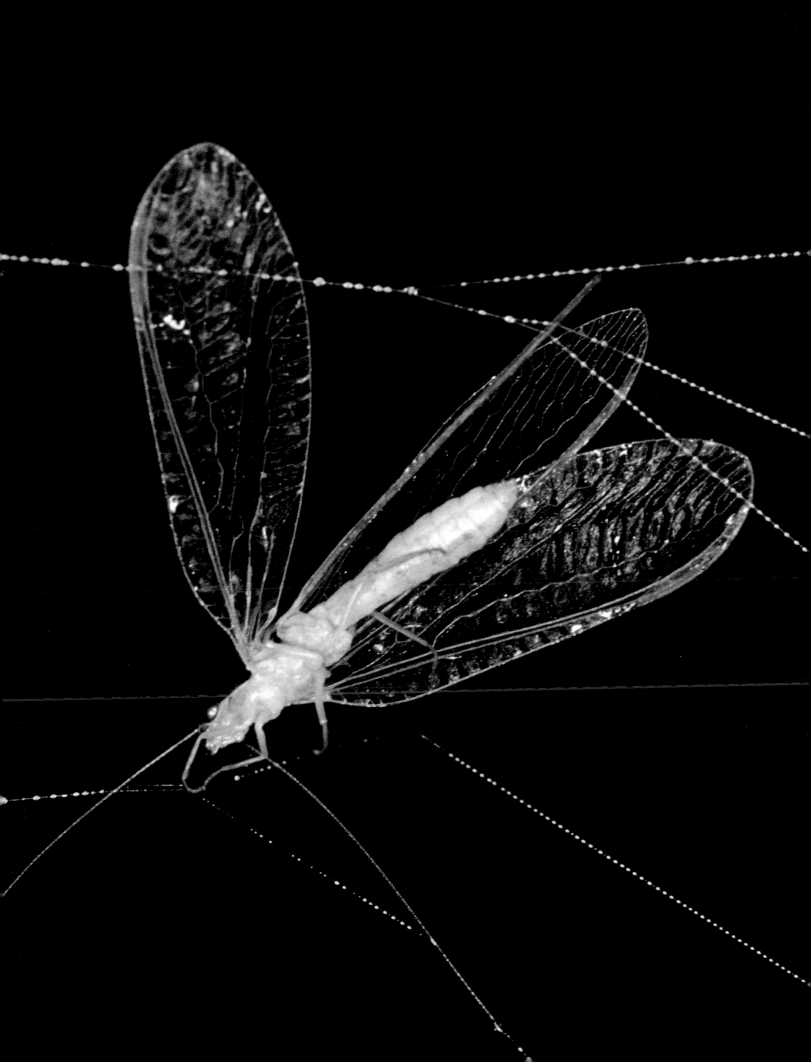

ABOVE A late instar nymph of the raspy cricket (*Para-gryllacris combusta*). This nymph has miniature versions of its parents' wings; its adult wings will be gained only in its final moult (five to ten moults, according to sex and species). When moulting, the nymph anchors itself to the underside of a leaf by its tarsal claws. It takes in air to expand and split its old cuticle, which it consumes after moulting.

outgrowths, which aided gliding or scudding, enabled them to extend their leaps from plant to plant, developed in time into wings.

Interestingly, too, the Australian jumping spider, known as the flying spider, *Saitis volans*, is equipped with gliding outgrowths. It uses these in exactly the same way it is suggested ancient insects used theirs.

The development of flowering plants lured many groups of insects upward, towards pollen and nectar so that they developed techniques of climbing and, eventually, flying. This also led to spiders developing their aerial snares, in order to keep abreast of their prey. Insects and spiders have helped shape one another's evolution.

All exopterygotes and endopterygotes are derived from ancestors that had wings, including the present-day wingless pterygota. There are some flightless insects within these two groups: their wings were lost or reduced as part of their evolution. In spite of our understanding of insect evolution, it remains a controversial subject how insects developed wings in the first place.

WINGS AND FLIGHT

Wing action

All flying creatures use a wing action in which the air is struck with greater velocity during the downstroke than with the upstroke. Otherwise, the upstroke would neutralise the downstroke and the insect would lose control, direction and speed. Adjusting the wing surface as it acts upon the air is crucial to flight: dragonflies, for instance, strike the air with the flat sides of their wings, and present the edges in rising.

The muscles activating the wings are numerous and complex: some are involved with wing adjustments during flight; others are used for spreading and folding the wings when at rest. Muscles are directly involved in operating the wings: the elevator-muscles are attached to the wings just inside the fulcrum (where the wings are hinged to the thorax); the depressor-muscles are attached immediately outside of this region. There are also indirect muscles, which are not attached to the wings themselves but to the inner walls of the flexibly moving thoracic area. These muscles alter the shape of the thorax as they alternately contract and relax, thereby forcing the wings to move up or down. This is the evolutionary path of development that was followed by butterflies and moths. Dragonflies have very powerful direct flight muscles but in most other insects, the direct flight muscles are feeble by comparison. In most insects, their indirect muscles are the largest in their entire bodies and these constitute the main motor mechanism of the wings: essentially up and down wing movement is all that is required.

Insects do not have more than two pairs of wings, and many—for example, beetles and many true bugs—use only one pair for flight. Those that do use both pairs for flight typically synchronise their wing beats. This is usually achieved by coupling the wings, either through a series of fine, hook-like bristles or spines (called a frenulum), as with many moths, or rows of hooks, as with bees and wasps. If these insects had no means of wing coupling, they would flutter about less efficiently. On the other hand, the wings of dragonflies are uncoupled and they work together in perfect synchronisation, allowing the dragonfly to turn sharply in the air at very high speeds.

The rate at which insects fly and the rapidity of their wing vibrations vary greatly among the different orders of insects. Those with narrow, rapidly vibrating wings move through the air faster than those that have broad wings. This is well illustrated by the hawk moths (family Sphingidae), which are among the most powerful of flying insects. They have very strong, narrow wings attached to extremely powerful thoracic muscles within a streamlined bodily structure. In contrast, large emperor moths (family Saturniidae) have a slow, flapping motion, making little headway against the wind.

Having the ability to fly allows insects to migrate *en masse* to more favourable locations during seasonal extremes of heat and cold. In certain regions there are species of ladybird beetles that migrate in their millions when carried by favourable winds. Some insects carry out great migration flights annually, such as the painted lady butterfly *Cynthia kershawi* (family Nymphalidae-Nymphalinae) and the wanderer (or monarch) butterfly *Danaus plexippus*

LEFT A European honey bee (*Apis mellifera*) feeding on the nectar of a bird-of-paradise flower (*Strelitzia reginae*). This is the only bee species found in Australia that leaves its sting behind after it has injected. Wild populations of this bee build nests in hollowed tree trunks, cliffs and holes in banks of streams. Vertical combs of cells are formed of wax secreted by worker bees.

plexippus (family Nymphalidae–Danainae). Although seemingly frail when compared to the sturdy wings of birds and the leathery wings of bats, the wings of certain insects can carry them thousands of kilometres over land and sea.

For purposes of scientific study, the flight of insects is categorised as follows:
• true flight—the wings are moved up and down, beating the air and impelling the insect forward
• gliding and planing—the wings are used to break falls
• soaring—the wings are held motionless
• hovering—the wings are moved rapidly and in such a way that the insect can remain almost stationary in mid-air.

Most winged insects display true flight.

Wing design and improvement

In some insects, the evolutionary modifications of their wing design have brought great benefits in terms of improvements in flight-power, although the specialised streamlining of their body shape has also contributed. The power of a hawk moth's flight, for instance, owes as much to its streamlined body shape as to its powerful muscles and wing shape, which are used in rapid flight and for hovering while feeding.

The wings of many exopterygotes are more suited for gliding—used to break their fall from tall plants, for example—than for actual flying. On the other hand, the four wings of many of the more advanced insects—the endopterygotes—are evolved for vigorous flight. With many insects—such as crickets, earwigs, cockroaches, mantids, phasmatids and beetles—it is the hindwings that do most of the actual flying.

LEFT An Australian painted lady butterfly (*Vanessa kershawi*) feeding on a dandelion (*Taraxacum officinale*). Many butterflies belonging to this subfamily (Nymphalinae; family Nymphalidae) are rapid flyers. Despite the fragility of its wings, the Australian painted lady may travel thousands of kilometres over land and sea to its breeding grounds. While some do not survive the journey, others arrive with wings in tatters or even reduced to stumps. In comparison, the wanderer butterfly (*Danaus plexippus plexippus*) has relatively rubbery wings that are better adapted to the stresses of migration, and consequently wanderers suffer fewer casualties.

The heavier forewings serve as a protective covering for the body and for the flying wings when the insect is at rest.

Modification in wing design has resulted in the forewings being greatly enlarged (for example, butterflies or moths), or hardened (for example, beetles), or even lost (for example, stylops). Hindwings have developed with associated direct flight muscles (for example, crickets or short-horned grasshoppers, butterflies, moths, wasps and bees). The hindwings of many exopterygotes are folded fan-like when at rest (for example, crickets and grasshoppers), or intricately folded and tucked away (for example, earwigs and beetles). By contrast, termite alates (sexually mature, winged castes) shed their cumbersome wings immediately after mating.

Many insects have glass-like wings—for instance, the majority of dragonflies, damselflies, cicadas, flies, lacewings, wasps and bees. Other insects, such as the moths and butterflies, have their entire wing surface densely covered with minute scales and hairs, often vividly coloured with pigments and arranged into patterns characteristic of the species. Light refraction also plays a large part in producing the vivid colouring of many forms, the scales themselves being colourless, their structure alone creating the striking iridescence which, apart from its beauty, also plays a significant role in survival.

OPPOSITE A newly emerged tailed emperor butterfly (*Polyura pyrrhus sempronius*). The process of emergence first involves pumping haemolymph (blood) into the wing veins to expand its wings; this is followed by its new cuticle drying. Then the waste fluids that have accumulated during its larval and pupal stages will be expelled. An hour or so later, the butterfly is ready for its first flight.

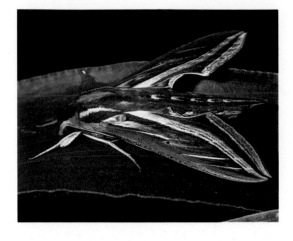

Wing venation and taxonomy

Each wing consists of two layers that are in close contact, and is supported upon a framework of hollow veins. The wing veins supply the wings with haemolymph (insect blood), circulating outwardly from the thorax. So long as an insect can absorb the radiant heat of sunlight, its haemolymph is warmed and is in full circulation for flying. Many insects cannot fly when temperatures drop below 17°C.

Study of the wing venation (the pattern of veining in the wing) and of the overall wing structure helps us to place insects into the different orders for taxonomic purposes and the different orders in relation to one another.

Insects experienced great selective pressures in the development of their wings during their evolution. Stick insects originally had long, narrow forewings; early beetles had elytra that did not sit snugly against the abdomen.

Nevertheless, in a basic design that has existed from the start, all flying insects have two

pairs of wings (modified or otherwise) located on their second and third thoracic segments, and the system of wing venation is essentially the same for them all. This uniformity in wing design, which applies to all flying insects, indicates that the wing design developed once only—unlike what occurred with vertebrates, whose flying appendages have evolved independently several times.

The main veins of an insect's wing typically alternate between being convex and concave in shape towards their bases. An insect's wing membrane is divided by longitudinal veins and cross-veins, which form a number of closed areas called 'cells'. These cells are designated by a numbering system for ease of classification. Cross-veins are transverse struts that have developed between the branches of the main veins in order to support the wing membrane. There are three principal types of vein-branching:
- dichotomic (a simple dichotomous branching found in most insects)
- pectinate (most clearly developed in lacewings and in many orthopterans)
- triadic (widespread in recent insects).

Careful study is required in determining vein features, comparing morphology within and between orders (including that of fossil finds).

When the interpretation of wing venation is difficult, another way that is sometimes used to determine insects' true relationships is by examining the tracheae of the larval wing sheath—but only for those orders in which no specialisations of the tracheational system has occurred—that is, in the orders Hemiptera, Neuroptera and Lepidoptera.

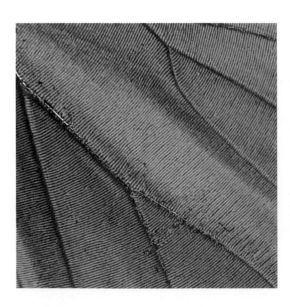

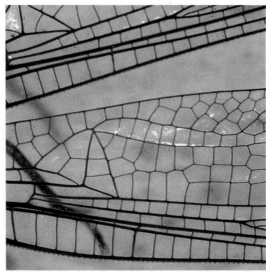

DIVERSITY AMONG THE GROUPS

The types of wings and methods of flight found among insects are intimately connected with their particular habits and lifestyle. Most adult insects have fully functional flying wings, which gives them many distinct advantages. The remainder of this chapter takes a look at the role of wings for particular insects in some of the orders, starting first with the primitive winged insects (the exopterygotes), then followed by the modern winged insects (the endopterygotes).

MAYFLIES
order Ephemeroptera

Mayflies have wings with many veins. They are the only insects known that can moult their wings and can fly before reaching maturity.

Forewings

The wing surface is fluted in structure, and the forewing venation is reduced in certain families. Wings are typically opaque at pre-adult (sub-imago) stage, and clear, sometimes with colour, in a mature insect (imago).

Hindwings

The hindwings have abundant irregularly spaced cross-veins, but are tiny, compared with the forewings, which are greatly reduced or even absent in some species. The anterior margins of the hindwings of many species have a well-developed wing-coupling device used during flight (similar to butterflies).

DRAGONFLIES
order Odonata: suborder Anisoptera

An adult dragonfly, which is gauze- or nerve-winged, has an admirably streamlined anatomy, its wings being its major asset. True flight, combined with soaring, is well demonstrated by dragonflies. The direct-flight muscles of the wings are chiefly involved with flying.

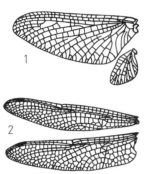

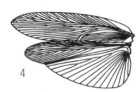
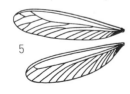

ABOVE Wing types:
1. Triangulated: mayflies.
2. Net-veined: dragonflies.
3. Membranous: stoneflies.
4. Leathery: cockroaches.
5. Equal-winged: termites.

Wings

The wings are attached to the thorax by a single axillary and controlled by their powerful thoracic wing muscles, which can propel them along at a swift pace of over 50 km an hour. The strong, supportive veins of their wings hold the front area of each wing rigid, but the hind portion remains very flexible. A dragonfly's forewings are smaller than its hindwings. Dragonfly wings:

- are membranous and usually clear, sometimes with large pigmented areas, and corrugated almost throughout
- have highly specialised wing venation (usually black, but brightly coloured in some species), which handles aerodynamic stresses
- have cross-veins and pleats bracing the overall design. However, the two pairs are not coupled in flight, but work independently.

Their ability to move the four wings independently of one another means dragonflies have outstanding manoeuvrability in the air. They must be able to make sharp, sudden turns, swerve, hover, accelerate or slow down, and even dart backwards at times, in instant response to the movements of prey.

STONEFLIES
order Plecoptera

Stoneflies are nerve-winged. Their wings are membranous and are without a coupling mechanism. They are unequal in size, the forewings being smaller than the hindwings. When the stonefly is at rest, the wings are folded together so that they are close to the body and held overlapped. The wings extend beyond the tip of the abdomen.

Forewings

The forewings have short anal veins, some basally fused together. Cross-veins, when present, are spaced irregularly throughout, with a special set located between the basal area of the forewings, but missing from the anal fan of the hindwings (with exceptions).

Hindwings

The hindwings fold fan-like and have a coupling device in the form of a fold. The venation of the wings is complex, with numerous supportive cross-veins.

COCKROACHES
order Blattodea

Cockroaches are straight-winged and, generally, their wings are used little for flying. When folded, they overlap one another and are held flat above the body.

Forewings
Those species with flying wings have tough, sclerotised forewings, which serve to protect the hindwings when the insect is in repose or moving about leaf litter and rotting timber.

Hindwings
The delicate, membranous hindwings are large and widely expanding, with distinctive characteristics that aid identification. They consist of a narrow pre-anal area supported by several radiating convex veins, separated by secondary furrow-like veins, enabling them to be folded longitudinally, fan-like, when at rest.

TERMITES
order Isoptera

The winged forms, which are known as alates, have two pairs of membranous wings that are much longer than the body. These are similar in shape and equal in length. Alates take flight only in order to mate and form a new colony. On alighting near a potential nest-site, they shed their wings. The female attracts the male by emitting pheromones. The pair form a nuptial chamber in the soil and begin a new colony.

Wings
In termites, the wing venation is reduced and strongly branched without supportive cross-veins. Three main veins normally exist, the anal veins being reduced in termites as, compared with other insects, they have a reduced anal area. The wings have a special basal suture, which is modified so that they can be easily shed following the termites' nuptial flight.

ABOVE A tropical dragonfly, (family Libellulidae) alert for prey. Its spiny legs are situated well forward on the thorax and form a basket to hold and turn any prey that is caught. It is crammed between the dragonfly's cutting mandibles.

PRAYING MANTIDS
order Mantodea

Mantids are straight- or fan-winged. When at rest, their wings overlap one another and are held flat above the body.

Forewings
The forewings of female mantids are often either reduced or entirely absent; when present, they are elongated, sclerotised and opaque but are used little for flying. Males of species with flying wings have tough sclerotised forewings which serve to protect the hindwings when at rest.

Hindwings
When present, the large, delicate, membranous hindwings are used for flying. They consist of a narrow pre-anal area supported by several radiating convex veins. These are separated by secondary furrow-like veins, enabling them to be folded longitudinally, fan-like, when at rest (similarly to those of winged cockroaches).

EARWIGS
order Dermaptera

Earwigs have pleated or folding wings.

Forewings
The hardened tegmina are small, smooth and shiny, without any veins; they serve to protect the flying wings.

Hindwings
The highly specialised hindwings are membranous with supportive cross-veins and are semi-circular. When in use, they unfold and expand fan-like. At rest, they are folded crosswise along concentric lines into a tiny package protected beneath the tegmina.

ABOVE Wing types:
1. Fan-like flight wings (hindwing): katydyds.
2. Semi-circular-winged (unfolded): earwigs.
3. Straight-winged: (forewing) and fan-like flight wing (hindwing): mantids.

RIGHT Cryptic-coloured grasshoppers like this male gumleaf mimic grasshopper (*Goniae* species) remain motionless unless disturbed. When threatened, they jump or fly onto leaf debris to merge with their background and wait for danger to pass.

KATYDIDS, CRICKETS AND SHORT-HORNED GRASSHOPPERS
order Orthoptera

Orthopterans are straight-winged. Both sexes are usually fully winged, although it is not uncommon to find forms in which the wings are either reduced or entirely absent—particularly among females of many species. This is especially pronounced among the crickets, which have modified their wings for stridulation (that is, making sound), or have lost them owing to a lifestyle of tunnelling or soil-dwelling. The direct and indirect flight muscles of short-horned grasshoppers are about equally developed. When approached, they 'sit on the heels' of their hindlegs the instant prior to leaping, and launch into the wind to lift their wings.

Forewings

When present, the forewings are typically narrow, opaque and leathery. Some are broad, usually to mimic leaves. The forewings of short-horned grasshoppers and crickets are held in a roof-like manner over the body when at rest, which protects the flying hindwings. The forewings are often modified to perform secondary functions, such as stridulation or protection of hindwings.

Hindwings

When present, the membranous hindwings are broad, with prominent veins to strengthen the flanks of the fan-like, longitudinal folds and cross-veins or temporary fusions. The membranous hindwings do most of the work in flight. They are often brightly coloured and are used to 'flash' to confuse would-be predators.

STICK AND LEAF INSECTS
order Phasmatodea

These are cryptic-winged insects. True flight is not possible due to their large bulky bodies and reduced wings. Gliding techniques break their falls from trees. Males of some species have fully functional wings but they are not strong fliers.

Wings

Being tough and leathery, the sclerotised forewings serve to protect the functional flying wings. When present, the forewings are often cryptically coloured and merge with the surroundings, thus providing camouflage. The forewings of females are often reduced. When at rest, the wings overlap one another and are held flat above the body, with the hindwings being longitudinally folded fan-like.

ABOVE A female Sydney gumleaf katydid (*Terpandrus horridus*) feeding on the nectar of a scrub apple (*Angophora hispida*). As in many insects, her wings mimic leaves.

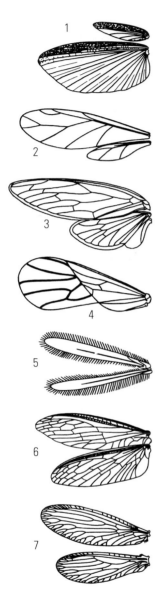

ABOVE Wing types:
1. Cryptic-winged: stick insects.
2. Clear membranous: aphids.
3. Hyaline (glass-like): cicadas.
4. Hemi ('half-winged') forewing: true bugs:
5. Fringe-winged: thrips.
6. Many-veined: alderflies.
7. Nerve-winged (neuron): lacewings.

APHIDS, CICADAS, TRUE BUGS, AND THEIR ALLIES
order Hemiptera

Hemipterans are glass-winged or half-winged, and their wings differ enormously between the various suborders. Those of plant lice and aphids (suborder Sternorrhyncha), for example, are clear and held roof-like over the body when at rest. Those of most true bugs (suborder Heteroptera), on the other hand, overlap one another and are held flat over the body (shield-like) when not in use. The thickened forewings of shield-bugs act as shields, protecting the membranous flying hindwings. The wings of almost all true bugs are further modified by having a transverse division that is distinguished by a basal, toughened or hardened area (the corium), on which the venation is often absent, and a distal, more delicate membranous area (the membrane), on which the venation remains.

Using air currents, aphids frequently travel vast distances over land and ocean on their migratory flights. Cicadas, however, do not normally sustain long flights. Cicadas head for the nearest tree, where they can quickly conceal themselves. A cicada's four clear wings are strong enough to transport it relatively briskly across open spaces from one tree to another. When chased on the wing by a bird, a cicada will make zigzag manoeuvres in order to confuse its predator as it cannot outfly a hungry bird.

Forewings

The forewings of hemipterans belonging to the suborder Auchenorrhyncha (for example, most Australian cicadas) are typically clear and the apical area is often more membranous than the remainder of the wing. The membrane is often demarcated from the basal half of the wing by a transverse separation called the nodal line, which can be readily distinguished in particular groups.

Hindwings

The hindwings of all members of the order Hermiptera are entirely membranous, and they often have a small, folding anal area. Wing coupling, when present, is achieved with interlocking wing margins and gripping devices.

THRIPS
order Thysanoptera

Thrips are fringe-winged. Their wings are often absent, but when they are present, they are minuscule, exceedingly narrow and shorter than the body, with the forewings being slightly wider and narrower than the hindwings.

In flight, thrips do not move their wings in the same way that most other winged insects do; the movement is something more akin to a rowing motion.

In some species of thrips, when they are at rest the wings are held flat upon the abdomen. In other species, they lie parallel to the abdomen. The venation of both pairs of wings is reduced to two longitudinal veins, which are margined with a long fringe that is comprised of long, socketed bristles known as setae. Wings are coupled by a pair of strong forewing setae that hook up with curved hindwing setae.

ALDERFLIES AND DOBSONFLIES
order Megaloptera

The wings of alderflies and dobsonflies have wings with many veins. Both pairs are delicate, membranous and almost equal in size and shape, with a well-branched venation system. As alderflies do not feed when they become adults, their flying ability is essentially focused on two things: finding a mate and avoiding capture until the female is fertilised and the eggs deposited. It is fascinating to watch an alderfly take to the air on the approach of danger. When threatened it will run to the top of a leaf or branch, take off and alight on another leaf or branch close by. It will do this over and over again whenever it is approached.

Wings

Alderfly and dobsonfly wings have abundant cross-venation and a marginal series of tiny veinlets, which are often accompanied by darkened areas that form sockets for stiff sensory hairs.

The anal area of the hindwings has an expandable and folding feature. Alderfly wings produce uneven flight, and at rest are typically held roof-like above the body. Their bases are usually widely separated, and are uncoupled in flight (except in some species).

LACEWINGS
order Neuroptera

Lacewings have wings with many veins. Their wings are held in a roof-like manner, high above the body. The two pairs of sub-equal wings have a complex venation, with numerous cross-veins. The veins are haired in some species of the family Berothidae.

The hindwings of certain species are very long and narrow, often having areas of the wing membrane pigmented with spots or markings —for example, owl-flies (family Osmylidae). Some of the small, circular markings are actually sensory organs used for picking up specific vibrations.

BEETLES
order Coleoptera

Beetles are sheath-winged. They have modified their forewings into heavily sclerotised wing cases, which are called elytra. Although derived from the functional flying wings of earlier ancestral forms, the elytra are no longer used for flight by most beetles; in fact, they create a drag effect. Instead, when folded, these hard, horny or shell-like forewings protect their delicate hindwings and also shield the entire hindbody (although there are some exceptions, such as rove-beetles, family Staphylinidae). The elytra, being particularly protective, also provide beetles with distinct advantages in occupying and surviving in an exceptionally wide range of different habitats.

Forewings

The highly specialised forewings of beetles are opened during flight (except among members of the subfamily Scarabaeidae–Cetoniinae). They are attached to the side of the mesothorax by a definite hinge mechanism. The elytra are typically without venation of any kind, but are often hairy, scaly and frequently sculptured with a series of longitudinal grooves or rows of pits, ridges and hollows.

Even though the elytra are not flying wings, they do contribute to the distinctive styles of flight found among different beetle species. For instance, in flight, the elytra of a cowboy beetle are not spread but are held together and slightly lifted to allow the flying wings to

unfold, forming a cushion of air beneath them. Christmas beetles, on the other hand, extend their elytra above and outwards, and by comparison are very clumsy in flight. The elytra also assist in producing the sounds that beetles make when whirring through the air.

Hindwings

The venation of the hindwings is peculiar, when compared with that of most other insects. In coleopterans, the apical area is mostly always able to fold immediately when not in use (some having a double fold). The flying wing venation of beetles varies in relationship to the complexity with which the wings are folded when at rest. The direct-flight muscles rotate the wings forward into the flight position and open the longitudinal and transverse folds.

LEFT A bright-yellow ladybird (*Illeis galbula*). Both larvae and adults actively feed on the fungi produced by white wax scale insects and they are often found in large numbers on affected plants.

ABOVE A long-beaked beetle (*Metriorrhynchus rhipidius*). The foul taste and smell of *Metriorrhynchus* beetles makes them highly unpalatable, thus deterring predators. Flies, moths, wasps and other beetles mimic their colour and shape to ward off predators.

OPPOSITE A clubbed lacewing (*Suhpalacsa flavipes*). Owl-flies like this are the strongest-flying of the lacewings and they capture winged prey in mid-air.

OPPOSITE A robber fly (*Bathypogon* species) feeding on a tachinid fly. The sturdy long legs of robber flies help accelerate them into the air to capture flying insects. Their power-ful flight muscles are housed in the domed thorax. Robber flies have a piercing rostrum, which they plunge into captured prey to extract the vital juices.

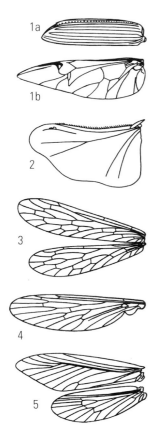

ABOVE Wing types:
1a. Sheath-winged, elytron (forewing): beetles.
1b. Unfolded flight wing (hind wing): beetles.
2. Flight wing (hind wing) twisted-winged: stylopids.
3. Long-winged: scorpion flies.
4. Flight wing (forewing): true flies.
5. Hair-winged: caddis flies.

STYLOPS
order Strepsiptera

Stylops are twisted-winged. With their general bodily structure and their hindwing structure, these insects are closely related to the beetles. Males use their hindwings for flying. The females are entirely wingless.

Forewings

The forewings are reduced to a small pair of small knob-like structures. Although hardened like the elytra of beetles, they do not serve to protect the flying wings.

Hindwings

The milky-coloured, membranous hindwings are large and fold fan-like when not in use. The veins are structured in an unusual manner, with a concave-shaped costal area and two strengthened veins.

SCORPION-FLIES
order Mecoptera

Mecopterans are long-winged. The wings are held roof-like over the abdomen when not in use.

Wings

Both pairs of membranous wings are almost the same size and shape as one another. However, actual wing shapes vary considerably among species, some being elongated and very narrow. All the main longitudinal veins and branches have supporting cross-veins. In the family Boreidae, the wings are sometimes sclerotised. The forewings have a wider base and costal area than the hindwings. As a primitive wing-coupling device, the hindwings normally have one or two frenulum bristles at the base of the costal region.

FLIES
order Diptera

Dipterans have two wings; their forewings are the functional flying wings. Their hindwings have, over time, become reduced to halteres, which are club-shaped balancers. Halteres have no flying action but are highly sensitive sensors of movement and act to counterbalance the fly in flight. In some species of true flies, both pairs of wings may be reduced or lost entirely, for example, in the wingless female soldier fly *Boreoides subulatus*, which occurs in the more mountainous regions of southeastern New South Wales and northern Victoria.

Forewings

The forewings have a narrow base and a strong costal margin that thickens towards the apex and sometimes extends around the wing completely. The membrane of the forewings varies among species in shape, size and colouring. It is often tinted in colour patches. The reduced venation at the apex of the wings of true flies suggests a modification that was tailored to improve their flight: the common housefly, for example, beats its wings at around 350 times per second, travelling at around 9 km an hour; mosquitoes beat their wings between 270 and 600 times per second.

Hindwings

The hindwings of true flies persist only as minute stalked knobs (halteres), richly supplied with nerves to assist the insect in maintaining its balance during flight. These highly reduced hindwings rapidly vibrate during flight and detect variations in ambient forces such as air movement, which may mean approaching danger.

CADDIS-FLIES
order Trichoptera

Most caddis-flies are hair-winged. In general appearance they are moth-like, but what distinguishes them from moths is that, in most species, their four wings are densely covered in fine hairs.

There are two methods of wing coupling, either by a jugal lobe located on the basal area of the forewing that links with a fold of the costal base of the hindwing, or by a row of tiny hooks located on the costal area of the hindwings that engages with a ventral ridge running longitud-inally behind the anal veins of the forewings.

Wings

The two pairs of sub-equal wings are folded flat or roof-like over the body when at rest. Wing venation is usually simple and complete, but in certain species it is reduced.

RIGHT A male orange cruiser butterfly (*Vindula arsinoe ada*) feeding on the sap flowing from a tree trunk. Males are territorial and stake claim to a particular tree branch or leaf in order to oversee a wide area where they wait for passing females. With their wings folded at rest, these butterflies are difficult to locate among foliage.

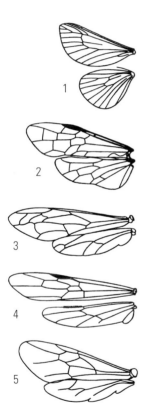

ABOVE Wing types:
1. Scale-winged: butterflies and moths.
2. Clear winged (hyaline or translucent): sawflies.
3. Clear-winged: solitary wasps.
4. Clear-winged: bulldog ants:
5. Clear-winged with highly reduced wing venation: bees.

MOTHS AND BUTTERFLIES
order Lepidoptera

Lepidopterans are scale-winged and are closely related to caddis-flies. True flight, combined with soaring, is well demonstrated by many butterflies. Many larger species fly with a slow flapping of their large wings. An 'average-sized' butterfly, by comparison, has been estimated to do around nine wing beats per second; the rapid wing beats of some hawk moths (family Sphingidae) can reach over 300 wing beats per second and fly up to 55 km/h.

Lepidopteran wings cannot operate efficiently in flight without various secondary locking—or coupling—devices. During flight, butterfly wings are characteristically coupled by an overlapping wing membrane. Moth wings are often coupled by a long, thin, spine-like process—the frenulum. This projects from the front edge of each hindwing, located close to where the wings are attached to the body. In females, this typically engages with a row of forward-pointing bristles on the forewings, but in males it engages a hook-like flap of wing cuticle that locks both pairs of wings together. In the females, the frenulum generally consists of three separate bristles; in the males it usually takes the form of a single long curved spine. These and the catches on the forewings are easily seen in hawk moths.

Lepidopteran wings are typically held roof-like when not in use, or dorsally folded above the body. Wing venation is typically reduced. The two pairs of flying wings have both surfaces adorned with broad, flattened scales. These tiny scales help them to escape from the sticky snares of aerial, web-weaving spiders: the scales are readily shed on contact, the hungry spider is left with nothing but a 'web full of dust'. A butterfly can lose up to a third of its wing area (mostly its hindwings) and still continue its lifestyle.

Usually broad-winged, butterflies and moths have developed wing-colouring features such as eyespots, flash-colouring, cryptic camouflage, and patterns in order to be recognised by the opposite sex (see Chapter Four).

Forewings

On a typical forewing of a lepidopteran, 12 veins radiate from a large, closed, basal cell—the first and last vein being developed from the wing base and the remainder, from the basal cell itself.

Hindwings

A typical hindwing has essentially the same vein arrangement but with only eight veins. In older existing groups, the venation of the hindwings closely resembles that of the forewings, except that the anal veins are unlooped.

WASPS, ANTS AND BEES
order Hymenoptera

Hymenopterans are typically hyaline-winged, and include a number of different types of wasps—sand wasps and parasitic, predatory, and nest-building wasps—as well as ants and bees. Two pairs of functional flying wings are present, except among certain families—for example, all worker ants (Formicidae), female flower wasps (Tiphiidae) and female velvet ants (Mutillidae). When not in use, the wings are folded one above the other longitudinally, but they are never held roof-like. The venation is distinctly different from that of other insects, and is reduced due to the fusion of veins.

Forewings

The wing membrane is very tough and usually glassy, with highly modified venation. The two main veins and cross-veins are strongly formed. The forewings are always longer and wider than the hindwings; they have a wing-coupling device and their point of attachment to the thorax is concealed.

Hindwings

The anal lobe of these Hymenopterans may have a distinct fold, according to the species. Wing coupling during flight is achieved by means of a row of minute hooks on the hindwings' front margin. These engage with the downwardly projecting ridge or fold on the hind margin of the forewings.

BELOW A nocturnal moth, the Oleander hawk moth (*Daphnis placida*), hovers at tree blossoms to probe the nectaries with its long proboscis, pollinating them as it feeds.

LEFT When ready to exit from its resin-hardened, oval-shaped cocoon, the emperor gum moth (*Opodiphthera eucalypti*) regurgitates fluid to soften the silk. It cuts open its cocoon using a sharp thorn located on the base of its forewing. This thorn is shed on emergence. The pupal phase can last several years, awaiting climatic conditions favourable for emergence.

CHAPTER FOUR

Behaviour and Survival

Insects often surprise us with behaviour that seems to indicate a high degree of 'intelligence', an assumption that may be due to such patterns as the complex social organisation of bees and ants. But are insects' lives governed by intelligence or instinct? The truth lies somewhere in between: while many insects are capable of learning and recall, much of their behaviour is instinctive. Over vast periods of time, insects have evolved patterns of behaviour or certain physical characteristics in response to their basic survival needs—perhaps as a means of evading or confusing predators. They have adapted in extraordinary ways, often in order to cope with changed circumstances in their environment. For example, insects can feed on an enormous range of food including decaying carcasses, animal excreta, horns, wood, hair, blood, wax, other insects and foliage, nectar and pollen. This chapter explores their many extraordinary means of survival.

OPPOSITE A monkey grasshopper (*Morabines* sp.) caught in the wheel-web of a St Andrew's cross spider (*Argiope keyserlingi*). Kicking its powerful hind legs, a grasshopper can tear a spider's snare to shreds and, with a well-placed kick, can mortally wound the spider. Even when swathed in silk, by regurgitating gastric juices that are capable of dissolving the threads, a grasshopper can escape. However, once the spider sinks in its fangs, the insect's fate is sealed.

There is little point in trying to determine whether insects are intelligent (they certainly use intelligence) or are merely slaves of instinct. It can be argued that they cannot recall past actions or plan for future ones, relying instead on a prearranged set of actions. The problem is that we do not have enough knowledge or understanding of this aspect of insects' lives to be able to determine the true equation.

It could be said that intelligence—the ability to respond appropriately—steers the material of the body of any life form. Without it, matter is undirected, formless, and chaotic. Insects, especially, absorb and manufacture chemicals which they use as repellents and attractants— messenger molecules. Each living cell has an endless number of messages it can send and receive, with only a small fraction of messages being activated at any one time. What, then, controls these messages and these processes?

Instinctive behaviours

Although we do not fully understand how the mind of an insect works, we do know that it receives messages by way of nerve fibres extending from its sensory organs, giving the nervous system the appropriate responses to stimuli. These behavioural patterns are built into an insect's nervous system so that when confronted with a situation within the range of its normal routine, it reacts with a precision that is often predictable.

For instance, an insect may need to act quickly—a fly can take to the wing in a twentieth of a second, as its reflex nervous system has comparatively huge connecting fibres that rapidly convey information and prompt an immediate response. The sensory ability of any creature determines the type of stimuli it can respond to, and its response to any given stimuli depends upon its form of motor equipment.

There are also patterns of behaviour involved with finding food, mating, nest-building, maintenance, host selection, grooming, and so on, which are each arrived at by a natural selection process suited to the particular needs of the species involved. For example, cave insects are almost blind; although sensitive to light, they cannot respond to shapes or colours. A butterfly caterpillar will respond to light by moving away from it, while the adult butterfly seeks the sunlight.

Or there is the behaviour of most moth caterpillars when nearing the pupal stage. The caterpillars spin a silk cocoon within a rolled leaf of the host plant (on which they have fed and grown). Before doing this, however, they deliberately secure the stalk of the leaf to its twig with abundant silk. The leaf, therefore, does not fall in autumn and the caterpillar survives.

BELOW Banded gumtree hoppers (*Eurymela* species) with *Iridomyrmex* ants. These ants feed on honeydew exuded by the gumtree hoppers and, in exchange, the hoppers are offered protection. The formic acid emitted by the ants is distasteful and so effective at deterring most predators that some gumtree hoppers live permanently in ants' nests. Banded gumtree hopper nymphs huddle when disturbed, but do not jump. The winged adults leap and fly when threatened.

RIGHT A female spider-hunting wasp (*Turneromyia* species) drags a paralysed huntsman spider (*Delena* species) to her burrow nest-site. Over millions of years these wasps have gained intimate knowledge of spiders, which they hunt to use as food for their own larvae to eat upon hatching (one spider per cell).

So instinct does appear to play a significant role in the life of an insect as it goes about its business, performing a given series of actions. A marked feature of instinct, as opposed to what we call intelligence, is that instinct shows very little accommodation to conditions that vary in any way from what is considered normal for that creature. We can best assess what is happening inside the insect's mind by observing what it does when confronted by circumstances that demand some form of decision-making process outside its normal routine but still remain within its natural surroundings.

An insect that is disturbed from the course of its normal routine usually seems unable to retrace its course of action, but it will continue the sequence of actions from the point it was engaged in before being interrupted. Some classic examples of this kind of behaviour have been observed among hunting wasps, sand wasps and mud-daubing wasps that stock their burrows or nests with live insects as food for their offspring when hatched. Should the wasp return to her nest to find the cells emptied, she does not replace the food supply (because that link in the process has already been carried out). Instead, she deposits her eggs anyway and seals the cells as though all is in good order.

Learned behaviours

Nevertheless, insects—and spiders—do demonstrate different levels of behaviour, some of which are akin to using life intelligence or, as J. H. Fabre once described it, 'discernment'. Insects, he said, 'possess latent powers held in reserve for certain emergencies. Long generations can succeed one another without employing them; but, should some circumstance require it, suddenly these powers burst forth ...'.

The wasps, ants and bees (order Hymenoptera) include many social species, so they provide the most readily available opportunities for observing and studying such differing levels of insect behaviour. From a careful study of their activities, it becomes apparent that in some way they do have a capacity for learning and remembering—they are not entirely 'pre-programmed'.

Even allowing that nest-building and nest-provisioning involve complex sequences of 'behavioural patterns', these tasks are subject to an enormously wide range of varying circumstances and conditions. Certain species of spider-hunting wasps (family Pompilidae), in particular, are flexible enough to change the usual order of sequence of actions when confronted by situations that prevent them from carrying out their normal routines. They also recognise landmarks, which they use to guide themselves back to their underground nest-sites.

Some also exhibit complex feats of memory and location-finding. The hunting wasps, for example, track down spiders and other prey, paralyse them and then drag their stunned prey over rough terrain to a subterranean burrow that they have prepared in advance. When sufficient food for its larvae has been stored, the wasp lays her egg or eggs, and takes no further interest in the nest-site or its contents.

There are numerous examples of insects using initiative to better their lives. At some stage in their long history, ants, for example,

LEFT An engineering feat, the leaf nest of the tropical green weaver or green tree-ant (*Oecophylla smaragdina*) is formed by chains of worker ants. They draw together leaves and adhere them with silk obtained from their larvae.

learnt to literally farm other insects that can supply them with nourishment. Aphids, plant-hoppers, scale insects, mealy bugs and caterpillars of certain butterflies (family Lycaenidae) all exude honeydew and sweet-tasting substances from specialised glands, which is eagerly sought after as a staple diet in certain ant communities. The ants build shelters for these creatures and rear them for their own use—even carrying their eggs into the nest and caring for them just like their own eggs.

The green tree-ants, *Oecophylla smaragdina*, somehow discovered that they could utilise the silk produced by their own offspring in the construction of their nests. The nest is formed by leaves drawn together by chains of workers and adhered with silk obtained from the silk glands of the ant larvae. Each worker ant involved with nest-building carries a larva in its mandibles in such a way that the larva's head faces forward. The ant then approaches the edge of the leaf and holds the larva's head against it momentarily. When the larva's head is withdrawn, a silken thread is drawn out and the larva's head is immediately pushed onto the edge of the leaf again. Numerous larvae are employed in this way until a stoutly woven sheet of silk has secured the leaves together, forming a rainproof shelter.

SURVIVAL STRATEGIES

Insects are heavily preyed upon, both as adults and in their pre-adult forms, and they have developed a diverse range of complex strategies and behaviours designed to confuse, hide from or escape their predators. With some insects (and spiders, too) this even includes shedding one or more of their limbs; in some groups (for example, phasmatids) the lost limbs are regenerated between moults.

Many species rely largely on concealment for their survival, adopting shapes or patterns of colour or shading that allow them to blend in with their habitat. Large populations of larvae, pupae and adult insects conceal themselves within the soil, under rocks and beneath fallen timber and tree trunks of both dead and living plants. Most insects use some kind of evasive action—flying, jumping, falling, running, mimicry, bouncing, rolling, or remaining motionless in order to feign death.

Some insects attempt to scare off potential predators using a variety of methods, such as mimicry of dangerous creatures, or by displaying flashes of colour, or false eyes or even false heads. Many insects are equipped with defensive tactics in reserve, should their first method fail. Switching from the use of

camouflage to using offensive smells is one method; making themselves distasteful by absorbing chemicals from their food, or covering themselves in frothy, ill-tasting fluids is another. Certain species may resort to spraying blistering chemicals, or to biting and stinging.

In general, the claws, mouthparts, raptorial limbs, spurs and spines of insects are primarily used for obtaining and manipulating food. However, in some cases, certain body-parts may be modified into mechanisms for attack or defence. For example, the females of numerous wasps, bees and ants are formidably armed with venomous stings—in wasps from the family Vespidae, the tail stings, which are ovipositors, have been modified to secrete poisons from specialised glands. In the social bees, the sting is used to defend the nest-site, but some families of solitary wasps use their stings to paralyse other insects, which are placed in their nest to be used for larval food.

Escaping the spider's snares

For insects, spiders are probably the worst of their enemies. In their effort to keep one step ahead of the spider's snares, insects have evolved numerous means of escape.

Large dragonflies and cicadas, for example, have powerful flight muscles with which they can tear a spider's web to shreds in their vigorous struggle, and usually they successfully free themselves. Many orthopterans regurgitate liquids that can dissolve the web's protein threads. Moths and butterflies (moths in particular as, like moths, most spiders are out at night) have evolved a highly effective means of escape. They simply shed their abundant wing-scales on contact with the sticky threads of the web and quickly fly on their way— literally 'brushing' off the temporary inconvenience. Spiders that try to use their fangs to penetrate the heavily chitinised exoskeletons of many beetles are generally thwarted by such armour. Many beetles are simply left to die, bundled in silk, but many also escape.

The huge mandibles of tree crickets, katydids and large longicorn beetles can cut a spider in two. The long, spiny, kicking legs of some tree crickets and short-horned grass-hoppers (locusts) can fatally rip the spider's body wide open. Large mantids seldom succumb when captured: they free themselves by severing the threads holding them, and even seize the spider in its own web. Afterwards, the mantid spends some time preening itself to dislodge the remaining threads from its body.

Numerous stinkbugs exude repellent odours and many of the larger ichneumonoid wasps also have highly offensive smells and tastes. Spiders are only too pleased to release such insects from their webs. Wasps often prove to be formidable prey for spiders, even when the wasp is temp-orarily held by the sticky threads—a spider that mistimes its move when snaring a wasp can end up being injected with the wasp's potent venom.

CONFUSION AND CONCEALMENT

Mimicry and cryptic camouflage

Inoffensive species commonly adopt warning colours to mimic more dangerous, distasteful or stinging insects such as hymenopterans. The warning colours of red, orange or yellow—often highlighted by surrounding bands or borders of black or white—most frequently occur among daylight-active insects. Through painful experience, predators learn to avoid such conspicuously-coloured insects. However, no insect is entirely inedible to some form of predator or scavenger.

Insects also mimic natural objects—ranging from tree bark to leaves in various stages of growth or decay, thorns, seeds, seedpods, lichen, twigs, pine needles, dry stems, grass blades, fungi, and bird and other animal droppings. This cryptic camouflage is achieved by the use of patterns, shapes and colours adorning the body or wings. It is the most common form of concealment for insects living in more exposed situations.

Insects camouflage themselves by mimicking parts of plants with an amazing degree of accuracy. Some insects, for example, have clear windows in their wings that simulate holes. A mimicked leaf or twig is copied in its tint, shape, size and even in its stage of growth. Knobs, thorns and even notches around the edges of the wings of many insects simulate eaten portions of a leaf. Many caterpillars—especially those in the family Geometridae—hide perfectly in foliage by imitating the twigs and leaves of the host plant.

Disruptive camouflage

Disruptive camouflage is a defensive feature found throughout the animal kingdom. It involves using pattern, shape and colour to visually break up the outline of the creature, enabling it to blend with its surroundings.

When approached by a predator, some butterflies in the family Nymphalidae try to become less prominent by tilting their wings towards the predator. This makes the butterfly less conspicuous by making it appear smaller, and helps it blend with the environment by reducing the size of the shadow cast by its body. Similarly, the bodies of some moth and butterfly caterpillars are subtly coloured and toned to reduce their prominence when casting shadows, helping them to blend with their surroundings.

Cryptically-camouflaged insects can sometimes deploy a back-up defence tactic by using flash-colouring. When threatened by a potential predator, an insect will suddenly flash brilliant orange, red or yellow colours, which confuse the predator long enough to provide the insect with an opportunity to escape. When the insect settles elsewhere it neatly folds its wings, making the bright colours disappear. The change in the colouring of the insect is so great that the insect seems to have vanished.

LEFT In its typical protective posture of twig-mimicry, the caterpillar of the twisted-winged moth, (*Circopetes obtusata*), is afforded a remarkable degree of camouflage. Its cryptic nature is carried through to the adult moth, which rests with its wings spread and curled, holding its body to one side—a convincing mimic of a dead leaf.

ABOVE A jewel shield-bug (*Scutiphora pedicellata*) is caught in the snare of a spider (*Eriophora* species). Spiders will often remove these 'stinkbugs' from their webs. However, shield-bugs can be made edible by leaving them bundled in silk until their odour subsides,

THE ROLE OF WINGS

RIGHT Disruptive camouflage in moths helps them blend with their surroundings. At rest during daylight the mottled shadowless form of the privet hawk moth (*Psilogramma menephron*) merges with the tree bark. Its large fleshy green caterpillar also blends with the foliage on which it feeds.

OPPOSITE The green lichen moth (*Pachythrix hampsoni*). The wings of moths in this genus are mottled. In daylight they remain motionless, blending into the mossy rainforest habitat.

BELOW When alarmed, the mountain katydid (*Acripeza reticulata*) uses flash-colouring—it displays bright colours, warning of its bad taste. If further annoyed, it will expand an orange-yellow membrane between its head and thorax that exudes distasteful fluid. Its final line of defence is to leap, close its leathery tegmen and merge with its surroundings.

Wings play a crucial role in species survival and the survival of individuals. One of their main functions, of course, is to escape from predators, especially ground-based ones such as reptiles. Flight is also the chief means by which most insects seek out a mate and disperse to favourable habitats. Flying abilities vary across the different insect groups—some are equipped only for short bursts of flight, just enough to get away; others are skilled flyers. Escaping from other winged predators—birds, bats or other insects—involves the use of different flying tactics or a combination of flying and being still, or taking advantage of patterns and colours on the wings to surprise or evade pursuers.

The wing patterns of many insects have evolved along some very interesting lines, especially in their use of colour, and often they are used to hide from predators or to startle them. A grasshopper or a moth, for example, which is usually well-camouflaged when resting, will use the bright colouring on its wings to flash at a predator if disturbed.

Butterflies adopt similar strategies. They, too, are coloured so as to blend in with their surroundings when not in flight. When they do take to the air their pattern of flight is fluttery—they rarely remain still for long. Even when feeding at flowers, butterflies flit from one flower to the next; if danger threatens, some species are able to accelerate skyward at an extraordinary rate of speed. Their keen eyesight and erratic flight pattern increases the

difficulties for predators, and the use of iridescent blue and green colours on the wings of many tropical butterflies makes them quite elusive as they fly through shadows and dappled light. In these light conditions, the sudden appearance and disappearance of highly iridescent colours causes confusion to any would-be predators.

The sudden display of primary eyespots, found in many moths and butterflies, is another way of using wing patterns to evade predators. The hindwings are adorned with concentric colour patches that often resemble vertebrate eyes. These are typically large and contrast with surrounding colours. When the moth is at rest, the eyespots are usually covered by cryptic-coloured forewings, but when it is threatened, the forewings are suddenly lifted to expose the two staring eyes. This can momentarily confuse a predator, giving the moth time to escape.

Other insects have clear wings, enabling their cryptically coloured bodies to merge more effectively with their surroundings. The wing design of cicadas was so successful from the start that present-day forms are remarkably unchanged from those of the earliest fossil finds. A cicada strongly relies on its wings both to move swiftly from tree to tree, and away from predatory birds. It also helps it to quickly merge with foliage and branches upon alighting.

DIVERSITY AMONG THE GROUPS

This part of the chapter details some specific strategies employed by particular insects. It deals with a fascinating variety of defensive strategies insects adopt to survive. Also covered are the strategies insects use to catch prey.

MAYFLIES
order Ephemeroptera

Survival strategies

The female lays an enormous number of eggs in the water—the sheer size of their populations is the main survival strategy of mayflies. In addition, parthenogensis occurs with some species of mayfly.

Predators

The carnivorous nymphs of other aquatic insects such as dragonflies, damselflies, diving beetles, and stoneflies prey upon mayfly nymphs.

Fish and tadpoles take a large proportion of mayfly nymphs on the creek-bed; they also swim to the surface to catch the females as they are laying their eggs. While they perform their swirling courtship dance above water, both sexes are vulnerable to attack by aerial web-weaving spiders and insectivorous birds.

BELOW An insect predator, the Gippsland water dragon (*Physignathus lesueurii howitti*). Silt and decaying plant life of creeks and streams provide a rich source of food for a large assortment of aquatic insect nymphs and larvae. These, in turn, are frequently included in the diet of water dragons, as well as providing food for tadpoles and fish.

DAMSELFLIES
order Odonata: suborder Zygoptera

Survival strategies

Some species of newly hatched nymphs hasten to seek shelter beneath a stone or a crevice on the banks of the stream; some burrow into the mud. As adults, they often avoid predators by remaining motionless. If that fails, their secondary defence is to quickly flutter away, alight on nearby foliage and remain still.

Predators

Water spiders (family Pisauridae) capture the nymphs of both damselflies and dragonflies, and freshwater fish include nymphs in their diet.

Damselflies lack the flight-power of dragonflies and so are more easily captured by predators such as mantids, assassin flies and web-weaving spiders. They are captured in the air and, when resting on foliage, by birds and reptiles.

DRAGONFLIES
order Odonata: suborder Anisoptera

Survival strategies

The dull nymphs blend in perfectly with aquatic vegetation; this is in strong contrast to the bright colours of the adults. To avoid predators, nymphs normally emerge from their nymphal skins using the protective cover of darkness, either before dawn so that their wings are ready for flight at sunrise, during overcast conditions or immediately before or after a thunderstorm.

The enormous compound eyes working in conjunction with a highly flexible neck give dragonflies 360° panoramic vision. Its eyes are particularly interesting. They have binocular vision and each compound eye has two divisions: the back part is focused for movement or sudden changes in light; the front provides the accurate focusing required to track fast-flying prey and to recognise the opposite sex. In addition, the three ocelli give frontal and lateral light and also detect movement. Sets of tactile setae located between its large, swivelling head and pronotum enable it to gauge its level of flight and adjust its wings in relation to its head and eyes.

A dragonfly will normally alight upon a leaf or reed stem that affords an unobstructed view, yet is out of easy range of predators. Should it detect the slightest movement, it can take to the air at a moment's notice. Its flight is efficient and noted for its manoeuvrability. Its flying skills are due to both pairs of wings being able to work independently or together—synchronised for sudden mid-air changes of direction, for hovering, or for making a direct burst of speed to overtake winged prey.

Try to catch an airborne dragonfly with a net and you will quickly discover its agility. To catch it head-on will inevitably prove impossible, and some of the larger species fly faster than swallows. To successfully net a dragonfly on the wing, follow through with a swift, deft, sweeping stroke of the net from behind the insect as it passes.

Predators

During the vulnerable period when it emerges from its nymphal skin, dragonflies can fall prey to fish and frogs. Fish are their chief natural enemies, yet the fish hatchlings provide food for dragonfly nymphs.

Alighting on foliage, adults are frequently captured by large mantids and hunting wasps. Despite their sight and prowess on the wing, dragonflies often meet an ignoble end in the viscid meshes of wheel-web snares constructed by the master-weaving spiders (family Araneidae), although the larger dragonfly species are seldom held for long in the web. Birds such as the keen-eyed bee-eaters (family Meropidae) frequently capture dragonflies in mid-air by intercepting their flight path.

Dragonflies do not sting or bite nor spread diseases, yet in spite of their survival skills, their survival is seriously threatened by destruction of their natural habitats with pollution, dredging, drainage and infilling of ponds and creeks.

STONEFLIES
order Plecoptera

Survival strategies
The wings of the stonefly closely match the surrounding rock surface or tree bark upon which the insect rests.

Predators
The nymphs form a large part of the diet of fish. They are also preyed upon by carnivorous nymphs and larvae of other aquatic insects such as dragonflies, damselflies, diving beetles, and other stonefly nymphs, too.

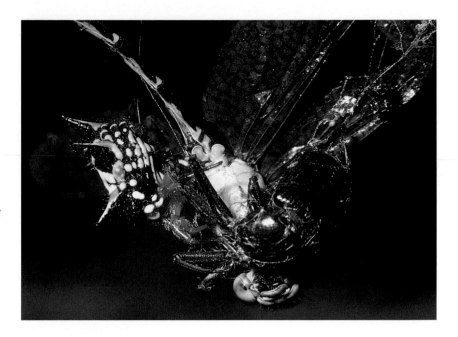

COCKROACHES
order Blattodea

Survival strategies
Like many insects, a cockroach is equipped with a pair of sensory organs called cerci on the end of its abdomen. These cerci are highly sensitive to the slightest movement of air currents. In response to the tiniest of movements, the nerves of the limbs are triggered into immediate action and the cockroach begins running, scuttling to find the nearest hiding place. The only successful way to closely approach one is slowly, and from the front.

While their running speed and sensory equipment are their chief defences, cryptic camouflage also plays a major part in cockroach survival strategy. Many species use the protective shelter of fallen timber, while others may burrow deeply beneath the soil. Cockroaches have specialised in exuding a 'repulsiveness' as another defensive strategy, one that is particularly effective when it comes to encounters with humans.

Predators
Despite their defensive strategies, cockroaches form the diet of numerous predatory creatures, including mantids, carnivorous grasshoppers, crickets and spiders. Deter their presence in your home by reducing the availability of food and shelter: repair leaky taps and pipes, keep pet bowls clean and seal any cracks in cupboards.

ABOVE A dragonfly (*Hemigomphus heteroclitus*) has met an ignoble fate entangled in the wheel-web snare of the Christmas spider (*Gasteracantha minax*). Wheel-weaving spiders exploit the flight paths of insects by constructing their snares in strategic positions to capture insects in transit.

ABOVE The spinifex termite (*Nasutitermes triodiae*) constructs huge mounds, which reach up to seven metres high. The soldier castes never build, feed the young or gather any supplies. Instead they act as bodyguards, defending the nest. Grass and debris feeders, these termites do not infest buildings.

TERMITES
order Isoptera

Survival strategies

The nest provides termites with their greatest protection, and perhaps the most famous nests are those found in the Northern Territory made by the magnetic termites (family Termitidae). Their massive, tombstone-shaped nests are built on a north–south axis in order to even out the nest's exposure to the sun. Most repair work is carried out during the wet season, the soil being more malleable when damp. Because of the orientation of the nest, its tall, wide sides, once reworked, dry out quickly and harden in the sunshine.

Depending on the species, however, various types of nests are built—the simplest being a large series of chambers and galleries excavated within moist or dry timber. The outside of the timber may show no sign of being eaten, but it is usually just a shell. Such a nest, which also supports a rich fauna of other arthropods, may be constructed in a tree or at its base, or as a mound above or below ground. Perhaps the most typical termite nests are the large dome-shaped, clay-covered mounds made by the milk termites, *Coptotermes lacteus*, commonly found in sclerophyll forests in southeastern Australia. Termites live in total darkness and build earthen tunnels from the nest-site to their food source.

Because a constant source of moisture is required, most species maintain a connection with the ground. To get around the problem of desiccation, they use ingenious methods, such as metabolically manufacturing their own water and taking water from the soil. In this way, the humidity within the galleries of their nests can consistently remain as high as 95 per cent.

In northwestern Australia, there are species that build almost impermeable clay mounds that often rise over 7 metres high. The upper part incorporates bulbous, vase-shaped galleries and vertical tunnels that lead to underground chambers, where temperature and humidity are stabilised. Moisture from these underground chambers and the soil fills the tunnels and galleries throughout the nest. During the night, the temperature can drop an average of 12° C and the vaporised moisture at the top of the nest condenses to drain into the vase-shaped galleries, from where it is retrieved. Termites collect water from the soil, sometimes tunnelling to depths as great as 100 metres.

Predators

If nesting flights cannot be made, the termites will eat one another to prevent a colony growing too large. Predators such as other insects, spiders, mammals, reptiles and birds readily devour the alates (winged castes) in particular.

PRAYING MANTIDS
order Mantodea

Survival strategies

Some of the larger tropical species of the plant-frequenting mantids (family Mantidae) have brightly coloured hindwings and, when threatened, will stand their ground, raising their wings high in an aggressive posture. A large mantis will strike out with its spiny forelimbs, and can also inflict a painful nip on a marauder.

Their cryptic colouring also allows them to move about undetected, especially the small mantids (family Amorphoscelidae). This, combined with their stealthy movement, gives them an added advantage when stalking prey.

Predators

Mantids are preyed upon by insectivorous mammals, birds, lizards, spiders, hunting wasps, and other predatory insects.

Tiny parasitic wasps (families Torymidae and Podagrioninae) attack the mantids' egg

capsules (oothecae). Small, round holes in the capsules are evidence of wasp activity that has destroyed the eggs within. Tree crickets (family Gryllacrididae) tear the egg capsules open using their strong mandibles, and feed on the contents of the capsules.

EARWIGS
order Dermaptera

Survival strategies

Earwigs are mostly nocturnal. During daylight hours they favour cool, dark places but at night they venture out from beneath bark, logs, rocks and stones, to feed on plants, decaying matter or other small insects.

Predators

Strangely enough, although the mother takes great care in guarding her eggs and young nymphs, her tolerance for this work is rather short-lived. Unless the young disperse and look after themselves, she becomes cannibalistic and eats them. Earwigs are attacked by parasitic tachinid flies (family Tachinidae), spiders, birds and bats.

KATYDIDS, CRICKETS AND SHORT-HORNED GRASSHOPPERS
order Orthoptera

This insect group includes both suborders: the long-horned, primarily nocturnal ensiferans, such as katydids, bush crickets and true crickets; and the short-horned, primarily diurnal caeliferans, such as short-horned grasshoppers (or locusts).

There are some differences in terms of the survival strategies between the two groupings, and they are treated separately for this purpose. However, all orthopterans are subject to the same range of predators.

Survival strategies—ensiferans

Katydids and bush crickets rely extensively on camouflage techniques to evade other creatures that pose a threat to them, but still rely on hopping with their long hindlegs to escape. Even as nymphs they attempt to evade predators through cryptic camouflage and by remaining motionless.

The katydids and bush crickets have forewings that perfectly match the foliage of the plants they frequent and they are amazingly

BELOW Ants are cleaners of the forest floor. This female worker red bulldog ant (*Myrmecia gulosa*) is delivering an exhausted mantis to the nest-site. The nest extends well below the ground with cleverly constructed avenues, rooms, tunnels and passages, all of which lead to a large central chamber where the ants meet.

RIGHT The ra
(Paragryllac
nocturnal a
hidden duri
night these
for weaken
defenceles:
their power
mandibles,
emerging c
and tear ap
cases of co
mantids and
insect rema
included in

BELOW A late instar nymph of a stinkbug, the cryptic shield-bug (*Poecilometis armatus*). Stinkbugs are infamous for their repulsive-smelling noxious secretions. Both adults and nymphs exude smells from special glands. Such chemical defence is characteristic of many heteropterans.

To a lesser degree, ants (family Formicidae), hunting wasps or digger wasps (family Sphecidae), parasitic flies (family Tachinidae), robber or assassin flies (family Asilidae), and mandibulate predators such as the bush crickets and tree crickets (family Gryllacrididae) and mantids (family Mantidae) also prey upon the hordes of cicadas.

Leaf hopper and tree hopper nymphs exude a substance, similar to that of aphids, which is a rich source of food, particularly for ants. For this reason, until they become adults, these nymphs are generally well protected from predators by the ants.

RIGHT The soft pale nymph of the 'cuckoo-spit' spittlebug (*Philagra parva*) creates bubbles by taking air into its abdominal tubular channel and expelling it through a film of liquid excreta. This frothy shelter offers protection against predation and desiccation.

ASSASSIN BUGS AND SHIELD-BUGS
order Hemiptera: suborder Heteroptera

Survival strategies—assassin bugs

Assassin bugs have a powerful, sharp rostrum. Most assassin bugs can inflict a painful stab with their rostrum when handled or stepped on, and are able to emit a foul smell.

They take their prey by using the rostrum to stab it, and immediately inject it with a deadly chemical mix. Unlike most other bugs, which have two channels incorporated in their rostrum—one for discharging digestive juices and the other for siphoning food—assassin bugs have one large channel for both activities. Once stabbed, the prey succumbs almost immediately as it is injected with the toxic fluid, which acts on its nervous system and breaks down its bodily tissues.

When an assassin bug is caught in a spider's web, these repellent odours can cause the spider to quickly sever the threads holding the bug and let it drop to the ground. Some species utilise their paralysing venom by squirting a jet of spray through the rostrum, achieving remarkable accuracy in their aim up to 30 mm away. For vertebrates this can cause such discomfort that the would-be predator is temporarily blinded.

Sounds are also produced by many species, using specialised stridulatory organs located beneath the head, which are scraped against the rostrum.

Survival strategies—shield-bugs

When threatened or handled, several species of shield-bug produce repulsive-smelling and foul-tasting fluids (from thoracic glands in adults and abdominal glands in nymphs). Many of the insects of this group can squirt fine mists of putrid-smelling fluids, thus they are able to deter numerous predators from eating them.

Predators

Despite their formidable weapons, assassin bugs still fall prey to birds and reptiles, which eat them with little or no ill-effects. Equally, while the odours that shield-bugs emit are intended to deter, many predators ignore them and feed upon the bugs regardless.

Parasitic hymenopterans, such as wasps in the families Scelionidae and Chalcididae, attack the eggs of all heteropterans. Tachinid flies also parasitise the eggs of heteropterans.

LACEWINGS
order Neuroptera

Survival strategies

Many lacewing species deposit their eggs a few millimetres above the substrate on stems. This practice deters marauding ants from carrying them off. The stems supporting the eggs are often coated with sticky globules that makes climbing them very difficult indeed. It also provides some protection for the nymphs when hatching, as some species have cannibalistic tendencies.

Predators

Tree crickets (family Gryllacrididae) are not deterred from eating lacewings' eggs. They are large and long-legged and can simply ignore the adhesive material that coats the stems, plucking the eggs off one at a time until they all are devoured. The adult lacewings themselves frequently end up trapped in spider webs, to be devoured later.

BEETLES AND WEEVILS
order Coleoptera

Survival strategies

Beetles utilise an enormous range of defences in order to deter predators. These include the use of armour, mimicry, warning colours, distastefulness, flying, climbing, running, camouflage and burrowing, making stridulatory sounds, and even dropping to the ground and remaining motionless.

Cryptically coloured beetles drop to the ground the instant they detect approaching danger and they will remain motionless among the ground-litter until they sense it is safe to move. Camouflage is important for many beetles, especially the weevils or snout beetles. They and other beetles such as the stag-beetles (family Lucanidae) also have another strategy—to stiffen and fold their limbs underneath their body, remaining frozen still for long periods until danger has passed.

Certain species can also jump, tumble or simply bounce away from danger, such as the flower-frequenting, tumbling, pin-tailed beetles (family Mordellidae) and the click beetles (family Elateridae), which propel themselves up into the air to avoid capture, and also make a clicking sound. As a means of communicating alarm or warnings, a number of beetle species, both in adult and larva form, are able to produce loud, stridulating sounds when disturbed or threatened. Many longicorn beetles (family Cerambycidae), bess beetles (family Passalidae), and others produce 'surprise sounds', calculated to startle predators. These stridulations are produced from file-shaped organs—specialised rows of tiny pegs and spines, located on the wing covers and limbs—which are rubbed backwards and forwards against each other.

Some species rely on their offensive smells and foul-tasting body fluids. A bombardier beetle (family Carabidae) can spray an explosive chemical cocktail of noxious gases, heated to boiling point. Other beetles depend on producing distasteful chemicals within their body as a means of defence. Beetles such as ground beetles (family Carabidae), rove-beetles (family Staphylinidae) and ladybird beetles (family Coccinellidae) are equipped with specialised glands that produce foul-smelling, foul-tasting and corrosive exudations.

Many beetles advertise their repellent nature by wearing bold warning colours of red and black, orange, yellow and black—for instance, the ladybird beetles. Warning colouration is often also employed, however, as a mimicry device. Flower-visiting beetles, especially longicorns such as *Aridaeus thoracicus* or those of the genus *Hesthesis*, often mimic warning colours and mannerisms of some of the large hunting wasps. Others

ABOVE The long rostrum or 'snout' in this female 'splinter-puller' elephant beetle (*Orthorrhinus cylindrirostris*) is an obvious feature of most weevils. It is equipped with mandibles at its tip. Most weevils have exceedingly hardened exoskeletons and sturdy limbs with broad pads. Their cryptic colouring and shape enable them to merge with the bark of the host plant.

RIGHT A male green fiddler beetle (*Eupoecila australasiae*) feeds on a bearded blue bellflower. These vibrant, highly active beetles advertise their presence during summer days with a loud buzzing flight as they feed on nectar, pollen, ovaries, stamens and petals. They are quick to fly if disturbed.

such as rove-beetles adopt threatening poses in order to bluff an enemy.

All these strategies are aimed at creating a distraction in order to confuse the enemy long enough for the hapless insect to make its escape, but some beetles have other defences. For instance, the exoskeleton and elytra of many beetles are too tough for predators to penetrate. Some, such as the cowboy beetle (*Diaphonia dorsalis*), have powerful leg muscles armed with sharp spurs and spines on their limbs and extensions of body segments ending in thorny protrusions. These can cause considerable discomfort to an assailant and force it to release its hold. Certain larger beetles (such as the ground beetles, tiger beetles and longicorn beetles) resort to inflicting a painful bite, using their stout cutting mandibles. Larvae of leaf beetles (family Chrysomelidae) exude a lethal fluid of hydrogen cyanide.

Predators

Regardless of their defences, many adults, larvae and pupae fall prey to a horde of predatory creatures, and form a good portion of the diet of birds, mammals, reptiles, fish, spiders, wasps and many other insects. Fungus, bacteria and viruses also take an enormous toll on beetles in various stages of their life cycle.

The larvae and pupae of beetles are generally quite well concealed in mud-clay cells, in wood-dust cocoons within the tunnels of timber, or simply naked in the soil. Nonetheless, beetle larvae are heavily preyed upon by a wide range of enemies, including soil-dwelling spiders, as well as by other beetle larvae (for example, families Cleridae and Carabidae). Several wasp species, including the flower wasps (families Tiphiidae and Scoliidae), use them as food for their young, and Tachinid flies (family Tachinidae) lay their eggs on ground-dwelling curl grubs.

LEFT Bundled in silk, a male golden-green stag beetle (*Lamprima aurata*) remains suspended in the wheel-web of a St Andrew's cross spider (*Argiope keyserlingi*). The exoskeleton of many beetles is impenetrable to spiders' fangs and they are often left hanging in the snare.

FLIES
order Diptera

Survival strategies

In their favour, flies have extraordinary alertness, keen eyesight, the power of flight and speed in taking to the air. This allows them to escape most predators, with the exception of their most deadly enemies—the spiders. Their greatest means of survival, however, is through sheer numbers. The eggs are often deposited in large masses and develop rapidly, hatching within a few days. The larvae generally thrive, feeding within decomposing organic matter. Most species pupate beneath the soil.

Predators

Flies fall prey to an enormous range of predatory arthropods, including dragonflies, damselflies, praying mantids, assassin flies (family Asilidae), and the predatory larvae of other fly families. Sand wasps (family Sphecidae) store flies as provision for their young. Spiders, birds, bats and reptiles also take great quantities of flies in their diet. To deter flies in the home, install flyscreens on windows and access doors, wrap all meat scraps, keep garbage bins well closed, and remove dog and other animal excrement from the garden.

MOTHS AND BUTTERFLIES
order Lepidoptera

Survival strategies—larvae and pupae

Primitive caterpillars conceal themselves within tree trunks, logs, branches, tree roots, bark and leaves (borers and miners), or build protective cocoon-like cases as they move about feeding (family Psychidae). Many of the advanced forms, however, are exposed when they feed and rely upon different means of concealment or other protective mechanisms. They therefore use a variety of strategies, cryptic camouflage being one of the main ones. Some mimic leaves, bark, flower buds, twigs, or bird or animal droppings. If detected, they may have other back-up strategies to startle, repel and confuse predators.

Caterpillars have a range of responses to perceived danger. Some simply drop to the ground when danger threatens. Others attach themselves to a silken thread, and rapidly lower themselves, remaining motionless until the threat has passed. These caterpillars then haul themselves back up again using the silken thread. Many caterpillars suddenly inflate their thoracic region, displaying primary eyespots or mouth-shaped patterns that startle a predator.

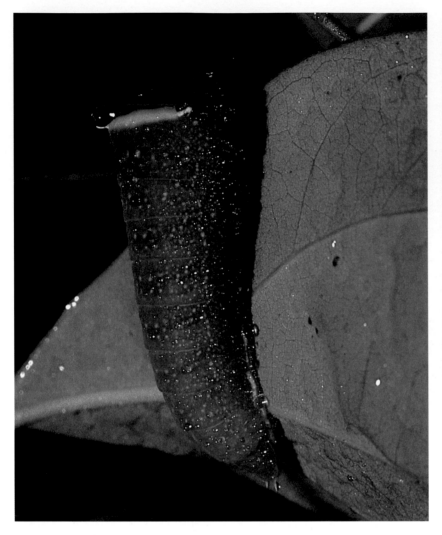

ABOVE A caterpillar of the blue triangle butterfly (*Graphium sarpedon choredon*) resting in daylight on a leaf of its host plant, camphor laurel. When disturbed, it inflates a yellow organ (osmeterium) and exudes a high concentration of plant oils, a deterrent to most predators.

ABOVE RIGHT The colourful caterpillar of the balsam hawk moth (*Theretra oldenlasndiae firmata*) commonly feeds on balsam and grapevine. It has a series of orange-centred eyespots along its body and a slender straight dorsal horn that it waves about as it crawls.

Certain caterpillars can suddenly display a brightly coloured red or purple gland from behind the head or, in some species, beneath the head—typical examples being the caterpillars of the peppered prominent moth (*Neola semiaurata*), banksia moth (*Danima banksia*), and orchard swallowtail butterfly (*Papilio argeus aegeus*). When everted, this gland emits highly pungent odours or fluids, according to the species, and deters any would-be predators.

Many caterpillars are extremely hairy, bristly, or even spiny. Some species have pockets that open to push out thick tufts or clumps of stinging hairs or spines, which can cause irritation and skin rash, as in the mottled cup moth larvae of the genus *Doratifera*. Others are distasteful, or even poisonous, causing a predator great discomfort about the mouth, eyes and nose, and can cause vomiting if swallowed, or even death. Some caterpillars can effectively deter a would-be predator by expelling brightly coloured

liquid or froth from their mouths, which contains a high concentrate of toxic plant juices.

The pupae of moths are frequently well concealed within timber or soil, beneath tree bark or within a curled leaf. Their silken cocoons are often coloured to match the surroundings. Butterfly pupae often defy detection to all but those with the keenest scrutiny. They are usually naked and have remarkable cryptic colouring and shapes, perfectly blended to merge with their surroundings.

Survival strategies—adults

Few creatures can match the fascinating beauty of a butterfly flying from flower to flower in the sunlight, and it is hard to resist trying to catch one in cupped hands as it alights. However, most attempts to hand-catch butterflies are bound to fail as their eyes readily detect movement. The 'nervous' flight pattern of butterflies, such as the blue triangle (or blue sailor) butterfly (*Graphium sarpedon choredon*),

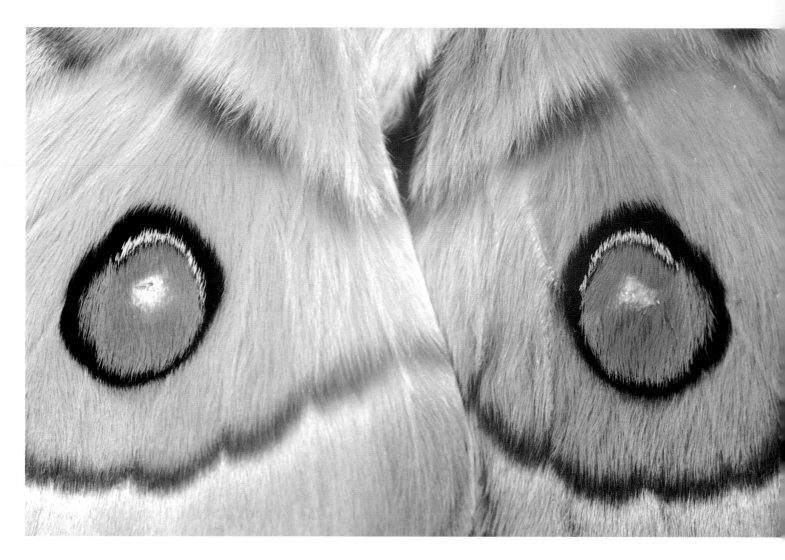

makes them extremely difficult for insectivorous birds to capture. Their power of flight and keen eyesight, combined with the use of cryptic camouflage, special wing patterns and flash-colouring are their best lines of defence, and the ones most frequently adopted.

Moths and butterflies both use cryptic patterns on their wings to conceal themselves when at rest. However, leaf-like wing designs in combination with disruptive patterns are the most frequently adopted forms of camouflage. Beautiful iridescent blues and greens adorn the dorsal wing surfaces of many tropical rainforest butterflies, such as the male Cape York birdwing butterfly (*Troides priamus pronomus*) with its bright iridescent green and yellow wings. Such iridescent colouring can make these butterflies extremely difficult to follow as they flutter in and out of the moving patches of dappled sunlight, or when flying about moving foliage, waterfalls or streams.

Many moths and butterflies also hide brightly coloured patches—eyespots or bright hues—which are part of a complex evasive strategy, almost like a game of 'now you see me, now you don't'. Predators may be startled by the sudden appearance of these brightly coloured patches, giving the moth or butterfly time to get away. On escaping, the insect settles elsewhere, remaining motionless, with its wings at rest and the bright colours hidden. The predator then searches in vain for colours it cannot find.

Among insect wing patterns, none are more remarkable than the eyespots—a more or less circular grouping of colour, edged with white or cream, giving the appearance of staring eyes. The general tinting of the wing area is frequently subdued to harmonise with the insect's customary surroundings, but the eyespots are invariably conspicuous and arresting, usually very pronounced on the hindwings. Sometimes the centre of the eyespot is without colour and entirely transparent, resembling a miniature,

ABOVE Bluff tactics of the emperor gum moth (*Opodiphthera eucalypti*). When startled, these moths may suddenly lift their forewings to display two prominent staring eyespots on the hindwings. Such threatening body language can momentarily confuse a predator, giving the moth a chance to escape, either by falling to the ground among leaf litter or by fluttering away and alighting else-where and remaining motionless.

amber. They are mostly large insects and have a potent sting, with large, biting mandibles; they are never shy to use these weapons.

Bees have the most highly developed form of sting, which is found in the worker honey bee *Apis mellifera*. This is the only species of bee in Australia known to leave its sting in the flesh of the victim. The bee continues to pump venom by means of attached muscles, but in the process, its entrails, along with its barbed sting and poison glands, are dragged out and it dies.

Parasitic wasps also have a long, often slender ovipositor. In several species, the female may use her ovipositor as a self-protective device if she is roughly handled, but it is not an actual sting: it has no accompanying toxins. If it pierces human flesh, its effect is normally akin to a pinprick.

Social habits leading to nest-building are another kind of survival strategy. The wasps' habit of hunting food for their young developed into a situation in which the females needed to stand guard over their catches to protect them from other predators. This led to the wasps hiding their catches by building cells within the ground or in plant tissue or specialised types of nest. In turn, this led to certain wasps developing highly complex social structures.

A wasp colony, such as mason wasps or paper-nest wasps (family Vespidae), is seasonal and exists for one year only (except in tropical regions, where they are ongoing). New colonies are started each spring by fertilised females, which have hibernated during winter. A queen wasp finds a nest-site in a sheltered location such as a hollow tree, or beneath a rock ledge, and begins collecting wood pulp (for a paper-nest) or clay to form the cells. After much skill and hard work, the first few cells are formed, and an egg is laid in

each. The queen rears the first brood by herself until, within a few weeks, the female workers in this first brood are able take over the work of extending the nest while the queen devotes her energy to laying more eggs.

It is the honey bee, however, that has reached the highest form of social life found among insects. Having evolved highly efficient methods of storing sufficient food to supply the colony during lean periods, bees began to develop ongoing colonies. When a colony becomes over-populated, the solution is to swarm—the old queen leaves to begin a new colony and a new queen takes over the old colony. Certain Australian native bees construct loosely knit colonies but none attains the highly organised social nests of the honey bee.

Ants also engage in highly sophisticated communal activities, mostly underground. They, too, swarm when the colony becomes over-crowded, the only time they use their flying wings. They take to the air in their millions for their nuptial and dispersal flight, after which the wings are discarded.

Ants have some unique practices, such as collecting broods from other ant nests and raising them as slaves. Some ants and plants have a symbiotic relationship—ant plants form a living home for the ant occupants. In addition, other insects such as silverfish or the larvae of Lycaen-idae butterflies take up residence in ants' nests (being known as inquilines), and are tolerated by the ants in a mutually beneficial relationship.

Green tree-ants (*Oecophylla smaragdina*) lack stings but they can bite fiercely; formic acid is also squirted into the wound from their tail end. Thousands of ants can suddenly fall upon an intruder milling about beneath their nest. Some effort is needed to remove their vice-like grip. Many refuse to let go and leave their head and mandibles still clinging on after the remainder of their body has been severed when brushed off.

Predators

Hymenopterans are preyed upon by many insects, including parasitic ones. They are parasitised by coleopterans, dipterans and other hymenopterans that grow to maturity feeding on hymenopteran larvae. They are also susceptible to nematode infections, fungi, viruses and bacterial diseases.

Assassin bugs, robber flies and lacewings are also opportunistic predators of hymenopterans, as are spiders, frogs, lizards, birds and mammals.

CHAPTER FIVE

Habits and Habitats

Nature's amazing tapestry is infinitely complex. Insects have been on Earth for hundreds of millions of years, evolving and adapting their forms and maintaining a balance within most terrestrial ecosystems found throughout the world. Insects make enormous contributions to the supply of much of the food we eat (by pollinating our food plants), to conserving the soil (through decomposition) and as prey for other animals on which our livelihoods depend. Yet we still treat insects as enemies, continually finding new ways to control, kill or eliminate them. Crops are dusted, houses sprayed and patios zapped. Slowly people are realising that our relationship with insects does not have to clash with our personal interests. But this necessitates a greater understanding of the particular roles that insects play and the importance of what they do in nurturing the environment. This chapter explores these roles.

OPPOSITE Just as we humans utilise the environment for maximum comfort and rearing our young, so too do insects make use of every conceivable micro-niche. This apparently uninhabited lush mossy forest in Carnarvon Gorge, Queensland, is actually home to a thriving community of insects, many of which live out their lives under bark, soil and leaf litter or in pools of water.

There is a web of dependency between all living things, including ourselves, which means that the way all of us—insects or humans, or other creatures—interact with our surroundings has consequences for the balance of life on Earth.

There are more insects on our planet than any other organism, both in species and sheer numbers. Without the insects, many kinds of plants, and many kinds of fishes, birds and reptiles would quickly disappear. Without the spiders, the world would be overrun with insects. It is likely that our present state of existence would be impossible if it weren't for these little creatures maintaining much of what we tend to take for granted.

Numerous insects have roles involved in tidying or cleaning up, in other words, the important processes of recycling or regenerating. For example, flies and ants rapidly transform and disperse dead animals and their rotting carcasses into rich nutrients that feed the soil. Wood-eating beetles hasten the process of decay in fallen timber; without them, the forests would choke with piled timber and cease to regenerate. Other insects are crucial in the propagation of plants, pollinating them, or are part of the essential food chain, by means of which other creatures survive. Predatory and parasitic insects perform a controlling role, keeping down populations of other potentially harmful insects.

With their adaptability and diversity of physical form, insects can occupy almost every mode of lifestyle and every type of ecological niche—natural or not—bringing the benefits of their ceaseless activity to all kinds of surroundings. They are the dominant life forms found in tropical rainforests, temperate forests, woodlands, grasslands, mountains, plains and deserts; they also inhabit streams and waterways.

Insects live as herbivores, as feeders on nectar and gatherers of pollen, as scavengers, parasites of animals and plants, and as predacious carnivores. Within each of these broad categories, competition is arranged in such a way that it is minimised. Among wood-eaters, for instance, while certain species feed on the sapwood of normally unhealthy timber, others feed on the bark or within rotting logs.

Because most insects are plant-feeders, our own interests often conflict with those feeding on our food crops. Also, because they are spread so diversely, insects tend to transgress our living spaces. It is due to such situations that humans see most insects as pests, as creatures to be exterminated. However, numerous species of winged insects have essential roles—for instance, in fertilising the plants that provide much of our food. If we act to wipe out all so-called 'pests', we also destroy the insects that we rely on.

THE NEED TO PRESERVE HABITATS

Because of this closely interdependent network of life forms, the conservation of natural habitats is a priority. Scientists have long understood the natural realm as being like a complex household, in which its occupants perform different roles in order to make the whole house work. It is from this idea that the science of 'ecology' (from the Greek word *oikos*, meaning 'house') developed. It is a science that deals with our understanding of the conditions of living organisms—a subject whose scope is vast. It is best presented in terms of 'levels of organisation', ranging from the smallest unit:

- the organism—the individual plant or animal
- the population—groups of individuals of any species
- the community—all the different populations within a selected area
- the ecosystem—the sum of all communities in a selected area, including the non-living environment
- the biosphere—the sum total of life on Earth.

In practice, no one level of organisation can be fully investigated without exploring others, as each larger unit includes all smaller ones. Just as a single organism includes organs, tissues and cells, an ecosystem cannot be studied in isolation.

Despite the lack of sharp boundaries between them, ecosystems are useful working units, for they can be as small or as large as we choose to make them. But studying an ecosystem does not just involve considering all organisms included within its confines, from the smallest bacteria to the insects and birds and other creatures. All aspects of the non-living environment must also be included—light, humidity, temperature, winds, altitude, nutrients, and so on—for these all affect the organisms.

The interplay of organisms and their environment may appear forbiddingly complex, the competition so intense, that nature's realm can appear as an anarchic or chaotic state, with every plant and animal competing for food and shelter. But, even though the struggle for

ABOVE, LEFT AND CENTRE Testimony to the visual capabilities of insects, flowers evolved a variety of forms and the use of the entire colour spectrum to lure insects. The diversity of flowering plant species is matched by an equal diversity of pollinating animals, especially insects. Clockwise from top left: *Eucalyptus macrocarpa* blossoms are favoured by beetles, butterflies and wasps; the heathlands of Kalbarri National Park, Western Australia, attract myriad beetles, flies, butterflies, moths, wasps, ants and bees; *Verticordia grandiflora* is pollinated by flies, wasps and bees.

OPPOSITE The bullseyes of rosy everlasting daisies (*Rhodanthe chlorocephala rosea*) quickly direct flies, butterflies and bees to the the nectar and pollen.

ABOVE Most flowering plants such as this heart-leafed flame pea (*Chorizima glycinifolium*) have modified and developed their flower structure to accommodate flower-visiting insects. Bright colours like these act as lures to attract insects.

ABOVE Some bell-shaped flowers like columbine (*Aquilegia canadensis*) have long spurs containing nectar accessed by entering its 'mouth'. Some insects evolved shortcuts and insert their proboscis into the spur base or chew into the walls.

RIGHT Californian poppies (*Hunnemannia fumariifolia*) house a microforest of stamens, and visiting insects become covered in pollen.

survival is intense, it more often goes unseen, as it proceeds so slowly and steadily.

Insects, because they are such ancient creatures, have been able to adapt themselves to specific conditions over a very long period of time—surviving catastrophic events, including ice ages, shifting landmasses, drying up of water, and mass extinctions of forests and vertebrates.

Interference with—or, worse, the destruction of—their supportive habitats will result in changes of conditions beyond the range of even the insects' remarkable degree of adaptability. Adapting to a changing environment invariably needs time for any organism. The preservation of natural habitats is our responsibility as wilderness is a vital requirement for the well-being of most life forms on Earth.

INSECTS AND PLANTS

What makes a natural forest thrive and become healthy? The answer is, of course, because it teems with insects. Of known insect species (including both larval and adult forms), 70 per cent are closely associated with plants in one way or another—at least 400 000 species are known to feed on plants. Many of these are flower-feeders—more than 165 000 species are known to specialise as nectar-feeders. Even those that are not associated directly with plants base their diet and life cycles on others that are. Insects dominate most ecosystems because of their intimate association with plants—a relationship that began in the Cretaceous Period (146 million years ago) as the angiosperms—the flowering plants—began to evolve.

Primitive flowering plants were fertilised solely by the winds until they developed a sticky coating of nectar around their grains of pollen. This nectar, which is a highly concentrated source of energy, then became a readily available food-source, especially for early climbing and flying insects. They then transported the pollen to other plants—pollinating them as they fed. This was the beginning of the co-dependent, steadily co-evolving relationship between flowering plants and insects.

But it is not only the flowering part of the plant that is important for insects. The roots, trunks, branches, twigs, leaves, buds, fruit, pods and seeds all provide major sources of nourishment as well. Not only is every part of a plant included in the diet of one insect species or another, all parts of the plant provide shelter of one kind or another for most arthropods. Insects have diversified and radiated in tandem with the flowering plants—each has intimately influenced the evolution of the other.

In the course of this parallel evolution, flowers themselves are modifications by the plants in order to attract insects to them. For their part, insects have developed specialised sense organs, and have modified their anatomy and lifestyle to accommodate the flowers. Both herbivorous and predacious insects are, in general, so closely associated with plants that numerous forms of insects have actually taken on the venation and colouring of leaves and petals, mimicking these patterns in their wing and bodily structure.

POLLINATION

Flowering plants, or angiosperms, have evolved specialised features in order to accomplish pollination, and to attract four major insect orders, particularly:
- the beetles—Coleoptera
- the flies—Diptera
- the moths and butterflies—Lepidoptera
- the wasps, ants and bees—Hymenoptera.

An angiosperm's most distinctive feature is its flower, which consists of both male and female reproductive structures. Over time, flowers have evolved in ways specifically designed to enhance their ability to reproduce and they use flower visitors—especially the insects—for this purpose. To this end, flowers have developed a wide range of ploys to lure the insects in, such as sweet-tasting nectar, scents and colours, and special landing platforms.

Flowers with relatively simple blossoms and exposed sex organs—for example, tea-tree (*Leptospermum* species), angophora or eucalypts—are pollinated by beetles, flies and short-tongued wasps. Flowers that typically have long corollas—for example, kangaroo-paws (*Anigozanthos* species)—are pollinated by butterflies, moths and long-tongued flies. Tubular-shaped inflorescences are particularly favoured by butterflies—these include the butterfly bush (*Buddleia davidii*) and lantana (*Lantana camara*). Symmetrical flowers that have brightly coloured, cup-shaped or bell-shaped corollas often have attractive markings and scents that guide insects to the pollen and nectar—for example, bacon-and-eggs (*Daviesia*, *Dillwynia* or *Pultenea* species) or irises (family Iridaceae) and poppies (*Papaver* species)—are pollinated by bees and long-tongued wasps. Among the most specialised flowers for bee-pollination are those of the pea family (Papilionaceae). Their complex corollas can only be opened by particular bees—those that know exactly how to access the concealed nectar. The highly adaptable hive bee will utilise the nectar and pollen of most flowering plants. The European foxglove flower is a fine example of a flower that bees like: it has a landing platform, nectar guides and recurved hairs to repel smaller insects.

Many insects feed only on nectar, but in the act of doing this they also pick up pollen and transfer it to the flower pistils. Pollen-transferring insects have brought about a further refining of the fertilising process—in that almost all plants have combined both sexes in the one flower, secreting nectar at the base of the flower. In turn, this has prompted some insects to develop tongues, modified from stylet mouthparts in butterflies, moths and long-tongued flies, or from mandibulate mouthparts in wasps and bees.

Flowering plants such as nasturtium (*Tropaeolum majus*) or columbine (*Aquilegia* species) secrete nectar from a long spur, situated behind the flower itself, and rely upon long-tongued insects to carry out the pollination process (in its native Peru, nasturtiums are fertilised by hummingbirds as well as insects).

On the other hand, several species of short-tongued, flower-visiting wasps and beetles—for example, some species of solitary hunting wasps and sand wasps, and flower-chafers, scarabaeid and cerambycid beetles—have learnt another way to procure the nectar from flowers with spurs and long tubular calyxes. They take a short cut—biting directly through the flower's outer walls without pollinating the plant.

USING OTHER PLANT PARTS

A very large proportion of insects are herbivorous, eating various parts of the plants they live on, from the leaves to the bark and sap. Various species of gall-forming wasps (for example, family Cynipidae) deform leaves, stems and flowers, because of their lifestyle. However, when the large, showy Christmas beetles (family Scarabaoidae) are feeding in prolific numbers on *Eucalyptus* leaves during summer, the ground beneath can become carpeted with leaf fragments, adding vital nutrients to the soil.

Many insect larvae—including those of numerous beetles, moths, butterflies, wasps and bees—develop relatively quickly (within a matter of weeks) to take full advantage of seasonal blossoms, seedpods and young foliage. Some insects feed on the outside of tree trunks or beneath bark and often leave scribbly carvings, from their tunnelling activities. Long- and short-horned grasshoppers, phasmatids, beetle larvae and sawfly larvae feed on foliage, whereas cicadas and true bugs typically feed on the sap of the leaves, stems, tree trunks and roots.

Other insect larvae spend lengthy periods (often years) developing. These are all protected

ABOVE AND TOP The duck orchid has a spring-loaded landing platform. When an insect reaches for the orchid's nectaries, the plant's trigger mechanism is tripped and the platform springs shut, temporarily capturing the insect and pushing it against the sticky grains of pollen. Some orchids use sexual deception in their quest for pollination. For example, *Cryptostylis* orchids have flowers that mimic the scent and shape of the female wasp *Lissopimpla exelsa*. Males will attempt to mate with one flower after another, distributing pollen from one visited flowers to another as they go.

RIGHT The broad-necked mantis (*Hierodula atricoxis*) can capture and hold formidable prey, including large insects, spiders and small skinks. If carelessly handled, it can savagely bite. Its cryptic figure goes unseen by unwary insects.

against climatic conditions because they predominantly feed within timber or beneath the soil. The females normally deposit their eggs on injured, unhealthy or otherwise overstressed plants, as their vulnerable condition provides easy access for their larvae to enter the timber and tunnel through it. For example, those larvae that feed and develop within the trunks and branches of living and fallen timber include darkling beetles (family Tenebrionidae), longicorn beetles (family Cerambycidae), stag-beetles (family Lucanidae), bess beetles (family Passalidae) and jewel beetles (family Buprestidae). The larvae of wattle-goat moths or wood moths (family Cossidae) also feed within the timber, but those of some large swift moths (family Hepialidae) feed on tree roots beneath the ground.

FORESTS

Australia's splendid rainforest pockets extend from the temperate regions in Tasmania to the tropical northeastern tip of Cape York Peninsula in far north Queensland, although lessening in extent along the coasts of southern Queensland and New South Wales.

Rainforests of both tropical and subtropical regions are termed 'vine forests', and they support a wealth of life forms. Temperate rainforests are termed 'fern forests' and their

inhabitants, by comparison, generally lack the vivid colouring or the bizarre shapes and species diversity of the tropics.

The different types of forest are fertile ground for insect activity. The forests are maintained by symbiotic exchanges of the great variety of life forms living there, from the tiniest creatures to the forest giants—all working together for the harmony of the whole.

When a branch or a tree falls in an open, woodland area, it is exposed to the sun and wind and dries out with minimum decay taking place, sometimes remaining unchanged for years. However, when timber falls in a damp, shaded area beneath the tree canopy in a rainforest or eucalypt forest, the process of decomposition can rapidly go through its various stages.

Some of the first visitors to start the work of breaking down the timber are the ambrosia beetles (subfamily Platypodinae). These stoutly built insects have a short, broad rostrum. The female ambrosia beetle tunnels galleries beneath the bark and packs them with cultivated fungi as food for themselves and their young larvae. Longicorn beetles, by contrast, burrow straight into the timber.

While all this activity takes place, the moist log is further attacked by fungal decay below the bark. Unlike the green plants, fungi do not contain chlorophyll. Being unable to manufacture their own food, fungi have to obtain their nourishment from either plants or other animals. As decay advances, countless invertebrates colonise the site, including millipedes, centipedes, spiders, earwigs, cockroaches and the larvae of many species of flies and beetles.

Through this natural process, essential growth factors are returned to the soil for the benefit of the whole woodland or forest and its inhabitants. Of course, this process occurs far more rapidly in tropical regions, where heat and moisture combine to speed up the recycling of fallen timber.

Tropical and subtropical rainforest

The most luxuriant remains of tropical rainforest occupy far north Queensland in the regions between the Daintree River and Tully, with smaller pockets along the east coast of Queensland. Here, in these closed forests, an abundance of well-hidden animal life exists in sensitive interrelated patterns—even though a casual look may reveal very little faunal activity. The pressure for survival has put pressures on numerous kinds of insects to compete with one another for microhabitats. This has led to the development of some amazing lifestyles.

Flora and fauna are interdependent in this complex forest system. A single tree occupies an enormous amount of space, which is sometimes thousands of times greater overall than the relatively small ground surface area occupied by its trunk. Balanced proportions of sunlight and moisture stabilise subtropical rainforests throughout the year.

These conditions have allowed for the development of an enormous diversity and richness of tropical rainforest insect fauna. For example, of the 397 described species of butterflies and skippers found in Australia, 325 are found in Queensland. Huge populations of beetle larvae (families Cerambycidae, Lucanidae and Scarabacidae) are active throughout the day as they chew, digest and break down the decaying, moss-covered logs and fallen timber to form the forest mulch.

The vegetation is in a continual process of decomposition, necessary for plant growth and regeneration. The cycle of decay and growth within the subtropical and tropical rainforest is too rapid to allow a build-up of thick, heavy humus that often accumulates on the floors of wet sclerophyll forests.

Shafts of filtered sunlight beam down between the tall timbers, through the fleeting spaces in the middle of the dense, green canopy of lianas and vines and jungle growth, creating an eerie dimension to the forest as they continually shift position. This continual movement of light lures butterflies to follow it and 'dance' within the sunlit patches, moving from one to another during the day. The twilight of the forest floor is only bright enough for dwarf-palms and ferns to grow; tree seedlings must wait their turn for a gap in the forest canopy, created when older trees fall down.

The velvet-green night of the forest brings forth the greatest activity as countless beetles and moths take to the air, and the sounds of their buzzing and fluttering wings contribute to the rich atmosphere.

One way many insects avoid the stresses of the dry season is by undergoing a resting period—known as diapause. This period of arrested growth is governed by day-length and humidity. It allows the insect to wait out unfavourable conditions—bridging prolonged spells of water and food shortage. During the wet season (lasting several months), the rainforest inhabitants prepare for their emergence at its end. When the heavy rains finally cease, the rainforest canopy bursts into bloom, the air laden with scented flowers and its steamy rooftop alive with buzzing insects. Species that go through a series of rapid generations during the wet are the reason for much of the activity in the late wet season.

Amid the abundant blossoms, bees, wasps, butterflies and flower-visiting beetles feed to their fill. Lining the forest edges along the trails, the lantana shrubs parade their lively coloured blossoms, which are constantly in motion as numerous nectar-feeding insects momentarily alight on one flower after another. Within the rainforest among the lawyer (or 'come-back-quick') vines, the longicorns and stag-beetles

BELOW The heat and moisture, flowers, leaves and fragrant woods of lush tropical rainforests support a staggering number of insect populations. In turn, the insects are a vital food source for a diversity of other animal species. The high level of biodiversity in such habitats means that, should they be destroyed, innumerable species would ultimately perish.

LEFT The combined work of fungi and beetle larvae in rainforests play a vital role in decomposition. They contribute enormously to the breakdown of fallen timber, returning it to fertilise the soil for plant regeneration.

move about the timber, the females seeking suitable host plants on which to deposit their eggs. The vast populations of beetle larvae relentlessly exercise their mandibles, chewing the timber.

The silence and stillness of the rainforest is intermittently broken by the calling of birds, frogs, mammals and other creatures, including the loud drumming of the large, northern green cicada *Cyclochila virens*—and, of course, by the crashing of decaying timber as rotten trees fall to the ground.

Temperate rainforest

Australia's coasts and mountain ranges are often the home of graceful stands and beautiful forests of eucalypts. These forests often merge with rainforests and open woodlands. Such forests are within easy reach of most Australians living near the coastline or in the mountains. There are hundreds of species of Australian eucalypts, which are among the tallest and fastest-growing species of broad-leaved plants in the world. These evergreen forests thrive in both wet and dry regions. In the drier regions, they have a distinct understorey that is predominantly sclerophyll (hard-leaved plants). On the other hand, the wet eucalypt forest has a characteristic understorey of tree ferns, with moss-covered fallen timber and rocks. The green leaves of the eucalypts can sustain a large fauna population. The falling leaves and branches accumulate on the forest floor, building up thick, heavy humus.

Throughout the cooler seasons, an enormous population of insect larvae, hidden from view among the leaves, beneath the bark, soil and timber, feed and grow in preparation for their pupal stage. The scene is set for an explosive event as the warmer season arrives, and the spiders prepare their tables. Once emerged, adult insects confront the most important task of their lives, that of mating and reproducing their kind to ensure that the forest is plentifully restocked with its vital inhabitants.

During the summer months, the forest teems with buzzing and climbing insects. Along the banks of streams and creeks, and up along the hillsides, there is an almost deafening chorus of cicadas, especially from the larger species. The buzzing in the treetops is the sound of beetles, butterflies, flies, wasps and bees winging from flower to flower. For some species, the feeding activities involved with pollen- and nectar-gathering continue from sunrise to sunset. There are also, in abundance, the large handsome Christmas beetles flying about the treetops celebrating the sunshine. These feed on the young leaves, which they firmly grasp with their huge tarsal claws. In some localities they are accompanied by the brilliantly coloured golden-green stag-beetles (*Lamprima aurata*), also clinging tenaciously to young leaf tips.

Exhausted fallen insects, leaves, flowers, tree bark and timber are relentlessly recycled by the hordes of ground-dwelling insects and their larvae beneath—nature's supreme economy, where nothing is wasted.

Woodlands and open country

Much of Australia's woodlands were once dense, lush forests covering vast regions of the continent. These forests dramatically shrank during the glacial periods, some 1.5 million years ago, and were pushed to the edge of the continent. Rainforest has widely been replaced by sclerophyll forest, which has then thinned

BELOW Male and female golden-green stag-beetles (*Lamprima aurata*), with the female feeding on unformed flower heads. The male located her, detecting the trail of pheromones (odour molecules) she exuded to attract nearby males.

out to become open woodland. These areas have been dramatically thinned even further, through logging, the introduction of grazing animals, mining, and burning-off for 'land development', and the clearing of timber generally, leaving vast areas of grasslands.

The trees and undergrowth of woodlands are frequently widely spaced, where insects such as the large short-horned grasshoppers (family Acridiidae) often occur in high numbers. They quickly advertise themselves by the clicking of wings as they fly from one patch of ground to another. Certain species, such as the yellow-winged locust (*Gastrimargus musicus*), have bright yellow hindwings, momentarily exposed during short bursts of flight. Butterflies such as the tailed emperor butterfly (*Polyura pyrrhus sempronius*) and the chequered swallowtail (*Princeps demoleus sthenelus*) are frequently seen flying about in the open sunlight near waterways.

In the flat, open country on the other side of the mountain ranges, pockets of thicker growth are dotted here and there. The trees and shrubs generally thin out and these sparser areas may appear somewhat devoid of fauna (besides introduced grazing animals). Nevertheless, a vast population of insect larvae remains out of sight behind leaves and bark, beneath the timber and, particularly, within the soil, aerating it as they burrow. The parasitic wasps, especially, control the number of beetle larvae, which they use to feed their young. The adult wasps feed on nectar, which the existing eucalypt blossoms supply aplenty.

INSECTS AND PEOPLE

Friend or Foe?

Insects react with us just as they do with every other form of life on the land surface of the Earth, and just as we do with them. Despite the importance of arthropods in the overall scheme of things, most of us persist in disliking them. We too-readily treat insects as pests, yet relatively few species actually harm us. Many people, too, have a genuine fear of approaching insects.

An insect may become a 'pest' when it preys on humans or feeds on something we value for our own use—our crops in the fields, our clothing, furniture, or the timber of our homes.

ABOVE Dry sclerophyll forest covers the Warrumbungles in New South Wales, an ancient region of volcanic origin. This type of habitat supports a vast diversity of insects, including commonly encountered species such as the leptops weevil, mountain katydid, emperor gum moth, chequered swallowtail, tailed emperor butterfly and mud-daubing sphex wasp.

LEFT Typical alpine habitat above the treeline at Mount Kosciuszko in New South Wales. The summer-flowering alpine snow daisies (*Celmisia asteliifolia*) attract numerous insects, with bees and flies rivalling one another for access to the pollen and nectar.

A single creature can be regarded as either beneficial or as a 'pest' depending on how its lifestyle and its work are viewed. Of all the numerous kinds of insects on Earth, we have only managed to breed and domesticate two for our own purposes: hive-bee species and silkworms. But that doesn't mean that the others do not perform useful tasks.

It is only in so far as insects compete with us that they are pests, or if we get in each other's way. For example, the wasp that stings us most likely would have been busy at the time cleaning up rotting fruit or hunting for caterpillars in the vegetable patch.

Although insect-borne diseases such as malaria and yellow fever affected hunter-gatherers, it is only since the establishment of agriculture and livestock farming over the last few thousand years—together with the associated land-modification practices—that humans and domestic stock have become far more exposed to many such diseases. This is particularly the case in tropical regions, where great tracts of virgin forest have been destroyed along with their inhabitants in order to make space for our food crops. Myriad forms of insects that formerly lived out their life cycles high in the forest canopies had to adapt to new habitats and hosts among the available food crops grown by humans. This brought these insects into greater proximity with humans, who had little or no immunity against some of the more harmful species.

Fear and loathing

Many people are reluctant to go near—let alone observe—the majority of insects, either through a fear of being stung or bitten or else because of some irrational fear of the creature itself. But what most people do not realise is that the risk of being bitten or stung by insects is normally very remote—unless they handle the creature carelessly, or threaten it by not observing commonsense rules.

Most insects have a relatively short lifespan and a number of essential tasks they need to carry out in that time—mostly based on doing what is needed to propagate their species. The great majority of insects are too busily engaged in their work to want to expend energy seeking out humans to attack.

If you have a genuine fear of insects and/or spiders, it is nothing to feel ashamed of. Simply admit it—which is the first step towards changing your phobia into a more positive and controlled response. You can watch insects or spiders from a safe distance, or look at them in films, videos and books, and you may eventually even grow to admire them for the roles that they play. Overcoming a horror of small creatures is not achieved by running away from them nor by unmercifully squashing them out of fear. I believe that animals can sense this fear; like hate, it may give off emanations. It is sensing this that infuriates some animals, and it may motivate them into defensive behaviour. This is why they often attack what they instinctively sense as being a threat to their lives.

The historical perspective

Throughout history, insects have had a distinct impact on human culture and populations—from their role in events such as the Black Death to a less dramatic but still critical role in economic plant propagation. But the nature of this interaction was for a long time understood poorly, if at all. Equally, the reverse is true. It is only now, as our knowledge has grown, that we have begun to appreciate the impact our own activities have on insects, and the consequences this has for the ecosystems of which they form a part.

The study of insects, called entomology, is a branch of knowledge that has only developed comparatively recently in the Western world. Even now there is much that remains unknown about the insect world—new species and even genera are continually being discovered.

OPPOSITE While we are quick to condemn insects, this field of sunflowers (*Helianthus annuus*), like most of our plant crops, depends on pollination by insects. These giant flowers attract just about any flower-loving insect in their locality including earwigs, katydids, flies, butterflies, beetles, bees and wasps. A native of South America, the sunflower has been cultivated in warm climates worldwide since the 16th century.

BELOW A European honey bee (*Apis mellifera*) pollinating a sunflower. Just as our crops depend on insects, over 20 000 species of bees on the world checklist depend entirely on flowers for their sustenance and the geographical and ecological distribution of bees directly correlates with that of flowering plants.

Systematic insect study really came into being with the major expansion of scientific exploration during the 17th century. Ulysses Aldromandus has often been credited as being the 'father' of entomology for his publication of *De Animalibus Insectis* in 1602. The first significant book devoted solely to entomology, however, emerged in 1634: the *Insectorum Theatrum*, attributed to Thomas Mouffet, which was not published until after his death. Early entomological books were mainly dedicated to the study of bees, owing to their obvious economic relevance, although books on butterflies also appeared at an early stage.

INSECT BITES AND STINGS

A number of insects have defensive mechanisms that may cause discomfort to humans—for example, caterpillars with spines that break off in the skin, or defensive fluids emitted when an insect, such as a shield-bug, feels threatened. But it is the mosquitoes, flies, wasps, ants and bees among insects, as well as certain spiders, that cause humans the greatest anxiety with their ability to administer stings or bites that do real harm.

Remember that is is more unusual than common to be bitten or stung. Insects, like most creatures, tend to react when they feel threatened. Therefore, the first step is to adopt commonsense behaviour around such insects: do not antagonise them, and keep clear of their nests.

Many wasps have what appears to be a sting but is in fact an oviposter. This is also true of other insects sometimes thought to have stings, crickets, for example. However, in certain wasps the oviposter also serves as a sting.

Social hymenopterans, those living together in colonies, can pose a greater problem for humans—if the nest is affected in any way, they swarm out to attack. How much harm they can inflict has to do with how many insects are involved, all biting or stinging together. Many ants can sting and bite viciously at the same time. Primitive species such as the bulldog ants (subfamily Myrmecinae) are particularly ferocious. The green tree ants (subfamily Formicinae) have evolved an acid-squirting apparatus in place of a sting.

The introduced honey bee *Apis mellifera* is the only species found in Australia that leaves its sting within the flesh of its victim. This is, of course, its one and only line of defence and, once used, means the bee's certain death.

The venom in hymenopterans' sting consists of histamine (in wasp stings) and hydroxytryptamine and enzymes (in bee stings). The stings of these insects are commonly encountered and are generally harmless to humans—except to those who are allergic to them. If stung by a bee, the first step is to remove the sting from your flesh. This is best done by scraping the sting sideways, using a fingernail; using tweezers more often causes further injection of venom. A cold compress will help alleviate any pain. You should seek medical attention immediately if the person who was stung begins to show any allergic reactions.

To relieve the pain associated with the stings of wasps, bees or ants, apply a generous amount of aloe vera (fresh or in tube form) on the wound until the swelling subsides.

With advances in printing methods in the late 17th century and early 18th century, a new wave of books containing extensive observations on insects began to appear. Among the first of these, published in 1705 and lavishly illustrated, was the impressive *Metamorphosis Insectorum Surinamensium*, by Maria von Merian. This work represented a major advance in the study of entomology, as it demonstrated the importance of studying the complete life cycles of insects, integrating the adult insects with their larvae.

By the second half of the 19th century, natural history museums were being established throughout Europe. There was considerable activity associated with building their collections, and exotic insects, spiders and plants were brought back from remote regions by collectors. All this stimulated an enthusiastic interest in natural history among the general public, which brought the butterfly net into popular use. Much of the knowledge about the lives of insects gained at this time was contributed by enthusiastic amateurs with a keen eye for observation and a deft hand at manipulating the net. In 1864, the Scott sisters, Harriet and Helena, became famous for their exquisite paintings of Australian flora and fauna in *Australian Lepidoptera and their Transformations*, published in England, with a text by their father, Walker Scott.

At that time, little more than a century ago, great expanses of land, timber and waterways were yet to be encroached upon. Great wildernesses still existed—complex ecosystems harbouring an enormous diversity of habitats. But since then many changes have occurred. The demand for wilderness has now outstripped supply in most regions on Earth. Gradually, all over the world, the landscape is being almost totally 'humanised'—or transformed into 'civilisation'.

However, human culture and wilderness are organically related. By exploiting and dominating the natural world to the point of destroying what is wild and free, we in fact diminish our humanity and endanger the web of life itself. As Henry David Thoreau once said: 'In wilderness lies the preservation of the world'. It is our duty, as well as our basic need, to reverse this trend toward destruction of our natural surroundings. We need to begin by preserving what wilderness remains—and, of course, its inhabitants.

HEALTHY GARDENS AND THRIVING INSECTS

One of the most common places where insects and humans come into contact—and often into conflict—is in the garden and around the home. Insects and spiders use our creations just as they use available niches throughout the natural bushland. They go about their lives right on our doorstep—building their nests underneath our houses and rooftops or pupating on our fences and garden walls; some even live comfortably inside our homes.

A home garden can provide ideal conditions for several insect species—insect herbivores and the carnivores that prey on them. But, even though we may aim for a balanced environment for our plants, we need to keep in mind that a home garden is necessarily an unnatural ecosystem. This is equally true of parklands and nature reserves, or even homes—all inhabited by insects—but also places where human action has affected natural balances. Nature reserves tend to suffer from less human interference than national parks in most States of Australia.

It is counterproductive to battle with any creature that 'dares' to enter our garden to eat or sample a leaf or fruit. Instead, it is better to learn how natural ecosystems work and to encourage, as far as possible, the proliferation of natural conditions in our gardens and employ natural means of resolving any problems. This means trying to adopt principles of biological management instead of depending on chemical pest control.

A healthy garden means having a lot of insects—a thriving community of insects that is in balance. Otherwise you will end up with a sterile, insecticide-laden plot of closely guarded, diseased plants—a poor garden that no bee or butterfly will visit, and with dead soil lacking even an ant's nest.

Creating a healthy garden

Regularly feed your garden a generous supply of compost and water as this encourages worms, which are highly beneficial to any type of soil. Select good-quality seeds—preferably non-hybrids—as these have a natural resistance to leaf-eating insects.

Another characteristic of a healthy garden is its ability to support predatory creatures—such as lizards, birds and spiders—as well as predatory insects—such as mantids, tree crickets, assassin bugs, tachinid flies and

ABOVE Imperial blue butterflies (*Jalmenus evagoras evagoras*) lay their white spiny eggs in clusters on the stems of black wattle (*Acacia decurrens*). Eggs are deposited in late summer to hatch the following spring and the larvae feed on the wattle's foliage. Although they are closely attended by black ants (*Iridomyrmex* species), which continuously feed on highly prized fluids exuded from their dorsal glands, they are frequently parasitised by braconid wasps.

parasitic wasps. All these help to maintain a balance in insect populations.

Apart from the predatory species, there are several kinds of insects, such as bees, ants or butterflies, which are useful in a home garden. Gardeners are increasingly encouraging certain insects into their gardens for their colours, sounds and interesting habits.

Most flowering plants advertise their blossoms to bees and other insects, as they cannot reproduce without them. Butterflies are admired the world over and, to attract them, some Australians create 'butterfly gardens' by planting delightfully scented blossoms of native trees and shrubs such as melaleuca, wattle, tea-tree, bottlebrush, grevillea, kangaroo paw and purple-top verbena. Butterflies are also attracted by other introduced flowering plants such as butterfly bush (*Buddleia* species), lantana hybrids, lavender, and all sorts of members of the daisy family, Asteraceae.

To attract their larvae, there is crepe myrtle, citrus, cotton bushes, sassafras, portulaca, snapdragons, everlasting daisies, native violets, native thistles and nettles, unmown native grasses (swordgrass or blady grass, for example). Growing specific food plants will attract butterflies and their larvae, and growing as many native plants as possible helps create a balanced ecosystem.

Of course, if we want butterflies, we need to accept that it means some of the plants will be eaten—no caterpillars, no butterflies. Apart from the notorious caterpillar of the cabbage white butterfly (*Pieris rapae rapae*), very few butterfly larvae feed on common garden crops; but, when they do, the damage they cause is always minor. The larvae of the orchard swallowtail butterfly (*Princeps aegeus*) and the small citrus butterfly (*Eleppone anactus*) typically feed on the leaves of citrus trees during spring and summer. Before the introduction of citrus trees into Australia, these species fed on the native plants *Geijera* and *Zieria* species.

In the home garden, insects are usually blamed for almost everything that fails to grow, but there may be other causes, too. To ensure the plant life in your garden stays healthy, look out for the following problems:

- Temperatures that are too high or too low, or incorrect quantities of light, water or nutrients, which can affect plant growth.

- Rust and black spot—these are fungal diseases, their spores settle on the leaves and stems of the host plant and, in obtaining nourishment from it, they weaken the plant. Sooty mould is a fungus that grows on the sugary exudate of scale insects. It shades the leaves, but it is not an actual disease.

- Sunburn, or abrasions and wounds made by pruning or mowing (plants can be ring-barked, for instance, when you mow too close to their trunks)—such damage weakens plants, making them prone to health problems, and allows easy entry points for wood-boring beetles and moths to lay their eggs and for their larvae to bore in. Some type of plant damage does indicate insect attack but insects tend to take advantage of plants that are already under stress or weakened. This is nature's way of promoting healthy plants, by eliminating those that are unhealthy.

- Borers' holes—insects occupying the bark and timber damage the tissue that carries the nutrients that enable the plant to grow. Unhealthy or injured plants are normally chosen over healthy plants by female longicorn beetles (family Cerambycidae), jewel beetles (family Buprestidae), stag-beetles (family Lucanidae) and wood moths (family Xyloryctidae and Cossidae).

- Defoliation—defoliating a plant reduces its ability to manufacture food, thereby affecting its growth. Such defoliation can be caused by snails and slugs or by the chewing, leaf-feeding insects and their larvae, when these occur in large numbers. Such insects include Christmas beetles (family Scarabaeidae), sawfly larvae, or spitfires (family Tenthredinidae), emperor moths (family Saturniidae), cup moth larvae (family Limacodidae), all of which are normally kept in check by a wide range of parasitic wasps such as those in the families Ichneumonidae and Braconidae.

- Stem and growth-tip damage, and plant galls—stem and growth-tip feeders such as aphids (family Aphididae), scale insects and lerp insects (family Psyllidae), and leaf-hoppers (family Membracidae), as well as the gall-forming insects such as thrips and chalcid wasps, singly or combined, can cause plant discolouration or malformation as well as kill plant tissue.

ABOVE With an open invitation during spring and summer, red-and-green kangaroo paws (*Anigozanthos* species) attract pollinating birds, bees, flower flies and butterflies such as the graceful large orchard swallowtail butterfly (*Princeps aegeus*).

Biological management

Standard methods of pest control use deadly chemicals, nerve poisons, hormone-changing drugs (growth inhibitors), and behaviour-changing chemicals. The toxins used in some of these pesticides are potentially hazardous in the long term to all life, humans included. It has long been known that many insecticides and pesticides are responsible for causing cancer in humans.

Biological management is a very different approach. It aims, not at total eradication, but at sustaining the populations of all insects (including unwanted ones) at a manageable level in order to support the predatory insects and other creatures that keep these populations in check. In other words, by understanding more about the laws of nature, we can work with them.

Many insect 'pests' are actually species that have been introduced (accidentally or otherwise), and breed and multiply out of proportion, without their natural predators or balancing agents to keep them in check. Generally, insects only reach pest proportions when there are no natural predators and when insect-susceptible plants are grown in large quantities.

Many insects are predators. These insects are generally larger than their prey, and their hunting activities often attract other predators such as birds and reptiles, which in turn eat them. Predatory insects have to know where to seek food and, once located, how to capture and overpower prey. Active searching, ambushing or trapping methods are employed, according to the species and its requirements. Many prey on whatever is available, while some are restricted to a limited range of prey. Because plant availability governs the total population of animals in any given area, or microhabitat, there are always many times more herbivores than carnivores, and still fewer secondary predators.

Apart from biological management, there are other alternatives to chemical control, for example, by light-trapping, by the removal of breeding grounds (such as introduced weedy plants, food scraps, outdoor water-filled containers and inappropriate food storage), and by encouraging birds. Crop plants can be protected with mesh or glass.

Most unwanted leaf-eating insects can be discouraged from establishing themselves in the garden by intermingling insect-deterring plants, such as garlic, thyme, rosemary and aromatic herbs among native and other plants.

A mixture made of pure soap and water sprayed on plants can be used to treat aphid infestations. This mixture works effectively on soft-bodied insects, such as aphids, and leaves hard-bodied insects unharmed. Sprays made of garlic, rhubarb and pyrethrin are highly effective against aphids, coccids, scale insects, mealy bugs and mites.

It is important that the use of any poison, from any source, is limited and selective so that predatory insects are not also destroyed. You could also talk to your neighbours about your efforts to develop a healthy garden. They may then become interested in following your lead and, at the same time, will likewise benefit from not spraying deadly poisons.

ABOVE Home gardens can provide ideal conditions for a large variety of animals, including insects and spiders. Pot plants, rockeries, undisturbed corners, ferneries, trees, shrubs, flowers and soil support a wide range of arthropods, which attract the interest of insectivorous birds and lizards. To deter unwanted plant bugs such as scale insects, coccids and aphids, grow aromatic herbs.

ABOVE A male flower wasp (*Hemithynnus variabilis*) feeding on tea-tree blossoms (*Leptospermum laevigatum*). Females of this species paralyse beetle larvae in the soil and lay an egg on each, thereby providing food for their own larvae.

ABOVE RIGHT A weevil (*Elleschodes hamiltoni*) feeding on a drumstick (*Isopogon*) flower. Coleopterans are among the chief pollinators of native trees and shrubs.

OPPOSITE The ribbon gum (*Eucalyptus viminalis*) is host to the red-eye cicada (*Psaltoda moerens*). Eucalypts generally attract many cicada species.

HOW TO CREATE A HEALTHY GARDEN

To create a healthy garden with a good ecological balance, there are several things to be done:

- Identify exactly which insects are causing harm and which are beneficial, and the roles played by each in this ecosystem. For instance, are they nectar-feeders and, hence, pollinators? Or do they prey on other insects and, therefore, naturally control 'pest' species? Are they plant eaters—but are there too many of them—or are they being kept in check naturally?
- Having identified the 'pests', find out what conditions they favour: reducing the places they frequent or breed in helps keep them in check. Use selective control methods that target only those insects that are causing harm. For example, soapy water will remove aphids without harming the insects that may prey on them, but a dose of insecticide will wipe out anything in range.
- Favour biological management over indiscriminate use of chemicals. For example, use natural

predators to deal with the problem wherever possible, choosing non-toxic solutions for sprays avoids long-term problems for the soil and your own health.

Take practical steps to ensure the plant life is, and remains in, good condition:

- When planting, the site chosen must suit the species—water availability, soil texture, structure and depth all need to be taken into account.
- Adopt measures that will encourage beneficial insect life and insects that are attractive and interesting—certain kinds of plants will attract particular species.
- Take a longer-term view of everything in the garden, allowing time for growth and change. A dose of insecticide may provide instant gratification, but it creates other problems. Natural predation may take a few insect generations to re-establish control and create the balance required, but it is healthier, safer and better for the environment.

RIGHT A male black prince cicada (*Psaltoda plaga*) on its host plant, a river oak (*Casuarina cunninghamiana*). Nymphs feed on root sap and spend several years steadily growing, aerating the soil as they tunnel. Fossil finds of cicadas 245 million years old in Triassic shale from Brookvale in New South Wales show that these ancient cicadas were almost indistinguishable from present-day cicadas.

cicada—have adapted very well to suburban situations, so long as there are plentiful native and cultivated shrubs and trees available.

There are always overlapping generations feeding beneath the soil, and their development and emergence is greatly influenced by climatic conditions. Numbers fluctuate cyclically depending on the previous generations and previous favourable seasons. Some species can build up enormous populations in a good season, but in unfavourable seasons, nymphs are able to postpone their emergence for a year or more. Bushfires can considerably reduce adult numbers, which means that in future years, far fewer will emerge until favourable conditions allow their numbers to be built up once again.

WATER-BUGS
order Hemiptera: suborder Heteroptera

Ambush predators

The aquatic and semi-aquatic bugs (superfamilies Nepoidea, Ochteroidea, Corixoidea, Naucoroidea and Notonectoidea) live in still or brackish water among aquatic plant-life. There, they ambush and capture other aquatic insects and any insects that fall into the water, the bugs being attracted by their struggling.

Range, habitat and behaviour

These insects are well represented in most parts of Australia, being rather prolific in tropical and subtropical regions. Some species, such as the giant water-bug, occur from Sydney northwards but are more abundant in subtropical and tropical regions. Water-bugs are found usually in or near water—in ponds, creeks, streams and billabongs, or along the muddy banks and among decaying vegetation. Some species of the family Enicocephalidae live on the forest floor beneath stones and decaying wood. Some forms, like the large water scorpions (family Nepidae), live around the edges of muddy ponds or slow-running waters, their colouring merging with their surroundings. Others such as the water-boatmen bugs (family Corixidae) are usually found among the weeds and leaf litter that have settled at the bottom of ponds.

While some aquatic bugs move across the water surface in a skating-like motion, using the surface tension of the water, many are excellent swimmers. Certain species can remain underwater for extended periods by using up the oxygen supplies they carry with them, trapped beneath their wing covers.

ASSASSIN BUGS
order Hemiptera: suborder Heteroptera family Reduviidae

Ambush predators
Assassin bugs are stealthy hunters and attack lepidopterous larvae and spiders, and also feed on a wide range of prey including grasshoppers, flies, ants and bees. One can inflict a painful stab with its sharp rostrum, but the pain associated with the stab is mainly due to the salivary fluids used to paralyse insect prey and break down its bodily tissues.

Range, habitat and behaviour
Assassin bugs are well represented in Australia, as almost half of the 30 subfamilies worldwide occur on this continent. They occur throughout the country but most species are found in subtropical and tropical regions.

Favourite haunts of these insects are flowering shrubs, tree trunks, leaves, beneath stones and fallen timber, birds' nests, and home gardens. Those of the subfamily Harpactorinae, bee-killer bugs, especially favour flowering plants, and position themselves on the flowers to seize bees. Female assassin bugs normally deposit their eggs in crevices among leaf-litter, moss and lichen.

LACEWINGS
order Neuroptera

Ambush and open-range predators
Almost all lacewing larvae and adults are predatory, but each stage feeds in different ways. Adults of the families Myrmeleontidae, Ascalaphidae, Osmylidae and Psychopsidae feed upon a wide range of flying insects including sap-sucking insects such as aphids, scale insects, thrips, whiteflies, mealy bugs and psyllids.

Ant-lions, the larvae of the family Myrmeleontidae, lie in wait among the ground debris for their prey or else they trap them by digging pits. They feed on ground-dwelling beetle larvae (curl grubs) and other insects, including ants, which fall into the conical pit-traps they dig. Their prey slip down the sides and are delivered into the waiting jaws of the hungry ant-lions beneath. Some green lacewings (chrysopids) are specialised feeders on honeydew-yielding hemipterans.

BELOW A male clubbed lacewing (*Suhpalacsa flavipes*). These beautiful insects have a round head capsule bearing large compound eyes and butterfly-like club-tipped antennae. They actively fly during daylight capturing small flying insects. If threatened, they alight on the nearest shrub and merge among foliage. Their larvae are equipped with large mandibles and hunt insect prey among ground debris and low herbage.

Range, habitat and behaviour

Lacewings are widely distributed throughout Australia. They occur in most ecosystems, from cold, subalpine streams to the desert regions. Most, however, are generally found in the temperate, subtropical and tropical areas within the wetter, eastern coastal zone, where aphids and psyllids thrive.

A number of lacewing species live underneath the bark of rough-barked trees in their larval stages, where they feed on a wide range of insect prey. Larvae of the family Ascalaphidae hide within leaf-litter, feeding upon small insect prey until fully grown. Ant-lions live in sandy soil or leaf-litter, with some species being cryptically coloured, closely resembling bark.

Lacewings commonly fly at night and are strongly attracted to electric lights. During daylight, they rest on low herbage and shrubs and are often found near streams and creeks, where they mate.

GROUND BEETLES AND TIGER BEETLES
order Coleoptera: family Carabidae

Open-range and ambush predators

Ground beetles (family Carabidae) feed on a range of prey including snails, worms and slugs and their eggs, mites, curl grubs and other beetle larvae but it would seem lepidopterous larvae are particularly favoured. When prey is captured, it is sliced apart by the beetle's sharp mandibles and swallowed in pieces.

BELOW Banks and beds of rivers, streams and creeks support enormous insect populations undergoing aquatic lifestyles as nymphs and larvae. These include mayflies, damselflies, dragonflies, aquatic bugs, lacewings, caddis-flies, aquatic beetles and flies. In spring and summer, flying insects can be prolific among the flowering shrubs growing on the banks.

Tiger beetles (family Carabidae) are fierce predators that actively hunt down other insects or capture prey by ambush. Their larvae are typically ambush predators that live in long, vertical tunnels in sandy soil and fallen timber.

Range, habitat and behaviour

Ground beetles and tiger beetles are both found throughout Australia but tiger beetles are far more common in subtropical and tropical regions. Several iridescent ground beetle species occur within the wetter, eastern coastal zone, where they are one of the predominant ground-dwelling insects in both larval and adult forms.

Tiger beetles are generally active by day and live in hot, open, sandy areas of heathland, riverbanks and beaches—in contrast to their nocturnally active cousins, the ground beetles, which typically shun sunlight.

Locations near water, such as swampy places and riverbanks are typical among the favoured habitats of ground beetles, although many species also live in arid regions. Normally they live out their lives in damp places beneath rotting logs, stones and bark, coming out at night in search of prey.

During several visits to Dorrigo in New South Wales, I have found many *Notonomus* and *Pamborus* species ground beetles to be plentiful beneath fallen, rotting timber. It was not uncommon to find these different species together under a single piece of rotting timber.

Many tiger beetles are brightly coloured with iridescent tints, too. They frequent tree trunks and rocks in the sunshine, rapidly moving out of sight around the tree trunk or flying away if disturbed. Many species frequent sunlit banks of creeks and streams and are extremely active in full sunlight, running about tree trunks in search of prey, although a few species live in burrows in soil and fallen timber.

ROVE-BEETLES
order Coleoptera: family Staphylinidae

Open-range predators

Rove-beetles are omnivorous, although typically scavengers. They seek out fly maggots on decaying carcasses, sometimes feeding on the the decaying meat. Their predatory habits are similar to those of ground beetles.

Range, habitat and behaviour

Rove-beetles occur in the tropics and subtropics, but are more common across the southern region of the continent. They have highly reduced elytra and an elongated form. They live beneath decaying vegetation including fungi, seaweed, animal dung, and beneath and within the animal carcasses. Some species can be found on flowers or feeding at sap flows. The most frequently encountered species is the devil's coach-horse beetle (*Creophilus erythrocephalus*); its large head capsule is bright red–orange with a black dot and its body is blue–black.

FLOWER BEETLES
order Coleoptera:
family Scarabaeidae
subfamily Cetoniinae

Pollinators

Flower beetles feed on the nectar of native shrubs and trees. The magnificently coloured green fiddler beetle *Eupoecila australasiae* visits angophora blossoms during November–January and is common in eastern Australia.

Range, habitat and behaviour

Flower beetles occur throughout Australia, and are found from the tropics in the far north to the temperate zones of the south.

The flower beetle group comprises beetles with a variety of popular names, such as rose chafers, flower scarabs or flower chafers. There are many fine, iridescent species that occur in tropical Queensland.

Mainly diurnal in their habits, flower beetles are commonly found around compost heaps, where they also breed. They are often brightly coloured and are quite powerful fliers that produce a rather distinctive buzzing sound when on the wing.

The large, orange-brown cowboy beetle (*Diaphonia dorsalis*), is one of the most frequently seen flower beetles. It may often be sighted buzzing about in sunshine during hot summer days—the males visiting blossoms and ripe stone fruit while the females are seeking out the best sites for egg-laying among decaying vegetation. When a suitable compost heap is found, the female emits sex pheromones that will attract the local males. Not long after mating, she deposits her eggs.

ABOVE A male green fiddler beetle (*Eupoecila australasiae*). Native shrubs and trees flower profusely during spring and summer, and during favourable seasons plants literally buzz with insect activity. Flower and longicorn beetles, flies, butterflies, flower and hunting wasps, bees and ants vie for the best spots to feed on pollen and nectar among the thronging crowd.

RIGHT A female enamelled-orange cetoniid beetle (*Micropoecila cincta*) feeding on the nectar of a scrub apple (*Angophora hispida*). These shrubs, as well as *Leptospermum* species, flower prolifically during spring and summer and attract hordes of flower-visiting insects.

LADYBIRD BEETLES
order Coleoptera: family Coccinellidae

Open-range predators

Both the adults and larvae of most species of ladybird beetles are carnivorous. They feed voraciously on aphids, as well as on mealy bugs, thrips and mites. Several carnivorous species are used as biological control agents owing to their vast appetites for unwanted pest species—particularly for cottony cushion scale insects and aphids, which commonly infest garden plants. The ladybird *Rodalia cardinalis* dramatically reduces cotton scale in citrus plantations.

One of the few non-carnivorous species is the 28-spotted ladybird beetle (*Epilachna vigintintisexpunctata vigintintisexpunctata*), which feeds on the flowers and leaves of pumpkin, potato and tomato plants.

Range, habitat and behaviour

These brightly coloured insects are abundant around all parts of Australia. Some species hibernate as adults, congregating in large groups beneath flaking bark, in crevices of rocks beneath ledges, and inside caves, where they rest until spring.

Their orange-coloured eggs are laid in batches of 3–50 on the undersides of leaves on plants where prey is abundant. In this way, immense numbers of aphids are devoured by both the growing larvae as well as the adults. Ladybird beetles normally secrete an offensive fluid that is highly distasteful to would-be predators.

ROBBER FLIES
order Diptera: family Asilidae

Open-range predators

Most species of robber fly—or assassin fly—attack whatever is readily available on the wing but some adult species pounce on stationary insects. The larvae of some robber fly species are also predacious, feeding on beetle and moth larvae within decaying, fallen timber.

The adults are aggressive and will attack almost any insect, even insects much larger than themselves, the victim being held in a vice-like grip by the six spiny legs forming a basket. The large tuft of stiff, forward-projecting hairs a robber fly has between its eyes and rostrum protects the head and eyes from its victim's struggles. Robber flies also feed on insects that are normally distasteful to many other predatory insects, such as butterflies.

Robber flies are equipped with a sharp, stout rostrum located beneath the head. An insect, when captured, is pierced and injected with a toxic fluid containing proteolytic enzymes that rapidly liquefies its bodily tissues, all of which the robber fly greedily siphons up.

Range, habitat and behaviour

Robber flies are widespread throughout Australia. The highest number of species are found in grasslands, heathland, forest tracks and clearings, where they remain motionless on grass-blades, twigs and branches, ever-alert for flying insects approaching or alighting. These aggressive flies form a large group of predatory insects occupying a wide range of habitats.

Some species mimic large orange-and-black wasp species such as the spider-hunting wasp (*Cryptocheilus bicolor*). The stoutly-built robber fly *Chrysopogon crabroniformis* superficially looks like the large mason wasp (*Abispa ephippium*).

BEE-FLIES
order Diptera: family Bombyliidae

Pollinators and parasitic predators
Adult bee-flies are flower pollinators. They hover in the sunshine and visit blossoms, moving from one flower to the next, usually not lingering for long at any one flower. The larvae feed on the egg piles of other insects such as

crickets and short-horned grasshoppers, and also readily attack lepidopterous larvae.

Range, habitat and behaviour
Representatives of this family occur throughout Australia. They are commonly found in temperate, subtropical and tropical regions. They also feature strongly in some of the drier areas of the interior.

Bombyliids are very diverse in their appearance and include some amazing mimic forms of wasps and bees, but only the subfamily Bombyliinae actually contains those referred to as 'bee-flies'. Adults are normally seen in sunny locations, resting on warm patches of ground adjacent to flowering shrubs and trees.

ABOVE A female robber fly (*Bathypogon* species) feeding on a native hive bee. Aggressive hunters, robber flies are natural predators of flies, cicadas, wasps and bees, seizing their prey in mid-air. Robber fly mouthparts are modified into a hard, piercing rostrum, which is plunged into prey to extract the vital juices.

RIGHT Skippers (*Trapezites phigaloides*) are named for their rapid, erratic flight. They are often numerous in grassy clearings in open woodland. They have an unusual manner of resting, with their forewings folded while the hindwings are held flat, like moths.

HOVERFLIES
order Diptera: family Syrphidae

Pollinators and parasitic predators
Adult hoverflies are among the prime pollinators of flowering plants. While the larvae of most species feed on aphids and their kind, the larvae of some species also attack slow-moving moth caterpillars.

Range, habitat and behaviour
In terms of the number of species present, hoverflies are not well represented in Australia. The drone fly (*Eristalis tenax*), an insect that was introduced into Australia, mimics honey bees in its action and appearance.

Hoverflies are readily distinguished by their remarkable habit of hovering—they appear to be motionless in mid-air. Many species mimic the appearance of wasps and stout-bodied bees. Generally, the larvae are maggot-like in appearance, feeding in overripe fruit and decaying vegetable matter. The larvae of some species live in soupy, decaying matter such as found around manure, and they have a breathing siphon that can be telescopically extended to the surface. Some hoverfly larvae live in a commensal relationship with ants.

Because hoverflies so closely resemble honey bees, until the 17th century, people believed that honey bees were born from the dead bodies of animals such as asses, oxen and sheep. Drone flies of the genus *Eristalis* breed in liquefying carcasses, within which the fully grown larvae pupate to finally emerge as adults.

TACHINID FLIES
order Diptera: family Tachinidae

Parasitic predators
Tachinid flies, which closely resemble blowflies, help to keep in check the populations of a wide range of other insects, including plague locusts (family Acridiidae), whose bodies they parasitise for their young to feed on. Typically, their eggs are laid on the larvae of lepidopterans or of scarabaeid beetles, and on other insect larvae. Thus, tachinid flies are parasitic as larvae but not as adults.

Range, habitat and behaviour
Tachinid flies are very numerous, being found Australia-wide in temperate, subtropical and tropical regions, with over 500 species described. They occur wherever insects are abundant, especially where large numbers of lepidopterous larvae are feeding on leaves.

During summer months in particular, tachinid flies are commonly found in woodlands and open country, resting in the sunshine on tree trunks and on bracken fern growing along forest tracks and clearings. The adults feed on various juices, such as sap flows and nectar, or on decaying fruit.

Immediately on hatching from the egg, a tachinid fly larva feeds on the flesh of its host until it is fully grown. It remains within the empty shell of the host until it emerges as the winged adult, having also undergone its pupal stage there. The females of some species shower their tiny eggs on the leaves of food plants eaten by lepidopterous larvae, which then also swallow the eggs. The tiny larvae, on hatching within the caterpillar's intestine, begin devouring their host and eventually pupate inside the dying body of the caterpillar.

MOTHS AND BUTTERFLIES
order Lepidoptera

Pollinators
The nocturnal flower-visiting lepidopterans, the moths, play an enormous role in the pollination of flowering plants and are among their chief pollinators. In comparison, the butterflies are relatively minor pollinators.

Range, habitat and behaviour
Even though lepidopterans are plentiful in Australia, the vast majority are moth species; there are only a few hundred butterfly species in Australia. Members of various moth and butterfly families—such as Geometridae, Sphingidae, Noctuidae, Hesperiidae, Pieridae, Papilionidae, Nymphalidae, Lycaenidae—occur in all regions of Australia, but they typically reach their peak of diversity in the tropics. Over 80 per cent of the described species of butterfly found in Australia are found in Queensland.

Butterflies require an abundance of plants and sunshine, thriving in the vicinity of water, and can be found in open fields, hillsides and forest clearings and tracks, or wherever flowers are abundant. Sap-flow sites on tree trunks also attract the adults, which congregate to feed on the bountiful supply of sweet liquid.

Most of us regard lepidopterous larvae as pests because of the damage certain (mostly moth) species—especially, perhaps, the cabbage white butterfly (*Pieris rapae rapae*)—cause to our food crops and other plants through their feeding habits. Most lepidopterous species are, in fact, beneficial in the overall scheme of nature, although unwanted in agricultural districts. Nevertheless, with their obvious beauty, butterflies are usually a welcome sight in home gardens.

ICHNEUMONOID WASPS
order Hymenoptera:
family Ichneumonidae

Pollinators and parasitic predators
Most adult ichneumonoid wasps feed on pollen, nectar and plant exudations. They are also 'parasitic' but only in the sense that they hunt the larvae of a wide range of endopterygote insects to use as food for their own offspring.

Range, habitat and behaviour
Ichneumonoid wasps form a great number of genera and species, and occur widely throughout Australia, being more diverse in the cooler, southeastern regions of Australia. Their range extends from cool, moist forests to arid regions, with many species confined to tropical north Queensland and northeastern regions.

They favour moist habitats, and in drier localities they more commonly occur along riverbeds and watercourses. Clearings in both sclerophyll and rainforest are among their favourite sites, as these habitats provide a bountiful supply of prey.

Their eggs are deposited on the bodies of caterpillars or beetle grubs. In many species they are injected into the body of the host using the female's long, sharp ovipositor. The tiny wasp larva, immediately upon hatching, bores its way into the body of its host, where it continues to feed on its host until adulthood. Until the wasp larva has completed growing, it leaves its host's vital organs intact, not killing it outright.

LEFT A female golden-haired sand wasp (*Sphex vestitum*) dragging a meadow katydid to her nest as food for her future offspring. Males often ambush and forcibly mate with females when they are laden with prey items. Adults feed on nectar, sap flows and honeydew.

BRACONID WASPS
order Hymenoptera: family Braconidae

Parasitic predators
Braconids include a large range of species that attack the larvae of flies, beetles, lepidopterans and aphids, which they parasitise as food for their young. Many smaller species parasitise lepidopterous larvae and it is not uncommon to see a caterpillar's dying and shrivelled body covered with the small, white, egg-like cocoons of braconids.

Range, habitat and behaviour
Braconid wasps have a wide distribution, similar to that of the Ichneumonid wasps, being found throughout Australia from cool, moist forests to arid locations. Many species are confined to the tropical north and northeastern regions.

During the summer months, adults can be seen running about foliage and the trunks of live and fallen trees. They typically move about in a delicate manner on long legs, waving their long (frequently white-tipped) antennae up and down to inspect trunks and leaves for the presence of larvae, such as longicorns or lepidopterans. When the female detects a potential host, she uses her long, sword-like ovipositor as a drill to insert her eggs into its body.

The braconid larvae develop within the caterpillar's body and, when they are ready to pupate, bore their way outside just prior to their host's death. There, they spin silken cocoons that adhere to the skin of the shrivelled caterpillar. Other species of braconid wasp larvae undergo their metamorphosis inside the dried skin of their host.

SAND WASPS
order Hymenoptera: family Sphecidae

Pollinators and parasitic predators
Adult sand wasps of both sexes normally feed on nectar, sap flows and ripened fruits for their own nourishment. However, the females alone hunt various arthropods to provide food for their offspring, generally preying on grasshoppers and their relatives, caterpillars, cicadas, flies, or on spiders. Individual species specialise in hunting particular types of prey. The wasp larvae parasitise these insects, feeding on them in the nest.

Range, habitat and behaviour
Sand wasps are represented throughout Australia. They are generally slender-waisted wasps with diverse lifestyles. Some species (for example, *Sphex* species) excavate burrows in sandy soil,

and are most readily seen in patches of open ground such as sand-flats, tracks, trails and clearings. The female sand wasps prepare the nest-sites before hunting, each nest being multi-cellular and each cell being stocked normally with more than one prey item.

Others, such as *Sceliphron* species, are known as 'mud-daubers'—the slender, black-and-yellow-banded species, the mud daubing wasp *Sceliphron laetum*, being one example. Mud-daubers use clay to build their nests, which are strategically attached to tree trunks or the undersides of rock ledges. They are commonly seen flying about sheds, garages and outhouses, where they construct their mud-clay nests, using well-ventilated locations on walls and ceiling corners. These wasps are most commonly found in the vicinity of creeks and streams, where they collect material for their nest-building along the banks. The females fly back and forth, making numerous trips until sufficient material has been gathered to complete the nest, which then has to be stocked with lepidopterous larvae for their own offspring when they hatch.

Even though their nests may be built close to one another, the occupant of each one leads her own life—apart from the act of mating, all hunting wasps have rather solitary lives. Depending on the species, the opportunistic males either wait around the streams and watercourses, where the females constantly visit to collect clay for nest-building, or they wait along forest trails where the females go hunting for insects to stock their nests.

FLOWER WASPS
order Hymenoptera: family Tiphiidae

Pollinators and parasitic predators
The male flower wasps, which are winged, are the pollinators. Flower wasps also play an important role in controlling the numbers of other insects by parasitising them for their larvae to feed on when they hatch. The wingless female seeks out beetle larvae (families Scarabaeidae and Carabidae) or mole crickets, paralyses them and deposits her eggs on them.

Range, habitat and behaviour
These wasps occur in most areas of Australia, particularly subtropical and tropical regions, and many species are restricted to Australia. During spring and summer months, the males can be found feeding at *Leptospermum* and *Eucalyptus* flowers growing in open woodlands, heathland, and along the tracks and margins of forests and alongside coastal dunes.

Female flower wasps are wingless and—an unusual phenomenon among insects—are smaller than the males. In order to reproduce, females climb to the tops of shrubs, tall grasses and flowerheads, and emit sexual pheromones to attract amorous males. When such a male arrives, the female grabs hold of him with her strong mandibles and is immediately lifted up into the air, where mating often takes place—on the wing.

After mating, the female drops to the ground and proceeds to actively search the ground for beetle larvae feeding beneath the soil—most commonly for larvae of flower beetles such as the cowboy beetle (*Diaphonia dorsalis*). She has the uncanny knack of finding them through her sense of 'smell'. When she locates one, she digs down below the soil until she reaches the beetle larvae and then lays her egg or eggs on it.

Immediately on hatching, the wasp larvae begin feeding on the paralysed insect's internal body-parts and, when fully grown, pupate within the dried husk of the host.

LEFT A paper-nest wasp (*Polistes variabilis*). Paper-nest wasps make their paper-cells by rasping wood from trees. This is chewed into fragments and mixed with saliva. Should the nest become overheated on hot days, the wasps fetch water and regurgitate it over the combs and then fan it with their wings. Their energy is provided through nectar, a natural source of sugar, but their own larvae are fed on masticated lepidopterous larvae.

PAPER-NEST WASPS
order Hymenoptera:
superfamily Vespoidea

Pollinators and predators

In numerous wasp species, both sexes obtain nectar for their personal nourishment, while many females collect pollen and nectar as provision for their offspring. Pollen-gathering wasps have long tongues like bees, and are able to obtain nectar from a far wider range of flower types than those with short tongues.

Range, habitat and behaviour

Paper-nest wasps (family Vespidae) have a worldwide distribution in tropical and temperate regions, and include a number of subfamilies.

In tropical climates, their paper-nests survive all-year round. In temperate zones, however, the workers die in autumn, leaving the queen to survive the winter months by hibernating within shelter. The queen re-emerges the following spring and begins a new nest. She looks after her newly hatched offspring by herself until they become adults and start helping with the rearing, too. Should the queen die, another individual takes over her role. Carbohydrates and proteins from a wide range of sources—including nectar, pollen, fruits and other insects such as caterpillars, bees and flies—are progressively fed to their growing offspring.

The accidentally introduced paper-nest wasps (subfamily Vespinae) are widespread—the European (or German) wasp (*Vespula germanica*) has established itself in eastern and southern parts of Australia, while the English wasp (*Vespula vulgaris*) is restricted to Victoria. Each colony is founded by an egg-laying queen and can grow to support thousands of sterile workers. The workers often prey upon other insects, which are masticated and fed progressively to the larvae. Flower nectar, ripe fruit and carcasses also supply their carbohydrate and protein requirements. If you find these insects on your property you must seek the service of a qualified integrated pest control company to have them removed as they are a pest species in Australia.

THE LIFE OF THE WORKER HONEY BEE

Queen honey bees are so highly specialised for egg-laying they are unable to perform any other tasks in the colony. So the nest is entirely constructed by the worker bees. Unlike social wasps, which build horizontal nests, the social bees build vertical combs or sheets of cells. There are two sizes of cells: the small ones are for workers; the large ones are for drones in the breeding season, and for storage of pollen and honey at other times. The queen bee, when laying eggs, gauges the size of each cell using her forelimbs to measure it.

For the first two weeks of a young worker bee's life, her principal occupation is nursing. She brings honey and pollen from the storage cells to feed the queen, the drones and larvae. Bees feed pollen, nectar and honey to their young (unlike most other hymenopterans, which feed their young on the flesh of other arthropods).

As the worker bee grows older, she is able to produce wax from glands beneath her body and so takes on a new profession—building honeycombs. This is her middle age. This period of her life includes other duties such as taking care of cleaning the hive and standing guard at the entrance to deter any intruders such as bees from other colonies, mice and marauding ants.

Nursing is, however, her most demanding job, as each larva eats over 1000 portions of pollen each day. New queen larvae are fed a special diet of royal jelly, and given so much attention that they fully develop from egg to winged adult in 16 days, whereas the larvae of workers fully develop in 21 days, and drones in 24 days. New queens are normally reared in late spring when the colony is about to reproduce.

When it is the time to reproduce, the mother queen departs with her swarm of faithful workers to begin another hive elsewhere and is replaced in the old nest by a new queen. A queen bee mates several times in the one season. A few drones can participate but most are left behind in a corner of the hive without food or are forced to leave and, once outside, quickly die of starvation and exposure.

BEES
order Hymenoptera: superfamily Apoidea

Pollinators

The bees perform their greatest service by pollinating flowers while collecting the nectar and pollen. This is of far greater value to the environment at large than any honey the honey bee produces in the wooden hive-boxes we provide them with for our own purposes.

There is much research being undertaken to investigate the use of native bees in the pollination of crops.

Range, habitat and behaviour

Wherever flowering plants grow plentifully, bees are found. Of all the known species of bees worldwide, only three species have been domesticated. The introduced honey bee (*Apis mellifera*) has threatened the survival of a number of Australian native species, particularly in certain areas, by competing for available blossoms.

Anatomically, bees are sphecoid-like wasps that utilise flower pollen as a source of protein. In this, they are almost unique among hymenopterans: wasp species generally (with only a few exceptions) feed their offspring on the flesh of insects or spiders, but bees feed their young on a staple diet of honey and pollen. Being entirely dependent on flowers for their required proteins and carbohydrates, bees must constantly visit blossoms to obtain nectar and pollen to feed their growing larvae within the nest.

The majority of bee species are solitary in lifestyle but some build their nests in a community, while others are social. Nests are most often built beneath the soil—some species favouring clay and compact soil, others choosing loose and sandy soils. Certain species choose hollows in dead trees and rock crevices for nest-sites, while open ground or plant-covered sites are utilised by still other species. The important requirement for a nest-site is its moisture level, which determines the burrow-depth as well; the nest-site also has to be close to plants that can provide nectar and pollen.

Among solitary bees there are no worker castes. Solitary native bees lay their eggs on lumps of pollen, moistened with nectar (one egg per cell). Having stocked the cells with food and having laid her eggs, the female seals the cells and has no further contact with the growing larvae.

ABOVE A native bee (family Megachilidae). In the course of nectar-feeding, most bees become heavily dusted with pollen grains, invariably picked up on the patches of stiff hairs situated on their limbs and undersides. These pollen-laden brushes transfer pollen from one flower to another, thereby cross-pollinating the flowers and thereby affording them genetic diversity.

CHAPTER SIX

Collection and Observation

As human interest and knowledge of nature increases, more people seek to understand the creatures that live among us. Spending time exploring the natural world reaps its own rewards. It is fascinating to watch an ant carry its huge bounty, a katydid leap into action or a dragonfly hover, motionless, then suddenly take off. Some insects evoke special feelings, like the first cicada song heralding the start of summer or bees hovering on spring's first blossoms. Their natural theatrics capture the imagination and spark our interest—what sort of ant can carry such a burden? Which butterfly visits those flowers? What kind of cicada is that? Observation is simple but we like to identify what we are watching—the sheer numbers and varieties of insects can make this difficult. For those wanting to develop their knowledge of insects, a reference collection is a real asset, and this chapter explores how to create one as well as some techniques for observing insects in action.

OPPOSITE Creating your own reference collection is a valuable asset for anyone interested in learning about insects. Each specimen in a reference collection should ideally have a data label written in waterproof ink (or laser-printed) containing relevant information such as locality, habitat, date and time collected, food plant and name of the collector. Expanded notes can be stored in a filing card system or made into a database on your computer.

In creating a reference collection, aim for a collection of specimens mounted in an orderly way with all the details of where and when each specimen was collected, plus any other valuable, relevant information. A male and female representative of a species, and examples of their larval and pupal forms, should be sufficient. Such collections are invaluable for making positive identifications and accurate line drawings, although relating a dead specimen to the live creature that you observed in its natural habitat is not always easy—the way it moves and its lifestyle are not available for study. A reference collection is useful if you are studying a particular phase of a species during a time of the year when it is not available. Or perhaps you may wish to refer to the egg, larva, pupa or adult stage of a particular species.

Collecting for collecting's sake can get out of hand and should be avoided. There is no useful purpose served by amassing huge series-collections of widely distributed species, because the variations of size, pattern, colouring or other aberrations are often widespread.

When collecting, do so lightly. Species now in existence are but rare survivors among the species that are now extinct. Although great surges in the populations of particular species may take place in one year, these will have occurred to compensate for unfavourable conditions in past seasons. Population fluctuations for many insect species occur in a cyclical pattern in various localities. Such patterns are natural, but they are also caused by human practices such as the destruction of wilderness habitats and the use of pesticides.

A trade has always existed in insects—in butterflies and beetles particularly—and the beauty and rarity of numerous exotic species creates a demand among collectors who are willing to pay well for unusual specimens. However, populations of the vast majority of insects are largely unaffected by the numbers taken for research and genuine reference collections. Prohibitions on capturing specific insects should only apply to a few rare, locally restricted species. The biggest threat to the survival of insects—and other life forms—is not the careful collector but the destruction of the ecosystems they all inhabit.

If you need to make identifications without a reference specimen, it is useful to make an identification key. This is a way of refining down the possibilities by making a series of choices between two alternatives. For instance—does the insect have two pairs of membranous wings, or one pair hardened? Or, an abdomen with forceps or without forceps? And so on, ruling features in or out until you arrive at a final choice to make an identification.

RIGHT Dried insects preserve well and most retain colour and shape. An orderly tray of specimens with data labels can inspire further interest for those studying natural history. To prevent museum beetles or other insects from destroying them, they need to be stored in a tightly enclosed case (glass-top or storage box) with a little net of naphthalene pinned to a corner. If you are allergic to naphthalene, a minute amount of beechwood creosote liquid in a small tube with a cotton wick can be put inside the lid. These chemicals prevent mould, but stored specimens must be kept dry and examined at intervals. If mould sets in, specimens can be cleaned using ethyl acetate with a fine brush, taking care with all appendages. In tropical regions, a dehumidifier helps prevent mould.

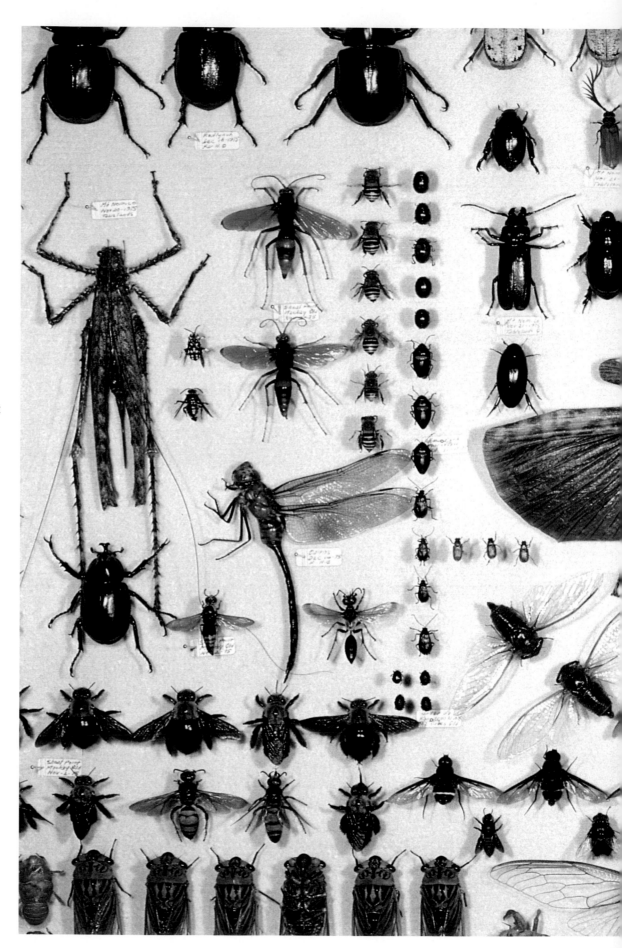

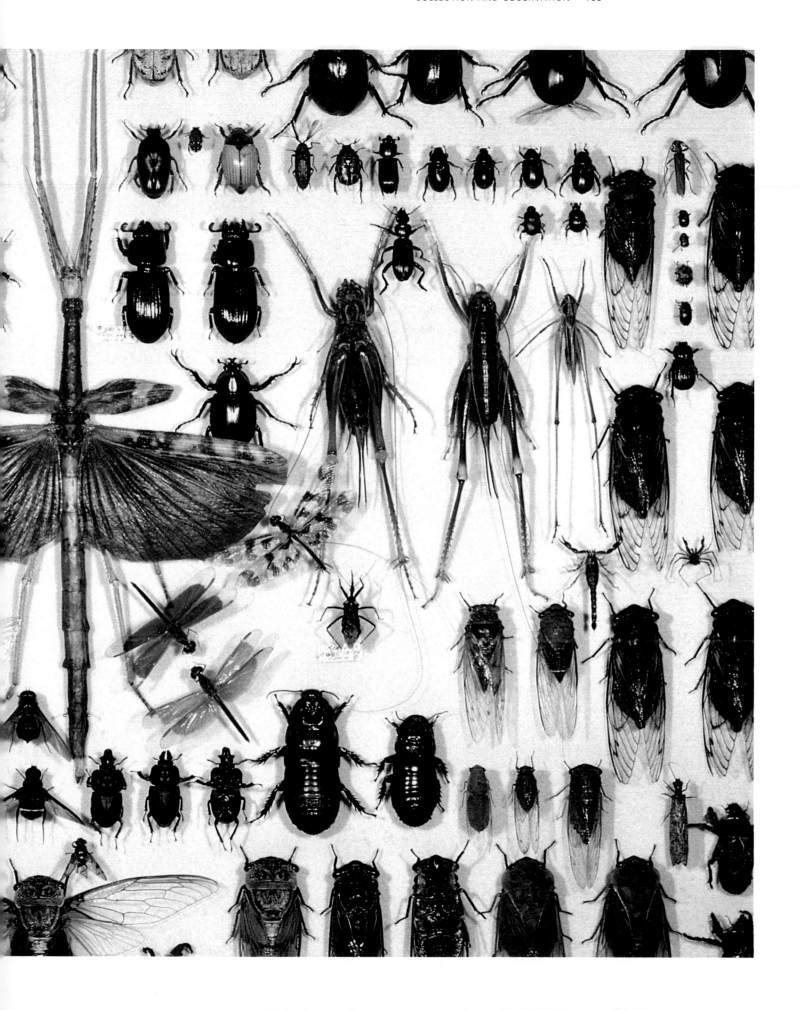

RIGHT For practical purposes, beetle specimens are best pinned through the base of their right elytron using standard stainless-steel entomological pins. Use size 2 for small- to medium-sized specimens, 3 for medium to large ones, and 4 and 6 for very large ones. Very minute specimens are best glued to a card, but use only a tiny amount of glue so as to not hide the body structures. Alternatively use 'minuten pins' inserted into a block of pith just large enough to take a size 3 pin. The data label can be placed directly onto this.

PRESERVATION AND PREPARATION OF SPECIMENS

Preservation

There are two methods suitable for preserving most insects. Wet-preservation method: Soft-bodied specimens and most nymphs, larvae and eggs should be drowned in 70% alcohol (for up to two hours) then stored in a solution of 75% alcohol and a little glycerin. Dry-preservation method: Pour a 40 mm layer of plaster of Paris into a clean jar and, when the plaster is set and dry, saturate it with ethyl acetate. Hard-bodied insects may be placed in this killing jar with the lid on for up to two hours. Once the insect is dead it may be placed in an envelope or pinned on a setting board until thoroughly dry, before being stored.

The wet-preservation method may also be used to preserve the internal structures of hard-bodied insects. Large insects, moths, butterflies, dragonflies and damselflies require specialised treatment; see Smithers' book for details.

Storage

Once dry, specimens can be stored in an air-tight box, usually 25 cm x 20 cm. Such boxes usually have polystyrene or cork bases and are fully lined with white paper. To prevent mould, put a little chlorocresol into a small glass container half-filled with cotton wool into the storage box. Insect pests, such as museum beetles and psocids, can be deterred by pinning a gauze bag of naphthalene to a corner of the box. Larger collections should be stored in cabinets housing numerous trays.

For all entomological equipment see:
Australian Entomological Supplies
PO Box 250, Bangalow NSW 2479
http://www.nor.com.au/business/austento
email: austento@nor.com.au

Remember that collecting insects in Australian national parks requires a permit.

Preparing specimens

Insects such as dragonflies, butterflies and moths, which need to be set with their wings displayed, are set on a setting board and then dried. This typically consists of a plywood base, which has a softer material, such as cork or polystyrene, glued to it. The softer material is used to receive the point of the mounting pin and pins are also used to hold the spread-out wings. A groove a little wider than the bodies of the insects being displayed is left for the body and legs to hang supported, so that the wings can be set flat and covered with strips of tracing paper, held in position by a number of surrounding pins until the insect is dried.

Presentation and display

Rows of insects lined up like soldiers on parade are fine for an arrangement of the orders, but tell little of the lifestyle of these insects and their relationship to other arthropods. As your reference collection grows, themes can be built up around the different species that have symbiotic relationships with one another, or at least have some interaction with one another.

Labelling is also an important part of a collection as it ideally contains all the relevant information about collecting the specimen, such as locality, date, collector, habitat, climatic conditions, food plant and the time of day.

RECORDING YOUR OBSERVATIONS

Drawing

One accurate drawing well done can be clearer than hundreds of words of description, and is a useful record of what you have found. A line drawing in black and white is a severe exercise in economy of means; it forces you to observe—to determine whether a particular detail is or is not present—and to record every piece of important information. As a discipline alone, drawing is

LEFT A reference collection of lacewings, beetles and wasps, with data labels including location, date and time collected. Dried and pinned insects are standard and practical methods of preservation.

well worth practising. A simple line drawing is what you are aiming for. Depending on how much representation of form you wish to give it, various methods of pen strokes can be used in the final stages.

To complete the drawing, shading and effects of roundness can be indicated rather than portrayed and the simplest methods are usually the most successful. To shade larger areas, two standard methods are very reliable: stippling and cross-hatching (or line shading). Stippling involves filling in an area with dots varied in size and spacing. You can erase unwanted lines and dots simply by the sparing use of white Liquid Paper. The basic requirements, apart from practice, are patience and deliberation.

Toolkit

This should include a non-smudging rubber, sharp pencils (2B and HB), a ruler, assorted nibbed pens (hollow-nibbed pens are ideal), waterproof Indian ink, a magnifying glass (X 3 magnification will give a complete coverage of the subject). You will also need a microscope for tiny specimens.

BELOW Most insects have an external chitinised skeleton and dry out naturally. Bulky insects enclosing large amounts of soft tissue sometimes need to have their body contents replaced with cotton wool in order to retain their shape. All setting is best done while the specimens are fresh.

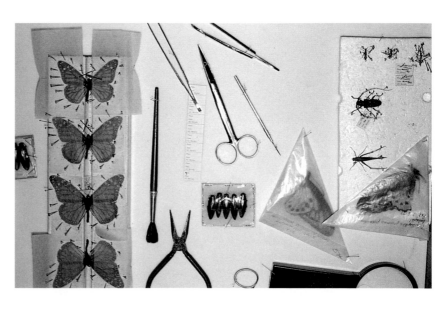

Relaxing dried specimens

When drawing an insect, you will often be copying from a cabinet-mounted specimen (wet or dried) and if the arrangement of parts of the specimen look unnatural, you can adjust this—but first, if the specimen is dried, it has to be 'relaxed'. Never attempt to move the limbs of a dried specimen before it has been relaxed.

Relaxing fluid can be made up by using water (about 25 mL) and a quarter of a teaspoon of chlorocresol to prevent the development of mould. Put some absorbent material such as cotton wool or a dishwashing sponge into the base of an airtight container and pour the relaxing fluid over it until it is saturated. Add a sheet of foam, as specimens should not be in contact with the fluid. Place the insects on this.

It can take 1–5 days to soften the specimen. Test it by gently touching one of its limbs; if it doesn't move, relax it further for another day or two. When fully relaxed, the body and limbs can be spread into a more natural position. Cut a piece of cork, foam or softwood as a support to pin the specimen on, making sure there is sufficient margin for safe handling. There is no point in making the support only slightly larger than the size of the specimen, for you may need to manoeuvre it to examine particular features more closely.

Shaping the outline

If the insect is not too small, you can copy it quite easily without magnifying it. First, make a preliminary sketch, as your initial aim is to supply line information only.

The creature viewed from directly above can be portrayed as symmetrical in the finished drawing, as this makes the process easier. When you have drawn one half of the subject (left or right) and you are satisfied that your drawing is reasonably accurate, you can trace it onto a fresh piece of paper with a 2B pencil. Then, turn the tracing upside down and align it with the half-drawing. Rub the paper firmly with a fingernail or the end of a paintbrush to transfer the image. You should now have a general shape that looks fine. When you are happy with the pencilled image, go over it with a mapping pen or drawing pen.

Make sure your drawing is of a size and shape that will reduce satisfactorily to fit onto a page without wasted space. An enormous drawing full of fine details will not reduce well—most of the detail is likely to disappear or become blurred. Equally, a tiny thumbnail sketch will not enlarge well. A line drawing will reproduce best if it is approximately four times larger than the subject.

It is also important to indicate the actual size of the insect that you have drawn. To do this, you need to do scale drawings, or use a scale, and supply the relevant measurements of the creature.

PHOTOGRAPHING INSECTS

Buy the best equipment that you can afford. This applies especially to lenses, because the images you capture on film are only as good as the optics that created them. There are a number of important aspects to bear in mind when photographing insects.

Technical tips

- Focusing

  Use the best lens for the job, and make certain that the head and eyes of the subject are in sharp focus. The rest of its anatomy will be acceptable in softer focus and can actually help highlight the features you wish to emphasise.
- Framing the subject

  Try to include as much of the insect and its immediate surroundings as is practically possible for its size. Careful cropping is essential in order to highlight a particular aspect of the subject that you intend the viewer to focus upon.

BELOW Mounting and setting. Pinning boards can be covered with polystyrene or cork and provided with a centre groove to accommodate the body of an insect. The groove needs a cork base to allow an entomological pin to hold the specimen in place. The wings are kept flat by paper, surrounded by pins until dry.

- Lighting the subject

  When photographing natural subjects, it is important to achieve really clear results. The use of a flash ensures this. For the best lighting, try to combine sunlight with the light of a flash, using the flash for various effects —for eliminating or accentuating shadows, for example. The flashlight should complement the natural light but not override it. Photographing the subject against a light-coloured background helps to make a good exposure (and the opposite is true if the subject is lightly toned—photograph it against a darker background). When photographing species that rely on cryptic camouflage for their survival, use frontal lighting only. Side lighting produces an obvious body shadow along one side. This could well ruin an otherwise convincing camouflage photograph.

- Film grain

  A fine-grain film is best for this type of close-up work. ASA 64 Kodachrome, Ektachrome or Fujichrome are ideal and can be enlarged without difficulty.

Getting scientific value from your photographs

Your photographs will have scientific value only if you show the outstanding features of the subject, its home-site, its nest-site, its young, and the features of its natural habitat. They should also include any other creature associated with the subject.

- Identifying features

  Try to photograph the creature so that an identifying feature of the species is clearly visible. If this is not evident in the photograph, it will be of little use for the viewer.

- Home-sites and nest-sites

  An insect's home-site or nest-site often provides valuable insights into the life history of a particular species and its relationship with other life forms. A good photograph of such a site helps recognise one easily in the field.

- The young

  Photographs showing the different stages of a particular insect are especially interesting because, even if the adults of a particular species are well known, their young may not be. When adults and immature stages are found together, the opportunity for a valuable record should not be missed.

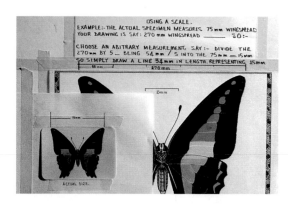

LEFT Scaling a drawing. Drawings need to include a scale to show the insect's actual measurement. This blue triangle butterfly (*Graphium sarpedon choredon*) has a wingspan of 70 mm.

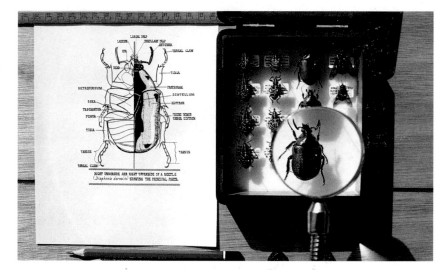

- Habitat features

  These tell their own story and give the viewer a considerable amount of information, such as plant relationships and soil and water relationships. This is an important aspect of photographing insects.

  A photograph of a dead insect is usually only a poor source of information about the appearance of the insect when it was alive. However, a full-colour photograph of a living creature in its natural habitat can often disclose more information than can be seen with the naked eye.

Artistic quality

This involves contrasts of colour, composition, selection of statement or viewpoint, and capturing the behaviour of insects in their natural habitat.

- Colour contrasts

  Select a viewpoint so that the subject is well defined in the photograph. The subject and its background will determine whether lighting from the front, the back or the side should be used. If you need to define the

ABOVE A drawing toolkit includes a non-smudging rubber, sharp pencils (2B and HB), a ruler, assorted nibbed pens and Indian ink. For tiny specimens, a magnifying glass (3 × magnification) will give complete coverage of the subject. To start, make a preliminary sketch, as the first aim is to supply line information only.

ABOVE In insect photography, the practical aim is to capture the insect in its ecological context rather than entirely fill the frame with it (unless specific features are to be shown close up). This male tailed emperor butterfly (*Polyura pyrrhus sempronius*) is drinking water at the edge of a stream, a frequent habit of these butterflies.

subject by using coloured background cards, they must be carefully chosen—shades of blue, green and brown are highly suitable. If so much clutter and debris surrounds the subject that it becomes difficult to recognise what the creature is, a colour card can be very useful in helping to define it in the finished photograph.

• Composition
Avoid the habit of always positioning the subject in the centre of the frame. Try to include some of the surrounding habitat. Keep a small pair of scissors or snips in your kit so that you can remove any obstructing leaf, stem or blade of grass out of the way of the camera lens.

• Statement of viewpoint
This comes down to a personal choice. What is the information or idea that you wish to convey? Photographs of insects vary enormously according to the viewpoint we select. Photographing them at their own level helps bring the viewer into their realm, but if we do it from above that will diminish them. Photographing a subject from the side or in profile will give a detached effect, while taking a shot from below adds a dramatic touch and can make an insect look quite formidable. So, you must consider carefully what it is that you intend to communicate.

• Knowing the subject
Knowing how your subject behaves is a distinct advantage. Animals have a discomfort zone, but if you remain outside it they will carry on with their activities. Enter their 'fear circle' and they will move away.

However, knowledge of their behaviour can be used to create wonderful photographs. For example, a beetle usually opens its wings in preparation for flight the moment it crawls to the end or tip of a twig held at an angle leading upwards. Series of photographs of insects showing their behaviour during feeding, courtship, mating, and so on, are potentially full of interest. Dragonflies, butterflies and cicadas offer opportunities galore for exciting photographic sequences as they emerge from their nymphal skins and pupae. If a butterfly is photographed feeding with its wings half-opened, you can show both the dorsal and ventral aspects of its wing patterns and colours as it moves from one flower to another.

Regardless of knowing your subject, having good equipment and the relevant skills, and being in the right place at the right time naturally produce the best results, along with patient determination. Even if you live in a large city, you can find nature reserves, parklands or natural areas where you can practise your skills in photography.

Equipment

In the field, the aim is to photograph the insect or spider in its ecological context, rather than fill up the frame with it (unless specific features are to be shown close up). Hand-holding the camera is the most practical way to do this when quick changes need to be made to frame the subject. A tripod is useful for setting up your camera to photograph a single flowerhead over a period of several hours.

Most insects are highly active and to photograph them as they go about their work can be a real challenge and may require considerable patience. A flash may be a helpful piece of equipment in nature photography as a short burst of light may stop an insect in its tracks. The use of a flash also allows for the use of smaller apertures, which provide the additional depth of field—the range of sharp focus—so greatly needed in close-up work. Extension tubes can be used in conjunction with the standard lens. A macro lens with a two-element dioptre combined with flash is also a good combination. If you don't want to scare off the highly mobile creature in front of you, fitting a dioptre onto the end of the lens for greater magnification is easier than screwing an extension tube between the lens and camera body.

A skylight filter should be fitted at all times to the front of your camera to protect the lens and to reduce flare to the minimum. Sometimes a polarising filter is useful, especially when photographing glossy spiders such as funnel-web spiders or insects in water habitats, where water reflections cause flare.

WRITING UP YOUR OBSERVATIONS

Making field notes

You will not get far in studying insects before uncovering some interesting aspects of their life histories that have not been written about, aspects no-one else seems to have noticed or recorded before. If you study almost any group of insects, you will be astonished to find how little is really known about them with certainty. However modestly you start out as a beginner, anxious to learn from the experts, sooner or later you will have some information that you feel compelled to pass on to others.

The first essential step when writing up your observations is to confine them to your immediate subject. Do not allow yourself to become baffled or confused by the immensity of the field of study. Choose one family, one genus, one small group of insects and study them thoroughly and precisely. In addition, when you begin to study arthropods, don't become side-tracked into playing with their names; there are endless scientific debates about taxonomy and changes are inevitable.

Collect your observations in an orderly way and file them properly—a filing-card system is fine. Transfer notes on odd scraps of paper or in old exercise books onto cards as soon as possible. Cards can be filed in an orderly arrangement and assembled with a definite purpose. In this way information can be built up quite easily for a paper (such as a review of a small group of arthropods) or a more extensive work. All work for publication is made much easier with this system.

Reports from the bushland

Two examples of field note observations I have made on insect-finding trips are included here to give an indication of the type of record one might keep.

1 SOUNDS OF SUMMER
Location: Waterfall, Royal National Park, New South Wales. Mid-December 1997, around 9 am—within a lush rainforest patch, a classic Sydney summer's day.

Resting at a creek—the noise of cicadas deafening. I observed six different species thriving in the region; each species giving one another short breaks between their singing. With these breaks, the females of the various species are able to locate the males of their kind. The black prince cicada (Psaltoda plaga) *was very common, as was the greengrocer cicada* (Cyclochila australasiae). *The scissors-grinder cicadas* (Henicopsaltria eydouxii), *also known as razor-grinder, were in their thousands, and cherry-nose cicadas* (Macrotristria angularis) *plentiful, along with double-drummer cicadas* (Thopha saccata), *and floury-millers* (Abricta curvicosta), *also known as floury-bakers.*

Two hours later I moved to the heathlands adjacent to dry sclerophyll forest, where the nectar-bearing blossoms of the scrub apple (Angophora hispida) *were in abundance. Greengrocer cicadas and cherry-nose cicadas were plentiful in the nearby stands of eucalypts. Numerous pairs of large green adult katydids* (Terpandrus horridus) *were engrossed in feeding on nectar from nearby shrubs, with many of the males continuously chirping as they fed. On one small flowering shrub were several large orange-and-black-bodied, female spider-hunting wasps,* Cryptocheilus bicolor, *taking nourishment along with the smaller male wasps of their species.*

2 NORTH QUEENSLAND STAG-BEETLE
Phalacrognathus muelleri (family Lucanidae)
Location: Mt Nomico, Atherton Tablelands, north Queensland. November–December 1978.

One rainy morning in rainforest on the Atherton Tablelands in north Queensland, I was searching for beetle larvae among the abundant decaying timber. One particular log situated in a wet gully took my attention. It had every sign of having insect activity within its rotting fibres. The tree had broken at its base, but remained leaning at quite an angle against adjacent tree trunks. I split a small section of it open with a tomahawk, immediately exposing a large female stag-beetle resting in its cell; its mirror-sheen cuticle glimmered in the available light. It had not been long free of its pupal wrappings, as its elytra had not fully hardened.

Using a stout knife-blade, I opened another portion of the rotting log and uncovered a fully formed insect, not yet emerged from the timber (a teneral adult) inside a cell at the base of the log. Above the long tunnel formed by the larva prior to its pupation were tightly packed wood chips, evidence of the activity that had taken place in forming this cell, in which the insect had undergone its metamorphosis. This second individual was a large male, measuring around 60 mm in body length, and even more striking in colouring, shape and size than the female. This individual had emerged sometime earlier than the female, as its elytra were fully hardened, and it became very active in response to being disturbed and exposed.

Upon cutting the rotting timber into sizeable chunks for ease of handling, another three males were exposed in the pupal stage. I carefully transferred the insects into a large container previously prepared with wood fibre and moistened blotting paper, keeping their cells intact as much as possible. The log measured about 140 mm in diameter and all the teneral adults and pupae were found at its base. The larvae had done most of their feeding much higher up from the ground but had moved down the trunk as they neared completion of their larval stage. This was evident from the remarkably long tunnels that opened into larger galleries at their base. The tunnel leading to each cell had been sealed with closely packed wood-dust by the larvae. Each cell measured around 30 mm in width by around 65 mm–70 mm in length, leaving a comfortable space around the occupant. Each pupa was enclosed in its own separate compartment, with only a few millimetres (10 mm–20 mm) of timber remaining between the heads of the insects and the world at large. Iridescent pearl-like hues gleamed through the semi-transparent cuticle, as each pupa neared its emergence from its juvenile wrappings. Frequent observation disclosed noticeable changes during their preparation for shedding their old pupal skin from the newly formed, soft, outer cuticle— through which slowly developing subtle colours of the adults could be seen.

I set up a vivarium to closely simulate the conditions of the natural habitat of these insects, and placed them inside. The observation tank was kept moist (but not wet) by regularly spraying with a fine atomiser charged with creek water. One individual in particular was in an advanced stage, its subtle iridescence pronounced just prior to shedding its old skin. After many hours of observation, I retired to the tent around 2.30 am. At daybreak I was met with a breathtaking sight—its transformation into a truly beautiful creature, pearly-pink and pearly-yellow with subtle hues throughout, its wing covers still expanding. Later that afternoon the beetle's new cuticle had changed into a deep maroon, and continued to change colour. Five days after its emergence, its exoskeleton had changed into a deep iridescent carmine, bordered by rich-green metallic margins and coppery tints. In its full glory, its entire body shone like a highly polished gem. The toothy, sculptured mandibles of the male beetle are enormous, projecting well forward of the head. The male's strong legs and strongly curved tarsal claws support the body clear of the substrate, its claws being able to hook into bark, securing a firm hold like that of a mountain climber. The colouring of the beetle had stabilised and its burnished exoskeleton had fully hardened. All pupae successfully emerged and were released. The male beetle under observation remained active and lived for four weeks (31 days) after its emergence.

REARING INSECTS

Rearing insects is an interesting activity, as much more is known of the adults, and they are more easily identified. The immature forms of many species often lead such vastly different lives to the adults, requiring different microhabitats, that in many cases a species can be positively identified only by rearing the immature stages under close observation. Information on the life cycle of a particular insect can be discovered in this way.

Insects can be kept in a vivarium or, for aquatic species or species with aquatic larvae, a small aquarium. This kind of observation is well suited to examining dragonflies, crickets or grasshoppers and cicadas. However, in many cases it is necessary to catch a live specimen to start a colony, which can prove difficult.

Try capturing an adult dragonfly on the wing, and it will quickly demonstrate its visual acuity and acquired flight skills, which to a casual observer can go largely unrecognised. Short-horned grasshoppers are also wary creatures, quick to avoid danger. Most are equipped with excellent hearing and vision complemented with leaping and flying skills. Try catching one by hand and it will demonstrate its tricks by leading you on a merry chase. During a sweltering summer's day, trying to catch a cicada can be exasperating. Even warily approaching a cicada singing in the sunshine usually results in its sudden departure. A cicada is easily approached only in certain circumstances: when settled at night; when emerging from the nymphal shell; when engrossed in feeding with its rostrum embedded into a tree trunk; on cool, damp days; or when an individual is nearing the end of its life.

Much can be learnt about dragonflies by closely observing their aquatic stages within a medium-sized aquarium. It provides opportunities to observe the dragonfly nymphs prepare themselves for feeding. They feed on a variety of water creatures including mosquito wrigglers (both larvae and pupae), small tadpoles, tiny fish and earthworms. After many weeks of being supplied with food, the nymphs usually associate the approach of the observer with their food supply and, in anticipation of a meal, they will come out from behind the rock or water plant. Keep smaller and younger nymphs separate from larger aggressive individuals to prevent cannibalism.

Many of the long-horned crickets such as tree-crickets (for example, family Gryllacrididae), the katydids (for example, family Tettigoniidae), true crickets (for example, family Gryllidae) and mole crickets (family Gryllotalpidae) demonstrate interesting courtship behaviour. Anyone who has ever had the experience of rearing generations of these insects in vivariums or cages could hardly fail to notice individuals communicating their intentions to one another by tapping one another's antennae, varying their songs and movements according to the response of the opposite sex. These activities are particularly commonplace among the meadow katydids of the subfamily Conocephalinae.

During the summer months I have frequently housed 20 or more greengrocer (yellow Monday) cicadas at a time in a wire cage hung from the ceiling of the porch to observe their ways. A suitable observation cage can be made of a light metal frame, about 60 cm by 60 cm, covered in lightweight, 12 mm wire mesh. Within the cage you should put a supply of fresh eucalypt branches, their stems immersed in a large bottle half-filled with water, centrally placed on the floor of the cage.

Occasionally a smaller than average-sized individual would discover an opening in the wire mesh that it could squeeze through. When returned to the cage it would soon return to the same opening to escape. Make certain that the necks of the water containers are covered with a few twigs so that if a cicada does fall in, it can climb out. It is not unusual for individuals to live for 4–6 weeks under these conditions, during which time they feed, sing, mate and lay eggs. Branches containing the eggs can later be taped to trees in the garden.

FOLLOWING PAGES Caterpillar of the emperor gum moth (*Opodiphthera eucalypti*). Each segment of the blue-green larva bears colourful tubercles that project small clusters of spines.

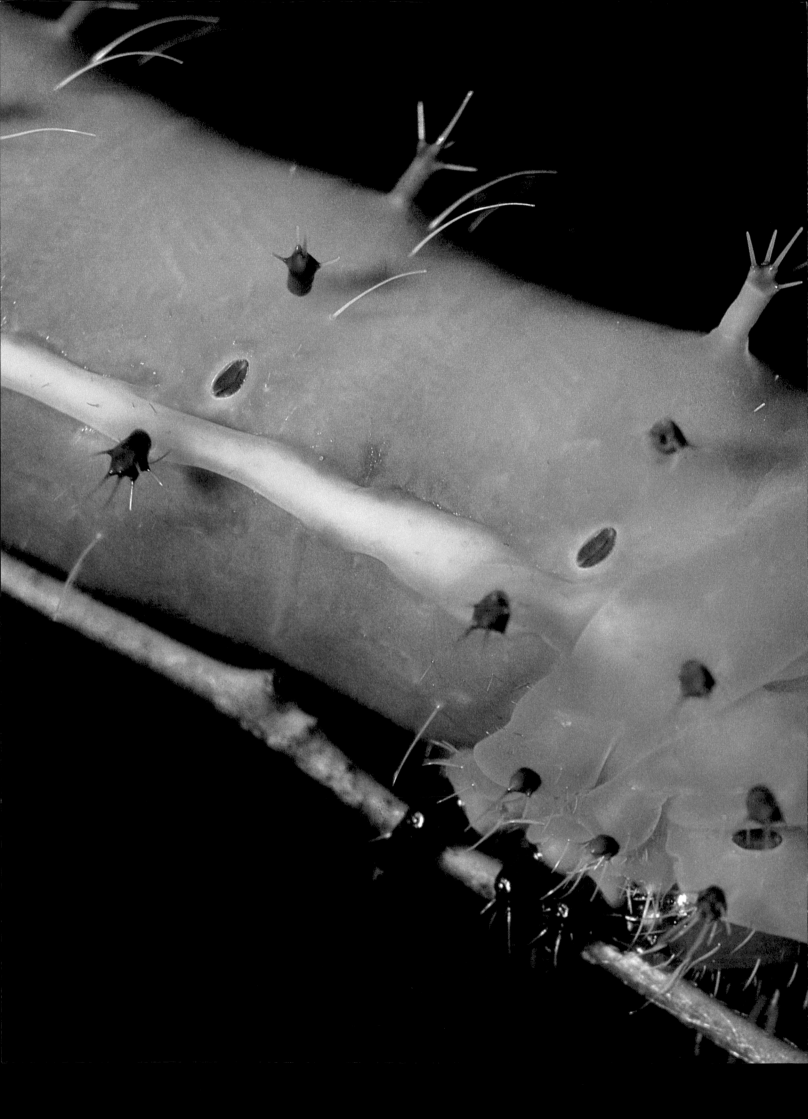

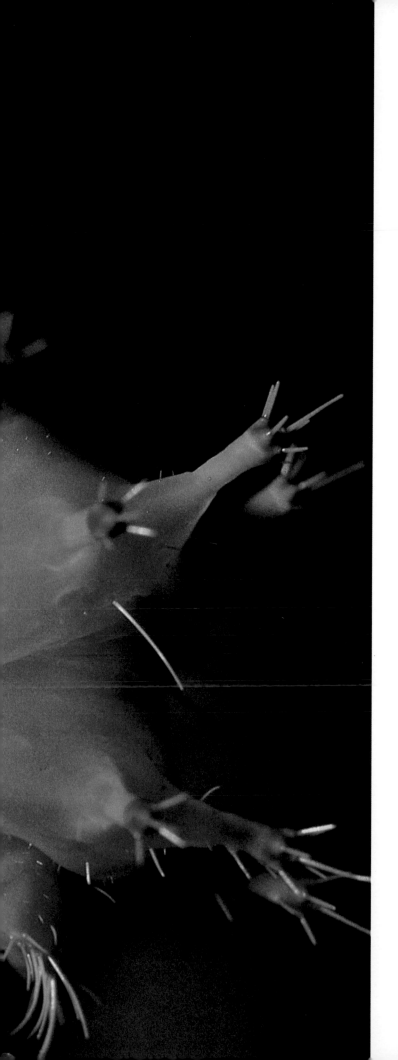

2

AUSTRALIAN

INSECTS

CHAPTER SEVEN

Pseudo Insects

Insects in the group (or assemblage) composed of pseudo insects are clearly derived from wingless ancestors. They include the springtails, proturans and diplurans. Scientifically they are classified as entognathous hexapods and comprise part of the superclass Hexapoda, which also includes the true insects. Until relatively recent times, these insects were treated as separate orders within the class Insecta. Now placed outside this class, each has been given the status of a class and order of its own. They do share some features with true insects: they have a distinctive head, a thorax, a many-segmented body and three pairs of legs. However, there are differences. Their anatomy differs from true insects—for instance, the mouthparts of the proturans are adapted for sucking food and are sunk well into the head region; also the number of abdominal segments differs. Most pseudo insects are obscure and very tiny and have not received the attention given to true insects.

BELOW Called springtails because many species are able to leap to extraordinary heights, they are among the oldest hexapods known, with fossil records dating back 400 million years. Some 2000 species are known to occur in Australia.

RIGHT Springtail habitat. Springtails live among leaf-litter, in animal nests, soil, dung, rotten logs and decaying vegetation. Some species frequent flowers, live in tree bark, wet sand, beneath rocks, coral reefs or on the water surface.

SPRINGTAILS
order Collembola

Springtails are small, jumping insects, no more than 10 mm long, with most species measuring less than 6 mm. An unusual feature of these insects is that as adults they moult up to 50 times without any additional growth. They only have six abdominal segments (unlike the 11 of most insects), and their organs of reproduction are similar to those of the proturans.

Springtails usually have a hind, fork-shaped organ (called a furcula) arising from the fifth abdominal segment, which acts as a spring to propel the insect into the air. When bent forward at rest, the furcula is held in position by a tiny, forked second appendage arising from the third abdominal segment. The furcula is formed from

embryonic legs (the potential legs that exist in embryo but are generally lost prior to hatching, unless adapted for other purposes).

Most springtails feed on decaying matter, but there are several species that feed on lichens, fungi, algae and pollen. The bright green lucerne-flea (*Sminthurus viridi*) may appear in its millions, damaging crops as it feeds. Some species have been recorded occurring in huge numbers, causing blockages in sewage beds. Populations can become so huge that they form layers up to 9 mm thick on the ground or water surface.

Range and habitat

Although rare in dry regions, their range is wide-spread, extending from subarctic to Antarctic regions, even occurring on snow. Certain species live on the water surface but most live in moist soil, leaf litter or under bark. A few species live in the nests of ants and termites. Some species occur on seashores, often being submerged by high tides, or on reefs between tidal marks.

Predators

Springtails have many predators including birds, fish and reptiles, 'primitive' spiders (mygalomorphs) and many open-range hunting spiders (families Miturgidae and Lycosidae), centipedes (family Scutigerellidae), ants (family Formicidae), mites (families Mesostigmatidae

LEFT Proturan habitat. Proturans live among leaf-debris, moss, in the soil and decaying timber. These minute, slow-moving cryptic hexapods are rarely seen, measuring less than 2 mm in body length.

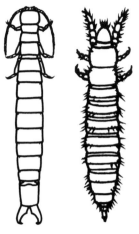

ABOVE Diplurans (left) are small, elongated hexapods distinguished by two abdominal cerci that arc pincers in some species. Proturans (right) are elongated wingless hexapods. Their forelimbs, held in front of the head, resemble antennae.

and Prostigmatidae), predatory flies (families Empididae and Dolichopodidae), predatory bugs (family Reduviidae), ground beetles (family Carabidae) and rove-beetles (family Staphylinidae).

PROTURANS
order Protura

These minute soil-dwellers, measuring 2 mm or less, were only discovered in 1907 and have not yet been given a popular name. They are structurally different from other arthropods, being characterised by having mandibles and maxillae retracted to form a pouch above the labium. Their mouthparts are slender and pointed and adapted for sucking. Proturans are colourless, wingless creatures without eyes, cerci or antennae, although their forelegs, which are larger and longer than their middle and hindlegs, serve as antennae. Their second and third pairs of legs are used for walking.

Range and habitat
Proturans are very common, occurring in many regions of Australia. As they only survive in very humid conditions, they are most usually found in woodlands, where they feed by sucking up liquid from moist soil, leaf debris and decaying timber. Various mites, spiders, ground beetles, crickets and centipedes feed on proturans.

DIPLURANS
order Diplura

Diplurans are soil-dwellers, mostly around 5 mm in body length, but some species in the family Projapygidae measure up to 50 mm. Many species are blind, worm-like soil-dwellers with bead-like antennae, and soft, creamy, elongated white bodies. The cerci of some species are modified into a pair of strongly sclerotised pincers, superficially resembling the rear forceps of earwigs.

In some species, there is a poison gland situated in the abdomen, which opens at the tips of the cerci.

Range and habitat
Diplurans occur in most parts of Australia, living in damp soil beneath logs and leaf litter, and feeding on decaying vegetation. They can frequently be found in large numbers: population densities are as high as 6000 per square metre in some woodland soils. Their worm-like activities enrich the soil, which benefits the plants.

Some diplurans live in the nests of termites and ants. Members of the family Projapygidae have an unusual way of preying upon small soil insects: they burrow into the soil head-first, leaving their pincers exposed to capture any passing prey. Adults can live for up to 12 months.

ABOVE Dipluran woodland habitat. Diplurans live in damp soil beneath decaying logs and leaf debris. Some woodland soils abound with these tiny creatures.

CHAPTER EIGHT

Primitive Wingless Insects

The primitive wingless insects comprise two groups, both within the class Insecta—the archaeognaths (subclass and order Archaeognatha), and the silverfish (subclass Dicondylia: infraclass Pterygota and order Thysanura). These are wingless insects whose ancestors never developed wings (unlike other wingless insects that had winged ancestors but at some evolutionary stage lost their wings). Both archaeognaths and silverfish were once formerly contained in the same taxonomic grouping but have since been separated—archaeognaths form their own subclass; silverfish have been placed in the recently erected subclass, Dicondylia. Silverfish are now believed to be close relatives of the winged insects (the Pterygota). Primitive wingless insects change little during their growth stages, with the last larval instar strongly resembling the adults. They do not mate: the female simply collects the sperm that the male deposits on the ground.

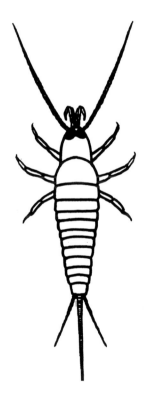

ABOVE Archaeognaths resemble silverfish superficially, but they are distinguished by their large compound eyes that meet in the middle, seven-segmented maxillary palps that protrude well in front of the head and their ability to jump. Body length is 3–18 mm.

ARCHAEOGNATHS (BRISTLETAILS)
subclass Archaeognatha:
order Archaeognatha

Archaeognaths, or the three-pronged bristletails, derive their name from their three slender, bristle-like tails and their antennae, which are also long and bristly. Their long antennae and chewing mouthparts are typical of true insects. Like silverfish, none have developed wings and their young are look-alikes of their parents, but are not as agile.

Archaeognaths have long, tapering bodies, 3–18 mm in length, their abdomen ending in a long appendage and two cerci. They are able to jump by flexing their abdomens. The jumping *Allomachilis froggatti* can leap short distances from the water surface.

A distinctive characteristic of archaeognaths is their ability to reproduce before they are fully grown, with their reproduction being sexual and seasonal. The males attach droplets of sperm to threads and leave these on the ground for the females to collect. The females lay their soft, globular-shaped, yellow–brown eggs in crevices and holes and the nymphs hatch in 2–9 weeks. Some species reach maturity at three months, while others require two years. They continue to moult throughout their lives.

Range and habitat
Archaeognaths are plentiful in tropical rainforests, wet and dry sclerophyll woodlands and coastal cliffs, a number of species occurring among leaf litter and under bark.

Most species feed on vegetable debris, algae and lichen, but also feed on their own cast skins. Heavy infestations of mites (order Acarina) kill archaeognaths, but their main enemies are spiders, ground beetles, crickets and centipedes.

SILVERFISH
subclass Dicondylia: order Thysanura

Silverfish are now the only representatives of the Apterygota. Those of the family Leidothrichidae (which are not found in Australia) are now regarded as being the most primitive living dicondylous insects known and are closest to the origin of the winged insects. The silverfish families that are found in Australia (Nicoletiidae and Lepismatidae) are more specialised.

Silverfish are torpedo-shaped, primitive wingless insects, with long, thread-like antennae and chewing mouthparts typical of true insects. Their long, tapering bodies, measuring up to 25 mm in length, end in one long appendage and two cerci. All silverfish are extremely agile.

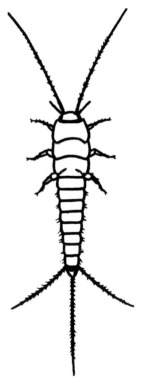

LEFT During daylight most archaeognaths hide among leaf debris and beneath bark, venturing forth at night to feed on lichen, algae and decaying vegetation. Their closely related allies, the silverfish, are agile insects that shelter beneath flaking bark and among leaf debris, feeding on bark and lichen. Some species live in nests of ants and termites, while some introduced species live in close association with humans.

They are aptly named, as the glittering scales covering their bodies help them slip away from predators. Should you attempt to seize or grab one, with its scale-covered body and streamlined form, it can easily slip through your fingers. Its scales immediately detach, leaving your fingers covered in their silvery dust. A distinctive characteristic of the silverfish life cycle is its ability to reproduce before being fully grown. Reproduction, generally, is sexual and seasonal; however, those of the genus *Nicoletia* are able to reproduce parthenogenetically. In most species the males form sperm capsules and leave them on the ground for the females to collect. Up to 30 soft, globular, yellow-brown eggs are laid into crevices and holes, and the nymphs hatch 2–9 weeks later. Some species mature at around three months and others require two years; they continue to moult throughout their lives.

While centipedes, crickets and ground beetles prey on silverfish, their principal enemies are ground-dwelling, open-range hunting spiders.

Range and habitat

Many species of silverfish live in close association with warm-blooded creatures, including humans—at least 10 species inhabit our homes and workplaces. Some species live within the nests of ants and termites. The introduced genera are cosmopolitan (family Lepismatidae): the domestic silverfish (*Ctenolepisma longicaudata*) commonly frequents kitchens and bathrooms. The cosmopolitan firebrat (*Thermobia domestica*) favours the warmth of bake-houses.

Silverfish feed during the cover of night on both vegetable and dead animal matter, but their main food sources are glues, especially sizing on books and wallpaper, and scraps of paper. Their fondness for starchy glues often results in the disintegration of older-style bound books, something for which they are well known. They will also eat linen, artificial silks and starchy foods, as well as their own cast skins and the dead bodies of other insects.

ABOVE Among the most primitive of living true insects, silverfish are distinguished by a body covered in tiny silvery scales, five-segmented maxillary palps and small eyes (when present) that do not meet. Body length reaches up to 25 mm.

CHAPTER NINE

Primitive Winged Insects

Insects in this subdivision, called the exopterygotes, have all evolved from winged ancestors. All growth is attained in the nymphal stage by shedding one outgrown cuticle after another until sexual maturity is attained. This process is called gradual (or, in the case of mayflies, partial) metamorphosis, that is, metamorphosis without a pupal resting stage. The life cycle of these insects unfolds in three marked stages of development—from egg to nymph to adult. The young of exopterygote insects are called nymphs and have visible wing-buds throughout their nymphal growth stage. Many nymphs have identical lifestyles and feeding habits to those of their parents. However, mayflies, damselflies, dragonflies and stoneflies differ from most other exopterygotes in that they typically undergo their early development in the water as active aquatic nymphs. Sexual maturity and full wing development occurs following the final moult, when adulthood is attained.

ABOVE A mayfly (*Atalophlebia costalis*). Mayflies are the only winged insects that undergo partial metamorphosis with a subimago that requires them to moult twice after leaving the water as nymphs. The subimago must again shed its skin and its wings before attaining sexual maturity.

MAYFLIES
order Ephemeroptera

Mayflies are distinguished by:
* their long forelegs that extend straight ahead
* their gauzy wings held erect above the body at rest
* their three long tails, usually present in both nymphs and adults
* being the only insects that moult their wings.

Mayflies are among the most delicate of creatures—even a touch can crush them. Members of the genus *Atalophlebia* have a wide distribution within Australia—this family (Leptophlebiidae) accounts for more than 70 per cent of Australian described species.

An adult mayfly is large-eyed, with a triangular-shaped head and soft, thin antennae. Its hind wings are tiny compared with the forewings. Bodily structure differs markedly between the sexes: the eyes of the male are divided, and his forelegs are exceptionally long and used for gripping a female in flight as they perform their brief mating flight. A female can produce up to 12 000 eggs.

Mayflies constitute the most primitive order of living winged insects and are the only known insects that fly and moult their wings before attaining maturity. Their life cycle has four stages, including partial metamorphosis: from egg to nymph, then to subimago, and finally to winged adult (10 mm–40 mm span).

The subimago has smoky-coloured wings. Before reaching sexual maturity it undergoes a further moult—including a wing moult—and its new, mature wings are clear. The insect is now ready for its 'marriage' flight, which is also usually the last day of its life. Hence the name of this order—Ephemeroptera, from *ephemeros* meaning 'living but a day' and *ptera*, the word for 'winged'.

Ecology

Most children are familiar with mayflies, as are anglers, who use them as bait—indeed, the lives of mayflies and fish are closely interrelated.

Mayfly nymphs are beneficial stream insects as they convert organic material into food for other aquatic life, forming an important link in the food chain, especially as food for freshwater fish. During their emergence season, adult mayflies also supply all insectivorous creatures with a bountiful supply of food.

DAMSELFLIES

order Odonata: suborder Zygoptera

Damselflies are distinguished from dragonflies by having:

- two pairs of slender wings, almost equal in length, that taper markedly towards the thorax
- both pairs of wings held above the body when at rest with most species
- a slower flying style, with a fluttering flight pattern
- nymphs equipped with three leaf-like gills stemming from the abdominal tip

- the nymph's face-mask being much shorter than that of the dragonfly nymph.

The abdomen of an adult damselfly is typically six times as long as its head and thorax combined. The relatively small thorax houses the powerful muscles controlling the relatively large wings (up to 90 mm). Like most insect groups, the venation of damselfly wings is so intricately varied that it is used as the basis upon which these insects are separated into their families. The thorax also contains the great nerve-centres that supply the insect with its sensory equipment and control of its limbs when it alights on a rock or on foliage. Sexes of the same species are often markedly different in colour.

Unlike dragonflies, damselflies fly slowly, in a fluttering flight pattern. Relatively feeble in flight, they normally search for insect prey that alights on foliage along the edges of streams.

Ecology

Being predatory, nymph and adult damselflies contribute to the biological control of mosquitoes. Damselfly nymphs in particular are an important food item for other creatures. A popular name for damselflies is 'darning needles', though they are harmless to humans.

ABOVE A male blue damselfly, often called 'blue darning needle' (*Coenagrion lyelli*). The three pairs of limbs of damselflies are progressively longer, the rear limbs adapted for the support required to grip a branch upon alighting.

DRAGONFLIES
order Odonata: suborder Anisoptera

Dragonflies are distinguished from damselflies by:
- forewings that are narrower than hind wings
- both pairs of wings horizontally spread at rest
- their fast, highly manoeuvrable flying style
- nymphs not equipped with leaf-like gills
- nymphs that are stouter and larger, with distinctive, retractable mouthparts.

A dragonfly has an indisputable beauty, and many species sport brilliant colours. Dashing above a sunlit stream, a dragonfly adds a sense of enchantment. Keen eyesight, a rapid response to danger, and powerful flying wings with a span of up to 160 mm are the main characteristics of a dragonfly in action. Their anatomical modifications are fine examples of adaption to their environment.

A dragonfly's eyes, which occupy most of its bulbous head capsule, are superb visual organs—those of some larger species have tens of thousands of facets (ommatidia), each with its own minute lens and retina. With its enormous compound eyes and highly flexible, slender neck that allows it to swivel its head almost 360°, a dragonfly has panoramic vision. The upper area of the eyes detects the slightest movement; the lower area can finely focus. Some larger species can recognise a member of the opposite sex from 40 metres while soaring in a circular pattern or dashing upstream and downstream. Three conspicuous ocelli provide additional light and also detect movement.

Its four wings can work independently or together, which gives it much greater manoeuvrability in the air. That, in combination with its excellent vision, wing power and speed, is what makes it possible for dragonflies to chase and catch fast-flying insects or evade predators so effectively, as well as to perform its vigorous, pre-nuptial courtship flights. Both nymphal and adult dragonflies are equipped with an impressive array of highly efficient devices modified for catching and holding prey.

Ecology

Both nymphal and adult dragonflies are predatory and perform an important role in the biological control of mosquitoes—hence, their popular name 'mosquito hawks'. The nymphs feed on a variety of water creatures including mosquito wrigglers (larvae and pupae), small tadpoles and tiny fish, as well as earthworms.

Dragonfly nymphs also form an important link in the food chain for other creatures. Dragonflies are sometimes also known as 'bee-butchers' and 'horse-stingers', although of course they do not sting at all, and, like damselflies, are harmless to humans (and horses). The large, colourful and widespread hawk dragonfly *Aeshna brevistyla* is often seen visiting home gardens.

STONEFLIES
order Plecoptera

Stoneflies are distinguished by:
- two pairs of soft, flattened, membranous wings held closely around the body at rest
- forewings that are slightly shorter and broader than the hind wings (up to 110 mm wingspan)
- nymphs that are equipped with gill tufts (leaf gills) stemming from the body, abdominal tip and limbs.

Stoneflies are four-winged, soft-bodied creatures that spend their nymphal life in water—like mayflies, damselflies and dragonflies. Stoneflies get their name from their close association with creeks and streams that have stony beds. The nymphs live beneath the stones in clear, running water or the wave-washed shores of freshwater lakes, feeding on plants.

Adults seldom venture far from water, and rest on rocks and trees along the water's edge, where they are well camouflaged. They take to the wing at dusk and fly up and down the stream, close to the water surface.

OPPOSITE A blue hawk dragonfly (*Aeshna* species). Dragonflies were successful in form and lifestyle early in their evolution, remaining virtually unchanged. Flight takes place by the alteration of wing surface acting upon the air. They strike the air with greater velocity on the downstroke than on the upstroke.

ABOVE Stoneflies are soft-bodied winged insects that live from sea level to high altitudes. Their aquatic nymphs form part of the freshwater food chain.

DRAGONFLIES IN THE PAST

Fossil-finds from the Triassic Period (245 million years ago) show that early dragonflies were gigantic, spanning 600 mm across their gauzy wings; even the nymphs had a body length of over 300 mm. One of the largest dragonflies now living, *Petalura ingentissima* (Petaluridae), which occurs in Australia, has a wingspan of just 160 mm and is 110 mm in length. Apart from having evolved smaller forms, all dragonfly species are remarkably uniform in bodily structure and have remained virtually unchanged in appearance and in lifestyle for millions of years. The similarity of these fossil-finds to presevnt-day forms suggests dragonfly origins lie even further back in time. When, comparatively recently, humans first appeared, dragonflies were already inconceivably ancient.

Plecopterans (whose name comes from Greek words for 'folded' and 'winged') are closely related to the orthopterans (such as grasshoppers and crickets), but are the only members of this grouping that have aquatic nymphs. With the cockroaches and mantids, stoneflies can be considered to be among the most ancient surviving insects of the orthopteroid group.

Ecology

The aquatic stonefly nymphs are extremely sensitive to pollutants, and their presence or absence at creeks and waterways is used as one indication of water quality when this is being monitored. Nymphs and adults both form part of the freshwater food chain, being food for many other creatures including several other predatory aquatic insect nymphs or larvae. Trout and salmon feed on the egg masses and hatchlings of stoneflies.

COCKROACHES
order Blattodea

Cockroaches are distinguished by:
- a greatly compressed bodily structure consisting of a large, shield-like pronotum dorsally covering the head
- a head capsule on a horizontal plane with the body
- mouthparts pointing downwards
- two reduced, 'lensless' ocelli located between the compound eyes

- both pairs of wings folded above the abdomen
- overlapping, toughened forewings, protecting the membranous flying wings.

Cockroaches tend to be universally detested. The smaller brown or reddish-brown cockroaches with their highly flattened bodies that are able to crawl into the most unlikely spaces are familiar to most people as household pests. A cockroach's most often-seen feature is its tail-end as it scuttles away from danger. But of all the species occurring in Australia, only nine are the introduced, house-frequenting species. By far the majority are native species, whose habitat is mostly confined to bushland.

Cockroaches were formerly classified as one family within the order Orthoptera, then later placed together with the mantids in another order. Now, however, cockroaches are treated as an order in their own right and, within this order, they are divided into:
- predominantly winged cockroaches (superfamily Blattoidea)
- burrowing cockroaches (superfamily Blaberoidea).

Predominantly winged cockroaches

Cockroaches in this group are members of the families Blattelidae and Blattidae. They can range in size from 3 mm–65 mm, most species having wings. Certain species can exude powerful offensive odours to thwart would-be predators.

These two families include the nine introduced species of domestic pests. The remaining species, however, are bush cockroaches that are native to Australia. Much of their life cycle is spent in and around leaf litter in bush or garden environments and many are active during daylight hours.

Burrowing cockroaches

Many burrowing cockroaches (family Blaberidae) are bulky insects with a body length of up to 70 mm. They are usually heavily armoured with thick, heavy-set bodies and spiky limbs, which are used for digging and burrowing into rotting timber and soil. The females of many native species feed their offspring on decaying leaf litter. Normally found in small colonies, the reddish-brown bush cockroach (*Panesthia laevicollis*) occurs among damp debris beneath fallen decaying timber. Although winged, they chew one another's wings off down to the base, as the wings get in the way when crawling about in their adopted habitat.

This group includes one of the largest cockroaches in the world—*Macropanesthia rhinoceros*, from northern Queensland, which measures up to 70 mm in length and spends its life cycle beneath the ground. The female forages at night, close by her burrow, for suitable food for her young, and drags leaf litter below ground. This species has become a popular pet for many people interested in studying insects; it does not carry disease and lives for many years under favourable conditions.

The highly flattened wood-frequenting cockroach (*Laxta granicollis*) has its head completely covered by the pronotum. The wingless female has numerous irregular nodules covering its entire dorsal surface. Males are fully winged and are often attracted to electric lights during spring and summer. These flattened, almost wafer-thin, cockroaches live among leaf litter, beneath flaking bark and decaying timber.

Ecology

Cockroaches are primarily scavengers, feeding on dead animal and plant material. Some species have relatively long lives—it is not uncommon for larger species such as the shiny red-brown house-pest, the American cockroach (*Periplaneta americana*) to live for 3–4 years. Most cockroaches are nocturnally active, and remain out of sight during daylight.

Cockroaches are of some considerable economic importance. They not only destroy our foodstuffs by eating them but also foul whatever they eat with their excreta to deter other animals from eating their finds. As many of us have experienced, these insects will eat an enormous range of what would normally be considered unusual and unlikely food sources— such as labels off containers or the bindings of books. They thrive in warm, damp situations, which is why they are commonly found in kitchens and laundries, preferring steam and hot-water pipes.

TERMITES
order Isoptera

Termites are distinguished by:
• a pale, elongated body (soldier castes have a large head capsule)
• two pairs of wings of equal size held flat above the body (reproductive castes), 12 mm–50 mm span
• several castes living in social colonies.

Termites are all small, pale-brown insects with a soft exoskeleton; workers have chewing mouthparts, bead-like antennae and compound eyes. They live in colonies of often thousands of individuals, divided into four or five castes.

The workers are structurally unspecialised individuals, which are blind and sexually

BELOW An American cockroach (*Periplaneta americana*). An introduced species, this is the largest cockroach that infests our homes and factories. Their egg capsules contain up to 16 eggs and each female produces as many as 50 egg capsules (800 eggs). These are normally adhered to the substrate in close proximity to food and water. Nymphs take 6–12 months to attain sexual maturity; the adults live up to four years or more. Their common name is misleading as this species probably originated in tropical Africa. Native species live a completely different lifestyle to the introduced domestic pest species and normally keep to the bushland. They generally live beneath fallen timber and feed on decaying vegetation. All native cockroach species assist in the process of soil regeneration. Some species spend their life cycle around the edges of streams and creeks.

undeveloped. They build and repair the nest and serve the king and queen.

Soldiers form another sexually undeveloped caste but in many species they are structurally specialised individuals with large heads and stout jaws. They defend the nest, act as guards for the queen and for foraging parties of workers. Should the nest be attacked, they use their heads to beat out warnings on the gallery walls.

Only reproductive castes (called alates) have wings and are sexually developed. Both pairs of wings are almost equal in length (hence the name of the order, from the Greek *isos* meaning 'equal' and the word for 'winged'), and are subsequently discarded. Alates are produced in enormous numbers during spring and summer. They leave the colony in swarms at dusk, shedding their wings when finding a mate, after which they establish new colonies.

Depending on conditions prevailing in the colony, 'supplementary reproductives' may also be present. These are pairs of males and females, which have the potential to reproduce.

Finally, there are the nymphs, which develop into whatever castes the colony needs at the time.

From the use of the popular name 'white ants' used for this group, there is a widespread but quite erroneous belief that termites are related to ants. Termites are actually greatly modified cockroaches that have evolved to live in social colonies. Their social structure is all that they have in common with ants.

Ecology

From an economic perspective, termites have an important role in the regeneration of soil. As earthworms are absent in many arid and semi-arid regions of Australia, the activities of termites allow air and water into the deeper layers of soil. However, because their food includes wood and vegetable matter, they also cause considerable damage to unprotected timbers in construction and housing, and also to furniture.

They form the diet of many other creatures, particularly of ants. Through their industrious nest-building, they also provide a wide range of microhabitats for several other creatures.

Termite colonies can be likened to perennial plants as their energy is also derived from above the ground and stored in galleries, corresponding to the roots of plants. Similarly, the nuptial flight of termites corresponds to the dispersal of winged seeds for propagation.

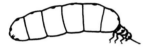

ABOVE The huge termite queen lives in a mushroom-shaped chamber of hard clay walls in the centre of the termitarium. As she lays eggs, the workers carry them to tiny cells to hatch and grow. They will shed their skins several times before reaching adulthood.

ABOVE The winged forms of termites are called alates. After leaving the nest, they mate, shed their wings and begin new colonies.

PRAYING MANTIDS
order Mantodea

Mantids are distinguished by having:
- a triangular-shaped head capable of swivelling in an almost 180° arc
- large, bulging eyes
- a long, slender neck, standing clear of the pronotum
- a pair of spiny, raptorial forelegs, held in typical prayer-like gesture and used for crushing and holding prey.

Mantids are extremely elongated creatures, with a soft exoskeleton and, normally, two pairs of wings. Their hind wings, which are always functional in the males, are for flying. A mantid is easily recognisable by its free-moving, triangular-shaped head capsule; its long, fine antennae, always alert to movement nearby; and its forelimbs characteristically held in a prayer-like position. Its large, bulging, ever-watchful eyes lend it an air of disdain for the world around it.

Mantids are ancient insects (perhaps even older than the cockroaches), and all mantid species are predatory and share the same well-defined bodily structure and lifestyles. Until recently, mantids were classed together with cockroaches, crickets, grass-hoppers and phasmatids. Now, however, they are treated as an order of their own, within which they can be arranged in two main groupings: plant-frequenting mantids and small, cryptic mantids.

The plant-frequenting mantids are green or brown, with a body length of 10 mm–130 mm. Some have brightly coloured flying wings. The large brown mantis *Archimantis latistyla*, a typical representative, measures up to 130 mm, and has a wide distribution—from coastal areas to inland regions, where it is the dominant species. Another fine example is the small green mantis *Orthodera ministralis*, measuring 40 mm long, which is commonly encountered leaping from leaf to leaf in pursuit of prey. This is readily distinguishable by its wide, flattened prothorax, blue–green colouring with bright blue markings on the inner face of the femur of its forelimbs.

Cryptic mantids are small, with a body length of up to 20 mm, and live on tree trunks or among leaf litter, where they take their prey.

Ecology

All mantids are carnivorous, and prey on a wide range of insects and spiders; male mantids are also included in the female's diet. Most species are fundamentally solitary insects that frequent grass, shrubs and tree trunks, although some live on the ground among leaf litter.

EARWIGS
order Dermaptera

Earwigs are distinguished by:
- forceps-like structures extending from the abdominal tip
- complex flying wings (when present), folded and protected by the reduced, hardened tegmina of the forewings
- short, annulated antennae
- an elongated, flattened, shiny exoskeleton.

Earwigs are instantly recognisable from their distinctive bodily structure, and particularly from their two stoutly formed rear pincers. Winged forms have amazing, intricately pleated flying wings that fold neatly away beneath their tegmina. Their pincers, which evolved out of greatly modified cerci, are purely defensive and are used like a forceps for carrying food to the nest-site, or during courtship displays.

People have long been wary of earwigs, in part owing to a wholly unfounded belief that they have a fondness for crawling into people's ears. It also stems in part from a fear of being pinched by their pincers. However, only a large species, such as the Australian giant earwig (*Titanolabis colossea*), has pincers strong enough to pierce human flesh—this is a rare occurrence.

Ecology

Earwigs are active at night and feed on plants (being minor pollinators), decaying matter or other small insects.

The introduced European earwig (*Forficula auricularia*) has proved to be serious garden pest as it feeds on the flowers and fruits of many plants, especially introduced plants. The native earwig (*Labidura truncata*) attacks coddling moth larvae (*Cydia pomonella*).

ABOVE A praying mantis (green form of an *Archimantis* species). After eyeing its prey—a meadow katydid (*Conocephalus semivittatus*)—and gauging its striking range, this stealthy hunter was positioned to strike and claim her intended meal but the alert little katydid jumped away. Mantids are commonly found in our cities and bushland. Some species are regarded as beneficial to humans as they feed on a wide range of insects that are regarded as pests.

LEFT A female giant earwig (*Titanolabis colossea*). Earwigs get their name from 'earwing' as their spread wings have the shape of a human ear. The female watches over her eggs until hatched and broods over the hatchlings the way a hen broods over her chicks.

THE ORTHOPTERANS—KATYDIDS, CRICKETS AND GRASSHOPPERS

The orthopterans date back to the Carboniferous Period (around 300 million years ago). Other closely related insects such as the mantids, cockroaches and phasmatids used to be included within the order Orthoptera (from *orthos* meaning 'straight' and the word for 'winged'). But the order is now restricted to katydids and the various crickets, and the short-horned grasshoppers, assembled into two main suborders:

- katydids and bush crickets, king crickets and tree crickets, true crickets and mole crickets—collectively known as ensiferans (suborder Ensifera)
- short-horned grasshoppers—collectively known as caeliferans (suborder Caelifera).

Each group is dealt with separately in the following pages.

Orthopterans are distinguished by:
- powerful hind legs
- leathery, elongated forewings, which typically serve as wing covers
- fan-like, membranous hind wings

- biting, chewing mandibles
- antennae that characteristically are long for ensiferans and short for caeliferans.

All orthopterans undergo gradual metamorphosis. They range in size considerably (body length varies from 5 mm–120 mm), but their most obvious shared physical feature is their powerful hind legs. Most orthopterans also have similar mandibles, suitable for chewing or biting.

Orthopterans are also world famous for their singing, which is an important element of their courtship. For ensiferans, the combination of touching one another with their long, thread-like antennae and the vibrations of their singing, stimulates the sexes into mating.

Sound-making
Numerous species have sound-producing organs, usually involving the forewings. The familiar chirping chorus heard in meadows, trees and shrubs is made by many of the long-horned species (superfamily Tettigonioidea). These insects have a row of tiny pegs

on the left forewing that they rub against a stiffened, modified wing vein on the right forewing. Part of the right forewing membrane—the 'mirror'—is circular, and modified to amplify the sound.

Some species of short-horned grasshoppers have a different method of producing their mating call. They do it by rubbing a row of tiny, peg-like protrusions, situated on the largest joint of the hind legs, against prominent ribs and veins of the forewings.

Many orthopterans have hearing organs. Long-horned grasshoppers and bush crickets (family Tettigoniidae) have theirs located on their forelegs. These can be seen as fine slits situated on an enlarged portion of the tibiae of the front legs. The organs with which katydids, crickets and short-horned grasshoppers receive sound is located on the forelegs; they also act as directional micro-phones as vibrations resonate upon them. Others have their organs of hearing located just behind their thoracic region on both sides of the abdomen; in some others they are located on the last segment of the thorax (the metathorax).

Some of these insects are equipped to distinguish sounds as closely separated as one-hundredth of a second (by comparison, human ears cannot distinguish separated sounds closer than one-tenth of a second). It is by the rhythm frequency that a female recognises a serenade from a male of her species. The mating song of the male long-horned grasshopper can be picked up by the female from a distance of 10 metres or more.

Depending on the species, crickets and grass-hoppers can produce at least five distinct sounds by rubbing their wings together in various ways:

- a spontaneous call during courtship
- the rival song between competing males
- a triumphant song prior to actual mating
- the mating song, causing the female to mount a singing male in her eagerness to mate
- the mating song of the female when ready to receive a mate.

Ecology

Orthopterans feed mainly on plants, and most short-horned grasshoppers are entirely herbivorous. However, many species of katydids, tree crickets and king crickets are carnivorous and regularly feed on the eggs, nymphs, larvae and adults of other arthropods.

Orthopterans are of great economic importance worldwide, as several species of locusts, grass-hoppers and crickets occur in cyclic plague populations, and feed on cultivated food crops,

causing famine in some countries. However, they are also important links in the food chain, forming a good part of the diet of many other creatures, including frogs, lizards, insectivorous birds and mammals. The yellow-winged grasshopper (*Gastrimagus musicus*) produces a single generation per year in temperate zones, but more than one in tropical zones.

KATYDIDS AND THE VARIOUS CRICKETS
order Orthoptera: suborder Ensifera

Ensifera is one of two main suborders of Orthoptera and includes:
- katydids and long-horned bush crickets (superfamily Tettigonioidea)
- true crickets and mole crickets (superfamily Grylloidea)
- king crickets, wetas and tree crickets (superfamily Gryllacridoidea).

Their long antennae readily distinguish ensiferans from the short-horned grasshoppers (or locusts). Many ensiferans, typically, have large appetites and a number of species with predatory tendencies feed on other insects as well as on vegetation.

Ensiferans are distinguished by:
- long, thread-like antennae, normally consisting of over 30 segments
- a long, sword-like ovipositor stemming from the tip of the female's abdomen
- the chirping sound they make as mating calls, and the stridulatory equipment used for this purpose.

Katydids and long-horned bush crickets

All these insects (family Tettigoniidae) are generally plant-feeders and nocturnally active (body length: 5 mm–80 mm). Most katydids and bush crickets have specialised ovipositors for inserting their eggs into young stems or leaves, although some species cement their eggs in rows on leaves or branches. A number of species also attack other insects, however, and feed on them, their eggs and their young.

The katydids, whose sparse and varied chirping calls can be heard echoing during warm summer evenings, are members of the largest subfamily of the tettigoniids (Phaneropterinae). These insects live among the foliage of trees, shrubs and tall grasses, remaining well camouflaged with their leaf-like wings. A typical example is the common green katydid (*Caedicia simplex*), which emits a soft chirping during the night from among the trees and foliage of gardens and bushland. However, all species can produce a musical chirping call. The mountain katydid (*Acripeza reticulata*) is a curious representative as both males and females have striking warning colours adorning the abdomen and flash these whenever threatened.

Meadow katydids are commonly known as bullyheads (subfamily Conocephalinae). They live among the grasses and are also mostly plant-feeders—a typical representative being the small green meadow katydid (*Conocephalus semivittatus*). These active insects can be heard chirping softly in low herbage and grasses throughout the warmer months, and are commonly found in home gardens, paddocks and meadows in patches of undisturbed grass and low-growing herbage.

True crickets and mole crickets

Gryllidae, the true crickets, constitute the largest family in this grouping. The fascination these insects have exercised over people stems from their shrill chirping performed throughout warm summer evenings. They produce the sound by rubbing together their highly modified wing covers, each of which has a file-like process and a stiffened vein serving as a scraper when used against the opposite one. The chirpy little black field-cricket (or black house-cricket) *Teleogryllus commodus* is typical of this group. It will remain out of sight beneath rocks and timber during daylight, emerging in the evening to resume its activities.

Mole crickets (family Gryllotalpidae), on the other hand, mainly dwell underground and are well-equipped for digging among the grass roots. Female mole crickets construct neat subterranean chambers the size and shape of a

BELOW A black field-cricket (*Teleogryllus commodus*). Field crickets are mainly vegetarian but will eat insects, dead animals and household scraps. During late summer, the female uses her ovipositor to insert her eggs into the ground, which hatch the following spring. Their hearing organs or 'ears' are situated in a pit on each front leg.

hen's egg, some 20 cm beneath the surface of the soil. This serves as their retreat and as a brood chamber in which their eggs are laid. The loud-shrilling, glossy mole cricket (*Gryllotalpa nitidula*) and the velvet mole cricket (*G. australis*) are typical representatives.

King crickets, wetas, and tree crickets

All these insects are grouped in the superfamily Gryllacridoidea, and are nocturnal in their habits. They go foraging during the night for their prey, which consists of a wide range of arthropods (both spiders and insects, including their eggs and young). The females of most of these long-horned crickets insert their eggs into the tissue of young stems or leaves of a wide range of plants, using their long, sword-shaped ovipositors.

The king crickets, also known as wood crickets, and wetas (both in the family Stenopelmatidae) are mainly large insects, and wingless. The males of certain species of

Stenopelmatidae are equipped with powerful—and sometimes enormous—mandibles, which are used to rip and tear prey apart. King crickets and wetas have a restricted range of distribution, being found on Australia's east coast, except for the genus *Onosandrus*, which occurs in Western Australia. A typical species is the large, king log cricket (*Australostoma opacum*), which is 45 mm long.

The tree crickets (family Gryllacrididae) constitute the most numerous family of this grouping and have a wider distribution. These are generally large, brown- and cream-coloured winged insects. Several species are also equipped with powerful mandibles. They frequent the ground, shrubs and tree trunks at night, where they move about feeding on both vegetation and live prey. A typical species is the commonly encountered large tree cricket (*Paragryllacris combusta*), which often enters our homes during warm summer evenings, normally hiding behind curtains and drapes.

ABOVE Female velvet mole crickets (*Gryllotalpa australis*) sometimes lay as many as 400 dusky yellow eggs. The roof of the nursery is constructed near the surface so that the sun's warmth can pass through and incubate the eggs. Mole crickets have well-developed flying wings and often fly into electric lights on summer nights.

OPPOSITE Having fallen from a *Eucalyptus* tree, this eucalypt stick insect (*Ctenomorpha chronus*) clings to a red-and-green kangaroo paw (*Aniganthos manglesi*). It will adopt its twig-mimicking stance here until nightfall, when most stick insects are active.

SHORT-HORNED GRASSHOPPERS
order Orthoptera: suborder Caelifera

Caeliferans are distinguished by:
- short, many-segmented antennae
- high populations during some seasons (with certain species)
- an insatiable appetite for plant matter.

Caelifera includes the short-horned grasshoppers, named for their short antennae, which instantly identify them. Two superfamilies present in Australia are Acridoidea (without cone-shaped heads), and Pamphagoidea (distinctly cone-headed). Short-horned grasshoppers are also commonly known as locusts and are entirely vegetarian in their feeding habits. They generally lay their eggs in the soil or sometimes in rotting timber, and none of the Australian species produce mating calls.

The most numerous group is Acridoidea, with just one Australian family—Acrididae. The females of this group are equipped with an ovipositor shaped in the form of a digging tool, and a typical representative is the locust pest or plague locust (*Chortoicetes terminifera*).

Of the superfamily Pamphagoidea, which are also known as pointed-nosed locusts, there is also a single Australian family—Pyrgomorphidae. A typical species is the smartly attired, green, cone-headed grasshopper (*Atractomorpha similis*), which is often found in home gardens, especially among long grasses and herbage in undisturbed corners. It will remain there perfectly concealed until disturbed, during gardening for instance.

BELOW A female blistered pyrgomorph grasshopper (*Monistria pustulifera*). If attacked, this leathery-skinned species regurgitates a frothy liquid (toxic plant juices) from special gland openings—an effective protection from predators.

STICK INSECTS AND LEAF INSECTS (PHASMATIDS)
order Phasmatodea

Phasmatids are distinguished by:
- long, stick-like or leaf-like bodies, cryptically coloured, to match their surroundings
- short, overlapping forewings (when present) that do not cover flying wings
- long, thin limbs held close to the body when at rest among foliage.

The most obvious features of stick insects and leaf insects are their size and their amazing stick-like and leaf-like forms, by means of which they mimic twigs or leaves. Most phasmatids have extremely elongated bodies (body length 30 mm–300 mm) and long slender legs that are often adorned with spines and flanges. Like their close relatives, the grasshoppers, crickets, cockroaches and mantids, they have chewing mouthparts and two pairs of wings.

Phasmatids were originally classified as a single family within the order Orthoptera, but they are now placed in their own order, with two families, Phasmatidae and Phylliidae.

Many of the larger species of stick insects are sometimes kept as pets and are particularly appealing because they carry no human diseases, cannot bite or sting, and may live relatively long lives, some for up to three years.

Stick insects
The family Phasmatidae includes all of the true stick-like insects, their body lengths ranging from 30 mm–300 mm. A typical representative of the group is the frequently encountered violet-winged stick insect (*Didymuria violescens*), which is from the subfamily Tropidoderinae, measuring up to 120 mm long. Another large species from the same subfamily is the 130 mm-long *Extatosoma tiaratum*. It is extremely spiny and curls its abdomen above its head as it rests in full disguise among the twigs and leaves. Certain species are larger—the giant Australian stick insect (*Acrophylla titan*), for instance, measures over 250 mm long. Its tightly folded, marble-patterned hind wings are beautifully coloured in purple-brown. The eucalypt stick insect (*Ctenomorpha chronus*) resembles twigs and stems of euclaypts. The male is fully winged, but the female has very short tegmina.

ABOVE A nymph of a spiny leaf insect (*Extatosoma tiaratum*). This species has developed an amazing degree of protective resemblance as its exoskeleton strongly resembles a leaf. Unless moving about, it usually remains unseen among the foliage and branches on which it feeds.

ABOVE Web-spinners are remarkable insects that have the ability to spin silken shelters using silk glands within their enlarged globular-shaped fore tarsi.

Leaf insects

True leaf insects (family Phylliidae) are remarkable for their mimicry of leaves. They have a maximum body length of 60 mm. A typical example is the short-antennaed leaf insect (*Phyllium siccifolium*), which is commonly found within sclerophyll forests in eastern Australia. Representatives of the subfamily Phylliinae are mostly thin, medium-sized insects that frequent tall grasses and shrubs.

Ecology

All phasmatids are herbivores, favouring the leaves and tender twigs of native plants, mainly eucalypts and acacias, and young eucalypt leaves in particular; most other plants are ignored. Most species are solitary but some are gregarious during certain seasons (owing to climatic conditions) and can occur in enormous populations cyclically, at which times they also provide food for other creatures, including birds.

When they occur in such large numbers, the foliage of eucalypts is denuded in their wake, although only a few species are known to defoliate eucalypt forests. Such heavy pruning

can kill trees but it certainly also robs the forest of fuel for bushfires, which may be a strategic move on their part. For it means that their eggs, which usually lay bare on the ground, will at least survive until the following season, when the plants have regrown their leaves.

WEB-SPINNERS
order Embioptera

Web-spinners are distinguished by:
• bulbous tarsal segments
• two small cerci at the tip of the abdomen, which are asymmetrical in males
• their production of silk.

Web-spinners have similar bodily structure to that of termites (order Isoptera) and earwigs (order Dermaptera), but are more closely related to stoneflies (order Plecoptera). However, these small- to medium-sized insects (body length 3 mm–12 mm) have a distinct feature all their own—swollen tarsal segments (fore tarsi), which house their silk glands. The presence of these tarsal segments distinguishes Embioptera from all other orders, as the ability to produce silk in the adult stage is rare among insects.

An adult male is usually winged and moves about in its search for females; but then, after mating, its life cycle is complete. Females are usually wingless and spend their lives in the silken galleries they manufacture. Web-spinners are gregarious insects with social tendencies— the females guard their eggs and the young nymphs until they are able to form their own silken galleries.

Web-spinners are mostly tropical insects, varying little in their lifestyle throughout the world. However, their habitats vary among the species—some live beneath bark or rocks, or in cracks in the ground; others live in humus or moss, or even inside termite nests. Web-spinners feed on vegetable matter, dead leaves, bark and living mosses and lichens.

BARK-LICE
order Psocoptera

Bark-lice (also known as booklice) are small, delicate, membranous-winged arthropods measuring 1 mm–10 mm in body length. They are closely related to animal-lice (order Phthiraptera), but differ markedly in lifestyle.

Booklice are commonly found on tree bark and among books and are characterised by a large, bulbous, mobile head capsule. They generally feed on minute particles of dried animal and vegetable material, and dead insects. Trogiidae and Liposcelidae are typical families. Some larger species such as *Myopsocus griseipennis* are seen in large numbers during summer months feeding on algae and fungi growing in cool, damp situations on fences or tiles.

ANIMAL-LICE
order Phthiraptera

Animal-lice are small insects, measuring 0.5 mm–10 mm in body length, that lack wings. They have developed specialised mouthparts that are modified for biting or sucking (depending on the species), and are placed in three suborders: Anoplura (sucking lice),

Mallophaga (biting lice), and Rhynchoph-thirina (elephant-lice).

All animal-lice feed on the blood or tissue of a wide range of vertebrates, including birds, reptiles, bats and seals. Fortunately, only two species parasitise humans: the crab-louse (*Pthirus pubis*), and the body- or head-louse (*Pediculus humanus*). The crab-louse does not transmit diseases. The body- or head-louse, however, is known to transmit diseases such as typhus and trench fever. These lice can infest people who are living in crowded or unhygienic conditions, and they have a particular liking for living in hair that is washed infrequently. Their eggs are commonly called 'nits' and these are often found cemented to strands of hair close to the scalp. Bird-lice and mammal-lice are host-specific and so, apart from their unpleasant associations, they rarely pose problems for humans.

LEFT Bark-lice live on and under bark, leaf litter, on foliage and beneath rocks and stones. They feed on lichens, fungi, algae, dead insects and plant tissue.

ABOVE Bark-lice are also commonly known as book-lice as they feed on skin and dust found in between the pages of books. They shelter in the book's spine.

ABOVE Animal-lice parasitise all orders of birds and most mammals. Their limbs are modified to move through feathers, fur and hair.

LEFT Most species of animal-lice parasitise marsupials or birds, such as this eastern yellow robin (*Eopsaltria australis*). Eggs are adhered to feathers and hatch soon afterwards.

RIGHT A male yellow Monday cicada (*Cyclochila australasiae*). This species has survived urbanisation and thrives in large cities, appearing in millions during peak seasons in late spring and summer. Several different variants of this well-loved insect exist, each affectionately named according to colour and body pattern. Its popular names have been around since the late 1800s and remain unchanged—the wholly orange-coloured 'yellow Monday', the orange and black 'masked bandit', the rich tan-coloured 'chocolate soldier', the 'black prince', the 'brown baker' and the well-known 'greengrocer'.

THE HEMIPTERANS—APHIDS, CICADAS, HOPPERS AND TRUE BUGS

The order Hemiptera includes insects of great diversity and enormous populations, testimony to their success. Different groups are dealt with separately on the following pages.

Hemipterans undergo a gradual metamorphosis, averaging (according to each particular species) 3–7 moults to reach maturity. In a few cases, however, the nymphs and the adults do not look anything like one another and they also lead completely different lifestyles—cicadas being the most obvious example. The order Hemiptera is assembled into three suborders, according to the insects' bodily structure and lifestyle:

- Sternorrhyncha (aphids, mealy bugs, scale insects and gall-forming insects), collectively called sternorrhynchans

- Auchenorrhyncha (cicadas, and various plant-hoppers), that are collectively called auchenorrhynchans
- Heteroptera (all 'true bugs'—aquatic and semi-aquatic bugs, assassin bugs, plant bugs and shield-bugs), collectively called heteropterans. The term 'true bug' is used here to describe heteropterans alone ('bug' is often misused as a word for any kind of insect, even for butterflies and spiders).
  Hemipterans can be distinguished by having:
- a head capsule that either has negligible movement, being held rigidly against the thorax (sternorrhynchans and auchenorrhynchans), or moves freely on the thorax (heteropterans)
- sucking mouthparts fused into a single, heavily sclerotised, beak-like rostrum
- short antennae with fewer than 10 segments.
- nymphs that have wing buds after early moults
- the body-shape of most true bugs (observed from above), which is formed from five closely fitting triangular shapes: the head and prothorax combined makes one; the scutellum forms the second; the basal section of each wing forms another two; the overlapping wing membrane forms the final one
- both pairs of wings being held when at rest: either roof-like over the body (sternorrhynchans and auchenorrhynchans), or flat over the abdomen (heteropterans).
  Water bugs and shield-bugs are distinguished by having:
- a head capsule, usually triangular-shaped, able to move from side to side
- hardened forewings (when present)—in shield-bugs these are fused
- a heavily sclerotised exoskeleton
- short antennae with fewer than five segments
- a beak or rostrum stemming from the head, which is held protected between the bases of the legs when the insect is at rest.

Ecology

All hemipterans feed by siphoning juices through their rostrum, so their diet is entirely liquid. The evolution of their specially modified mouthparts has given hemipterans enormous opportunities for exploiting what would otherwise be unavailable food sources. The rostrum is uniquely adapted for piercing the tough-walled cells of their host plant's epidermis, thus enabling hemipterans to tap into and feed on the sap. However, when occurring in high numbers, hemipterans can cause considerable damage to food crops and plants.

Sternorrhynchans and auchenorrhynchans feed entirely on plant juices. Some heteropteran species suck the blood of other animals, like the bed bug (*Cimex lectularius*), which was introduced into Australia at the time of European settlement. Other predatory species—such as assassin bugs—feed on the fluids of animals, including other arthropods. However, heteropterans feed mainly on a wide range of plants in gardens, parks, reserves and bushland.

Auchenorrhynchan females have sharp, spear-shaped ovipositors. They use these to slit tiny rows into the tree bark. One egg is laid into every slit, and the eggs hatch during warm weather. However, this slitting can sometimes cause the tree to bleed, producing large quantities of flowing sap, which sets into hard crystals in the sunshine.

A curious feature of many sternorrhynchan and auchenorrhynchan species is that they will often be found in company with ants. Sometimes they are even protected by the ants, which are attracted by the copious quantities of honeydew many species produce from their body glands. This is a symbiotic relationship in which both types of insects benefit; the hemipterans gaining protection from the ants.

LEFT Banded gumtree-hoppers (*Eurymela* species), attended by *Iridomyrmex* ants. These insects are normally attended by ants, which feed on the sweet honeydew they exude. The nymphs are decidedly gregarious and huddle even closer if disturbed.

ABOVE Pink-white wax scale insects (*Ceroplastes destructor*). These insects pack closely together, enclosed in thick waxy encrustations. In Asia this wax is used commercially to make candles, cosmetics and medicines. The closely related cochineal insects are boiled in water, dried, and ground to make valuable orange and red dyes for colouring cotton, foodstuffs and drinks.

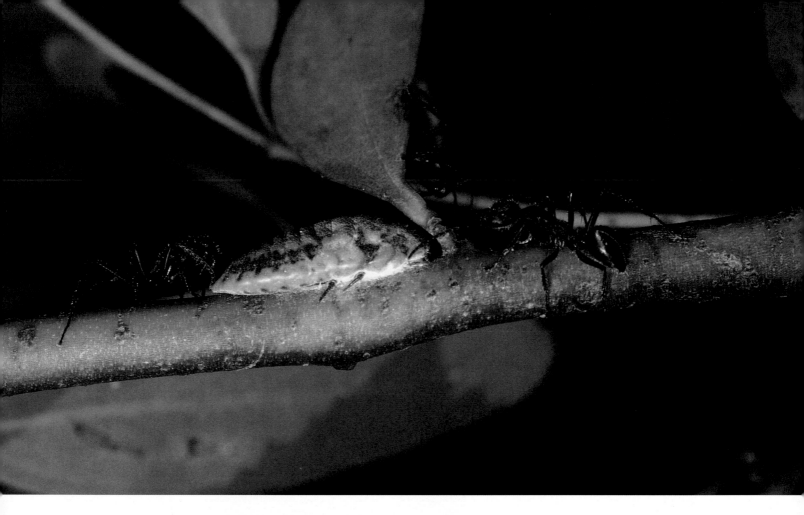

ABOVE A mealy bug or giant scale insect (*Monophlebulus pilosior*). Mealy bugs are large, soft-bodied scale insects clothed with a dense mealy wax and trailing filaments. The honeydew exuded by these insects is greatly prized by ants—here the mealy bug is being attended by golden-tailed ants (*Polyhachis* species). An orange and purple-coloured species, it lives on eucalypt trunks and covers its eggs with a mass of fine fluted 'wool'.

APHIDS, MEALY BUGS, SCALE INSECTS, GALL-FORMING INSECTS AND ALLIES
order Hemiptera:
suborder Sternorrhyncha

Aphids

Aphids are all rather tiny insects, measuring 1 mm–6 mm, most species being green, pink or black. They have soft exoskeletons and an enlarged central abdominal region with two slender tubes rising from the tip of their abdomen. Their life history is a complex story, involving generations of parthenogenetic reproduction (see Chapter Two). Consequently, adults may be winged or wingless according to the season. There are three families of aphids throughout the world, all of which are represented in Australia.

Common aphids (family Aphididae), popularly known as green-flies or plant-lice, are well-known, especially to gardeners. The best-known is the rose aphid (*Macrosiphum rosae*). Normally bright green in colour, but sometimes pink, it swarms upon young stems and buds of plants, especially roses. There are some indigenous species—including *Aphis acaenovinae*, which feeds on most plants of the family Rosaceae; and *Aphis platylobii*, which feeds on plants of the family Fabaceae.

Mealy bugs

Mealy bugs are mostly soft-bodied insects that lack any form of protective covering, although some species have scaly plumes stemming from their abdominal tips. They are large, sluggish creatures, some females of the larger species attaining a length of 40 mm. The large females have incredibly short legs, with which they are only just able to move about, if necessary.

Mealy bugs are considered the most primitive group in the superfamily Coccoidea (which also includes scale insects and gall-forming insects), and a typical example is *Monophlebulus pilosior*, which feeds on eucalypts. They also are often attended by ants, which eagerly drink the honeydew they exude.

Scale insects

Scale insects constitute the largest coccoid family. They are highly specialised and have bodies up to 3 mm long and are covered entirely with an armoured scale. The tiny nymphs are active briefly, before settling down to feed.

A female securely attaches itself to leaves or stems by deeply embedding its rostrum in the host plant, and forms its protective covering of waxy scale, beneath which it lives. The males are free-living and move about in search of females, being readily transported on winds.

Once the females, which are legless, settle down to feed, they remain attached to the host plant for the remainder of their life cycle—and sometimes the plant's.

White wax scale insects (family Coccidae) are soft-bodied and covered in waxy scales. They can gather in enormous numbers on a single plant. An example of this group is the pink-white wax scale insect (*Ceroplastes destructor*), which feeds on citrus trees.

Gall-forming insects

The distinctive woody galls, especially common on the stems of eucalypts and acacias, are often produced by the plant in response to the irritation caused by the tunnelling and feeding activities of the females of the genus *Apiomorpha*. The galls form a brood chamber for the females; the males, which are smaller, often spend their developmental phase within the outgrowths of the maternal gall.

Gall-forming insects (family Eriococcidae) have a body maximum length of 6 mm. The females remain sealed within the gall, living out their lives within it. The males, by contrast, are winged and very active, moving freely from one plant to another.

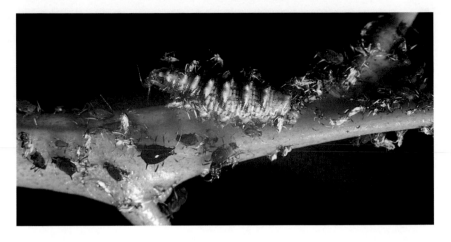

Ecology

Only 20 known species of aphid are endemic to Australia. The remaining 143 species are of foreign origin or cosmopolitan, and are serious pests of cultivated plants, but especially of introduced plants.

Many species of scale insects cause problems for their host plants because they promote fungal growth. The pink wax scale insect *Ceroplastes rubens* causes the spread of sooty mould, which grows on the sugary exudate from scale insects and can cover leaves, slowing plant growth.

Where scale insects occur on shrubs and trees, you will often also find ants, aphids and predatory insects such ladybird beetle adults and larvae. The ants protect the scales so that they can feed off the copious honeydew the scales produce. The aphids try to avoid their predators, the ladybirds, by staying close to the ants.

ABOVE Aphids (*Macrosiphum* species) being attacked by predacious hoverfly larva. Native aphid species are few; the numerous harmful species that attack crops, fruit trees, vegetables and flowers are all introduced.

LEFT Closed woody galls on *Eucalyptus* leaves formed by *Schedotrioza* species, a gall-forming insect. Galls on leaves and plant stems are caused by a wide range of insects within the orders Hemiptera, Coleoptera, Lepidoptera, Diptera and Hymenoptera, as well as by gall mites. Eggs and larvae in the plant tissues cause irritation to the plant, which then responds by growing some remarkable shapes around the annoyance, each being characteristic of the plant species and the insect species involved.

CICADAS
order Hemiptera:
suborder Auchenorrhyncha
superfamily Cicadoidea

In Australia summertime is associated with the shrill songs of cicadas, which normally reach a crescendo at dusk. From a patch of shrubs can come a sudden burst of song—the chorus of cicadas singing their hearts out—and just as suddenly it will cease. Although cicadas are not restricted to any one particular food plant, they tend to congregate on any available tree or shrub rather than disperse themselves over a wide area.

These large, often brightly coloured, insects are familiar to most of us mainly because they have readily adapted themselves to cities and suburban environments. Most people enjoy their chorus but, when the larger species drum together in high numbers, it can become almost deafening. Nevertheless, they are generally regarded with affection, as suggested by the variety of their common names (many dating from the 18th century)—such as hairy cicada, greengrocer, yellow Monday, brown-baker, masked-devil, masked-bandit, double-drummer, black prince, bladder cicada, cherry-nose, whisky-drinker, fiddler, floury-baker, floury-miller, scissors-grinder and razor-grinder.

Cicadas are distinguished by:
- their loud, incessant singing (except those in the family Tettigarctidae, which are not known to produce sound)
- three glittering, diamond-like ocelli on the crown of the head, and two large, bulbous eyes
- two pairs of membranous wings—hyaline (glass-like or clear) in most species, or opaque or smoky in some species—held roof-like over the body
- long, heavily sclerotised sucking mouthparts (the rostrum) beneath the head
- enlarged femora of the forelegs (remnants of the specialised digging equipment used during the nymphal stage)
- a pair of sound-producing organs (timbals), and a pair of sound-receiving organs (tympanums), which all males are equipped with—except in the family Tettigarctidae
- a consistency in lifestyle and bodily structure between species (except in Tettigarctidae)—size and colouring being the only variants.

Cicadas are placed in the suborder Auchenorrhyncha along with leaf hoppers and tree hoppers. The sound-producing cicada species (family Cicadidae) constitute the largest group in Australia but there are also just two species of hairy cicadas (family Tettigarctidae). Australian cicadas have clear or smoky wings but some overseas species have brightly coloured wings.

Cicadas are 10 mm–60 mm long, and have wingspans of up to 140 mm. There are variations in pigmentation, colouring and patterns in cicadas. Species that are usually green can often vary in colour—from yellow or orange to turquoise to pink or brown. On the other hand, the colouring, body patterns and wing markings of most species are fairly consistent and very helpful in identification.

The silent, hairy cicadas (family Tettigarctidae) are the only known 'fossil' cicada species and clearly resemble species from Mesozoic and Tertiary strata. Members of this family have body lengths of 10 mm–30 mm, and wingspans up to 100 mm. The hairy cicada (*Tettigarcta crinita*) is the larger of two living species, and is found on the southeastern mainland, particularly in high country and alpine regions, sometimes in large numbers. The smaller of the two species, the Tasmanian hairy cicada (*Tettigarcta tomentosa*), is found only in Tasmania.

All cicadas, like other hemipterans, rely on plant fluids for their nourishment throughout their life cycle. They take these in by way of a sucking, siphoning action, using their sharply pointed rostrums. Because they take in large amounts of fluids, they need to avoid excessive haemolymph dilution, and they do this by quickly eliminating surplus liquid. So much of this liquid is regularly discharged at once that an apparent shower of rain falls from trees where high populations of cicadas are congregating.

With the first indication that summer is beginning, and when the conditions are right, the nymphs begin to emerge from the soil, each climbing a tree in order to undergo its startling transformation from being an earthbound creature (see Chapter Two). Under the most favourable conditions, an adult cicada can live for around six weeks—a short burst of freedom compared to all the years they spend as nymphs in darkness underground.

The cicadas' celebration of summer continues for many weeks but, as the season

OPPOSITE A double-drummer cicada (*Thopha saccata*). At 120 decibels, males of this huge insect are the loudest insects on Earth, followed by the large greengrocer (*Cyclochila australasiae*). Unlike most large cicadas, which throw their voice, this species produces a directional mating call. Its populations fluctuate from extremely high to low in some seasons. It ranges from southern New South Wales to north Queensland. Clinging alongside it is a large ridgeback locust (*Goniaea australasiae*).

progresses, they lose their vitality and drop to the ground in large numbers. Many are mutilated by birds, and lie beneath trees with torn wings, broken limbs, or their entire abdomen missing. So long as their head and thorax are intact, they can still crawl about on their remaining limbs. The males' great muscle columns are often exposed by the tearing of a bird's beak. But even in this state some of the hardiest individuals continue purring sad notes, remnants of their once joyful songs.

Ecology

Cicada nymphs spend many years underground, feeding on tree roots, and can occur in enormous populations that include nymphs at varying stages of growth. In exchange for nourishing themselves on the abundant cool sap, the nymphs greatly assist the roots of the host plant by aerating the soil, and allowing water to penetrate the ground more deeply. Eucalypts, banksias, jacarandas, poplars, weeping willows, peppercorns, as well as most cultivated fruit trees, are examples of plants that supply the needs of some species such as the greengrocer cicada (*Cyclochila australasiae*).

As adults, cicadas form a part of the food chain, supplying numerous creatures with food, including spiders and predatory insects such as large assassin flies and mantids. When cicadas are plentiful, local insectivorous birds and other predacious creatures feast on them. Cicada nymphs and adults are susceptible to several species of fungi, which sometimes results in large populations being wiped out.

BELOW This male grass-hermit cicada (*Cicadetta tristrigata*) clearly shows the principal body segments typical of adult cicadas—the head, thorax, abdomen and genitalia.

Cicadas' music-making

The mating calls of cicadas were among the first sounds made by terrestrial creatures. There are a number of distinct types of singing, especially among the larger species:
- spontaneous chorus singing
- rival, competitive singing
- triumphant singing prior to mating
- broken or erratic singing when sensing approaching danger.

Cicadas also produce other sounds, not regarded as singing:
- a disjointed cry of alarm when captured, which can be so noisy that a predator will loosen its hold momentarily, affording the cicada a chance to escape
- an erratic-sounding 'death rattle' produced by the breakdown of the nervous system in the exhausted male at the end of his life.

Female cicadas (like many true bugs, grasshoppers, katydids, crickets and some moths) have highly attuned hearing. They are able to recognise high-frequency sounds produced by the males of their species, but they remain silent themselves.

The calls of the males assemble the local populations of a particular species into groups of both sexes. For this reason songs vary greatly among the different species—from the intermittent hissing of the floury-baker cicada (*Abricta curvicosta*) to the high-pitched drumming of the double-drummer cicada (*Thopha saccata*). Males of the same species often congregate to increase their vocal presence amid the deafening chorus of other local species.

A male cicada has a unique anatomy for producing these songs. Its abdomen is mostly hollow, the organs being tightly compacted into the abdominal walls. The timbals or 'drums' which produce the sound consist of a pair of ribbed membranes located within the first segment of the abdomen above the tympanums or sound receivers (which are commonly mistaken for the timbals). Both the tympanums and the timbals are protected by covers.

The cicada produces and varies its song by using its specialised muscles to rapidly vibrate its timbals, at a rate of up to 4000 times per second, in combination with abdominal movement. As the sounds are produced, they resonate within the air-filled cavities of the abdomen, and are greatly amplified because of its hollowness.

TREE HOPPERS, LEAF HOPPERS AND FROGHOPPERS
order Hemiptera: suborder Auchenorrhyncha, infraorder Cicadomorpha

The great majority of species of the super-family Cicadelloidea are leaf hoppers (family Cicadellidae). Two families account for the considerably fewer species of tree-hoppers (Eurymelidae and Membracidae). Froghoppers belong to a different superfamily (Cercopoidea) but are closely related. Tree hoppers and leaf hoppers are distinguished by:
- leathery forewings held roof-like over the more membranous hind wings
- adults that are superficially cicada-like, in miniature, but typically without sound-producing organs
- in some species an intimate association with ants, which protect them in exchange for their sweet exudations from abdominal glands.

Tree hoppers
There are two families of tree hoppers. All species of tree hoppers feed on the sap of young stems and branches of eucalypts and, for some species, casuarinas.

Those in the family Membracidae are the smaller of the two, with a body length of no more than 6 mm, and are characterised by their amazing thoracic shapes—all modifications of the prothorax. They have an enlarged pronotum, often adorned with bizarre-shaped domes and spines that extend above the body. In some species the enlarged pronotum is longer in its vertical height than the length of the body itself. When viewed from above, these insects appear as elongated triangles, ornamented with a single or double horn.

Members of the family Eurymelidae have a maximum body length of 10 mm–20 mm. Many species in this family are strikingly coloured creatures adorned in dark iridescent-blue, with splotches of bright yellow, red and white; pastel shades are not uncommon, too. Perhaps the best-known ones are the colourful gumtree-hoppers (*Eurymela* species), which feed on eucalypts and casuarinas, and whose nymphs are the ones most often attended by ants. The ants have a voracious appetite for the honeydew that these insects so readily exude.

Leaf hoppers
All leaf hoppers feed on the sap of the young stems, branches and trunks of eucalypts. Their flattened body shape leaves no shadow as they move about during daylight. The leaf hoppers *Ledromorpha planirostris* and *Cephalelus ianthe* are fine representatives of the group.

Most species are green or brown, and are less than 20 mm in body length, although some may be as much as 30 mm. The majority can only be distinguished from their close allies by the shape of the genitalia of the males, and the ovipositors of the females.

Froghoppers
Froghoppers have a wingspan of 25 mm or larger, and occur throughout Australia, being represented in three families: Cercopidae, Aphrophoridae and Machaerotidae. They are closely related to the leaf hoppers in their general bodily structure and, in common with them, have leathery forewings that are held roof-like over the membranous hind wings. Their forewing venation is very different. There are also some differences in lifestyle, although they all feed off sap and adults are able to jump. Although very similar in appearance to the adults of related families, froghoppers do, superficially, look frog-like.

Froghopper nymphs are called spittlebugs because they produce spittle. They are instantly recognisable from the sticky bubble surrounding them. Usually found on *Eucalyptus* tree trunks, they also feed on various other plants. As one feeds on the sap, it continually moves from side to side in order to recharge its supply of

ABOVE A late instar nymph green leaf hopper (*Ledromorpha* species). Nymphs of these leaf hoppers closely resemble large seeds. Wafer-thin, they remain remarkably well camouflaged. They cling to the leaves and trunks of eucalypts, feeding on sap.

OPPOSITE Gumtree-hoppers (*Eurymela bicolor*). These colourful, cicada-like insects feed on *Eucalyptus* sap. All species of this family (Eurymelidae) are gregarious and are found wherever eucalypts thrive. Both adults and nymphs have mutual interactions with ants, which attend them for their honeydew. Plant stems are used as communication channels to signal one another, the subtle vibrations sensed through their limbs and bodies.

oxygen—this action causes the frothy mass of bubbles to form. It lives within this frothy mass, which acts to deter potential predators. The mass diminishes as the insect nears maturity, at which time the pale yellow nymph remains motionless awaiting its transformation into an adult. Not long afterwards, it emerges from its nymphal skin and, when its wings have dried and hardened, it moves about the leaves and tree trunks. Two generations occur during the year, one in September and the other in January.

Ecology

Large numbers of nymphs and adults crowd together on the young shoots, feeding on the plant sap. Tree-hoppers and leaf hoppers are frequently attended by numerous ants, although some species (especially those of the family Eurymelidae) are more favoured than others. The ants rely for their sustenance on the honeydew these insects exude and, in fact, it provides a large part of their diet during particular times of the year. In exchange, the ants protect them from many would-be predators.

LANTERN FLIES AND VARIOUS PLANT HOPPERS
order Hemiptera: suborder Auchenorrhyncha infraorder Fulgoromorpha

Lantern flies and long-winged plant hoppers

Lantern flies (family Fulgoridae) and long-winged plant hoppers (family Derbidae) share a common feature: their wings extend beyond their abdomens. They are both types of plant hopper but lantern flies are distinctive for their 'horned' heads.

Australian lantern fly species do not have the huge, projecting hollow 'head' that is characteristic of lantern flies elsewhere. But some Australian tropical species do have a long, narrow 'snout' or horn protruding in front of the actual head capsule. They are very diverse in appearance, being found in such a variety of shapes and colours that often they are not recognised as lantern flies.

Lantern flies all have membranous wings, with a span of up to 150 mm (though

Australian species have a 25 mm–40 mm wingspan). They favour tropical regions, and feed on tree sap obtained by puncturing the woody bark with their sharp rostrums. Their family name is taken from Fulgora, the ancient Roman goddess of lightning, because it was once believed these insects emit light; in fact, they do not.

The long-winged plant hoppers are smaller, 10 mm in length, with a wingspan of up to 30 mm. Many species of this family are easily distinguishable from other plant hopper families because of their long, narrow flying wings extending well clear of the body. Members of this family feed on tall grasses.

Plant hoppers

A number of different families are included under this heading, but most plant hoppers are typically small, pinkish, green or yellowish insects. Along bush trails, in particular, you might catch a glimpse of moth-like insects clustering in large numbers on shrubs and vines. The wings are clear but heavily barred with black or brown. This is the passion-vine hopper (*Scolypopa australis*), which is widely distributed but mostly occurs in tropical and subtropical regions. Nymphs and adults sit together in rows along the passion-vine stems and other plants.

Flatid plant hoppers (family Flatidae) are typically triangular in profile. Most are brightly coloured and have opaque wings spanning 10 mm–20 mm. They congregate on plant stems, mimicking thorns or buds. A typical example, and one often seen, is the bright green, flatid plant hopper (*Siphanta acuta*), distinguished by the way its broad, triangular-shaped, opaque wings are held to form a steep roof over the abdomen. Members of this species are often found on eucalypt stems, feeding on the leaves, and their nymphs produce copious wax filaments.

Broad-flat plant hoppers (family Eurybrachyidae) have a wingspan of 40 mm or more, and are typically flat and broad in shape when viewed dorsally. Normally solitary in their lifestyle, they may be found climbing or resting on eucalypt trunks during daylight, where they feed on the sap. Typical examples are those of the genus *Platybrachys*, which have body patterns, colouration and markings that make them difficult to detect in their natural habitat. The well-known green plant hopper *Sextius*

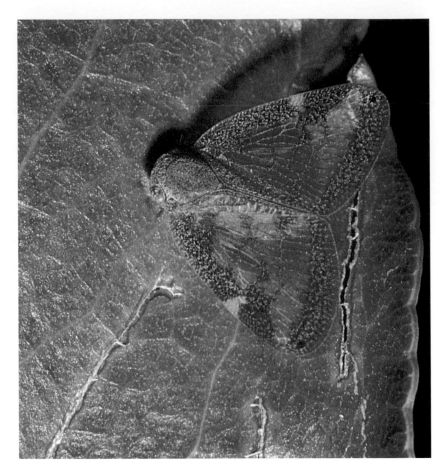

Some aquatic bugs move across the water surface but many are excellent swimmers. Certain species can remain underwater for long periods of time, using the oxygen supply trapped beneath their elytra, before having to resurface for more air. They typically feed on both live and drowned insects, seized above and below the water surface.

Water measuring bugs and water striders

These bugs are wonderfully adapted to spending their entire lives on the water, their bodies being densely covered with water-resistant hairs. They move across the water surface in short bursts of speed. Because they have long, slender limbs and are very light, they can do this without breaking the surface tension of the water.

The water measuring bugs (family Hydrometridae) are no more than 10 mm in length. The water striders, or pond-skaters, (family Gerridae), being up to 30 mm in length, are larger with an elongated body. They move about investigating the tell-tale ripples on the surface made by drowning and struggling insects that have fallen in from trees or shrubs.

Fish-killer bugs and water scorpions

Fish-killer bugs (family Belostomatidae) attain a body length of 50 mm–75 mm, and the giant water bug is a typical representative of this family. This creature is also known as the 'toe-biter' because of its unpopular habit of 'biting' the feet of people wading or dangling their legs in a stream or creek. However, all it is doing is investigating movement of what might be prey, and its 'bite' is no more than a nip made by its large, raptorial forelimbs. It is a large insect, 70 mm long, and is known to capture and feed on small fish and tadpoles. Its distribution is wide, being found from Australia to India, and it is commonly attracted to electric lights. Sometimes hundreds will fly into car headlights in certain areas, particularly in the vicinity of water.

The large, male water bug *Diplonychus rusticus*, which is 40 mm long, is also sometimes encountered. It comes up for air with a big cluster of white eggs fastened to its back. The female of this species forcibly seizes a male when she is ready to lay her eggs and proceeds to cement them in clusters upon his back. He then carries them about until they hatch.

ABOVE Passion-vine hoppers (*Scolypopa australis*). These moth-like plant hoppers are very conspicuous with their richly veined wings. They are gregarious and settle together in vertical rows on their host plant. Nymphs and adults are often found on leaves feeding on passion-vines.

virescens, feeds on native wattles, especially favouring the black wattle (*Acacia decurrens*).

Ecology

A large number of Eurybrachyidae species are widely distributed and many are pests of cultivated crops. They cause far more damage by carrying plant diseases from one plant to another than they do from sucking the sap itself. Native plants are not, of course, severely affected by their feeding.

WATER BUGS
order Hemiptera: suborder Heteroptera infraorder Neomorpha

Aquatic and semi-aquatic bugs are found throughout Australia, usually in water or along its edges. They comprise a large number of families, with individual species ranging in body length from 3 mm–75 mm, and include the giant water bug or fish-killer bug (*Lethocerus insulanus*), which is one of the largest hemipterans in the world.

Water scorpions (family Nepidae) have a body length of 40 mm or longer. Members of this family grasp prey by using their raptorial forelimbs (some heavily set), which are similar to those of fish-killer bugs. But water scorpions can be readily distinguished by their long, tail-like siphons used for taking in air when they break the water surface at regular intervals. These insects live among aquatic vegetation and feed on small aquatic life, favouring murky water in ponds, lakes and streams.

Water-boatmen and back-swimming bugs

In their general appearance water-boatmen (family Corixidae) and back-swimming bugs (family Notonectidae) are often confused with each other. But they can be readily distinguished by their styles of swimming. Water-boatmen use oar-like rear legs to propel themselves through the water, leaving ripples trailing as they move. Back-swimming bugs swim backwards, upside-down, and use all six legs for propulsion.

Water-boatmen have a body length of 10 mm and a typical representative is the water-boatman *Agraptocorixa eurynome*.

Back-swimming bugs (or back-swimmers) are slightly larger, with a body length of 15 mm. Unlike the water-boatmen, they have a convex dorsal surface, large compound eyes and thickly fringed hairs on the limbs. Females use their ovipositors to bore into the stems of aquatic plants, where they deposit their eggs.

ASSASSIN BUGS
order Hemiptera:suborder Heteroptera
infraorder Cimicomorpha

All assassin bugs (superfamily Reduvioidea; family Reduviidae) are predatory, stealthy hunters that feed on other arthropods. Assassin bugs in Australia have a maximum body length of 25 mm (up to 40 mm worldwide) and a number of species are brightly coloured—in red and black, or yellow and black—while others are brown or grey, to merge with their surroundings.

A typical example, although larger than most, is the bee-killer bug (*Pristhesancus plagipennis*), which usually hunts among the flowers. Other species, such as the assassin bug *Havinthus rufovarius*, are nocturnal hunters; they remain concealed beneath the bark of tree trunks during the day to emerge at night seeking their prey.

The feather-legged bug (*Ptilocnemus femoratus*) drugs ants prior to sucking their haemolymph: its saliva breaks down and dissolves the ants' internal tissues. It stations itself along ant trails on plants or on the ground. As soon as an ant approaches, the bug raises itself on its long legs to expose a specialised gland, which is eagerly licked by the foraging ant. Suddenly the ant is unable to walk and falls down helpless, and the bug's sharp rostrum is driven into the ant's soft tissue region

TOP The back-swimmer is an aquatic bug readily distinguished by the domed upper surface of its body and its manner of propelling itself backwards through the water.

ABOVE The water-boatman is an aquatic bug readily distinguished by the long fringes of hair on hind legs and tarsi, used to propel itself through the water.

LEFT Camouflaged in fungi, this assassin bug (*Ploiaria regina*) has just captured a harvestman (*Opiliones* species). Assassin bugs are stealthy hunters and many are masters at concealing themselves, their shape and colour merging with the surroundings. Their body shapes and sizes are extremely variable, and range from thickset to almost thread-like forms, some spiny and brightly coloured, some hairy. Others are flat with flange-shaped abdominal expansions.

ABOVE A female cotton harlequin jewel bug (*Tectocoris diophthalmus*). The scutellum or shield protects the upper abdomen and flying wings. It boldly advertises its unpalatableness to would-be predators by displaying bright colours, a warning of toxic taste and offensive odour. The name 'bug' is not a synonym of 'insect' and, when correctly applied, it refers only to the sucking insects of the suborder Heteroptera.

connecting the head and thorax. Many ants are drugged and die where they fall, without being eaten. This is because the lethal fluid is eagerly licked up by many more ants than the assassin bug can eat.

Ecology

The bee-killer bug is regarded as a pest by apiarists. It frequents flowering plants to await flower-visiting insects such as bees, flower flies and butterflies. It kills large numbers of bees as they are returning to their hive, laden with pollen. After sucking the body fluids of each bee, the bug drops each dried, empty body, one after the other, leaving a pile of dead bees beneath it.

PLANT BUGS
order Hemiptera:
suborder Heteroptera
infraorder Cimicomorpha

Although plant bugs are placed in the same infraorder as assassin bugs, and some species of mirid bugs do feed on the eggs of other insects or upon smaller soft-bodied insects, most plant bugs feed on the sap of shrubs and other plants, including crop plants.

Mirid bugs (family Miridae), also known as dimpling bugs, are the most numerous family in this grouping. They are up to 15 mm in length, and many species mimic ants and braconid wasps in their colouring, form and manner of moving about tree trunks and foliage. These bugs generally congregate in large numbers on their host plants.

Ecology

Plant bugs often cause dieback of the buds and young leaves when congregating in large numbers on their host plants, which is common with some species.

SHIELD-BUGS
order Hemiptera:
suborder Heteroptera
infraorder Pentatomomorpha

As a common name, 'shield-bug' usually refers to some families of bugs—such as jewel bugs or stinkbugs. But it is also often used for some of the other plant bugs, as some form of 'shield' is a distinguishing feature for most true bugs. When viewed from above, true bugs have what resembles a shield on their backs, often formed by a very large scutellum or by the shape of their forewings when closed. Here, 'shield-bug' is being used to describe members of the infraorder Pentatomorpha, comprising species ranging in size from 2 mm–30 mm.

Many of the so-called 'true bugs' are well known for their noxious secretions—particularly stinkbugs, which often attract close attention because of their bright colours. Female shield-bugs are well known for their maternal care of their eggs and young nymphs.

Most shield-bugs are to be found on the plants they feed from. However, members of one group spend most of their life cycle underground—the burrowing bugs (family Cydnidae), which have a maximum body length of 8 mm. They feed on rotten vegetation and emerge from the ground to mate and disperse, sometimes in extreme numbers. They will often congregate around electric lights and are also capable of emitting a very unpleasant odour.

Lygaeid bugs

Lygaeid bugs (family Lygaeidae) are also known as seed bugs or chinch bugs. They are elongated insects, most being rather small with a body length of 20 mm. During the summer months they swarm upon plants, piercing the leaves with their rostrums as they siphon up the plant juices—the sweet juice of ripening stone fruit being one of their favourite foods.

Alydid bugs

Alydid bugs, or pod-sucking bugs (family Alydidae) are very elongated, with a body length of 14 mm or longer, and have long, thin limbs and antennae. They are seed- and pod-suckers, and originally fed on native plants such as hibiscus. However, their diet has extended to include introduced crop plants. Some species are brightly coloured but most are grey or brown, and several species mimic wasps and ants in colour, shape and movement. Male and female alydid bugs are often found together in pairs on the food plants.

Coreid bugs

Coreids (family Coreidae) are also called squash bugs. One of the best-known members of this family, and typical of the group, is the widely distributed crusader bug (*Mictis profana*). This is a largish insect, with a body length of 25 mm, and while it is basically dark-brown it is strikingly adorned with a yellow–orange St Andrew's cross pattern on its forewings. The male differs in appearance to the female by having large, swollen hind femora (or thighs). It is an active insect that readily takes flight in the sunshine. When threatened, the crusader bug has the unpleasant habit of squirting highly offensive fluids from the rear of its abdomen. These bugs are also known as leaf footed bugs as many species have broad flanges on their limbs.

BELOW An orange female cotton harlequin jewel bug (*Tectocoris diophthalmus*) with two colourful nymphs. Also known as 'broody bugs', the females adhere their egg-clutches to the stems of their host plant and defend them until they hatch, sometimes over-wintering without feeding. She watches over her brood long after they hatch—until they disperse and fend for themselves.

RIGHT A female bronze–orange stinkbug (*Musgraveia sulciventris*). Both nymphs and adults feed on the sap of orange, grapefruit, lemon and lime trees. These insects can spray a severely repulsive odour if alarmed. The young bugs have an extremely flattened ovoid-shaped body and are bright orange with a dark abdominal marking.

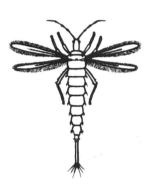

ABOVE Thrips are distinguished by their very narrow wings marginally fringed with long socketed setae. At rest, the wings are held parallel to the body.

BELOW Thrips commonly feed on fungi, pollen, plant tissue and tiny arthropods.

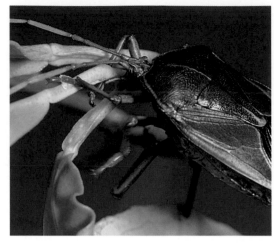

Stinkbugs and jewel bugs

One family of stinkbugs (family Tessaratomidae) appears to have a limited range of distribution, being confined to the eastern coast of Australia, from Narooma (New South Wales) in the south to Emerald (Queensland) in the north, and bounded by the Great Dividing Range. These bugs have a body length up to 40 mm or larger. A typical representative is the handsome, bronze–orange stinkbug (*Musgraveia sulciventris*), a largish insect which undergoes five moults before attaining maturity, reaching a length of around 25 mm. It often frequents citrus orchards and home gardens.

Pentatomid stinkbugs (family Pentatomidae) have a maximum body length of 30 mm. Familiar examples of this group, the cryptic bugs of the genus *Poecilometis*, are often found on the bark of tree trunks. Many species of Pentatomidae feed on seeds and some feed on plant saps. But this family also includes predatory shield-bugs such as the predatory pentatomid bug (*Cermatulus nasalis*), and the vine-moth bug (*Oechalia schellembergii*), which feed on other insects. Predatory shield-bugs have a strong, stout rostrum that is used as a spear to impale unwary prey, especially slow-moving caterpillars, and drain them of vital body fluids.

Jewel bugs (family Scutelleridae) have a body length of 8 mm–20 mm, and are recognisable from the large scutellum (shield) entirely covering their abdomen and protecting their flying wings. Jewel bugs are well known for the loving attention they devote to their offspring. One well-known species is *Scutiphora pedicillata*, a brilliantly coloured insect occurring in eastern Australia. The beautifully coloured, cotton harlequin bug, which is also named

'broody bug' (*Tectocoris diophthalmus*) is a typical member of this family. These insects are extremely variable in body patterns and colouring—the females being mostly bright orange–yellow with a number of darker coloured splotches; the males are iridescent reds, blues, purples and greens. They occur in areas of New South Wales and Queensland feeding on soft-wooded, juicy plants such as cultivated cotton and native and introduced hibiscus shrubs.

The mating habits of cotton harlequin bugs are typical of all shield-bugs (and, indeed, of most hemipterans). The male first mounts the back of the female and then turns around to continue mating end-to-end, both facing in opposite directions. Between 50 and 500 ovoid eggs are neatly laid in clusters, adhered to the stem of the host plant. Hatching can take weeks to several months depending on the season. The tiny nymphs mass together after hatching and undergo several moults before reaching maturity.

Ecology

All shield-bugs (in common with other hemipterans) feed through a long, tubular mouth that sits neatly beneath the head when at rest and has a sharp rostrum to pierce young plant-tips and draw out the sap. This causes the tips to wilt and, when shield-bugs congregate and feed in high numbers, the host plants will sometimes die—lygaeid bugs, for instance, adversely affect stone-fruit trees; the young shoots and tips of wattle die as a result of crusader bugs sucking the sap. So despite the attractiveness of many shield-bugs, with their striking colouring, several species can cause significant problems for food crops and home gardens.

The bronze–orange stinkbug, although a native, is commonly found in citrus orchards and causes dieback of young shoots on citrus trees. The harlequin bug *Dindymus versicolor* is widely distributed, and feeds on apples, figs, pumpkins and melons. The introduced green vegetable-bug (*Nezara viridula*) became established in Australia 100 years ago and quickly became a serious pest of tomatoes, beans and lucerne.

Despite the loving attention shield-bugs bestow on their young, a number of introduced parasitic wasps are frequently successful in attacking the eggs. This has dramatically reduced the rate of hatching from the eggs, bringing some control over the numbers of pest species.

The only shield-bugs that are specialised predators—the predatory shield-bugs (family Pentatomidae)—because they attack certain caterpillars, are themselves useful in helping to keep the populations of crop pests in check.

THRIPS
order Thysanoptera

Thrips are distinguished by having:
- clawless feet
- unusual fringed wings
- 'rowing' wing movements in flight.

Thrips are tiny and elongated, with body lengths between 0.5 mm–15 mm. These insects have clawless tarsi (feet) and slender wings, which are fringed with long, thin hairs—hence the name of the order, thysanoptera, from *thusanos* meaning 'a fringe'. In flight, their wings have a distinctive rowing motion.

Thrips feed on plant juices and have piercing and cutting mouthparts that enable them to scrape and suck the tissues and juices of plants. Many species create bubble-like galls on the leaves of native plants.

Some thrip species reproduce asexually, by parthenogenesis. Before a female gives birth, her abdomen sometimes swells to an enormous size. As with other exopterygotes, the nymphs of thrips undergo a gradual metamorphosis. However, their metamorphosis is different in having resting phases—similar to those of the pupal phase in the higher insects. Further, unlike a pupa, a nymphal thrip in the resting phase of metamorphosis is able to crawl away if disturbed.

During some seasons, thrips reach dense populations and are carried by the wind to land just about anywhere, often even alighting on clothes hanging out to dry on the clothesline. Sometimes they crowd on the flower heads of grasses, all moving as one in a seething mass.

ABOVE A cryptic shield-bug (stinkbug), *Poecilometis armatus*). Cryptic colouring offers protection from predators. If attacked, its secondary line of defence is to spray foul-smelling chemicals onto the would-be assailant.

CHAPTER TEN

Modern Winged Insects

Insects in this subdivision, called the endopterygotes, have also evolved from winged ancestors. However, unlike the exopterygotes, these insects undergo a complete metamorphosis involving a pupal stage. They are often referred to as being 'modern insects', meaning they are more advanced on an evolutionary scale. The immature stages of the life cycle of insects in this group have become so specialised that their transformation to the adult stage requires the pre-imaginal instar or pupal stage. Thus, their life cycle has four phases: the egg, the larval stage, the pupal stage and, finally, the winged adult. The young of endopterygotes are called larvae and they differ markedly from the adults in both their form and their lifestyle. In addition, during the larval stage, their wings develop internally within closed pouches of the body wall. Sexual maturity and full wing development occur following the pupal stage, when adulthood is attained.

ALDERFLIES AND DOBSONFLIES
order Megaloptera

Alderflies and dobsonflies are distinguished by:
- two pairs of broad, membranous flying wings
- expandable hindwings that fold fan-like when at rest
- compound eyes that protrude laterally on a broad, flat head
- three ocelli in dobsonflies; none in alderflies
- long, slender, thread-like antennae
- strong, biting mandibles.

Alderflies (family Sialidae) and dobsonflies (family Corydalidae) are large soft-bodied insects with a wingspan of 20 mm–100 mm. They are generally found around freshwater streams in both temperate and tropical regions. All species have a predatory larval stage, during which they live an aquatic existence. The larvae live beneath submerged logs and rocks and actively prey on a wide range of aquatic arthropods. The adults do not feed and stay close to larval habitats, living only long enough to mate and continue the cycle. Both alderflies and dobsonflies undergo a distinctive pupal stage before they emerge as adults.

The larvae of both families are important links in the food chain, and are taken in large numbers by trout. Adults are also commonly taken by trout because they fly close to the water's surface at dusk, making them an easy target for hungry fish.

LACEWINGS
order Neuroptera

Neuroptera is an ancient order, and it contains many forms which have remained virtually unchanged since the Permian Period some 270 million years ago. More than 90 per cent of Australian lacewing groups rarely occur elsewhere. The family Ithonidae is known only in Australia and the ancient family Nymphidae occurs only in Australia, including Lord Howe Island, and New Guinea. In spite of their evolutionary age, neuropterans undergo the more modern form of metamorphosis, consisting of four distinct stages in their life cycle, as do all other endopterygotes.

RIGHT Dobsonfly adults have a broad head with compound eyes that protrude laterally, a large prothorax, soft abdomen and two pairs of flying wings coupled during flight. All of the segments are well developed and flexible.

Lacewings are distinguished by:
- two pairs of broad, membranous flying wings of almost equal size
- wings held roof-like when at rest
- mandibulate mouthparts pointing downwards
- thread-like antennae, except among owl-flies (family Ascalaphidae), which are club-tipped.

Lacewings are small to large soft-bodied creatures with a wingspan of 3 mm–150 mm. Their two pairs of many-veined wings, often attractively patterned and coloured, are held roof-like over the body when at rest. All lacewings are predatory, both in their larval and adult forms, and they commonly fly at night.

This order constitutes a very interesting, and somewhat diverse group of insects,

especially as so many of the families superficially resemble other insects. For instance, there are mantid-like forms (family Mantispidae), moth-like forms (family Ithonidae), or larval forms that resemble curl grubs or beetle larvae (family Ithonidae).

Powder-winged lacewings (family Coniopterygidae) are very small, with a wingspan of 3 mm–8 mm, and the tiny adults are covered in a white to grey-coloured waxy material.

Most species of hairy winged lacewings (family Ithonidae) have grey–brown wings, with a wingspan of 28 mm–64 mm. But some species have patterned wings and superficially resemble moths. The adults in this family often swarm during mating flights.

ABOVE The female Australian dobsonfly (*Archichauliodes guttiferus*) has a wingspan of 70 mm. Dobsonflies skim the surface of running water at dusk. The carnivorous aquatic larvae live beneath rocks and fallen timber in streams and feed on small aquatic invertebrates; they, in turn, are often eaten by trout. The fully-grown larvae pupate under rocks along stream edges. Dobsonflies are closely related to lacewings.

RIGHT Lacewings are delicate gauze-winged insects with two pairs of net-veined wings. All species are beneficial to humans as both the larvae and adults feed on insects that attack our food crops.

OPPOSITE A female blue-eyed lacewing (*Nymphes myrmeleonoides*). A large species, it lays up to 40 eggs, each attached to the substrate by stiff silk stems in a characteristic necklace pattern. The female dabs a drop of gummy liquid from her abdominal tip onto the substrate, then raises her abdomen to draw the liquid up into a slender stalk. This stalk immediately hardens and an egg is deposited on its tip. The larvae live in leaf litter, preying on small invertebrates, and when fully grown, spin a silk cocoon in which to pupate.

Broad-winged lacewings (family Osmylidae) have the same wingspan as those in the family Ithonidae (28 mm–64 mm) but their wings are broader and patterned more strikingly. The adults emerge during the warmer months.

Adult mantisflies (family Mantispidae) have a wingspan of 6 mm–54 mm. They can be distinguished by their mantis-like grasping forelegs. During their larval stage they feed upon the eggs of spiders. Some species in this group are brightly coloured, mimic social wasps and feed on flowers.

There are three families from the super-family Hemerobioidea—brown lacewings (family Hemerobiidae), green lacewings (family Chrysopidae), and silky lacewings (family Psychopsidae). Adult brown lacewings are pale-coloured insects with a wingspan of 6 mm–26 mm, and normally hold their wings flat above the body when resting. Adult green lacewings generally have green bodies, with delicate, clear wings; in some species these are brightly marked with spots and patterns. The wingspan is 10 mm–64 mm. Silky lacewings are mostly large species with broad, brightly patterned wings and a wingspan of 14 mm–64 mm. Certain species in this family, such as *Megapsychops illidgei*, are distinctly butterfly-like in their wing shapes.

Members of the superfamily Myrmeleontoidea constitute the largest group of lacewings in Australia. Families in this group include large lacewings (family Nymphidae), ant-lion lacewings (family Myrmeleontidae), owl-flies (family Ascalaphidae), and spoon-winged lacewings (family Nemopteridae), which have a wingspan of 14 mm–40 mm and feed on flowers.

Large lacewings are considered to be the most primitive of this superfamily. They have a wingspan of 20 mm–90 mm, long, fine antennae and inhabit open woodland in eastern Australia. Females lay their eggs on long stalks, well clear of the substrate. The well-known blue-eyed lacewing (*Nymphes*

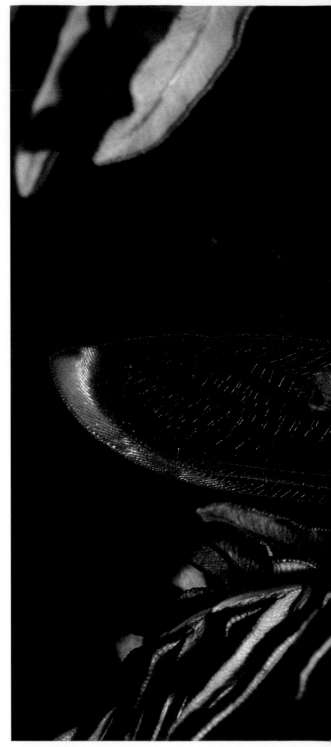

myrmeleonoides) is often seen fluttering from shrub to shrub in sclerophyll forests. The female of this species has the unusual habit of depositing her stalked eggs in a necklace-shaped string, not far from water.

Adult ant-lion lacewings have long, thin wings with distinctive markings, and a wingspan of 12 mm–148 mm. Their larvae, known as ant-lions, excavate pits to trap their prey and some

are cryptically coloured. Although similar to the ant-lion lacewings, most species of owl flies have clear wings, spanning 18 mm–96 mm. Owl fly species with patterned wings have the wing apex suffused with a dark brown colouring. These beautiful insects are highly developed lacewings, with long clubbed antennae and musk-like odours. Their resemblance to butterflies is only superficial. They fly during daylight.

Ecology

All lacewings are predatory, both in their larval and adult forms, and occupy varying habitats (depending on the requirements of each species). Lacewings are all directly beneficial to humans as they feed on lepidopteran eggs or on a wide range of insects that interfere with cultivated food crops and introduced plants —such as aphids, scale insects and psyllids.

THE COLEOPTERANS—BEETLES AND WEEVILS

Beetles are ancient creatures. The earliest known fossils of beetles have been uncovered from the later Permian Period, some 260 million years ago. Even today some living relicts are still found—such as in the family Ommatidiae—living, unchanged examples of beetles that are known in fossil form.

The order Coleoptera is extraordinarily diverse, with greatly different lifestyles, sizes and appearance. It is assembled into four main suborders: Archostemata, Myxophaga, Adephaga and Polyphaga—the largest and most diverse group being Polyphaga. As Archostemata is so rare and Myxophaga is a tiny group of minute beetles, this book focuses on the two latter suborders.

Most beetles are unlikely to be mistaken for any other insect group (except for some shield-bugs or native cockroach species). Some beetles, however, mimic the shapes and colours of wasps and ants so well that even the discerning eye of a professional entomologist can be momentarily tricked.

Australian beetles include some strikingly attractive insects, some with glorious tints and ornate sculpturing. Many have names that are particularly Australian—such as Christmas beetle, cowboy beetle, splinter-puller, washer-woman. Some larger species are often favourites among children because of their curious habits or appearance.

Beetles and weevils are distinguished by:
- heavily sclerotised bodies and hardened, modified elytra
- elytra that open but do not beat in flight
- membranous flying wings (when present), which fold beneath the elytra when at rest
- chewing, cutting or biting mouthparts
- among weevils—one common feature is a snout, equipped with cutting mandibles at the tip.

Coleopterans have been so successful in adapting to almost every available kind of microhabitat and to an extraordinary range of lifestyles that they make up the largest group of animals on Earth. Numerous species live an aquatic existence; others survive scorching desert heat and prolonged droughts. They are the most prolific insects both in terms of the number of species and their actual overall populations—the total number of coleopterans accounts for over 40 per cent of all known insects. The subgroup of weevils (superfamily Curculionoidea) alone consists of more than 60 000 described species worldwide, including over 6000 for Australia—the largest fauna family in the animal kingdom. During summer months, when their populations are at their peak, beetles are often found congregated around street and patio lights but many coleopteran species are seldom seen because they shun daylight.

Their enormous success stems mainly from their anatomical modifications—in particular, the development of the forewings into a tough, protective sheath called the elytra (the name of the order is derived from the Greek word *koleos* meaning 'sheath', and *ptera*, the word for 'winged'). Because of their elytra, beetles can penetrate niches where more vulnerably winged insects cannot venture— burrowing into soil and timber, or wedging themselves beneath flaking bark and rock crevices.

Most beetles rely for protection on their hardened exoskeletons and elytra. Some beetles, however— especially those with large, cutting mandibles and offensive body chemicals—do have a wide range of defences (see Chapter Four).

With their particular bodily structure, beetles are able to conserve the air and water they absorb more efficiently than most other insects—another factor in their success, allowing them to occupy arid habitats, for instance. An insect's cuticle takes in unsaturated air and water. But many coleopteran species are able to seal the edges of their elytra onto the abdominal margin, thus creating a kind of internal air-pocket in the space created by the closed elytra and the upper abdominal surface. This also means that their spiracles, being enclosed in this air-pocket, are not exposed (as they are in many insects).

This air-pocket has been utilised particularly well by species such as the carnivorous diving beetles (family Dytiscidae). It enables them to remain underwater for lengthy periods by breathing the air in the bubble that becomes trapped in this space.

RIGHT On emerging from the soil, the large wattle-pig weevil (*Leptopius tribulus*) crawls up the trunk to high foliage to feed on young leaves. After mating, the female (pictured) deposits her eggs, her life cycle completed. Larvae feed on roots and stems of living timber of *Acacia* trees, and pupate in the soil during winter months.

Coleopterans are highly developed and, like other endopterygotes, undergo a complete metamorphosis. The growing larvae bear little resemblance to the adults they become, and the pupal stage is necessary to bridge the two forms.

Ecology

In nature's scheme, coleopterans have important roles to play: they break down unhealthy or dying timber; they consume the remains of other insects, plants and animals; and they bury the excreta of other animals. Many beetles feed on fungi, too. Overall, they are significant contributors to the process of creating the natural rich soil so vital for sustaining a healthy environment.

However, several species are categorised as pests (based on their consumption and damage of materials we value for our own use), especially since many species consume grains and seeds. Some 400 species have been recorded in stored products.

Coleopterans are equipped with chewing and biting mouthparts much like those of grasshoppers. Larvae and adults of most species feed on plant material in one form or another, and beetles have a mutually dependent relationship with woodland and forest habitats. Many have roles as biological controllers of insect and plant pests.

The most dominant feeders of timber are the darkling, longicorn and jewel beetles (families Tenebrionidae, Cerambycidae and Buprestidae), and weevils (family Curculionidae). Unhealthy timber is primarily broken down by their wood-eating larvae and further disintegrated by stag and bess beetles (families Lucanidae and Passalidae). In a natural forest situation, the enormous populations of curl grub larvae, such as those of the flower chafers and Christmas beetles (family Scarabaeidae), perform the work necessary to aerate the soil as they feed on plant roots and decaying vegetation, replenishing the rich soil the forest requires for regeneration.

ABOVE A male cowboy beetle (*Diaphonia dorsalis*). Adults are day-flying and visit nectar-bearing plants during spring and summer to feed on the pollen, ovaries and stamens. Their loud buzzing flight announces their arrival. The males locate the opposite sex by the trails of pheromones (odour molecules) emitted by females to inform males of their exact whereabouts.

GROUND, TIGER, DIVING AND WHIRLIGIG BEETLES

order Coleoptera: suborder Adephaga
superorder Caraboidea

Although all these beetles are members of the same superfamily (Caraboidea), and all are predatory, one family (Carabidae) is terrestrial while the other two (Dytiscidae and Gyrinidae) are mainly aquatic. These beetles are mainly distinguished by:

- very pronounced, large, cutting mandibles, in terrestrial species
- modified (oar-like) hindlegs, in aquatic species.

Ground and tiger beetles

Carabidae constitutes one of the largest beetle families, with ground beetles being considerably more numerous than tiger beetles. They have a body length of 1 mm–60 mm and are long-legged and fast-moving. Most species in both their larval and adult stages are predacious on other insects. All members of the Carabidae are terrestrial and occur in a wide range of climates from deserts to cold mountain regions.

Ground beetles are nocturnal predators and are distinguished by their large heads with bulging eyes and their huge, cutting mandibles. Many are black and glossy, others brightly coloured and iridescent. They rarely fly; many species have reduced hindwings. They often inhabit damp environments along stream edges. Others live beneath the flaking bark of trees. If threatened, many will emit a pungent odour.

Tiger beetles are diurnal predators, and are usually coloured in attractively iridescent hues. They have a deflexed head capsule with large, protruding eyes and a large labrum. Some tiger beetle species frequent tree trunks in hot sunshine and, with their long legs, can move with alarming speed in pursuit of prey and quickly take to the wing on approach of danger.

Diving and whirligig beetles

Diving beetles (family Dytiscidae) are closely related to the Carabidae, but live predominantly aquatic lives. They are ovoid, flattened beetles, with a body length of 1 mm–40 mm. Their cuticle typically is smooth for ease of moving through the water. Each time they rise to the water surface for air, a bountiful store of oxygen is trapped beneath their elytra and thus, with each dive, they can remain below for long periods. Their modified (oar-like) hindlegs propel them through the water at speed when chasing prey or escaping danger. The tarsi are flattened and paddle-like, fringed with a dense pile of swimming hairs. Some of the larger species capture tadpoles and small fish. The adults are attracted to artificial lights, where they sometimes congregate in large numbers.

The gregarious whirligig beetles (family Gyrinidae) have a streamlined body shape, 4 mm–20 mm long, and are commonly found swimming about on the surface of ponds and streams. With their compound eyes divided by a thin strip of cuticle into an upper and lower portion, they appear to have four eyes. Whirligig beetles feed on both vegetation and live prey (depending on the species). Their forelegs are modified to seize and hold dead or exhausted insect prey, while their hindlegs are modified into oar-like shapes, with swimming hairs, to propel themselves about on the surface of the water. If need be, whirligig beetles can dive below the water surface or fly.

WATER BEETLES

order Coleoptera: suborder Polyphaga
superfamily Hydophiloidea

Polyphaga, the largest and most diverse beetle suborder, comprises well over 90 per cent of beetle species. Among a number of distinguishing features of beetles in this immense group is the concealed prothoracic pleuron, modified hindwing venation and tarsi of the larvae ending in one claw.

Both families of water beetles (Hydrophilidae and Histeridae) are about 2 mm–40 mm in length and closely resemble the diving beetles (family Dytiscidae), despite being in a completely different suborder. However, water beetles have a more dorsally convex shape and their forelimbs and middle-limbs are oar-shaped so that they are adapted for swimming. Their swimming power is supplied mostly by the greatly enlarged tarsi and coxae of their hindlegs. Many water beetles are semi-aquatic in lifestyle and most feed upon vegetation, some even frequenting flowers. Sometimes they will prey on insects that get into trouble on the water.

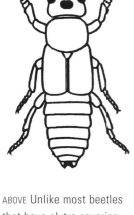

ABOVE Unlike most beetles that have elytra covering their backs, the elytra of rove-beetles (*Creophilus erythrocephalus*) expose over half the abdomen. When attacked they exude loathsome-smelling fluids.

ABOVE A beetle larva's sclerotised cuticle, as in this clerid beetle (*Trogodendron fasciculatum*) chrysalis, is to protect the pupa, especially species living in soil and rotting timber. Adult clerids are effective hunters that run down other insects on tree trunks.

ROVE-BEETLES, CLERID BEETLES AND LADYBIRD BEETLES
order Coleoptera: suborder Polyphaga various carnivorous families

The larvae and adults of most beetles in the suborder Polyphaga consume plant material. However, three families, although from different superfamilies, have members that are decidedly carnivorous: they mainly prey on larvae and adults of other insects. These are the rove-beetles, clerid beetles and ladybird beetles.

Rove-beetles
Rove-beetles (family Staphylinidae) measure 1 mm–25 mm long and are distinguished by their tiny elytra, which do not entirely cover the abdominal segments (unlike most other beetles). Their flying wings have reduced wing venation (with a few exceptions) and they are specially folded to tuck beneath the reduced elytra. Rove-beetles curl their remarkably flexible abdomens above their bodies while running about. If attacked, they exude highly offensive smells. Some species mimic ants and wasps.

The two largest groups of specialised predators are the subfamilies Staphylininae and Paederinae. A typical example is the devils' coach-horse beetle (*Creophilus erythrocephalus*), a rather large, black beetle with a bright red head capsule. It lives beneath animal carcasses and carrion, actively preying on fly larvae (maggots).

Clerid beetles
Clerid beetles (family Cleridae) measure 5 mm–40 mm in length and have an elongated and parallel-sided bodily structure. They are readily distinguished from other beetles by their large eyes and, on most species, cryptic-patterned patches of close-knit, erect hairs. Adults frequent tree trunks in search of prey, and larvae are also predatory, feeding on the larvae of other insects within decaying timber.

Ladybird beetles
Ladybird beetles (family Coccinellidae) are characterised by their dome-shaped bodies and bright colouring. Most are small, with a body length of 1 mm–12 mm, and are bright yellow, red, orange or even blue. Except for *Epilachna* species, which feed on leaves (especially pumpkin), most ladybirds prey on aphids, scale insects and mites. The larvae and adults of the brightly coloured 13-spotted ladybird beetle (*Harmonia conformis*) have an insatiable appetite for aphids.

SCARABAEOID BEETLES
order Coleoptera: suborder Polyphaga, superfamily Scarabaeoidea

This superfamily covers a wide range of beetles —dung beetles, stag-beetles, bess beetles, flower beetles, Christmas beetles, rhinoceros beetles, cockchafers, and geotrupid beetles. These are arranged in a number of families and subfamilies—one of these families, the Scarabaeidae, is the second-largest family of beetles (after the weevils, family Curculionidae). Scarabaeoid beetles are mainly distinguished by:
- antennae forming a lamellate club
- mandibles usually dorsally hidden by a plate (clypeus)
- C-shaped larvae, most of which feed on decaying vegetation beneath the soil.

Stag-beetles
One of the most distinctive characteristics of stag-beetles (family Lucanidae) are the antler-like mandibles of the males, which can be enormous in certain species. In Australia, stag-beetles have a body length (including their mandibles) of 10 mm–70 mm. There are even larger ones elsewhere. The forelimbs are equipped for burrowing in rotting timber. They can sometimes be found in large numbers clinging to, or feeding on, the leaves of eucalypts and sap flows.

Many stag-beetles are brilliantly coloured in iridescent hues of blues, reds, greens and purples, particularly *Lamprima aurata*, which can be seen flying about sclerophyll forests in the sunshine during summer months. This species can be found feeding at sap flows, especially on the sugary sap of the ribbon gum (*Eucalyptus viminalis*).

The largest and most spectacular species is, without doubt, the king stag-beetle (*Phalacrognathus muelleri*). It has a brilliant glossy cuticle, coloured in iridescent green, bronze and copper, and some individuals are up to 70 mm long. Males may have enormous 'antlers' (varying in size among individuals).

ABOVE Larvae and adults of the 13-spotted ladybird beetle (*Harmonia conformis*) feed on aphids. When startled, the adult secretes drops of yellow haemolymph (blood), toxic to vertebrates. It then drops from the plant and remains motionless.

ABOVE Affectionately known as Christmas beetles, these iridescent scarabaeoid beetles (*Anoplognathus* species) swarm in eucalypt treetops. They feed on young leaftips in the sun during late spring and summer, clinging onto gum leaves with their large, unequal-sized claws.

RIGHT The mandibles or 'jaws' of most beetles are brown or black no matter how vividly coloured the head, body and elytra are, but those of the male golden-green stag-beetle (*Lamprima aurata*) are even brighter and more iridescent than the rest of its body.

Flower beetles

Most flower beetles, also called flower scarabs (family Scarabaeidae, subfamily Cetoniinae) are active during daylight hours. Many species are strikingly patterned, with brightly iridescent or enamelled colouring. They mainly feed on flower nectar and pollen from native shrubs and trees.

These insects have a somewhat flattened body structure and are 5 mm–32 mm long. Powerful flyers, their elytra are slightly raised in flight but held together above the outstretched flying wings, producing a distinctive buzzing sound. The cowboy beetle (*Diaphonia dorsalis*) and the bright green fiddler beetle (*Eupoecila australasiae*) are typical examples.

Christmas beetles

The main characteristics distinguishing Christmas beetles (family Scarabaeidae, subfamily Rutelinae) are their opal-like colouring and their large, unequal tarsal claws. The handsome, iridescent Christmas beetles— so-named because they appear during summer, particularly December to January—are 3 mm–50 mm in length. They are often found in natural bushland in large numbers on eucalypts, feeding on the foliage, or flying about in the sunshine. The pearly coloured Christmas beetle (*Anoplognathus boisduvali*) and the large golden Christmas beetle (*A. viriditarsus*) are typical examples.

Bess beetles

Bess beetles (family Passalidae) usually have a small pointed horn on their heads. Most are glossy black and distinctive in appearance and lifestyle. The elongated body, 20 mm–60 mm in length, is dorsally flattened and the elytra are longitudinally striated. Adults pulverise the fibrous tissue of decaying timber and feed it by mouth to the growing larvae. These beetles produce sounds by rubbing rows of tooth-like denticles on the elytra against similar structures located on the lower surface of the wings. Making sounds helps keep the family group together as the larvae are able to make similar sounds, too.

RIGHT A male golden-bronze Christmas beetle (*Anoplognathus montanus*). Scarabaeoid beetles have far larger claws than the females. The wing covers serve as sheaths protecting the flying wings and upper body that typically extend to the abdominal tip and prevent desiccation when they are closed.

Rhinoceros beetles

The males of several species in this subfamily (family Scarabaeidae, subfamily Dynastinae) are popularly known as rhinoceros beetles because of their prominent horns jutting out from the prothorax. A number of large species found in tropical regions are also, because of their size, known as goliath beetles.

These beetles are 8 mm–70 mm in size (but larger with prothoracic horns) and most species are black or brown in colour, the large rhinoceros beetle (*Xylotrupes gideon*) being a typical example. In many species, the entire body is covered in a fine fur when the adult first emerges but this is soon lost as it becomes more active. Rival males are renowned for their wrestling, which they do to win the female's attention and favours, and their horns are often used to pick up females and carry them off for mating.

Cockchafers

Cockchafers or rosechafers (family Scarabaeidae, subfamily Melononthinae) are typically black or reddish brown in colour with a body length of 2 mm–35 mm. Mainly nocturnally active, these beetles occur in large numbers, feeding on foliage. Among the diurnal species are the flower-visiting beetles of the genus *Phyllotocus* and the small, iridescent, bright green and purple beetles of the genus *Diphucephala*, which congregate in enormous numbers at times during the summer months, feeding on the young foliage of acacias and eucalypts.

Cockchafer larvae feed on a great variety of plant-material in varying stages of decomposition, as well as on plant roots, and by so doing continually recycle the soil, aerating it in the exchange. The growing larvae make their way through the soil with ease in spite of their awkward, sluggish form.

Dung beetles

Dung beetles (family Scarabaeidae, subfamily Scarabaeinae) are, typically, stout-bodied and very rounded in form, with a body length of 2 mm–45 mm. Most are shiny black but many species have highly glossy iridescent colouring, often with marked sexual dimorphism.

Males frequently assist females in digging tunnels and gathering their specially-formed

ABOVE A jewel beetle (*Stigmodera macularia*) feeding on blossoms of the scrub apple (*Angophora hispida*). When disturbed, they usually fall, fold their legs and antennae close beneath the body, and lay motionless. Some species are exquisitely beautiful, flaunting stunning colour patterns and iridescence. All jewel beetle larvae are timber-feeders. Females have their last two abdominal segments modified to house an ovipositor, which is used to push their eggs into narrow crevices in bark.

balls of animal dung. They roll these balls to their underground nest-sites (or brood chambers)—sometimes over relatively great distances and rough terrain—and lay an egg beneath each one. Dung beetle larvae, after hatching, feed on the dung, which is also what the adults feed on.

Geotrupid beetles

Geotrupid beetles (family Geotrupidae) are usually reddish brown to yellowish, but sometimes black. They are stout-bodied, strongly convex in shape, with a body length of 5 mm–25 mm and show marked sexual dimorphism. The male has a prognathous head, normally with lamellate antennae that form a small club at the distal end, and it is typically equipped with a long, slender horn.

These beetles burrow deep tunnels into the soil and lay their eggs beneath subterranean fungi, decaying material or dung.

CLICK, SOFT-WINGED AND SOLDIER BEETLES
order Coleoptera: suborder Polyphaga superfamily Elateroidea

Click beetles

Also popularly known as skipjacks, click beetles (family Elateridae) are characteristically elongated in form, and have a body length of 4 mm–50 mm. The entire abdomen is covered by their hardened elytra. Their antennae are almost always serrated.

These beetles feed on nectar from flowers and are readily distinguished by the manner in which they snap their thorax against their abdomen. The click beetle *Lacon variabilis* is a typical example.

When disturbed, these beetles click themselves up into the air to quickly get out of harm's way. They are able to do this by means of a mechanism that is unique among insects: two acute spines, one protruding from each side of the rear of the prothorax, which fit into deep grooves on the mesosternum (on the second thoracic segment). Should the beetle land on its back, it can quickly right itself by propelling itself well into the air to either take flight or land back on its feet.

Soft-winged beetles and soldier beetles

These two families of beetles are quite similar in size—the soft-winged beetles (family Lycidae) are 5 mm–20 mm long, and the soldier beetles (family Cantharidae) are 3 mm–18 mm long. A characteristic feature of them all is their soft body and soft elytra.

They are readily distinguished, as well, by their flattened form and soft bodies, and by their pronounced antennae (serrated in Lycidae, and filiform in Cantharidae). Soft-winged beetles are typically reddish yellow, coppery and black, while soldier beetles are typically yellow and blue–black.

The head of a soft-winged beetle is triangular or rostrate, and partly covered by the pronotum. Its elytra have longitudinal ridges, often with rows of window-like puncture patterns. The larvae live in leaf litter and beneath bark, feeding on decaying vegetation and moulds.

Soldier beetles and some soft-bodied beetles can exude highly offensive fluids and odours, which deter would-be predators—soft-winged beetles are very distasteful. In some seasons, soldier beetles utilise plants to congregate, occurring in such numbers at times that they totally cover the plants. The soldier beetle *Chauliognathus lugubris* is a typical example.

JEWEL BEETLES
order Coleoptera: suborder Polyphaga superfamily Buprestoidea

Jewel beetles (family Buprestidae) are 3 mm–65 mm in length and are easily distinguished from most other beetles by their elongated bodies, readily retractable limbs, large eyes and short antennae. They also often feature brilliant iridescent colouring.

Many species feed on nectar, while others feed on foliage. A typical example is the large jewel beetle *Stigmodera macularia*, which has yellow elytra that are deeply pitted with blue-black spots and an iridescent blue body and limbs. It is usually found feeding on a wide range of blossoms in sclerophyll habitats.

Jewel beetle populations vary enormously from season to season for various reasons, including bushfires, availability of their food plants or climatic conditions.

OPPOSITE An iridescent scarabaeoid cockchafer (*Diphucephala aurulenta*) feeding on bush pea flower (*Pultenaea villosa*). This genus contains several similar-looking iridescent green- to purple-coloured species, their elytra prominently sculptured. They generally swarm about wattles and eucalypts during summer, feeding on the foliage.

DARKLING BEETLES, LONGICORN BEETLES AND LEAF BEETLES

ABOVE A female chestnut-brown longicorn beetle (*Paroplites australis*). Emerged from its pupal wrappings, the female utilises her old larval tunnel to await the arrival of amorous males. She broadcasts her location by exuding musk-scented pheromones (odour molecules), which the males pick up via their antennae.

RIGHT A chestnut-brown longicorn beetle (*Eurynassa australis*). Longicorns may be found resting on the bark of trees, with sickly trees yielding the greatest numbers. This species, like many large longicorns, makes squeaking noises when threatened by rubbing its hindlimbs against the edges of its elytra.

DARKLING BEETLES, LONGICORN BEETLES AND LEAF BEETLES

order Coleoptera: suborder Polyphaga, infraorder Cucujiformia

These insects are representatives of two different superfamilies: Tenebrionoidea (darkling beetles), and Chrysomeloidea (longicorn beetles and leaf beetles). One feature they have in common is that their larvae are timber borers but, as adults, they no longer feed on timber.

Darkling beetles

Also known as bark beetles, darkling beetles (family Tenebrionidae) have a body length of 2 mm–30 mm and are usually dull black or brown, but some species are iridescent. They are often found congregated beneath loose bark, feeding on vegetation. Many species feed on fungi, others feed on waste animal matter and foliage. This large family (the most numerous in its superfamily) consists of highly diverse species placed in subfamilies and also includes the pie-dish beetles, with *Saragus incisus* and *Heleus waitei*, being typical examples.

Longicorn beetles

Longicorns (family Cerambycidae) vary in size from 3 mm–85 mm (but some exotic species are over 150 mm). They are easily distinguished from other beetles by their extremely long antennae, large mandibles, distinct claws and long legs. Longicorns generally feed on plant material; some feed on nectar or on sap flows, too. Their larvae are timber borers.

Typical of the group is the large, chestnut-brown longicorn (*Paroplites australis*), up to 60 mm in body length. Another familiar species is the prionid longicorn beetle *Eurynassa australis* (subfamily Prioninae), which is often found on the trunks of acacias and eucalypts in sclerophyll forests during the summer months.

Leaf beetles

Leaf beetles (family Chrysomelidae) constitute one of the largest families of beetles. They range in body length from 2 mm–15 mm. Most species have a smooth, often glossy exoskeleton adorned in bright colours, like ladybird beetles. Some species are elongated and others flattened. Most feed on foliage of eucalypts and acacias.

The iridescent colours such as in the tropical, iridescent leaf beetle (*Aspidomorpha holmgreni*) are outstanding; this species has shiny gold, green and red metallic tints colouring the thorax and elytra. However, these colours quickly fade at death. Typical leaf beetles are *Paropsis dilatata* and *Paropsis pantherina*, usually seen in large numbers during summer months, feeding on eucalypt leaves.

WEEVILS

order Coleoptera: suborder Polyphaga, superfamily Curculionoidea

The weevils comprise the largest beetle family, all members sharing the distinctive characteristic of having an elongated snout (rostrum) that extends well ahead of the eyes—the reason they are also commonly known as snout beetles. They range widely in size, from 1 mm–60 mm.

The exoskeleton of weevils is characteristically very tough, defying the jaws of many a predator. Their antennae have a distinct elbow and are usually club-tipped. Their mouthparts are at the tip of the snout. The most typical examples of weevils are the blue diamond weevil (*Chrysolopus spectabilis*) and the large wattle-pig weevil (*Baryopadus tribulus*), whose larvae feed on the roots and trunk-bases of wattle.

Female weevils use their long snouts as a drilling tool to bore holes in seeds, fruit, timber and plant stems, where they deposit their eggs so that their larvae, which are typically C-shaped, have readily available food when they hatch. The surrounding plant tissue also serves, when they emerge, to protect them from predators.

Among other weevil families there are the Belidae and Brentidae. Belidae consists of

slender-bodied beetles with a small head capsule and a long forward-projecting rostrum, *Belus suturalis* being a typical species. Brentidae consist of remarkably elongated, parallel-sided beetles, with a marked sexual dimorphism between individuals—*Ithystenus hollandiae* and *Ectocemus decemmoculatus* are representative species.

STYLOPS

order Strepsiptera

Stylops are parasitic on hemipterans and hymenopterans. Those of the suborder Stylopidia are the only known parasitoids among the insects that keep their host alive while undergoing pupation. The female stylops is wingless and lives her entire life within the abdomen of the host insect, not killing it but continually draining it of energy by feeding on its haemolymph.

Stylops are small parasitic insects with distinctive antennae and a remarkable pair of pleated or twisted hindwings—which gives rise to the name of this order (from the Greek *strepsis* meaning 'twisted' and *ptera*, the word for 'winged'). These are the flying wings, with a wingspan of 1 mm–8 mm; only the males have wings. The highly-modified forewings are reduced to tiny, club-shaped structures (with flies, the hindwings are reduced). Stylops are very closely related to the Coleoptera (beetles) but, because of their highly specialised structure and unique lifestyle, they are placed in a separate order.

All larvae feed on a wide range of hosts such as auchenorrhynchans (leaf hoppers), heteropterans (true bugs or shield-bugs), and hymenoterans (wasps, ants and bees). The pupal stage is usually undergone attached to the living

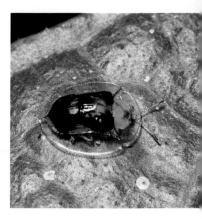

ABOVE Leaf beetles, such as this iridescent tortoise beetle (*Aspidomorpha holmgreni*), vary enormously in body structure and patterns, and are often brilliantly coloured.

ABOVE Stylops resemble beetles superficially in the structure and position of their fore- and hindwings and for this reason they are sometimes included in the order Coleoptera.

LEFT A beautiful male Botany Bay blue diamond weevil (*Chrysolopus spectabilis*) was among the first insects collected in Australia by Sir Joseph Banks, when Captain James Cook landed in Botany Bay. Its larvae feed on roots of living *Acacia* trees, while the adults feed on the young foliage.

RIGHT The bulbous genitalia on the elongated abdomen of the male scorpion-fly are often curled above the body like that of a scorpion. In flight, the slender body, narrow wings and long limbs superficially resemble large craneflies.

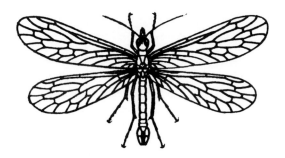

host within its final larval skin which forms a puparium (as in flies). The hosts are rarely killed from the feeding habits of the larvae as the females, which are wingless, require a living host to be able to complete their life cycle and reproduce. Upon attaining adulthood, the males fly off but the females remain within the host.

SCORPION-FLIES
order Mecoptera

Scorpion-flies (also known as hanging flies) have some resemblance to lacewings, except for their mouthparts and long spindly legs with long tarsi, used for grasping and manipulating prey. They are long-winged, with a maximum wingspan of 50 mm.

Adults generally favour damp conditions and are active, flying and moving about the surface of leaves and flowers, the males readily capturing small insect prey. Before producing their eggs, females more commonly feed on nectar. They have a complex courtship, as the female is only attracted to a male that is in possession of prey as an offering for her during courtship and mating.

Mecopteran larvae are caterpillar-like and unusual in that they have compound eyes. They live in cool, damp situations close to the ground, feeding on dead insects, and undergo 4–6 moults before they are fully grown. When fully fed, they form earthen cells just beneath the surface and spend a relatively long period in a pre-pupal state, but the actual pupal stage itself is brief before the adult insect emerges.

Scorpion-flies get their common name from the way that males of certain species carry their terminal tail segments—curved in the air, in the manner of a scorpion. However, scorpion-flies have no sting whatsoever and are entirely harmless to humans.

ABOVE A marsupial flea (*Pygiopsylla hoplia*). Fleas are wingless, parasitic insects with a laterally flattened body. They exhibit enormous leaping power. All species feed on the blood of birds or mammals. The pupae of some species have wing-buds, vestiges of the wings of their ancient ancestors. The wings became redundant as their warm-blooded animal hosts developed hair and feathers.

FLEAS
order Siphonaptera

Fleas are distinguished by:
• a highly laterally compressed body
• large, lateral ocelli (when present), and no compound eyes
• a head rigidly attached to the prothorax
• mouthparts adapted for piercing and sucking
• long legs specially developed for jumping.

Fleas are highly specialised, wingless, parasitic insects (body length 1 mm–10 mm), and are also long-lived. An adult human flea can live for 500 days. The highly compressed bodily structure of the adult flea enables it to move easily among its host's fur or feathers. Its long legs give it the jumping power we are all familiar with—a flea can launch itself into the air to a height of 20 cm (equivalent, in our terms, to a human jumping something like 27 metres into the air).

Fleas lay their eggs generally in the soil, or in places close to available hosts. The eggs can remain dormant for very long periods, becoming active only when a host is nearby. The larvae live as scavengers, normally in the host's nest, feeding on vegetable material and dead animal matter such as skin and feathers.

When pupating, fleas can remain dormant in the pupal stage for long periods, just as they did in the egg stage. As then, they are normally stimulated to emerge by vibration, which is why sometimes you can walk into an empty, unoccupied room and be suddenly attacked by fleas. Interestingly enough, in certain species the pupae have wing-buds—the vestiges of wings on ancient ancestors. Wings became redundant when their warm-blooded animal hosts developed hair and feathers.

Ecology
Fleas are parasitic on a wide range of warm-blooded animals, for example, domestic animals, humans, rabbits, bats and migratory birds, and aquatic animals such as the platypus. Some species—such as the human flea, the dog flea and the cat flea—are serious domestic pests. Other species are capable of transmitting diseases: plague is carried by rat fleas and transmitted to humans. Efforts to biologically control rabbit populations have used fleas as carriers of the agent of control.

THE DIPTERANS—FLIES

True flies are one of the latest groups in the geological record and are closely related to scorpion-flies, which resemble their earliest forms. One of the main evolutionary developments in dipterans, which is also one of their most distinctive features, is the modification of their hindwings into halteres (or club-shaped balancers). All flies are essentially two-winged (hence the name Diptera, from words with that meaning).

True flies are distinguished by their:

- large, compound eyes, sometimes dominating the entire head capsule
- single pair of membranous flying wings, located on the mesothorax
- highly reduced hindwings that are tiny, club-shaped balancers, named halteres
- highly modified sucking or piercing mouthparts
- short, simple antennae (branched in craneflies and mosquitoes).

Ecology

The order Diptera is the fourth-largest insect order and includes many insects—such as march flies, house flies/bush flies, fruit flies and mosquitoes—that commonly annoy or bite humans, and other animals. In fact, dipterans stand out from all other insect orders in terms of their medical and veterinary significance—as carriers of disease.

The mosquito is one example of a carrier (different species carry different diseases, all with serious consequences for human populations). Just one mosquito-borne disease—malaria—was, until recently, responsible for one-fifth of all human sickness. The need to control mosquito breeding-grounds has also had distinct ecological and social effects.

Fruit, vegetables and other crop plants have also been badly affected by various dipteran groups. In Australia, however, cultivated plants suffer less from fly pests than in many countries—with the Queensland fruit fly (*Dacus tryoni*), being one of the most serious of fruit-attacking insects.

Against this, Diptera also includes some of the most highly beneficial insects—ones that, through their predacious or parasitic lifestyle, play vital roles in helping to control populations of both plants and animals. Certain groups parasitise the nymphs and larvae of numerous species throughout the orders, thus keeping the populations of these other insects in check. Many others feed on flower nectar and play significant roles as plant pollinators.

Overall, however, the natural role of flies is carried out in the main by the maggots, their larvae, with their insatiable appetites: they greatly speed up the decomposition of animal carcasses, manure and rotting vegetation, and keep down disease in their natural habitats.

ABOVE A robber fly (*Blepharotes splendidissimus*) waits for passing prey, normally captured in flight. Powerful flight muscles are housed in its domed thorax. A male robber fly must approach a female cautiously as she is likely to attack him. Larvae live under leaves, bark, or within rotten logs, feeding on decaying plant tissue and other insect larvae.

CRANEFLIES

order Diptera: suborder Nematocera
families Tipulidae, Trichoceridae and
Tanyderidae

Craneflies, which are sometimes also called daddy-long-legs, are all long-legged. Most have delicate, slender bodies, and a wingspan of 6 mm–75 mm. They are often mistaken for huge mosquitoes; however, their size distinguishes them. Craneflies are found in moist habitats and they frequent hollow tree-stumps; or they may be found beneath rock ledges and cool places near waterways.

Cranefly larvae are largely aquatic, although some species feed in damp soil and decaying timber. They are popularly known as 'wire-worms', which are equipped with powerful jaws able to cut into the lower stems and roots of plants. They ascend at night to feed on tender grass stems.

There are three families of cranefly found in Australia—craneflies (Tipulidae); long-necked craneflies (Tanyderidae) and winter craneflies (Trichoceridae).

Tipulidae is the largest family in the entire order Diptera, which comprises all true flies. Most cranefly species are quite small, and they have a long, thin bodily structure. All craneflies lack ocelli. The adults drink water but otherwise do not feed.

Long-necked craneflies are among the most primitive dipterans known. They are medium to large in size, with long necks—and their pronotum and neck sclerites are well developed. Often they are to be found in cool, moist forests, along with the Tipulidae family of craneflies.

A few subalpine species of craneflies are larger, and these have attractively coloured wings. A typical example is the beautifully coloured long-necked cranefly (*Eutanyderus oreonympha*), which is found throughout the alpine regions of southeastern Australia.

Winter craneflies generally resemble members of the Tipulidae family, but they have ocelli. These craneflies are nocturnal. They have been not been recorded outside the cooler regions of southeastern Australia, and the adults occur only during the coldest months of the year. Tree stumps and tree trunks are often used as shelter.

MOSQUITOES AND MIDGES

order Diptera: suborder Nematocera
superfamilies Culicoidea and
Chironomoidea

Mosquitoes and midges are placed in different superfamilies, but the larvae of these insects are all aquatic. What they also have in common is the profound irritation they can cause humans and other creatures through their biting—although mosquitoes, of course, have more serious effects as they are sometimes carriers of diseases.

Mosquitoes

Mosquitoes are placed in the family Culicidae, the largest in the superfamily Culicoidea. They have a wingspan of 3 mm–4 mm and most males have plume-like antennae. Female mosquitoes have mouthparts that have been modified into a long proboscis which is used to siphon the blood of vertebrates. Females need a blood meal in order to produce eggs. Males are typically of a lighter build than females and only drink water—they do not feed. All mosquito larvae are aquatic and breathe through a siphon on the water surface.

Many species carry and transmit diseases that are dangerous to humans, such as malaria and yellow fever and, in Australia, dengue and Ross River virus.

Midges

There are several families of midges, some of which feed on the blood of other animals, including humans—such as the Ceratopogon-idae, and the Simuliidae, which although they are midges are popularly known as biting black sandflies. Other midges feed on moist vegetation. The two families of midges (Ceratopogonidae and Chironomidae) dealt with here are among the more numerous of those in the superfamily Chironomoidea. Of these, the biting midges (family Ceratopogonidae) are smaller in size, with a wingspan of 1 mm–7.5 mm. They are equipped with a stabbing rostrum and, by their sheer numbers alone, commonly cause great irritation to humans and many animals. Some species feed on the haemolymph of other insects. Their larvae are minute and live an aquatic existence, favouring brackish water.

OPPOSITE Long-necked cranefly (*Eutanyderus oreonympha*) is one of the large subalpine species. Adult craneflies have modified mouthparts that form a proboscis for sucking water and nectar but they do not feed very much. Like all dipterans, craneflies have one pair of wings (the rear pair) reduced to club-shaped halteres. Larvae feed within submerged logs.

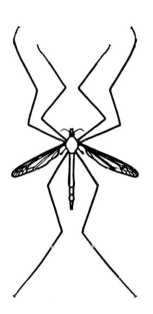

ABOVE A typical cranefly (*Gynoplistia* species) clearly shows its main features.

ABOVE Flies are readily distinguishable from almost all other insects by the presence of one pair of flying wings. Their large compound eyes and sucking or piercing mouthparts are also distinctive features.

BELOW A female giant robber fly (*Blepharotes splendidissimus*). The domed thorax houses huge flight muscles that accelerate this assassin from its perch to swiftly capture flying insects. These include bees, wasps, dragonflies and cicadas, which are seized and held by the robber fly's long, powerful, bristly legs.

Midges in the family Chironomidae have a wingspan of 1 mm–8 mm, and bear a resemblance to mosquitoes. But these midges lack a stabbing rostrum and they are characterised by having a hump-shaped thorax. Their antennae are plume-like; many are black or brown in colour, while some are red, yellow or green. Swarms of these insects are commonly seen around creeks and streams. In most species, the larvae are aquatic.

MARCH FLIES
order Diptera
suborder Brachycera
superfamily Tabanoidea

March flies (family Tabanidae) are between 6 mm–25 mm in length and are distinguished by their stout build and well-developed rostrums. March flies typically have large eyes that meet in the centre of the head capsule and (in most species, except those of the genus *Dasybasis*, which have hairy eyes) reflect highly iridescent colours.

These flies, also known as horseflies, are infamous for their annoying habit of biting humans, but it is only the females that bite. They are equipped with sharp, blade-like mandibles and maxillae that are used to pierce the flesh of their intended host. When the fly withdraws its beak, the blood flows. The males are strictly nectar feeders and as such, they contribute to plant pollination.

ROBBER FLIES AND BEE-FLIES
order Diptera
suborder Brachycera
superfamily Asiloidea

Robber flies

Robber flies (family Asilidae), also known as assassin flies, are distinguished from most other flies by:

- a robust build
- a beard of stiff, forward-projecting setae (hairs) beneath large eyes
- a stoutly pointed rostrum
- thorax and limbs covered in bristly hairs
- a wingspan of 2 mm–75 mm.

Robber flies prey on other flying insects. The facets of its large compound eyes are enlarged towards the upper portion of its head, allowing it to see any insect flying above its concealed position among low shrubs and fallen timber. The eyes are protected by the tuft of hairs between its eyes and its rostrum. A typical example is the giant robber fly (*Blepharotes splendidissimus*), which can capture cicadas, beetles and even dragonflies in mid-air. Some species also mimic wasps in their colouring and movement.

Robber flies generally can capture insects much larger than themselves. A robber fly will drive its rostrum into its prey and drain its life-juices, while holding it firmly with its strong, spiky limbs. The robber fly's saliva anaesthetises its victim. The robber fly's larvae are also predatory and live within rotting timber, feeding on other insect larvae.

Bee-flies

Bee-flies (family Bombyliidae, subfamily Bombyliinae) are small-to-large insects, with long proboscis for probing flower nectaries. Their bodies are covered with hairs that retain pollen. Bee-flies pollinate the flowering plants on which they feed for nectar. Their wings have a span of up to 70 mm and are held flat and wide when at rest. With their powerful wing muscles, they can hover in mid-air between short bursts of flight. The beating of their wings produces a loud buzzing similar to the sound that bees make. Bee-flies have particularly keen eyesight and are very difficult to approach when they are on the wing.

HOVERFLIES
order Diptera
suborder Brachycera
superfamily Syrphoidea

Hoverflies (family Syrphidae) have a wingspan
of up to 30 mm. They typically hover amid
flowers and are speedy flyers. Certain species are
known as drone flies. Their colours mimic wasps
and bees, and their bodies are densely covered
in fine hairs, by which they pollinate the
flowering plants they feed on. A typical example
is the bee-mimicking drone fly (*Eristalis tenax*),
often seen on daisies. Some species' larvae prey
heavily on aphids, while others feed on decaying
vegetation and fungi.

FRUIT FLIES AND VINEGAR FLIES
order Diptera
suborder Brachycera
superfamilies Tephritoidea and
Ephydroidea

Both fruit flies (superfamily Tephritoidea, family
Tephritidae) and vinegar flies (superfamily
Ephydroidea, family Drosophilidae) are tiny
insects that are attracted to overripe fruit.

Although these two families are members of
different superfamilies, they are placed together
here because they are often confused when seen.
They are quite frequently encountered in the
kitchen hovering over the fruit bowl or in the
greengrocer's store.

ABOVE A female bee-
mimicking drone fly (*Eristalis tenax*), a hoverfly,
feeding on a *Jasminum*
flower. Adult hoverflies are
equipped with long tongues
and they frequent flowers,
playing a significant role in
the pollination of plants.
This long-tongued bee-
mimic is commonly mistaken
for a bee, giving it some
degree of protection from
predators.

RIGHT A soldier fly (*Boreoides subulatus*). A close relative of tachinid and march flies, the wing-less female is larger than the slender-winged male. Females advertise their availability by exposing themselves on the decaying timber that they fed on during their larval stage.

ABOVE A long-legged tachinid fly (*Senostoma longipes*). Adult long-legged tachinid flies frequently visit blossoms to feed, and rest on the sunny side of tree trunks. Their parasitic larvae feed on the larvae and adults of other insects.

Fruit flies

A distinctive feature of fruit flies is that their wings, which have a maximum span of 23 mm, are usually patterned. Also, when at rest or moving about, their wings move in an oar-like rotation. Members of many species can be seen performing courtship displays.

It is the larvae of fruit flies, not the adults, that damage fruit. Most species feed within fruit, plant stems, decaying timber, or on flowerheads. The adults lay their eggs on the fruit, and the larvae, when they hatch, tunnel inside it. Adults drink juices such as from sap flows or from fruit.

Vinegar flies

Vinegar flies are tiny, with a wingspan of up to 12 mm. These are the flies that are usually observed gathered around the fruit bowl and, in this case, it is the adults that cause damage. They are especially attracted to overripe fruit, where they will congregate in large numbers, feeding on the fermenting juices. Their larvae feed mainly on yeast-infected vegetation and fungi.

HOUSE FLIES, BUSH FLIES, BLOWFLIES, FLESH-FLIES AND TACHINID FLIES
order Diptera
suborder Brachycera
superfamily Muscoidea

These flies have a wingspan of up to 40 mm. Apart from the tachinid flies, which breed in decaying matter, the larvae (or maggots) of the other families feed on flesh or carrion.

House flies or bush flies

These flies (family Muscidae), with a wingspan up to 14 mm, are probably the most familiar to Australians. Around the home is the common house fly (*Musca domestica*) and outdoors, the bush fly (*Musca vetustissima*). Flies of the genus *Neomyia* are especially common around human habitation. These flies are also known as bluebottle flies. Many species use their highly specialised 'tongue' to suck the blood of vertebrates, and both species carry and transmit diseases such as typhoid. The larvae of these flies feed on a wide range of material, including carrion, dung, fungi and decaying vegetation.

Blowflies

The sets of bristly hairs on either side of the thorax beneath the halteres distinguish blowflies (family Calliphoridae); their wingspan is up to 20 mm. A female blowfly can lay up to 600 eggs, normally depositing them on carrion and animal carcasses, on an open wound or on other bodily openings such as the nose, eyes and mouth. The larvae of most species of blowfly feed on dung and carrion, but some parasitise other insect larvae. One particularly handsome representative of this family is the green, iridescent-coloured blowfly (*Amenia imperialis*), often seen resting on eucalypt tree trunks in sclerophyll forest.

Flesh-flies

Flesh-flies (family Sarcophagidae) have a wingspan to 36 mm and plume-like antennae. They are characteristically marked with three longitudinal stripes along the back of the thorax. A typical example is the large flesh-fly *Sarcorohdendorfia hardyi*, often seen in gardens and woodlands near waterways The females are viviparous, producing live maggots, which they deposit directly onto the food source. Larvae of most species feed on decaying vegetation and carrion. Some larvae parasitise other insects.

Tachinid flies

Many tachinid flies (family Tachinidae), which have a maximum wingspan of around 35 mm, resemble flesh-flies and blowflies. Typical examples are the long-legged tachinid flies of the genus *Senostoma*, commonly seen resting on eucalypt tree trunks; some of the large, handsome, robust species of the genus *Rutilia* have iridescent hues.

Tachinid flies perform a highly beneficial role in culling the populations of a wide range of other arthropods, including spiders, on which they deposit their eggs. The larvae hatch and feed on the host's flesh within its body.

CADDIS-FLIES
order Trichoptera
superfamilies Rhyacophiloidea,
Hydropsychoidea and Limnephiloidea

Caddis-flies are distinguished by:
- wings that are sub-equal (but more often the forewings are broader)
- widely separated compound eyes on a moth-like head
- weakly developed mouthparts with only the palps visible
- filiform antennae held forward (very long in some species)
- parts of the body and all wings densely covered in hairs (most species).

Caddis-flies are closely related to insects of the order Lepidoptera, especially to some of the moths, and are moth-like in general appearance (wingspan 6 mm–70 mm). What distinguishes caddis-flies from moths is the wings, which are densely covered in hairs. Although their mouthparts are reduced, adult caddis-flies can still take up water and nectar.

Caddis-fly larvae live in water, beneath rocks, stones and submerged logs, in either fast-flowing streams or still lakes (depending on the species). Some species are herbivores, some are filter feeders and others are predators. Some species have developed tracheal gills; others take in oxygen through their body cuticles. Although caterpillar-like in appearance, they lack the abdominal fleshy pro-legs that are typical of lepidopteran larvae. The larvae and pupae are preyed upon by trout, amphibians and reptiles, while birds and bats feed on the adults.

Many larvae construct, inhabit and pupate below the water surface within remarkable protective cases. Some incorporate sand grains in the construction of their shelters, and others incorporate twigs, snail shells, leaves or tiny pebbles. It is all held together with silk and attached to a stone or rock. When the creature has undergone its transition and is ready to emerge as an adult, it moves to the water surface to cast off its old cuticle and dry its expanded wings. Then it is ready for flight.

Ecology

All caddis-flies are associated with water environments or cool, damp conditions, favouring pollution-free water in which to grow as larvae. They play an important role in the food chains of fresh-water streams, and are part of the staple diet of many freshwater fish, other aquatic animals and terrestrial creatures. The larvae also effectively control the growth of freshwater plants, since their feeding on the plants keeps them pruned.

The larvae are probably better known than the adults, as they are often discovered by people fishing in freshwater streams. The presence or absence of larvae in freshwater habitats is used as a measure of water quality. A number of the commercially made 'flies' used for fishing lures are modelled on caddis-flies.

ABOVE Caddis-flies are small to moderate moth-like insects closely related to moths and butterflies. Their wings, body and limbs are covered with fine hair-like scales. However, their wing venation and mouthparts distinguish them from moths and butterflies.

BELOW Caddis-fly habitat. Caddis-flies form an important part of the food chain in freshwater ecosystems. Water quality is gauged by their presence (or absence)—the larvae are highly sensitive to pollution

THE LEPIDOPTERANS—BUTTERFLIES AND MOTHS

Lepidoptera, which includes moths, skippers and butterflies, is the second-largest insect order after the Coleoptera (beetles and weevils) and, like Coleoptera, is one of the more recently evolved. Lepidopterans, too, are highly versatile—their success is directly attributable to the development of flowering plants.

The earliest lepidopteran adults had chewing mouthparts and ate the spores of ferns and the pollen of the earliest forms of flowering plants (angiosperms), which produced seeds enclosed in fruits. The development of the long, coiled tongue that lepidopterans use for taking in nectar came about as flowering plants and these insects co-evolved. Nearly all modern lepidopteran adults have no biting mouthparts. All their food is taken in liquid form, derived from nectar and sap flows from tree trunks, from ripe and fermenting fruits, juices of decomposed plants and animals, from puddles after rain, and from honeydew exuded by aphids.

Lepidopterans are distinguished by:

- four wings that are large in relation to body size and are often brightly coloured
- wings, body and limbs densely covered with overlapping scales
- modified scales associated with scent-producing organs
- mouthparts modified into a sucking proboscis, held straight when feeding and coiled at rest
- large, compound eyes
- a mummy-like pupal stage—naked or in a silken cocoon
- an intimate association with flowering plants.

Lepidopterous larvae (caterpillars) are characterised by:

- heavily sclerotised head capsule, mouthparts and, in most cases, true limbs
- six sclerotised, thoracic legs and up to 10 pro-legs
- mouthparts consisting of chewing mandibles.

Moths *vs* butterflies

There are far fewer butterflies than moths: worldwide, of the total number of described lepidopteran species, 20 000 are butterflies and the remaining 145 000 are moths. They are classified mainly according to wing venation, palps and antennae, and arranged into various suborders and infraorders. Some people refer to butterflies as 'day-flying moths', for one of the chief differences in lifestyle between them is that most moths are nocturnally active whereas most butterflies fly by day.

The other main characteristic distinguishing them is the way in which their wings are coupled during flight (see Chapter Three)—for moths it is by a frenulum; for butterflies, by an overlap between wings.

The cryptic patterns of butterflies are generally on the backs of their wings so, when folded at rest, the bright colours of the dorsal surface are hidden. Moths differ in having their cryptic patterns on both the dorsal and ventral surfaces of their wings—particularly the forewings, which often conceal brightly coloured patches on the hindwings when at rest.

Another distinction occurs when pupation takes place: moth larvae generally spin silken cocoons as protection while pupating, whereas butterfly larvae tend to pupate naked.

BELOW A freshly emerged female wattle goat moth (*Xyleutes encalypti*) clings to the trunk of a black wattle (*Acacia decurrens*) after a late afternoon rainstorm. These moths normally emerge from 4 pm onwards. Their huge larvae are among those known as witchetty grubs.

It is also very common for male and female lepidopterans of the same species to differ from one another in bodily structure, colouring, patterns and size. Because of this, males and females have occasionally been described as distinct species until they are observed in courtship and mating. There are, however, observable differences between the sexes of most moths. The antennae in females are thread-like; in males, plume-like. Males have scent pouches on their hindwings and claspers on the tips of their abdomens; none of these are present in females.

Patterns of flight behaviour also differ between the sexes. Female butterflies usually fly in the vicinity of the caterpillar's food plant. The lifestyle of the male butterfly is very different to that of the female, as he does not need to search for specific food plants for the offspring. The male has territorial flight patterns and flies out in the open, usually well above the ground, openly flaunting himself to advertise his colours and flying powers. Male moths and butterflies are generally smaller, slimmer and more brightly coloured than the females.

Butterflies typically have the following characteristics:

- active by day, generally visiting flowers in full sunlight
- wings held folded together upright above their backs when at rest
- thread-like antennae, clubbed at the tips
- larvae often with a naked pupal stage.

Moths typically have the following characteristics:

- active nocturnally (except day-flying moths), many visit flowers and some are strongly attracted to artificial light
- wings held folded roof-like, wrapped about the body or horizontally spread when at rest
- thread-like, feather-like or (less commonly) clubbed antennae
- eyes covered with hairs (in certain species)
- larvae usually with a sheltered pupal stage.

Ecology

Lepidopterans have highly significant and directly beneficial roles as pollinators. They do not transmit diseases of plants, animals or humans, and neither sting nor bite. They have also been used in biological control—one example is the successful introduction of the moth *Cactoblastis cactorum* to control the introduced prickly pear in Queensland. Many butterflies also serve as key indicators of environmental disruption.

Lepidopteran larvae consume (across all species) a broad range of foodstuff, from plant material to

animal matter (including, for example, wool and wax). Certain species of larvae also perform a useful function by reducing leaf litter to enrich the soil. But lepidopteran larvae do contribute substantially to losses involving our agricultural crop plants, too. Nevertheless, even if some caterpillars feed on our crops, most are too busy pruning the abundant foliage in their natural habitat.

Several species of lepidopteran larvae are carnivorous, preying on the eggs and living larvae of other arthropods, including the eggs of other lepidopterans and of spiders, as well as the eggs and larvae of ants, and on aphids.

Lepidopteran caterpillars, in particular, are vitally important links in the food chain, being the staple diet of numerous creatures, particularly small insectivorous birds and mammals, and a wide range of other insects. They have also featured in human diets—the witchetty grub and the bogong moth being well-known examples of lepidopterans used for food by Aboriginal groups.

ABOVE The sword-grass brown butterfly (*Tisiphone abeona abeona*). Confined to Australia, this butterfly has attracted much attention due to its geographical variations—there are eight recognised subspecies. Larvae feed on a range of swordgrasses, which include *Gahnia clarkei*, *G. erythrocarpa*, *G. melanocarpa* and *G. sieberana*.

ABOVE The swift moth (*Oxycanus* species) has wings shaped and coloured like leaves, which can make it difficult to locate. The adults normally emerge after rain. They can fly rapidly and are often attracted to electric lights. The larvae feed on living timber.

RIGHT An empty pupal case of the giant swift moth or ghost moth (*Zelotypia stacyi*) dwarfs one of Australia's largest geckos (*Underwoodisaurus milii*). Larvae feed on the living timber of *Acacia* and *Eucalyptus* trees.

SWIFT MOTHS
order Lepidoptera: suborder Glossata
infraorder Exoporia
superfamily Hepialoidea

This family (Hepialidae) has some of the largest and most beautiful moths known. A typical example is the bent-wing swift moth (*Zelotypia stacyi*), which has a wingspan reaching the family maximum of 230 mm. Swift moths (or ghost moths) often hang from plants by their forelegs. Most larvae feed and tunnel within the stems and roots of living shrubs and trees.

CASE MOTHS
order Lepidoptera: suborder Glossata
superfamily Tineoidea

Case moths (family Psychidae), or bag moths, derive their name from the cocoon-like cases in which the larvae live. The caterpillars of various species use silk to make these cases, often attaching leaves and twigs. At certain times of the year they are a common sight moving around the garden and feeding, sometimes invading the house. The Saunders case moth (*Oiketicus elongata*) is a typical representative of this group.

Some adult females never leave their case. They use sex pheromones to attract the winged males but in other case moths, the females are fully winged. The males, with a wingspan that rarely exceeds 25 mm, have extraordinarily elongated abdomens, with expandable abdominal segments. These allow a male to insert his body well inside the female's case in order to mate with her. Having mated, the female then lays her eggs within the case.

The larvae leave the case after hatching and, suspended on fine silken threads, they make their way to the nearest foliage. Here they will immediately begin constructing their own protective shelters.

WOOD MOTHS
order Lepidoptera: suborder Glossata
superfamily Cossoidea

Wood moths (family Cossidae) are also known as goat moths, and their larvae are well known as witchetty grubs, an important dietary item among some Australian Aborigines.

Wood moths have the heaviest bodies of all moth species. They have a wingspan of 10 mm–240 mm and reduced mouthparts. As adults they do not feed but live off fat reserves stored from their larval stage. A typical representative is the large wattle goat moth (*Xyleutes encalypti*). Its larva lives underground, mostly feeding off the roots of wattles (*Acacia* species). After pupating, it emerges from the soil, usually in the late afternoon during the summer months. Its large pupal casing, up to 110 mm in length, is often obvious, protruding from the soil near the wattle.

CUP MOTHS
order Lepidoptera: suborder Glossata
superfamily Zygaenoidea

Cup moths (family Limacodidae), which have a wingspan of up to 74 mm, are not often observed, mainly owing to their cryptic colouring and nocturnal activity. Their stoutly built, slug-like larvae are probably better-known. These larvae have retractable tufts of stiff, stinging spines that stand up when the larva is touched or threatened and can cause would-be predators a severe local irritation. When danger has passed they are retracted again.

The caterpillars of cup moths pupate inside cocoons that are very strong and resist great pressure from outside, but yield to slight pressure from within. On one end of their cocoon there is a hard, silken, domed 'lid', which allows the moths to emerge from their pupal wrappings after pupation has taken place.

A typical representative is the mottled cup moth (*Doratifera vulnerans*). This species is well known from its extremely tough cocoon, like a gum nut, commonly found strongly adhered to the bark of eucalypts and cultivated fruit trees.

GEOMETRID MOTHS
order Lepidoptera: suborder Glossata
superfamily Geometroidea

Geometrid moths (family Geometridae), also known as emeralds, comprise one of the largest families of moths. Their wingspan is from 12 to 120 mm. It is characteristic of these moths to rest with their wings spread flat and wide. Most species of this group of moths have mottled patterns on their wings, and this cryptic colouration helps them to blend with their surroundings to a remarkable degree. Typical geometrid moths include the green emerald moth (*Terpna mniaria*) and another tropical species, the four o'clock moth (*Dysphania fenestrata*).

LEFT A male Saunders case moth (*Oiketicus elongata*). The winged male fertilises the female by extending his expandable abdomen inside the base of her case. The eggs are laid within the case.

ABOVE A cocoon of the case moth (*Hyalarcta huebneri*). The larvae construct mobile shelters from stout silk, which they cover by adhering short lengths of irregularly spaced twigs and leaves of their host plant. The silk cocoon case is attached to a twig of the host plant with a band of strong silk and the larva undergoes pupation head-downwards. The wingless female never leaves her shelter, as it serves as a brooding chamber for eggs.

This moth gets its common name from its habit of flying about during the late afternoon.

The larvae of these moths are popularly known as loopers or inch-worms, because of the way one moves along a leaf or twig—it arches the front of its body forward first, to secure a foothold, and then moves its rear segments up behind to close the gap.

SKIPPERS

order Lepidoptera: suborder Glossata, superfamily Hesperioidea

Skippers (family Hesperidae) are close relatives of the papilionoid butterflies but differ from them in certain respects. The skippers are distinguished by:
- a wingspan of 20 mm–50 mm
- the unique way in which they rest with their forewings held upright and their hindwings spread flat
- antennae widely separated at their bases, thickened at the tips, but not actually club-shaped
- being browns and yellows (most species).

In most cases the caterpillars feed on grasses and similar plants, and hide themselves within rolled grass blades. A typical representative is the symmomus skipper (*Trapezites symmomus symmomus*), which has a wide-ranging distribution from eastern Victoria to north-eastern Queensland. Its larva feeds on the leaves of *Gahnia* swordgrass.

ABOVE A female mottled cup moth (*Doratifera vulnerans*) freshly emerged from its cocoon. The extremely tough pyriform cocoons offer much protection from the elements but these are not impenetrable to parasitic wasps. Mottled cup moth larvae feed on the leaves of *Eucalyptus*, *Angophora* and apricot trees.

OPPOSITE A caterpillar of the mottled cup moth (*Doratifera quadruguttata*), with its spines retracted (head end far left). The larvae feed on leaves of eucalypts, ornamental and fruit trees. The brightly coloured larva resembles a sea anemone, and is armed with expansible tufts of sharp stinging spines (setae), which the caterpillar is not shy to use if handled. These give a painful sting to the assailant.

RIGHT The symmomus skipper (*Trapezites symmomus symmomus*) is the largest species of its genus. The larvae remain well hidden during daylight, deep at the base of its grass food plant *Lomandra longifolia*. Keen eyesight and an erratic flight pattern make this elusive butterfly difficult for predators to capture.

OPPOSITE A female orchard swallowtail or large citrus butterfly (*Princeps aegeus*). This species has adapted to feeding on cultivated citrus plants such as grapefruit, lemon, orange and lime. It also feeds on the leaves of a number of other exotic plants, including parsley and camphor laurel.

BELOW A caterpillar of the geometrid four o'clock moth (*Dysphania fenestrata*) on its food plant, *Carallia*. The brightly coloured adult usually takes to the wing in the late afternoon, flying until after dark, hence its popular name.

PAPILIONOID BUTTERFLIES
order Lepidoptera: suborder Glossata
superfamily Papilionoidea

Most Australian butterflies are placed in the superfamily Papilionoidea. This group contains butterflies with a maximum wingspan of 160 mm, in four families: Papilionidae (swallowtails), Pieridae (whites, sulphurs, jezebels), Nymphalidae (admirals, browns), Lycaenidae (blues, coppers, hairstreaks).

Swallowtails
Swallowtails (family Papilionidae) have a wingspan up to 160 mm. All species are active in daylight, feeding on nectar. Their caterpillars are equipped with an osmeterium as a defence against would-be predators.

Papilionidae and Pieridae are very closely related; their pupae attach themselves to a leaf or steam by a cremaster (anal hooks) and a silken girdle. They remain in the head-upright position during metamorphosis (unlike the Nymphalidae butterflies, which normally hang upside down as they have no central girdle).

The family Papilionidae consists of the largest and most beautiful Australian butterflies. The brightly coloured and popular blue triangle or blue sailor butterfly (*Graphium sarpedon choredon*) is a fine example. The Cape York birdwing butterfly (*Troides priamus pronomus*), with a wingspan of 160 mm, is a magnificent example of the birdwing group.

Whites, sulphurs and jezebels
Whites, sulphurs and jezebels (family Pieridae) have a wingspan of 90 mm, and their wings are mostly white or yellow. However, eight species of the genus *Delias* are adorned with conspicuous reds and yellows on their undersides, the upper sides being white, bordered in black—the jezebel butterfly *Delias nigrina* is a typical representative of this group.

Admirals and browns
Admirals and browns (family Nymphalidae) have a maximum wingspan of 90 mm. Their wings are mostly brown, often brightly marked with splotches of white, yellow, orange or red, and many species have eyespots of concentric bands of coloured scales, which may be present on both the upperside and the underside of the wings, depending on the species. When pupating, the pupae of this group always hang by a cremaster from a leaf or branch, head-down.

The familiar monarch or wanderer butterfly (*Danaus plexippus plexippus*) is a typical representative of the family Nymphalidae. Another typical member of the family is the sword-grass brown (*Tisiphone abeona abeona*). The handsome tailed emperor butterfly (*Polyura pyrrhus sempronius*) is the only Australian representative of the subfamily Charaxinae.

Blues, coppers and hairstreaks
Blues, coppers and hairstreaks (family Lycaenidae) have a maximum wingspan of 70 mm. The upper surface of their wings is usually covered in iridescent blue scales. Many adults have tails on their hindwings, and they move the hindwings about when sitting on a leaf or twig in the sunlight. This serves to protect the butterfly, as a predator is often more likely to attack the moving tail than a still one. The attractive imperial blue butterfly (*Jalmenus evagoras evagoras*) is a fine example of this group.

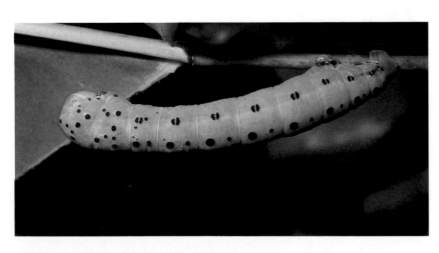

ABOVE The blue triangle butterfly (*Graphium sarpedon choredon*) inhabits coastal areas from south of Sydney to Cape York. Some 85 per cent of Australian butterflies occur in the belt of land stretching from the Kimberley Ranges across the north of the continent, to the east coast.

The moth butterfly (*Liphyra brassolis major*), an unusually large representative of the group, occurs only where green tree-ants (*Oecophylla* species) are plentiful, as its caterpillars live in a close relationship with the ants in their aerial nests built among the foliage of evergreen trees.

In fact, a number of species of Lycaenidae have extremely interesting life cycles—during their larval stage they are closely associated with the nests of ants. The caterpillars live inside the ant nest and feed on ant larvae, but their tough leathery skin protects them from being eaten by the ants and they are tolerated because of the sweet substance they exude, which the ants consume. The caterpillars pupate inside the nest and, after emerging as butterflies, they shed copious amounts of scales as they struggle to leave the ant nest. The ants' mandibles are filled with the scales and they are thus unable to prevent the newly emerged butterflies escaping from their clutches. Sometimes the ants carry too many of these caterpillars into their nest and the colony dies out because the caterpillars devour all the ants' young.

EMPEROR MOTHS, SILK MOTHS AND ANTHELID MOTHS
order Lepidoptera: suborder Glossata
superfamily Bombycoidea

All these families form part of the superfamily Bombycoidea, which also encompasses a number of other groups worldwide and within Australia, including insects with wingspans ranging from 20 mm–270 mm. One of these families, Bombycidae, includes the famed silk moth (*Bombyx mori*), the larvae of which are used in silk production.

Emperor moths

Emperor moths (family Saturniidae) have a wingspan of 60–270 mm. They have reduced mouthparts and do not feed as adults but live off fat reserves stored from their larval stage. Male emperor moths have large, plumed and complex antennae, capable of picking up the pheromone vapours that a female of the same species emits from scent glands at the tip of her abdomen. Through this scent, the male moth can detect her whereabouts from many kilometres away and he will fly upwind until he locates her. Females may attract many male suitors but will only mate with one of them.

The most widespread species of emperor moth is the beautiful, large emperor gum moth (*Opodiphthera eucalypti*), which occurs from Victoria to the tropics. Another Australian representative of this family is one of the largest moths known—the tropical species, the tailed Hercules moth (*Coscinocera hercules*), with a wingspan of a massive 270 mm.

The large caterpillars of these moths build rather tough cocoons in which to pupate. These cocoons may be hardened by a varnish-like substance that the caterpillar exudes as it constructs its shelter.

Anthelid moths

Anthelid moths (family Anthelidae) have a wingspan of 25 mm–160 mm, and hold their broad, pointed wings widespread and flat when at rest. These moths have an amazing habit of remaining still among leaf-litter or on foliage. They do not move even when they are prodded; their cryptic colouring merges in perfectly with their surroundings. Their caterpillars are very hairy and, like tussock moth caterpillars, are commonly known as 'hairy bears'.

The family Anthelidae occurs only in Australia and New Guinea. A typical example of this family is the huge white-stemmed gum moth (*Chelepteryx collesi*), which is commonly found in eastern Australia.

LEFT Some *Delias* species, such as this female wood white jezebel (*D. aganippe*), are common winter butterflies. Their flight is slow and usually high around treetops. Their conspicuous colouring makes them particularly easy to identify. Their larvae feed on mistletoe (*Amyema* species). Both the larvae and pupae are often found in large numbers on the host plant.

ABOVE An imperial blue butterfly (*Jalmenus evagoras evagoras*). Larvae feed on leaves of a wide range of *Acacia* trees including *A. dealbata*, *A. cunninghamii* and *A. falcata*.

HAWK MOTHS
order Lepidoptera: suborder Glossata
superfamily Sphingoidea

Hawk moths (family Sphingidae) have a wingspan of 40 mm–190 mm, and perhaps the most distinctive body shape of all moths. The robust body of a hawk moth and its strong, long, narrow forewings and short hindwings combine to give it aerodynamic power not found with most other insects. In some species the tongue is extremely long, and is used for feeding from flowers with deep corollas.

Hawk moths have large caterpillars, which are typically adorned with a harmless, prominent horn stemming from the rear segment. Species typical of this group of moths include the handsome, large hawk moth (*Gnathothlibus erotus eras*), the privet hawk moth (*Psilogramma menephron*) and a large hawk moth with orange-coloured hindwings (*Metamimas australasiae*), which ranges from southern coastal New South Wales to Cairns, Queensland. Its larvae are restricted to feeding on eucalypts.

NOCTUID, TIGER AND TUSSOCK MOTHS
order Lepidoptera: suborder Glossata
superfamily Noctuoidea

Noctuid moths (family Noctuidae), tiger moths (family Arctiidae) and tussock moths (family Lymantriidae) are all part of the superfamily Noctuoidea, which contains moths with wingspans ranging from 10 mm to 170 mm, and also includes another four families with Australian representatives.

Noctuid moths
Noctuid moths (family Noctuidae) have a wingspan of 10 mm–170 mm. In certain species the ocelli are prominent on the head capsule.

Among those included in this very large family, and typical of it, is the bogong moth (*Agrotis infusa*), well known for its annual migratory flights. They are best known during certain years when they are blown off course by westerly winds and arrive at the east coast *en masse* during summer months. The old lady's cloak moth (*Speiredonia spectans*), another typical

ABOVE A male emperor gum moth (*Opodiphthera eucalypti*) in its pink form, displays large staring eyespots on its hindwings. The larvae of this species feed on leaves of eucalypt and peppercorn trees. Adults have non-functional mouthparts and derive their energy from fat reserves accumulated during their larval growth.

example, is familiar to many through its habit of entering houses and hiding behind doors and drapes where it rests during daylight, with its wings spread flat and wide, showing their iridescent purple sheen.

With the peppered prominent moth (*Neola semiaurata*), however, it is its remarkable caterpillar, rather than the adult, that people are most familiar with. Whenever threatened, the caterpillar can display its prominent eyespots to warn of its unpleasant taste, or else flash a defensive gland that emits a highly repugnant smell, sufficient to deter any would-be predators.

Tiger moths

Tiger moths (family Arctiidae) have a wingspan of 10 mm–85 mm, and their distinctive warning colours advertise their distastefulness to would-be predators. Members of the genus *Arctiini* have wings typically adorned in black, with splotches of bright yellow, orange and white, and their abdominal segments are striped with similar warning colours. Typical examples of this group include *Spilosoma glatignyi*, *S. curvata* and also *Arctiini* species. The latter are often quite numerous during summer months, flying about in the sunlight visiting flowers.

Tussock moths

Tussock moths (family Lymantriidae) have a wingspan of 16 mm–100 mm. They are easily distinguished by their very furry bodies. These moths are sluggish, and can be found resting on foliage during the day, hidden by their drab colouring. The caterpillars of these moths (like those of anthelid moths) are very hairy and are also known as 'hairy bears'. The species *Euproctis edwardsii* and *Teia anartoides* are typical representatives of this family. The females have a dense terminal tuft of deciduous scales, utilised to cover and camouflage their eggs.

ABOVE A large hawk moth (*Metamimas australasiae*). The larvae feed on eucalypt leaves while adults feed on flower nectar at night. They are distributed from coastal New South Wales to Cairns, Queensland.

THE HYMENOPTERANS—BEES, WASPS AND ANTS

Hymenoptera is a large and complex order comprising two suborders. The suborder Sumphyta includes sawflies and wood wasps. The other suborder, Apocrita, includes all of the wasps, ants and bees, which are then further divided into 14 superfamilies.

Hymenopterans range in size from 1.15 mm to over 50 mm and they can be found occupying most terrestrial habitats.

They can be distinguished by:

- the distinctive waist-shape where the thorax and abdomen meet (especially pronounced in most ants and many wasps)
- two pairs of membranous, transparent wings, with few veins
- all vespoid wasps (superfamily Vespoidea) carry their wings longitudinally folded when at rest, distinguishing them from all other hymenopterans
- forewings which are always longer than hindwings
- both pairs of wings coupled in flight
- three ocelli and, especially with bees, large compound eyes
- mandibulate mouthparts equipped for biting, cutting, chewing (in all bees and certain wasps mouthparts are tongued, for sucking and lapping)
- short antennae, strongly elbowed in many groups
- a prominent ovipositor (very pronounced with ichneumonoid wasps), modified into a sting in many families, especially nest-building wasps and social bees
- grub-like larvae (with some exceptions, including sawflies)
- social behaviour and labour division—far more evident among the bees and ants than among the

wasps—although numerous solitary species show no sign of social behaviour whatsoever.

All female wasps have highly modified ovipositors, which serve a variety of purposes (only in certain species have they evolved into sting mechanisms). These ovipositors are used for:

- sawing into plant tissue to create cavities in which to deposit eggs
- drilling through tree bark to deposit eggs on beetle larvae feeding within the timber
- injecting paralysing fluids into the bodies of other arthropods, before laying eggs on them
- finding and identifying host insect larvae
- draining the body fluids of other insects.

The plant-feeding sawflies (superfamily Tenthredinoidea) were among the first hymenopterous insects to appear on Earth—during the early Mesozoic Era, approximately 200 million years ago. However, fossil records show that the first true wasps made their appearance around 60 million years ago. The development of social life among wasps began with the first wasps that provided food for their young, the solitary wasps (superfamily Sphecoidea). From this came the need to build nests and work cooperatively to gather food and feed the larvae.

The world of the nest-building species is largely a female one as their communities consist of all females except for brief periods during the mating season when males are produced. The males are ousted from the colony once they have fulfilled their one and only function in life—fertilising the females.

In some respects, ant colonies are similar to bee colonies. After the nuptial flight, and having shed her wings, the fertilised female or queen ant begins nest-building alone. As soon as the first brood emerges from its pupal wrappings, it takes on the work of caring for the larvae and nest-building, while the queen devotes her energy solely to egg-laying.

Through their teamwork and social behaviour, as a group, hymenopterans have developed an extraordinarily wide range of skills. They are now generally regarded as being the most advanced insects, because of their caring for their young, and their foresight in providing food and storing it. Most of all, perhaps, they are advanced in terms of their social organisation. Some species have evolved communities that are among the most highly organised found in the animal world. Parthenogenesis is universal.

Bees have certainly developed the highest forms of social cohesion among arthropods. Ants are

BELOW A black-and-white spider-hunting wasp (*Turneromyia* species) drags a paralysed huntsman spider to her nest-site. These pompilid wasps seize their prey by their mandibles and drag it backwards along the ground to their prepared nest-sites. The 30 cm-long burrow is excavated with several short side-burrows, each designed to house a spider. After an egg is laid on the spider, that cell is then sealed.

unrivalled in their complex organisational skills, being the only arthropods known to farm other creatures. Nevertheless, the popular belief that all wasps, ants and bees live in highly developed communities is a myth. The degree of social organisation and cooperation varies greatly among the species.

Ecology

Hymenopterans are among the most highly beneficial of insects in maintaining a balance in the animal and plant kingdoms—they control the populations of other arthropods and are also important plant pollinators.

Their role in controlling arthropod populations is carried out in many ways, reflecting the great diversity of life cycles and physical characteristics among hymenopterans. Various wasp families, such as Ichneumonidae and Braconidae, contribute significantly to the maintenance of population

balances. The offspring of many wasp families parasitise, and feed off spiders and other insects. Some wasps (such as those in the family Vespidae) feed their young the masticated bodies of lepidopterous larvae and other insects. Ants collect unhealthy, dead and exhausted insects from the ground and foliage and they generally clean up the forest floor. Having dragged these creatures off to their nests, they feed their larvae on the masticated bodies.

Although most hymenopteran larvae feed off other arthropods, most adults feed on flower nectar and pollen, sap flows, overripe fruit and honeydew. The young of most bees and some wasps are fed pollen and nectar. Since they are significant flower-visitors, hymenopteran adults play a major role in pollinating flowering plants. Ants also are significant in dispersing plant seeds.

ABOVE A red bulldog ant (*Myrmecia gulosa*). Australian bulldog ants are considered the prototype of primitive ants. Closely related species have been found perfectly preserved in amber. These are the oldest hymenopteran representatives known from fossil records dating back to the Triassic Period (245 million years ago) in Australia and central Asia.

ABOVE A female sawfly (*Pterygophorus analis*). Sawflies or leaf-wasps were the first hymenopterans, originating almost 200 million years ago in the early Mesozoic era. Sawfly larvae look and act much like butterfly and moth caterpillars. They feed on *Eucalyptus* leaves.

SAWFLIES
order Hymenoptera: suborder Symphyta
superfamily Tenthredinoidea

There are three families of sawfly in Australia—Tenthredinidae, Argidae and Pergidae—with the latter having the most species. Sawflies are the most common members of their suborder, which also includes wood wasps (stout-waisted adults that also have caterpillar-like larvae). These are the most primitive hymenopterans.

Sawflies are distinguished by:
• no waist
• distinctive, complete wing venation
• short antennae
• strong, cutting mandibles in adults and larvae
• a saw-like ovipositor, and no sting
• larvae that are caterpillar-like.

Sawflies are stout-bodied insects (body length 3 mm–55 mm) and are often showy, with iridescent colouring. They buzz loudly when they fly. The saw-like ovipositor folds away, much like a pocket-knife blade. Most females lay their eggs into the plant tissue on which the larvae feed.

Their caterpillar-like larvae are distinguishable from lepidopteran caterpillars by the lack of a ring of fine hooks at the ends of the pro-legs. These are the only hymenopterous larvae that must fend for themselves as soon as they emerge from the egg, which they do by feeding externally on plant leaves (sometimes eucalypts). They feed during periods of high leaf-growth, pruning the trees and encouraging vigorous regrowth.

When fully fed and grown, masses of larvae descend from the tree and burrow beneath the soil to pupate. Underground, they spin hard silken cocoons, placed up against each other, forming a large clump of cells. Pergidae larvae are commonly known as spitfires. This is because of their habit of ejecting highly concentrated, regurgitated globules of *Eucalyptus* oil from their mouths, which successfully deters all would-be predators. Spitfires congregate in large clusters on *Eucalyptus* leaves and raise their heads and tails in unison when threatened.

HATCHET-BODIED WASPS
order Hymenoptera:
suborder Apocrita
superfamily Evanioidea

Hatchet-bodied wasps (families Evaniidae, Aulacidae and Gasteruptiidae) are 2 mm–15 mm in length, dark-coloured—deep red or black—and cosmopolitan, but vary more in tropical regions. They have a stoutly built thorax linked to a laterally flattened abdomen by a long narrow waist attached to the dorsal surface of the thorax above the level of the hindcoxae. The rapid, up-and-down movement of the wasp's wedge-shaped abdomen as it moves about strongly resembles a tiny hatchet, giving rise to its common name.

These are solitary wasps, the adults usually being seen during spring and summer months on flowers or running about the trunks of standing and fallen trees. Very alert and active, they will quickly take to the air when disturbed, and alight elsewhere. Although essentially cosmopolitan, their lifestyles and their forms are more diverse in tropical and subtropical regions.

Females lay tiny eggs inside the oothecae of cockroaches and mantids, and the hatchet-bodied wasp larvae parasitise the occupants. Other hosts include longicorn beetle larvae.

ICHNEUMON WASPS AND BRACONID WASPS
order Hymenoptera:
suborder Apocrita
superfamily Ichneumonoidea

Parasitic hymenopterans are represented in several superfamilies, one of the most numerous being the Ichneumonoidea, which contains both ichneumons and braconids. Most species of the parasitic wasp families are, by necessity, smaller

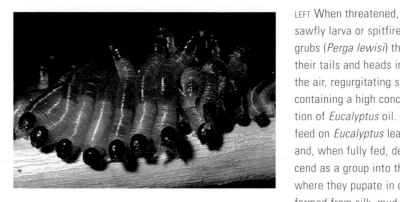

than most other hymenopteran species, the largest among them being the ichneumon wasps. Ichneumons and braconids have much in common, in terms of their lifestyles, and ichneumons are also distinguished by the fact that many ichneumon species exude an offensive odour when handled or threatened.

Ichneumon wasps
Ichneumon wasps (family Ichneumonidae) are 2 mm–120 mm in length, including the ovipositor. They have long, thread-like antennae with multiple segments. These wasps typically have forewings with two recurrent veins and hindwings with a long median cell beyond the marginal veins.

Most ichneumon species have a long, slender ovipositor (commonly mistaken for a sting), which can be more than three times the length of the body. The ovipositor is used to pierce plant tissue and the cuticles of spiders and other insects so that an egg can be laid in the plant or in the body of the victim. Many

LEFT When threatened, sawfly larva or spitfire grubs (*Perga lewisi*) throw their tails and heads into the air, regurgitating spittle containing a high concentration of *Eucalyptus* oil. They feed on *Eucalyptus* leaves and, when fully fed, descend as a group into the soil where they pupate in cells formed from silk, mud and regurgitated *Eucalyptus* oil.

BELOW A hatchet-bodied wasp (*Evania appendigaster*) feeding on blossoms of scrub apple (*Angophora hispida*). Hatchet wasps are parasitic insects that specialise in seeking out cockroach egg-capsules. Adults can be found frequenting flowers during summer, feeding on nectar and pollen and waving their wedge-shaped abdomens up and down.

OPPOSITE Replenishing her energy, a large female spider-hunting wasp (*Cryptocheilis bicolor*) is engrossed in feeding on the nectar of a blue-leafed ironbark blossom (*Eucalyptus nubila*). Adult wasps typically feed on nectar, fruit juices and sap flows.

ichneumon wasps have learned to feed on the body fluids of other soft-bodied insects by using their ovipositor to pierce the insect's cuticle. If held in the hand, an ichneumon may attempt a feeble jab at the flesh with its ovipositor, but this usually amounts to no more than a pinprick. Depending on the species, a female ichneumon deposits between ten and several thousand eggs within the body of large hosts, such as butterfly or beetle larvae.

Braconid wasps

Braconid wasps (family Braconidae) are very closely related to ichneumons and have similar habits in that they also parasitise the eggs, young and adults of insects from various orders. Their wings differ in being dark-coloured (often banded with clear areas) and folded closely together above the body when at rest. The wasps measure 1 mm–80 mm, including their very long ovipositors. When threatened or handled, they emit an odour repulsive to predators. Most species have bright bands of yellow and black or orange and black adorning their bodies.

Ecology

Ichneumons and braconids are important biological control agents, keeping the populations of other insects in check. Both types of wasp parasitise lepidopterans, dipterans and coleop-terans, as well as larger species of hymenopterans. Ichneumons kill enormous numbers of larvae of these groups. Braconids parasitise not only the larvae but also the eggs and adults; they also attack hemipterans and orthopterans. Some of the larger braconid wasp species prefer the larvae of wood-boring insects, such as longicorn beetles.

RIGHT A female spider-hunting wasp (*Cryptocheilus bicolor*) excavates a nest burrow. Unlike social wasps (family Vespidae), which mouth-feed their young, the pompilid wasps have no contact with their offspring, other than providing one spider per cell for each larva to feed on.

CHALCIDOID WASPS
order Hymenoptera:
suborder Apocrita
superfamily Chalcidoidea

Chalcidoid wasps are distinguished by:
• their greatly reduced wing venation
• swollen femora
• curved tibiae of the hindlegs
• a pronotum not extending to the tegula.

Chalcidoidea is the largest hymenopteran superfamily. Many of these wasps have iridescent colouring but are inconspicuous due to their size—most species measure only 1 mm–3 mm in length. Most are gall-forming insects, feeding on plant tissue and seeds. The galls are formed when the plant responds to injuries inflicted by the larvae. However, a number of species are parasitic on the eggs, larvae and pupae of other insects (including those of bees and wasps). Many chalcidoid wasps are host-specific, specialising in parasitising lepidopterans.

SPIDER-HUNTING, HAIRY FLOWER AND SAND WASPS
order Hymenoptera:
suborder Apocrita
superfamilies Vespoidea and
Sphecoidea

Many wasps create cells in the ground or in rotting timber as brood chambers for their young, which they provision with paralysed arthropods for their larvae to feed on after hatching. Such wasps are known as fossorial (or digging) wasps, and their females usually have modified limbs and a prothorax suited to digging or burrowing in the soil.

These wasps hunt for prey to feed to their larvae. The adults generally obtain their own food from nectar or sap flows. These wasps hunt a wide range of creatures but many species specialise. They search the ground and foliage for their prey, capture and paralyse it, and then drag or carry it to the burrow or nest-site. They then lay an egg on the paralysed creature and seal the cell. The larva, once hatched, parasitises the live arthropod and feeds on it until it is ready to change into an adult.

The main families of wasps that are fossorial and hunt food for their young are the spider-hunting wasps (family Pompilidae), hairy flower wasps (family Scoliidae) and some species of sand wasps (family Sphecidae); some of the flower wasps (family Tiphiidae) are also fossorial but they do not create chambers in this way. All these wasps are up to 40 mm in body length.

The spider-hunting wasps (family Pompilidae) and the hairy flower wasps (family Scoliidae) are part of the superfamily Vespoidea. The flower wasps (family Tiphiidae) are also in this superfamily, but are grouped here with the velvet ants (family Mutillidae). The most prolific group—the sand wasps (family Sphecidae)—is in its own superfamily, Sphecoidea.

Spider-hunting wasps

Spider-hunting wasps are distinguished by:
- a smooth, shiny body
- long, slender legs; hindlegs typically longer
- a pronounced vein lobe on their hindwings.

Spider-hunting wasps (family Pompilidae) include handsome and often large species, and can be seen running about tree trunks and over patches of ground in the summer sunshine. They are 3.5 mm–35 mm in length, and typically coloured orange and black. The females have a vicious sting if handled or attacked.

All pompilid wasps hunt spiders as food to provide for their young. The spiders are overpowered with great determination, para-lysed and carried away to prepared burrows (often excavated in sandy soil). Some pompilid species, however, lay their eggs on spiders captured by other pompilids, before the spider is dragged below ground.

Depending on the wasp species and the size of the spiders, one or more spiders may be stored in one cell. When fully grown (having left the spider's vital organs to eat last), the wasp larva spins a papery-silk cocoon in which to pupate.

Hairy flower wasps

Hairy flower wasps (family Scoliidae) are orange–yellow and black, some predominantly black and generally very hairy. They have strongly built forelimbs for digging into soil or rotting wood. Adults measure up to 40 mm in body length.

Females hunt beetle larvae (mostly family Scarabaeidae) for their own larvae to feed on. They have the uncanny knack of knowing the exact location of an intended host. The wasp stings and paralyses each beetle larvae and lays one egg per larvae. Adults feed on the nectar of *Eucalyptus* flowers during summer months.

Sand wasps

Sand wasps are all solitary and all are members of one large family (family Sphecidae), which includes the true stinging wasps. They have a slender, stalk-like petiole (or waist) and distinc-tive abdominal segments, range in size from 1.5 mm–40 mm and are distinguished from all other hymenopterans by the structure of the pronotum and by their simple body hairs.

Some species of sand wasp build their nests within burrows in the ground while another group in this family, the mud daubing wasps, are clay-nest builders (see Chapter Five).

VELVET ANTS AND FLOWER WASPS
order Hymenoptera:
superfamily Vespoidea
families Mutillidae and Tiphiidae

Velvet ants are, in fact, ant-like wasps and are very similar in appearance and lifestyle to the flower wasps, especially to the female flower wasps of the subfamily Thynninae.

These are among the most curious-looking wasps. The females are wingless, with short, curly antennae and have a vicious sting if handled. When moving about on the ground they resemble giant, stoutly-built ants. However, they lack the characteristic nodiform ant-waist of true ants. Because of their ant-like structure many species have acquired such common names as solitary ants, velvet ants and blue-ants.

The males of both families are fully winged and typically wasp-like. They often visit flowering shrubs as they fly about in warm sunshine.

Velvet ants

Velvet ants (family Mutillidae) are dark in colour—black to dark red—and measure 3 mm–25 mm in length, the females always much larger than the males. They are not flower-frequenters but they haunt tree trunks and patches of open or bare ground, where mating also normally takes place. They are more commonly found inland and prefer moving about during the hottest time of the day in the summer months.

Velvet ants are parasitic in nest-sites of other hymenopterans—burrowing wasps and bees. A typical representative is the rust-red coloured velvet ant (*Ephutomorpha ferruginata*), which has a white patch of hair on its abdomen. This

OPPOSITE A winged male flower wasp (*Hemithynnus variabilis*) feeding on the nectar of tea-tree blossom (*Leptospermum laevigatum*). The male frequents flower-ing trees and shrubs in hot sunshine. When a wingless female wasp is located, he immediately swoops down, grasps her with his legs, and carries her away to mate on the wing, with her hanging head-down.

LEFT A paper-nest wasp (*Polistes* species) represents a typical wasp. The two pairs of membranous wings are strongly coupled in flight by rows of fine hooks on the leading edges of the hindwings. These fasten onto the forewing margin.

ABOVE A paper-nest wasp (*Polistes variabilis*). If the nest-site is disturbed, adults can become aggressive, but if undisturbed, they can be observed performing their work. To make the paper-nest, the wasps rasp wood and plant tissue from trees with their jaws, chew it into fragments and mix it with their saliva. Their larvae are fed on lepidopterous larvae that are stung and brought to the nest. The meat is masticated and mouth-fed to the young.

species wanders about open patches of sandy ground searching for the burrows of sand wasps (family Sphecidae). Having found one, it waits for the female sand wasp to return with her prey (usually a meadow katydid, *Conocephalus* species or another similar-sized insect), and the velvet ant lays her egg on the paralysed insect. The female sand wasp, unsuspecting, lays her own egg on the host, too, but the velvet ant's larva emerges from the egg first and devours the katydid before the sand wasp larva hatches.

Female velvet ants have a formidable sting and can cause great discomfort if handled. Males never have venomous stings as they are unnecessary for their quite different lifestyle. They expend much energy on the wing in search of females and replenish this by feeding on flower nectar, a natural source of sugar.

Flower wasps

Flower wasps (family Tiphiidae) are often yellow and black with dark red legs, and are between 2 mm–40 mm in length. They most commonly frequent sandy coastlines where tea-trees (*Leptospermum* species) and angophoras are in full flower during spring and summer, but they also occur inland.

The wingless females are stoutly built, smaller than the males, fossorial, and have a vicious sting if handled. After mating, the female can be seen moving about the ground in an ant-like manner searching for soil-dwelling insects on which to deposit her eggs.

MASON WASPS AND PAPER-NEST WASPS
order Hymenoptera:
suborder Apocrita
superfamily Vespoidea
family Vespidae

Mason wasps and paper-nest wasps have in common:

- short, strong-cutting mandibles
- simple tarsal claws and two spurs on the tibia of their mid-pair of legs
- semi-social to social habits—forming temporary colonies, in which all members toil to feed the young
- the need to hunt to provide food for their young
- adults that usually only feed on nectar, though some species will occasionally consume portions of the masticated meat
- larval food that is mainly masticated caterpillar and beetle larvae. A few species feed their young on nectar and pollen, but this is rare.

Mason wasps

Mason wasps (subfamily Eumeninae) are mostly solitary, large, handsome and stoutly built insects, up to 35 mm long. They are typically deep orange–red with black abdominal bands Some species have a long, thin petiole or waist.

Most species build mud-clay nests attached by clay cement to rock overhangs, tree trunks, fence posts or similar. They also use abandoned tunnels of timber-boring moth and beetle larvae or tunnels in the soil formed by cicada nymphs. Clay-mud is used to build a protective shelter around the site; some species form mud turrets around the entrance. Insect larvae are paralysed and stored in the nests for their young to feed on. The males visit the nest-sites where the females are, as the eggs require frequent fertilisation.

Paper-nest wasps

Paper-nest wasps (subfamilies Polistinae and Vespinae) are between 5 mm–32 mm long. These social wasps build a variety of paper nests produced from masticated wood-pulp. The nest is attached to a roof or other overhang by a sturdy wood-pulp stem; unlike mason wasp nests, the cells face downwards. The wasp larvae, when fully fed, prepare for pupation by spinning a silken cap over the mouth of each cell.

ANTS

order Hymenoptera:
suborder Apocrita
superfamily Vespoidea
family Formicidae

Most members of this enormous family are
social insects that live in colonies within which
the division of labour has resulted in the
creation of different castes, for example, queens,
wingless workers or soldiers. Each caste has
distinguishing anatomical features and a
specialised role within the colony. The degree of
social organisation varies between species. True
ants have a characteristic nodiform waist, and a
body length of 2 mm–30 mm.

Most of the living ant genera have existed
from the end of the Cretaceous Period, some 70
million years ago. The first ants were large,
heavily armoured insects. Ants are now placed
in the superfamily Vespoidea. Although this
superfamily also contains the fossorial wasps as
well as other wasp families to which ants are
closely related, such as Mutillidae (velvet ants)
and Vespidae (mason wasps and paper-nest
wasps), ants still represent a distinct group.

Ants consume a wide range of food and are
highly adaptable. They help clean up habitats by
their relentless toil and highly organised
activities—dispersing plant seeds and removing
dying insects and other dead creatures, and
farming other insects. Overall, ants are probably
the most widespread of insects.

ABOVE A female red bulldog
ant (*Myrmecia gulosa*).
Insects are masticated and
fed to larvae. Between work
schedules, the adults feed
on nectar, honeydew and
sap flows.

RIGHT A female blue-banded mortar bee (*Amegilla pulchra*) deeply probes flower nectaries. These bees live in tunnels excavated in hard soil or in soft mortar between the bricks of buildings. The larvae are housed in wax-lined cells, each provided with beebread—dry pellets of pollen and honey.

BEES
order Hymenoptera:
suborder Apocrita
superfamily Apoidea

All bees are stout-bodied sphecoids, having evolved from the stoutly-built sand wasps (superfamily Sphecoidea). Bees can be distinguished from wasps by their branched body hairs, which gives them their furry look, while wasps have single hairs, if any.

Though bees are usually associated with hives and honey, and are thought of as social insects, most species are solitary, and behave like solitary wasps. Apart from the honey bee (*Apis mellifera*), the bees dealt with here are native to Australia, and most lack a sting.

BELOW A female green carpenter bee (*Lestis bombylans*) on crab apple blossom (*Malus sylvestris*). This species is similar to *L. aerata,* but is not as golden-green. Nests are constructed in dead and dying flower stems of *Leptospermum,* grasstrees and other plants, which are hollowed out and divided into separate cells.

As far as flowers are concerned, bees only exist to pollinate them. However, bees pay little attention to any sparsely flowering plant species and visit whatever is available in any given habitat. As a bee collects nectar, it is dusted with pollen which it unknowingly transfers to other flowers of the same species, thereby fertilising them. Australian native bees feed mainly on nectar from species of the family Myrtaceae, which includes the eucalypts, angophoras, melaleucas and callistemons.

All bees supply pollen, nectar or plant material to their young, and their food store—honey—is also an important food for humans.

Carpenter bees
Carpenter bees (family Anthophoridae–Xylocopinae) have long tongues. Pollen-gathering hairs (named scopa) are located on the femoral segments of their hindlimbs. With a body length of 7 mm–25 mm and a wingspan of up to 45 mm, they are among the largest and most colourful of the bees. *Xylocopa* species are very hairy and are often iridescent in colouring.

Brood tunnels can extend to 300 mm in length and are made in solid wood by female carpenter bees. The noise of their chewing can be heard from several metres away. They also construct their nests within the dying flower stems of grass trees, *Xanthorrhoea australis*, or inside the dead branches of other plants.

This family contains the genera *Thyreus* and *Nomada* in the subfamily Nomadinae, known as cuckoo bees. These bees raise their young, as their name suggests, in the nests of other bees, especially of smooth-bodied bees (family Halictidae) and other ground-nesting bees.

Hive bees
The hive bees (family Apidae) include the highly social bees. They are long-tongued, have a body length of 5 mm–15 mm, a wingspan of up to 25 mm, and have hind tibiae lacking apical spurs.

Hive bees include honey bees. More has probably been written about the honey bee than any other insect. With their highly efficient, productive colonies, these bees have reached the highest forms of social life among insects.

Burrowing bees
Burrowing bees (family Anthophoridae, subfamily Anthophorinae), also known as mortar bees, are mostly hairy, medium to large insects, with a body

length of 7 mm–20 mm and a wingspan of up to 35 mm. Typically, they have modified hindlimbs used for gathering pollen. Many *Amegilla* species have banded abdominal markings in a bright, iridescent blue hue. Burrowing bees generally build their nests underground, excavating them in soil. They collect pollen and nectar to feed the larvae and it is stocked within a paper-lined, oval-shaped cavity at the very base of the burrow.

Smooth-bodied bees

These bees (family Halictidae) are cosmopolitan, small to medium-sized, with a body length of up to 15 mm and a wingspan up to 20 mm. They are dark, often iridescent, and have short, pointed tongues. Their forelegs and middle-legs are adapted for collecting pollen.

Burrows are irregularly shaped and built close together, either in the ground or in decaying

timber. As larvae food, the bees carry pollen to their nest-site, which is in the form of large balls. One egg is laid on top of each moist pollen ball; these are stored in paper-lined chambers that branch off the main shaft of their burrows.

Leaf-cutting bees

Leaf-cutting bees (family Megachilidae) are all solitary bees, ranging in body length from 7 mm–25 mm. They have long, slender tongues, and the back of the abdomen is modified for gathering pollen.

Many species form their nests by using leaf fragments, particularly from rose-related plants, which are carefully cut to shape using their strong, sharp mandibles. These leaf fragments are then carried to holes in tree trunks, rock crevices or into the soil or rotting timber. The holes are then filled with a succession of neat cup-shaped cells.

ABOVE A European honey bee feeding on nectar of a wild fennel flower (*Foeniculum vulgare*). Brought to Australia from England in 1822, it is the only bee that leaves its sting behind after puncturing the flesh. In spite of their potent tail sting, honey bees are heavily preyed upon by dragonflies, assassin bugs, mantids, robber flies, scorpion flies, spiders and birds.

COMMON NAME	MAJOR GROUP CLASSIFICATION	IN THE WORLD		IN AUSTRALIA	
		FAMILIES	SPECIES	FAMILIES	SPECIES
PSEUDO INSECTS					
Springtails	order Collembola	20	6000	14	1630
Proturans	order Protura	4	500	3	30
Diplurans	order Diplura	9	800	5	31
PRIMITIVE WINGLESS INSECTS—APTERYGOTES					
Archaeognaths (Bristletails)	order Archaeognatha	2	350	1	7
Silverfish	order Thysanura	4	370	2	28
PRIMITIVE WINGED INSECTS—EXOPTERYGOTES					
Mayflies	order Ephemperoptera	23	2500	9	84
Dragonflies and Damselflies	order Odonata				
Damselflies	suborder Zygoptera	19	1660	11	107
Dragonflies	suborder Anisoptera	7	3340	6	195
Stoneflies	order Plecoptera	15	2000	4	196
Cockroaches	order Blattodea	6	4000	5	426
Termites	order Isoptera	7	2300	5	348
Praying Mantids	order Mantodea	8	1800	3	162
Earwigs	order Dermaptera	10	1800	7	63
Katydids, Crickets and Grasshoppers	order Orthoptera				
Katydids and Crickets	suborder Ensifera	10	9000	8	1806
Short-horned Grasshoppers and allies	suborder Caelifera	18	11 000	6	1021
Stick Insects and Leaf Insects	order Phasmatodea	3	2500	2	150
Web-spinners	order Embioptera	8	200	3	65
Bark-lice and allies	order Psocoptera	35	3000	26	299
Animal-lice and allies	order Phthiraptera	16	3000	14	255
Bugs, Cicadas and allies	order Hemiptera				
Aphids, Mealy Bugs, Scale and Gall-forming Insects and allies	suborder Sternorrhyncha	23	12 115	16	1054
Cicadas*	suborder Auchenorrhyncha	2	2250	2	252
Tree Hoppers, Leaf Hoppers and Froghoppers	suborder Auchenorrhyncha	9	25 175	6	844
Lantern Flies and Plant Hoppers	suborder Auchenorrhyncha	20	8919	14	436
Water-bugs and allies	suborder Heteroptera	20	2791	15	229
Assassin Bugs	suborder Heteroptera	1	5000	1	300
Plant Bugs	suborder Heteroptera	13	10 800	7	806
Shield-bugs	suborder Heteroptera	29	14 770	23	727
Thrips	order Thysanoptera	8	4500	4	422
MODERN WINGED INSECTS—ENDOPTERYGOTES					
Alderflies and Dobsonflies	order Megaloptera	2	300	2	26
Lacewings	order Neuroptera	19	5000	14	623
Beetles and Weevils	order Coleoptera				
Oldest surviving beetles	suborder Arachostemata	3	200	2	10

COMMON NAME	MAJOR GROUP CLASSIFICATION	IN THE WORLD		IN AUSTRALIA	
		FAMILIES	SPECIES	FAMILIES	SPECIES
Minute aquatic beetles	suborder Myxophaga	4	100	1	2
Ground, Tiger, Diving and Whirligig Beetles	suborder Adephaga	9	45 000	7	2733
Water Beetles and allies	suborder Polyphaga	4	2000	2	360
Rove-beetles, Clerids and Ladybirds	suborder Polyphaga	3	40 000	3	2250
Scarabaeoid Beetles	suborder Polyphaga	11	50 000	7	3360
Click, Soft-winged and Soldier Beetles	suborder Polyphaga	16	20 000	8	1397
Jewel Beetles	suborder Polyphaga	1	15 000	1	1200
Darkling, Longicorn and Leaf beetles	suborder Polyphaga	3	76 000	3	5700
Weevils (snout beetles)	suborder Polyphaga	11	65 300	6	6640
Stylops	order Strepsiptera	9	532	6	159
Scorpion-flies (hanging flies)	order Mecoptera	9	500	5	27
Fleas	order Siphonaptera	16	2380	9	88
Flies	order Diptera				
Craneflies	suborder Nematoicera	3	12 000	3	716
Mosquitoes, Midges and allies	suborder Nematoicera	8	5800	8	756
March Flies and allies	suborder Brachycera	11	3500	1	243
Robber Flies and Bee-flies	suborder Brachycera	2	7000	2	1031
Hoverflies and allies	suborder Brachycera	2	2000	2	199
Fruit Flies and Vinegar Flies	suborder Brachycera	4	4000	2	382
House Flies, Bush Flies, Blowflies and Flesh-flies	suborder Brachycera	4	12 780	4	929
Tachinid Flies	suborder Brachycera	1	8200	1	542
Caddis-flies	order Trichoptera	43	7000	25	478
Moths and Butterflies	order Lepidoptera				
Oldest surviving moths	suborder Zeugloptera	9	9	9	9
Swift Moths and allies	suborder Glossata	5	500	3	154
Case Moths and allies	suborder Glossata	1	1325	1	353
Wood Moths and allies	suborder Glossata	3	500	2	205
Cup Moths and allies	suborder Glossata	9	1235	4	227
Geometrid Moths	suborder Glossata	1	13 700	1	2310
Butterflies and Skippers	suborder Glossata	5	20 000	5	397
Emperor, Silk and Anthelid Moths	suborder Glossata	14	3068	6	245
Hawk Moths	suborder Glossata	1	850	1	65
Noctuid Moths and allies	suborder Glossata	9	35,800	7	2676
Sawflies, Wasps, Ants and Bees	order Hymenoptera				
Sawflies and Wood Wasps	suborder Symphyta	14	2100	6	176
Hatchet-bodied Wasps and allies	suborder Apocrita	3	1050	3	233
Ichneumon Wasps and Braconid Wasps	suborder Apocrita	3	100 800	2	2044
Chalcidoid Wasps	suborder Apocrita	21	100 000	20	3646
Hunting and Sand Wasps and allies	suborder Apocrita	3	12 000	3	1000
Velvet Ants and Flower Wasps	suborder Apocrita	2	6500	2	1250
Mason Wasps and Paper-nest Wasps	suborder Apocrita	1	800	1	369
Ants	suborder Apocrita	1	15 000	1	3000
Bees	suborder Apocrita	10	40 000	7	1652

FOOTNOTES

p262   *oldest surviving cicadas are Australian.

p263   The figures given in this table for worldwide totals are provided as a guide only and as a comparison with the Australian figures.

There are thought to be at least 10 million insect species in the world, including an estimated 140 000 species in Australia.

In the compiling of this list of families in Australia, the CSIRO publication *The Insects of Australia* has been used as the basis for the classification and current information on species numbers for Australian insects, which appears to the right of each family.

PSEUDO INSECTS

Springtails—Class Collembola
Neanuridae 220
Odontellidae 60
Brachystomellidae 70
Hypogastruridae 35
Onychiuridae 20
Isotomidae 300
Entomobryidae 300
Paronellidae 70
Cyphoderidae 30
Oncopoduridae (root-feeding) 5
Tomoceridae 50
Neelidae 20
Sminthuridae (globular
  springtails) 400
Dicyrtomidae 50

Proturans—Class and Order Protura
Eosentomidae 9
Protentomidae 1
Acerentomidae 20

Diplurans—Class and Order Diplura
Campodeidae 10
Projapygidae 2
Japygidae 12
Heterojapygidae 4
Parajapygidae 3

PRIMITIVE WINGLESS INSECTS

Archaeognaths—Subclass and Order Archaeognatha
Meinertellidae 7

Silverfish—Subclass Dicondylia: Order Thysanura
Nicoletiidae (silverfish) 12
Lepismatidae (firebrats) 16

EXOPTERYGOTES

Mayflies—Order Ephemeroptera
Siphlonuridae 1
Baetidae 13
Oniscigastridae 3
Ameletopsidae 3
Coloburiscidae 3
Leptophlebiidae 54
Ephemerellidae 1
Caenidae 5
Prosopistomatidae 1

Damselflies—Order Odonata
Suborder Zygoptera
Hemiphlebiidae 1
Coenagrionidae 30
Isostictidae 14
Protoneuridae 11
Lestidae 14
Lestoideidae 2
Megapodagrionidae 21
Synlestidae 7
Amphipterygidae 5
Calopterygidae 1
Chorocyphidae 1

Dragonflies—Order Odonata
Suborder Anisoptera
Aeshnidae 43
Gomphidae 38
Neopetaliidae 2
Petaluridae 4
Corduliidae 53
Libellulidae 55

Stoneflies—Order Plecoptera
Eustheniidae 15
Austroperlidae 9
Gripopterygidae 143
Notonemouridae 29

Cockroaches—Order Blattodea
Blattidae (chiefly winged forms) 209
Polyphagidae 5
Nocticolidae 2
Blattellidae 140
Blaberidae (chiefly wingless forms) 70

Termites—Order Isoptera
Mastotermitidae (northern termites) 1
Kalotermitidae (drywood termites) 46
Termopsidae (dampwood termites) 5
Rhinotermitidae (subterranean termites) 30
Termitidae (magnetic termites; allies) 266

Praying Mantids—Order Mantodea
Amorphoscelidae (small cryptic
  mantids) 45
Hymenopodidae 1
Mantidae (typical mantid forms) 116

Earwigs—Order Dermaptera
Pygidicranidae 7
Anisolabidae 11
Labiduridae 15
Apachyidae 3
Spongiphoridae 15
Chelisochidae 8
Forficulidae 4

Katydids, Crickets and Short-horned Grasshoppers—Order Orthoptera

Suborder Ensifera
Cooloolidae (cooloola crickets) 3
Stenopelmatidae (king crickets) 15
Gryllacrididae (tree crickets) 125
Rhaphidophoridae (camel crickets) 30
Tettigoniidae (katydids, bush-crickets) 900
Gryllidae (true crickets) 715
Myrmecophilidae (ant crickets) 6
Gryllotalpidae (mole crickets) 12

Suborder Caelifera
Eumastacidae (monkey locusts) 200
Pyrgomorphidae (stick locusts) 24
Acridiidae (locusts) 712
Tetrigidae (grouse locusts) 70
Tridactylidae (femur crickets) 9
Cylindrachetidae (mole locusts) 6

Stick and Leaf Insects (Phasmatids)—Order Phasmatodea
Phasmatidae (stick insects) 95
Phylliidae (leaf insects) 55

Web-spinners—Order Embioptera
Notoligotomidae 6
Australembiidae 32
Oligotomidae 27

Bark-lice and Allies—Order Psocoptera
Lepidopsocidae 25
Trogiidae (bark-lice and booklice) 9
Psoquillidae 1
Psyllipsocidae 3
Liposcelidae (bark-lice and booklice) 15
Pachytroctidae 3
Sphaeropsocidae 1
Amphientomidae 2
Epipsocidae 1
Caeciliidae 30
Stenopsocidae 1
Amphipsocidae 4
Lachesillidae 3
Ectopsocidae 25
Peripsocidae 20
Calopsocidae 2
Pseudocaeciliidae 20
Trichopsocidae 1
Archipsocidae 2
Elipsocidae 10
Philotarsidae 30
Mesopsocidae 1
Hemipsocidae 4
Psocidae 60
Psilopsocidae 1
Myopsocidae 25

Animal-lice and Allies—Order Phthiraptera
Boopiidae (dog and kangaroo-lice and allies) 49
Gyropidae 2
Laemobothriidae 4
Menoponidae (poultry-chewing lice) 50
Ricinidae 2
Philopteridae (feather-chewing lice) 117
Trichodectidae (mammal-chewing lice) 6
Echinophthiriidae 2
Haematopinidae (wrinkled-sucking lice) 5
Hoplopleuridae (rabbit-lice) 7
Linognathidae (smooth-sucking lice) 6
Pediculidae (human-lice) 1
Polyplacidae 3
Phthiridae 1

Order Hemiptera

Aphids, Gall-forming, Scale insects, Mealy Bugs and Allies Suborder Sternorrhyncha
Psyllidae (lerp insects) 330
Calophyidae (gall insects) 3
Phacopteronidae (gall insects) 3
Homotomidae (fig psyllids, gall insects) 3
Carsidaridae (star psyllids) 4
Triozidae (gall-forming insects) 36
Aleyrodidae (whiteflies) 31
Aphididae (aphids) 157
Adelgidae (pine aphids) 3
Phylloxeridae (gall aphids) 3
Margarodidae (mealy bugs) 40
Ortheziidae (mealy bugs) 3
Pseudococcidae (mealy bugs) 240
Eriococcidae (gall-forming insects) 172
Dactylopiidae (cochineal insects) 5
Asterolecaniidae (scale insects) 25
Cerococcidae (scale insects) 5
Lecanodiaspididae (scale insects) 22
Coccidae (scale insects) 78
Kerriidae (lac insects) 7
Conchaspididae (scale insects) 1
Halimococcidae (scale insects) 2
Diaspididae (scale insects) 240

Cicadas, Tree Hoppers, Leaf-hoppers and Allies—Suborder Auchenorrhyncha
Tettigarctidae (cicadas) 2
Cicadidae (cicadas) 250
Cercopidae (froghoppers) 9
Aphrophoridae (froghoppers) 12
Machaerotidae (froghoppers) 10
Cicadellidae (leaf-hoppers) 664
Eurymelidae (tree hoppers) 92
Membracidae (horned tree hoppers) 57
Delphacidae (plant hoppers) 64
Cixiidae (plant hoppers) 42
Meenoplidae (plant hoppers) 10
Fulgoridae (lantern flies) 21
Achilidae (plant hoppers) 24
Derbidae (plant hoppers) 49
Dictyopharidae (plant hoppers) 10
Tropiduchidae (plant hoppers) 7
Issidae (plant hoppers) 29
Flatidae (plant hoppers) 96
Nogodinidae (plant hoppers) 8
Eurybrachyidae (broad-flat plant hoppers) 44
Lophopidae (plant hoppers) 3
Ricaniidae (plant hoppers) 29

Aquatic and Semi-aquatic Bugs, Plant Bugs, Shield-bugs and allies—Suborder Heteroptera
Peloridiidae (wet-moss bugs) 5
Enicocephalidae (leaf litter bugs) 28
Aenictopecheidae (leaf litter bugs) 2
Ceratocombidae (moisture-bugs) 4
Dipsocoridae (moisture-bugs) 24
Schizopteridae (moisture-bugs) 60
Mesoveliidae (slender water-bugs) 4
Hebridae (leaf litter bugs) 7
Hydrometridae (water measuring bugs) 8
Hermatobatidae (marine bugs) 3
Veliidae (surface water bugs) 39
Gerridae (water-striders) 32
Leptopodidae (slender stream-bugs) 2
Omaniidae (coral-bugs) 1
Saldidae (shore-bugs) 16
Nepidae (water scorpions) 10
Belostomatidae (fish-killer bugs) 4
Ochteridae (saline-lake bugs) 8
Gelastocoridae (toad bugs) 23
Corixidae (water-boatmen) 31
Naucoridae (small toe-biters) 8
Notonectidae (back-swimming bugs) 40
Pleidae (back-swimmers) 4
Anthocoridae (flower bugs) 24
Cimicidae (bed bugs) 1
Polyctenidae (bat bugs) 2
Nabidae (predacious bugs) 20
Miridae (dimpling bugs) 600
Tingidae (lace bugs) 148
Thaumastocoridae 11
Reduviidae (assassin bugs) 300
Aradidae (flat bugs, bark bugs) 175
Termitaphididae 1
Idiostolidae 3
Piesmatidae 4
Colobathristidae (linear bugs) 1
Berytidae (stilt-legged bugs) 7
Lygaeidae (seed bugs, chinch bugs) 401
Largidae 7
Pyrrhocoridae (stainer bugs) 12
Stenocephalidae 2
Hyocephalidae 2
Coreidae (leaf-footed bugs) 57
Alydidae (pod-sucking bugs) 9
Rhopalidae (scentless plant bugs) 6
Urostylidae (shield-bugs) 1
Plataspididae (shield-bugs) 16
Cydnidae (burrowing bugs) 43

Acanthosomatidae 52
Lestoniidae (shield-bugs) 2
Tessaratomidae (stinkbugs) 15
Scutelleridae (jewel bugs) 26
Dinidoridae (curcurbit, pumpkin bugs) 3
Pentatomidae (stinkbugs) 391

Thrips—Order Thysanoptera

Merothripidae 3
Aeolothripidae 24
Thripidae 128
Phlaeothripidae (tube thrips) 267

ENDOPTERYGOTES

Alderflies and Dobsonflies—Order Megaloptera

Sialidae (alderflies) 4
Corydalidae (dobsonflies) 22

Lacewings—Order Neuroptera

Coniopterygidae (powder-winged lacewings) 50
Ithonidae (hairy-winged lacewings) 14
Osmylidae (broad-winged lacewings) 40
Neurorthidae (delicate lacewings) 2
Sisyridae (sponge-flies) 16
Berothidae (berothrid lacewings) 30
Mantispidae (mantisflies) 45
Hemerobiidae (brown lacewings) 35
Chrysopidae (green lacewings) 55
Psychopsidae (silky lacewings) 13
Nymphidae (large lacewings) 23
Myrmeleontidae (ant lion lacewings) 250
Ascalaphidae (owl flies) 40
Nemopteridae (spoon-winged lacewings) 10

Beetles and Weevils—Order Coleoptera

Suborder Archostemata

Ommatidae (oldest-surviving beetles) 4
Cupedidae (oldest-surviving beetles) 6

Suborder Myxophaga

Microsporidae (minute shiny beetles) 2

Suborder Adephaga

Superfamily Caraboidea
Rhysodidae (black shiny beetles) 8
Carabidae (ground beetles and tiger beetles) 2500
Haliplidae (boat-shaped beetles) 5
Hygrobiidae (stout oval beetles) 3
Noteridae (diving beetles) 5
Dytiscidae (predacious diving beetles) 185
Gyrinidae (whirligig beetles) 25

Suborder Polyphaga

Superfamily Hydrophiloidea
Hydrophilidae (small water beetles) 175
Histeridae (carrion water beetles) 185

Superfamily Staphylinoidea
Hydraenidae (algae beetles) 55
Ptiliidae (minute water beetles) 75
Leiodidae (spiny-legged beetles) 135
Scydmaenidae (small-waisted beetles) 300
Silphidae (carrion-burying beetles) 3
Staphylinidae (rove-beetles) 1600
Pselaphidae (elongated beetles) 900
Superfamily Eucinetoidea
Scirtidae (ovoid compacted beetles) 70
Eucinetidae (small fusiform beetles) 10
Clambidae (minute oval beetles) 20
Superfamily Scarabaeoidea
Lucanidae (stag-beetles) 85
Passalidae (bess beetles) 40
Trogidae (carcass beetles) 53
Geotrupidae (underground scarabs) 140
Ceratocanthidae (round beetles) 2
Hybosoridae (curved-mandible beetles) 40
Scarabaeidae (scarabs and chafers) 3000
Superfamily Dascilloidea
Dascillidae (serrated antennae) 2
Rhipiceridae (flabellate antennae) 13
Superfamily Buprestoidea
Buprestidae (jewel beetles) 1200
Superfamily Byrrhoidea
Byrrhidae (pill beetles) 40
Elmidae (air-bubble beetles) 150
Limnichidae (coral beetles) 30
Heteroceridae (mud beetles) 15
Psephenidae (water-penny beetles) 15
Callirhipidae (ribbed beetles) 10
Ptilodactylidae (pubescent beetles) 15
Chelonariidae 1
Superfamily Elateroidea
Rhinorhipidae (deflexed-headed beetles) 1
Brachypsectridae (chinned beetles) 1
Eucnemidae (wedge-headed beetles) 160
Throscidae (pseudo click beetles) 20
Elateridae (click beetles) 800
Lycidae (soft-winged beetles) 240
Lampyridae (fireflies) 25
Cantharidae (soldier beetles) 150
Superfamily Derodontoidea
Derodontidae 1
Superfamily Bostrichoidea
Jacobsoniidae (scale-antennaed beetles) 5
Nosodendridae (convex-ovoid beetles) 3
Dermestidae (museum beetles) 150
Bostrichidae (auger beetles) 60
Anobiidae (spider beetles) 225
Superfamily Lymexyloidea
Lymexylidae (eucalypt pinhole beetles) 10
Superfamily Cleroidea
Trogossitidae (cadelle beetles) 40
Cleridae (predatory beetles) 350
Acanthocnemidae (campfire beetles) 1
Phycosecidae (prognathous-headed beetles) 3
Melyridae (soft-bodied beetles) 300

Superfamily Cucujoidea
Protocucujidae (window-winged beetles) 4
Sphindidae (mould beetles) 8
Nitidulidae (dried-fruit beetles) 300
Rhizophagidae (grass compost beetles) 12
Boganiidae (prominent-jawed beetles) 13
Phloestichidae 12
Silvanidae (grain beetles) 60
Cucujidae 15
Laemophloeidae (flat-grain beetles) 50
Propalticidae 3
Phalacridae (spore-feeding beetles) 100
Hobartiidae (carrion beetles) 2
Cavognathidae (bird-nest beetles) 3
Cryptophagidae (compost beetles) 50
Lamingtoniidae (transverse-banded beetles) 1
Languriidae (subcylindrical-bodied beetles) 30
Erotylidae (mushroom beetles) 50
Biphyllidae (fermentation beetles) 35
Bothrideridae (mould and leaf beetles) 40
Cerylonidae (fungal and spore beetles) 40
Discolomidae (polypore-fungi beetles) 15
Endomychidae (pseudo ladybirds) 50
Coccinellidae (ladybird beetles) 300
Corylophidae (dead vegetation beetles) 60
Lathridiidae (minute mould beetles) 55
Superfamily Tenebrionoidea
Mycetophagidae (hairy fungus beetles) 10
Archeocrypticidae (leaf-litter beetles) 20
Ciidae (large club-antennaed beetles) 120
Melandryidae (wedge-shaped beetles) 50
Mordellidae (pintail beetles) 120
Rhipiphoridae (feather-horned beetles) 60
Colydiidae (sculptured antenna beetles) 120
Monommidae (large-eyed beetles) 1
Zopheridae (ironbark beetles) 50
Chalcodryidae 2
Tenebrionidae (darkling beetles) 1500
Prostomidae (prostomid beetles) 6
Oedemeridae (slender soft-bodied beetles) 85
Meloidae (blister beetles) 60
Mycteridae 20
Pythidae 20
Salpingidae 30
Anthicidae (ant-like beetles) 200
Aderidae 100
Scraptiidae 25
Superfamily Chrysomeloidea
Cerambycidae (longicorn beetles) 1200
Chrysomelidae (leaf beetles) 3000
Superfamily Curculionoidea
Nemonychidae (weevils) 15
Anthribidae (weevils) 150
Belidae (weevils) 175
Attelabidae (weevils) 100

Brentidae (elongated weevils) 200
Curculionidae (elephant weevils) 6000

Stylops—Order Strepsiptera

Mengenillidae 20
Corioxenidae 9
Halictophagidae 40
Myrmecolacidae 22
Elenchidae 3
Stylopidae 65

Scorpion-flies—Order Mecoptera

Nannochoristidae 3
Bittacidae 14
Meropeidae 1
Apteropanorpidae 1
Choristidae 8

Fleas – Order Siphonaptera

Pulicidae (dog, cat, rabbit and human
fleas) 19
Rhopalopsyllidae 4
Hystrichopsyllidae 2
Pygiopsyllidae 41
Stephanocircidae 9
Macropsyllidae 2
Ischnopsyllidae (molossid bat-fleas) 7
Leptopsyllidae (mouse-fleas) 1
Ceratophyllidae (rat and chicken fleas) 3

Flies—Order Diptera

Craneflies, Mosquitoes, Midges, Gnats and
Allies – Suborder Nematoicera
Division Tipulomorpha
Tipulidae (craneflies) 704
Trichoceridae (winter craneflies) 6
Division Tanyderomorpha
Tanyderidae (long-necked craneflies) 6
Division Blephariceromorpha
Blephariceridae (net-winged
midges) 25
Superfamily Culicoidea
Chaoboridae (pseudo mosquitoes) 10
Dixidae (pseudo mosquitoes) 11
Culicidae (mosquitoes) 275
Superfamily Chironomoidea
Chironomidae (midges) 202
Ceratopogonidae (biting midges) 174
Simuliidae (biting black sandflies) 38
Thaumaleidae (small stout midges) 21
Division Psychodomorpha
Psychodidae (moth flies) 115
Division Bibionomorpha
Anisopodidae (mottle-winged gnats) 4
Perissommatidae (winter gnats) 4
Scatopsidae (minute black gnats) 57
Bibionidae (smoky-winged gnats) 32
Cecidomyiidae (gall gnats) 112
Sciaridae (fungus gnats) 61
Mycetophilidae (fungus gnats) 250

Other Flies—Suborder Brachycera
Division Orthorrhapha
Superfamily Tabanoidea
Pelecorhynchidae (non-blood-sucking
flies) 34
Rhagionidae (snipe flies) 54
Athericidae (non-blood-sucking flies) 12
Tabanidae (march flies, horseflies) 243
Stratiomyidae (soldier flies) 92
Xylomyidae (large femora flies) 1
Xylophagidae (slow-flying flies) 4
Nemestrinidae (tangle-vein flies) 52
Acroceridae (bladder flies) 34
Superfamily Asiloidea
Therevidae (stiletto flies) 112
Scenopinidae (window flies) 83
Asilidae (true robber flies) 640
Apioceridae (flower-loving flies) 75
Mydidae (mydas flies) 35
Bombyliidae (bee-flies) 391
Superfamily Empidoidea
Empididae (dance flies) 88
Dolichopodidae (long-legged flies) 320
Division Cyclorrhapha
Superfamily Lonchopteroidea
Lonchopteridae (bristle-headed flies) 1
Superfamily Phoroidea
Ironomyiidae (living relic flies) 2
Platypezidae (smoke/campfire flies) 11
Sciadoceridae 1
Phoridae (scuttle flies) 90
Superfamily Syrphoidea
Pipunculidae (hoverflies) 30
Syrphidae (hoverflies) 169
Superfamily Conopoidea
Conopidae (thick-headed flies) 75
Superfamily Sciomyzoidea
Sciomyzidae (snail-killing flies) 11
Helosciomyzidae (fungus-feeding flies) 8
Coelopidae (kelp flies) 11
Sepsidae (ant-like flies) 16
Chamaemyiidae 12
Lauxaniidae (fungus-feeding flies) 367
Superfamily Diopsoidea
Tanypezidae 3
Psilidae 2
Superfamily Tephritoidea
Lonchaeidae (lance flies) 21
Piophilidae (cheese/skipper flies) 7
Otitidae (oar-winged flies) 4
Platystomatidae (boatmen flies) 236
Pyrgotidae (scarab flies) 100
Tephritidae (fruit flies) 135
Superfamily Nerioidea
Pseudopomyzidae (damp-forest flies) 1
Cypselosomatidae (cave flies) 3
Neriidae (banana-stalk flies) 2
Micropezidae (stilt-legged flies) 18
Superfamily Heleomyzoidea
Heleomyzidae (sun flies) 67

Sphaeroceridae (dung, heel flies) 60
Chyromyidae (yellow and black flies) 3
Superfamily Opomyzoidea
Clusiidae (wet-forest flies) 29
Odiniidae (wet-forest flies) 3
Agromyzidae (leaf-miner flies) 150
Fergusoninidae (eucalyptus flies) 25
Xenasteiidae 2
Carnidae 1
Superfamily Asteioidea
Neurochaetidae (upside-down flies) 3
Periscelididae 13
Teratomyzidae (fern flies) 24
Aulacigastridae 7
Asteiidae 6
Anthomyzidae 1
Superfamily Ephydroidea
Ephydridae (shore/marsh flies) 85
Curtonotidae (glassy-winged flies) 1
Drosophilidae (vinegar flies) 247
Cryptochetidae (mealybug flies) 4
Superfamily Chloropoidea
Tethinidae 8
Canacidae (beach flies) 9
Milichiidae 16
Chloropidae (grass flies/flit-flies) 300
Superfamily Brauloidea
Braulidae (bee-lice flies) 1
Superfamily Muscoidea
Anthomyiidae (vegetable flies) 9
Fanniidae (lesser houseflies) 11
Muscidae (house flies/carrion flies) 180
Calliphoridae (blowflies/bluebottles) 140
Sarcophagidae (flesh-flies) 67
Tachinidae (parasitic flies) 542
Gasterophilidae (horse bot-flies) 3
Oestridae (bot-flies) 3
Hippoboscidae (louse flies/keds) 30
Streblidae (bat flies) 7
Nycteribiidae (bat flies) 16

Caddisflies—Order Trichoptera

Superfamily Rhyacophiloidea
Hydrobiosidae 57
Glossosomatidae 10
Hydroptilidae 101
Superfamily Hydropsychoidea
Philopotamidae 19
Stenopsychidae 9
Hydropsychidae (moth caddisflies) 27
Polycentropodidae 12
Ecnomidae 57
Psychomyiidae 2
Superfamily Limnephiloidea
Limnephilidae 3
Plectrotarsidae 5
Oeconesidae 1
Tasminiidae 6
Chathamiidae 1
Conoesucidae 21

Antipodoeciidae 1
Helicopsychidae 6
Calocidae 18
Helicophidae 6
Kokiriidae 5
Philorheithridae 13
Odontoceridae 4
Atriplectididae 1
Calamoceratidae 10
Leptoceridae (long-horned caddis-flies) 83

Moths and Butterflies— Order Lepidoptera
Suborder Zeugloptera
Superfamily Micropterigoidea
  Micropterigidae (oldest surviving moths) 9
Suborder Aglossata
Superfamily Agathiphagoidea
  Agathiphagidae (kauri moths) 1
Suborder Glossata
Infraorder Lophocoronina
Superfamily Lophocoronoidea
  Lophocoronidae 6
Infraorder Exoporia
Superfamily Hepialoidea
  Palaeosetidae 2
  Anomosetidae 1
  Hepialidae (swift moths, ghost moths) 151
Infraorder Heteroneura
Superfamily Nepticuloidea
  Nepticulidae 250
  Opostegidae 80
Superfamily Incurvarioidea
  Heliozelidae 45
  Adelidae 28
  Incurvariidae (leaf-cutter moths) 110
Superfamily Palaephatoidea
  Palaephatidae 30
Series Ditrysia
Superfamily Tineoidea
  Psychidae (case moths) 353
  Eriocottidae 1
  Tineidae (clothes moths and allies) 440
  Roeslerstammiidae 42
  Galacticidae (web moths) 10
  Bucculatricidae 28
  Douglasiidae 1
  Gracillariidae (leaf-blotch miners) 450
Superfamily Yponomeutoidea
  Yponomeutidae (ermine moths) 60
  Argyresthiidae 1
  Plutellidae 78
  Glyphipterigidae 240
  Heliodinidae 4
  Lyonetiidae (leaf-mining moths) 160
Superfamily Gelechioidea
  Oecophoridae (house moths and allies) 5550
  Batrachedridae 50

Hypertrophidae 200
Depressariidae 120
Coleophoridae (case-bearing moths) 30
Elachistidae 30
Agonoxenidae 1
Ethmiidae 14
Blastobasidae 25
Cosmopterigidae 850
Gelechiidae 1580
Lecithoceridae 205
Scythrididae 35
Superfamily Cossoidea
  Cossidae (wood moths/goat moths) 202
  Dudgeoneidae 3
Superfamily Tortricoidea
  Tortricidae (leaf-rollers) 1230
Superfamily Castnioidea
  Castniidae (sun moths) 45
Superfamily Sesioidea
  Brachodidae 45
  Sesiidae (clear-winged moths) 19
  Choreutidae (triangular-winged moths) 26
Superfamily Drepanoidea
  Zygaenidae (foresters) 56
  Limacodidae (cup moths) 115
  Epipyropidae 16
  Cyclotornidae 40
Superfamily Immoidea
  Immidae 20
Superfamily Copromorphoidea
  Copromorphidae 18
  Carposinidae (small fruit moths) 108
Superfamily Epermenioidea
  Epermeniidae 30
Superfamily Alucitoidea
  Tineodidae 14
  Alucitidae (many-plume moths) 20
Superfamily Pterophoroidea
  Pterophoridae (plume moths) 40
Superfamily Hyblaeoidea
  Hyblaeidae (beak-mouthed moths) 5
Superfamily Thyridoidea
  Thyrididae 81
Superfamily Pyraloidea
  Pyralidae 1670
Superfamily Geometroidea
  Geometridae (loopers) 2310
Superfamily Drepanoidea
  Drepanidae (hook-tipped moths) 13
Superfamily Uranioidea
  Uraniidae (day-flying moths) 36
Superfamily Hesperioidea
  Hesperiidae (skippers) 122
Superfamily Papilionoidea
  Papilionidae (swallowtail butterflies) 18
  Pieridae (whites, sulphurs, jezebels) 32
  Nymphalidae (admirals, browns) 85
  Lycaenidae (blues, coppers, hairstreaks) 140

Superfamily Bombycoidea
  Lasiocampidae (snout moths) 90
  Anthelidae 121
  Eupterotidae 14
  Bombycidae (silk moths) 3
  Carthaeidae (dryandra moths) 1
  Saturniidae (emperor moths) 16
Superfamily Sphingoidea
  Sphingidae (hawk moths) 65
Superfamily Noctuoidea
  Notodontidae 145
  Thaumetopoeidae (processionary moths) 55
  Lymantriidae (tussock moths) 129
  Arctiidae (tiger moths) 342
  Aganaidae 8
  Herminiidae 40
  Noctuidae (noctuids/semi-loopers) 1957

Sawflies, Wasps, Ants and Bees— Order Hymenoptera
Suborder Symphyta
Superfamily Siricoidea
  Xiphydriidae (wood wasps) 7
  Siricidae (wood wasps) 1
  Orussidae (wood wasps) 11
Superfamily Tenthredinoidea
  Tenthredinidae (common sawflies) 4
  Argidae (sawflies) 13
  Pergidae (sawflies) 140
Suborder Apocrita
Superfamily Stephanoidea
  Stephanidae (sirex parasite) 7
Superfamily Trigonalyoidea
  Trigonalyidae (wasps) 13
Superfamily Megalyroidea
  Megalyridae (wasps) 25
Superfamily Ceraphronoidea
  Ceraphronidae (wasps) 60
  Megaspilidae (wasps) 40
Superfamily Evanioidea
  Evaniidae (hatchet-bodied wasps) 40
  Aulacidae (wasps) 31
  Gasteruptiidae (wasps) 162
Superfamily Ichneumonoidea
  Ichneumonidae (ichneumon wasps) 1244
  Braconidae (braconid wasps) 800
Superfamily Proctotrupoidea
  Monomachidae (wasps) 3
  Diapriidae (wasps) 325
  Heloridae (wasps) 1
  Peradeniidae (wasps) 2
  Austroniidae (wasps) 3
  Proctotrupidae (wasps) 40
Superfamily Platygasteroidea
  Platygasteridae (wasps) 100
  Scelionidae (parasitic wasps) 445
Superfamily Cynipoidea
  Ibaliidae (sirex wasp parasites) 2
  Liopteridae (wasps) 2

Figitidae (wasps) 3
Cynipidae (wasps) 10
Charipidae (wasps) 12
Eucoilidae (wasps) 40
Superfamily Chalcidoidea
  Mymarommatidae 3
  Chalcididae (chalcid wasps) 250
  Leucospidae (wasps) 11
  Eurytomidae (seed chalcids) 150
  Torymidae (wasps) 215
  Ormyridae (wasps) 9
  Agaonidae (fig wasps) 50
  Pteromalidae (dart-tailed wasps) 525
  Perilampidae (wasps) 65
  Eucharitidae (wasps) 97
  Eupelmidae (wasps) 177
  Tanaostigmatidae 8
  Encyrtidae (wax/scale parasitic
    wasps) 600

Aphelinidae (parasitic wasps) 250
Signiphoridae (wasps) 10
Tetracampidae (wasps) 6
Eulophidae (wax/scale parasitic
  wasps) 750
Elasmidae (wasps) 60
Trichogrammatidae 140
Mymaridae (fairy wasps) 270
Superfamily Chrysidoidea
  Scolebythidae (wasps) 2
  Colebythidae (wasps) 2
  Sclerogibbidae (wasps) 3
  Embolemidae (wasps) 4
  Dryinidae (wasps) 90
  Bethylidae (wasps) 100
  Chrysididae (cuckoo or ruby-tailed
    wasps) 76
Superfamily Vespoidea
  Rhopalosomatidae 3

Pompilidae (spider-hunting wasps) 231
Mutillidae (velvet ants) 500
Tiphiidae (flower wasps) 750
Scoliidae (hairy flower wasps) 25
Vespidae (potter, social wasps) 369
Formicidae (ants) 3000
Superfamily Sphecoidea
  Sphecidae (thread-waisted or sand
    wasps) 744
Superfamily Apoidea
  Colletidae (solitary burrowing
    bees) 860
  Stenotritidae (bees) 30
  Halictidae (smooth-bodied bees) 382
  Ctenoplectridae (bees) 1
  Megachilidae (leaf-cutting bees) 171
  Anthophoridae (carpenter and
    burrowing bees) 194
  Apidae (hive bees) 14

Photographic Acknowledgments

All photographs are by Bert Brunet with the exception of the following:
Kathie Atkinson: front cover
Anne Robertson: photograph of the author front flap
David Hain: p89
Shaen Adey/NHIL: p118, 135, 140cr, 143t, 144, 145, 156
Jaime Plaza van Roon/NHIL: p136, 137, 138t, 139
Anthony Johnson/NHIL: p148
Denise Greig/NHIL: p149

NHIL: New Holland Image Library
t = top
c = centre
r = right

Some non-indigenous insects—for instance, longicorn beetles and termites—introduced in the past are now well established in Australia. The problem with introducing exotic species is that they lack natural enemies and can usually establish themselves effectively if undiscovered. Proper inspection at ports of entry into Australia (as laid down in the Principles and Practices of the Australian Quarantine Service) prevents many potentially harmful plants and insects from entering this country.

Other non-indigenous insects that have been accidentally introduced have been found, subjected to control and prevented from establishing themselves in Australia. But there are many others that could have drastic ecological and economic consequences if they were introduced and succeeded in establishing themselves. Some of the more significant of these include the following:

Russian wheat aphid or cereal aphid (*Diuraphis noxia*; superfamily Aphidoidea) can destroy final yields of barley crops totally and wheat crops by as much as much as 80 per cent. This aphid is a major problem in many countries and in recent years it has expanded its range considerably.

spiralling whitefly (*Aleurodicus dispersus*) is already established in Australia and is resistant to all control attempts. Other whiteflies not yet established here are the bayberry whitefly (*Parabemisia myricae*), the ash whitefly (*Siphoninus phillyreae*) and the woolly whitefly (*Aleurothrixus floccosus*). All these species (all family Aleyrodidae) can extensively damage fruit crops and have spread their range of distribution in recent years.

tea bugs (*Helopeltis antonii*, *H. cinchonae*, *H. bradyi* and *H. theivora*; all family Miridae) live on a wide range of crops, greatly disfiguring leaves and fruit. They are known pests of cultivated fruit, cashews, cocoa and tea throughout Asia. There are several undescribed species of native *Helopeltis*.

New Zealand grass grub or grass beetle (*Costelytra zealandica*; family Scarabaeidae) is, during its larval stage, a serious pest of pasture and crop plants throughout New Zealand. The adult beetles can completely defoliate trees, particularly stone-fruit trees during spring and summer months.

colorado potato beetle (*Leptinotarsa decemlineata*; family Chrysomelidae) is a serious pest of potatoes in the USA.

cotton boll weevil (*Anthonomus grandis*; family Curculionidae) is the most costly agricultural pest in the USA, from the damage it does during its larval and adult stages by feeding on cotton.

mango weevil (*Sternochaetus frigidus*; family Curculionidae) is a serious pest in South–East Asia and attacks both cultivated and wild mango fruit. No effective control measures are so far known for dealing with it once it is established.

hession fly (*Mayetiola destructor*; family Cecidomyiidae) is a serious pest of grain crops such as wheat, barley and rye. By means of diapause, the hession fly can withstand unfavourable conditions for lengthy periods.

leaf-mining flies are capable of breeding on a wide range of plants, including cultivated crops, especially chrysanthemums, and do extensive damage to both living flowers and cuttings. There are four known species that must not be allowed into Australia: *Liriomyza trifolii*, *L. huidobrensis*, *L. sativae* and *Amauromyza maculosa* (all family Agromyzidae).

fruit flies are serious pests of fruit and vegetables in many countries. The species involved can be categorised into two main morphological groups, one of which includes the genus *Dacus* and the others of the genera *Anastrepha*, *Ceratitis*, *Epochra*, *Euleia*, *Myrioperdalis*, *Playparea* and *Rhagoletis*—all family Tephritidae.

screw-worm flies (family Calliphoridae). There are several species of screw-worm flies occurring in various regions of the world. However it is the Old World screw-worm fly species *Chrysomya bezziana* of New Guinea that is regarded as being the most serious threat to Australia. The female lays her eggs on fresh wounds of warm-blooded animals (for example, sheep and cattle). After hatching, the larvae burrow into the underlying tissue. As they feed and grow, the seething mass of maggots emit a strong offensive smell and cause serious damage,

resulting in production losses and death unless the animals are found and treated. The larvae can affect humans as well as domestic livestock, companion animals and various wildlife species.

stem-borers (family Pyralidae) are serious pests of cultivated crops such as sugar-cane, rice, maize, millet, and other cereals in many parts of the world. There are four known species that will attack any or all of these crops: the early-shoot-borer (*Chilo infuscatellus*), the spotted-stalk-borer (*C. partellus*), the gold-fringed-borer (*C. auricilius*) and the stem-borer (*C. terrenellus*). There are also five known species of rice stem-borers (all family Pyralidae), which attack only rice and are serious pests, particularly in Asia and the Middle East. Of these, two have been recorded from northern Australia—the striped rice-borer (*Chilo suppressalis*) and the white rice-borer (*Tryporyza innotata*). The three Asian species are the yellow stem-borer (*Tryporyza incertulas*), the dark-headed borer (*Chilo polychrysa*), and the pink borer (*Sesamia inferens*).

citrus-borer (*Citripestis sagittiferella*; family Pyralidae) severely damages fruit by characteristically riddling it with holes while feeding during its larval stage. The navel orange worm (*Paramyelois trasitella*; family Phycitidae) is a serious pest of walnuts and almonds in parts of the USA. The larva of the banana skipper (*Erionota thrax*; family Hesperiidae), from New Guinea, is a serious pest of banana plantations.

gall wasp (*Bruchophagus muli*; family Eurytomidae) is a native of Papua New Guinea, where it is a serious pest of lime fruit.

sirex woodwasp (*Sirex noctila*; family Siricidae) is an introduced European species which is a major pest of *Pinus radiata* pine plantations. Its larvae feed within the timber and the tree is often killed as a result of the toxic fungus *Sphaeropsis sapinea*, which accompanies the presence of the wasp larvae.

fire ants (*Solenopsis ritcheri* and *S. invicta*; family Formicidae) are serious pests that affect humans, animals and crops in the southern USA and can cause painful stings.

Glossary

abdomen hindmost section of the three distinct parts of the insect body; it houses the organs of reproduction and the digestive and excretory systems.

aedeagus a part of the male genitalia which is inserted into the female during mating.

alate the name for a winged and sexually developed individual ant or termite; alates are produced in enormous numbers during spring and summer, and leave the colony in swarms at dusk, shedding their wings when finding a mate, after which they establish new colonies.

antennae (sing. antenna) pair of sensory organs consisting of a number of sections of varying structure, located on the head of insects.

anterior forward-facing region.

aorta main dorsal blood vessel.

apical/apically the region at or adjacent to the tip of the wing or other structure.

apterous wingless.

apterygotes a group of incects whose ancestors never developed wings (classified as Apterygota).

Arthropoda largest phylum of the animal kingdom; it includes all animals possessing a hardened outer skeleton with jointed limbs—the arthropods.

biodiversity the diversity of all life forms inhabiting marine, aquatic and terrestrial environments.

biological control the deliberate control of damaging animals, or other creatures, and feral plants, such as by the introduction of an insect species that naturally preys on the undesired species.

bristle a short, stiff hair (or similar) rising from a socket of the body or limbs.

bug a member of the insect order Hemiptera, suborder Heteroptera.

caste a particular group within a colony of social insects whose individual members have a distinct body form peculiar to the group they belong to—for instance, reproductive females, reproductive males, soldiers or workers.

cerci (sing. cercus) pair of sensory appendages located at the rear of the abdomen and retained in most exopterygotes (for example, cockroaches, grasshoppers, crickets).

chitin a strong, flexible, fibrous substance which is the basis of the exoskeleton of an insect; it is a protein material resembling cellulose, but combined with added nitrogen.

chrysalis a butterfly pupa.

class the taxonomic category between the phylum and the order.

clypeus protective, sclerotised flap, covering and protecting the mouth.

cocoon protective, silken case formed by some larvae to enclose themselves while undergoing the pupal phase of metamorphosis.

colony individuals living as a group and mutually dependent.

commensal/commensalism two different species living together in harmony; only one benefits positively; the other is unharmed.

compound eye an eye consisting externally of thousands of hexagonal facets (ommatidia), each one serving as a single corneal lens.

coxa (pl. coxae) first basal segment of the legs, forming the attachment points on the underside of the thorax.

cremaster the attachment point of a pupa to the plant or twig.

crochets tiny hooks on the abdominal pro-legs of lepidopterous caterpillars.

crosspollination the transfer of pollen from the male flower parts of one plant to the female flower parts of another or vice versa.

cuticle the outer, non-cellular layer of the insect exoskeleton.

diapause arrested growth and development occurring during unfavourable climatic conditions—to enhance survival.

dimorphism where individuals of the same species may be in two or more distinct forms. When males and females are distinctly different it is called sexual dimorphism.

disruptive colouration highly effective means of camouflage, incorporating patterns that merge with the insect's surroundings.

distal at the far end (opposite of proximal); away from the centre of the body.

distalia collective term used for all sections of antenna apart from the scape and pedicel.

diurnal active during the day (opposite of nocturnal).

dorsal upper surface of an insect's body.

ecdysial lines the indication lines on a larva's head, along which the head capsule splits open at ecdysis.

ecdysis the process of an insect casting off its old cuticle or exuviae—as the insect nymph or larva grows, its cuticle becomes too tight for the insect to expand further. The cuticle is then shed (moulted) to be replaced by a larger cuticle, which had been developing underneath the old one.

ecology the study of animals and plants in relationship to their environment.

ecosystems the populations of flora and fauna and their environment functioning as an interdependent unit.

elytra (sing. elytron) the strongly sclerotised forewings of beetles (order Coleoptera), which form tough, protective shields for the functional membranous hindwings used for flying.

endemic found only in a particular region or country.

pyriform cocoon extremely stiff pear-shaped cocoon constructed by cup moth larvae, serving as protection during the long pupal stage of development.

raptorial describing limbs modified to seize, capture and hold prey—as typically found in the forelegs of praying mantids.

respiration process by which organisms utilise oxygen from the environment to obtain and sustain life-energy.

rostrum the beak-like, anterior portion of the head in certain insects (such as weevils or assassin flies), used for piercing and sucking the tissues of plants and animals.

scale a modified seta which has evolved into the broad and flattened covering of the wings and bodies of certain insects (for example, silverfish, moths and butterflies).

scape the first and, usually, largest section of the antenna.

sclerites the tough, sclerotised plates forming the segments of the exoskeleton.

sclerotin the substance that, when added to chitin, creates the hardened tissue of the insect body—especially the sclerotised material forming parts of the body such as the mandibles, elytra, head capsules, body segments.

scutellum dorsal, shield-shaped sclerite of the metathorax.

segment subdivision of the exoskeleton, each one separated by flexible joints in the body and appendages (fused in areas of the body in certain insects).

serrated the saw-like shape of the antennae of certain beetles and moths, or sawflies' ovipositors.

seta (pl. setae) slender bristle (or 'hair') rising from a socket on the main part of the body or a limb.

sexual dimorphism when the two sexes of the same species differ markedly in appearance or behaviour.

species the taxonomic category below genus, in which is placed animals or plants that share or potentially share a common gene pool.

spermatheca a sperm sac—a specialised receptacle found within the female insect for storing spermatozoa that is received from the male.

spermatophore sperm-package transferred to the female by the male during mating.

spiracle laterally located breathing hole, or external opening, through which air passes to the tracheae.

sternites ventral sclerites of any segment.

sternum (pl. sterna) ventral plate of the thorax, and scalloped to accommodate the coxae.

stridulation production of sounds (as in crickets and grasshoppers, for instance) by rubbing or flexing together highly modified surfaces of the body, wings or limbs.

stylets the elongated mouthparts of hemipterans, which is operated by maxillary and mandibular levers of the siphoning sheath (proboscis); stylets are used to pierce the tissue of plants or the host when feeding.

subimago not sexually mature but fully winged—the first of the two fully winged developmental stages of mayflies, immediately preceding the imago (or adult stage).

suture grooves dividing the segments and sclerites of an insect's body.

symbiosis an intimate association of living organisms, whereby the relationship provides benefits to both partners.

synthorax see pterothorax.

tarsus (pl. tarsi) refers to the distal segments making up the final region of the leg.

taxon (pl. taxa) the name for any one of the hierarchical categories into which organisms are classified—species, order, class, and so on.

taxonomy the description and naming animals and plants, and assigning into categories, as a basis for their classification.

tegmen (pl. tegmina) the forewings of insects in several orders such as Blattodea, Mantodea, Phasmatodea.

tegula (pl. tegulae) a small scale-like basal plate, which hinges between the base of the forewing and the wing's operating mechanisms.

tergum (pl. terga) dorsal area of any body segment—the dorsal protective plates of the body being usually called the tergal plates.

thorax part of the insect's body that bears the legs and wings. Comprised of three segments—prothorax, mesothorax, metathorax.

tibia (pl. tibiae) the fourth segment of the leg, forming the long shank located between the femur and the tarsus.

timbals the delicate, sound-producing, ribbed membranes situated on either side of the abdominal segment (for example, as found in cicadas).

trachea (pl. tracheae) in insects, one of the tubes conducting air from the outside throughout the interior of the body.

tracheal system the network of fine, internal cuticle-lined tubes carrying oxygen directly to the nerves, muscles and tissues throughout the body, the air-flow being controlled by valves.

trochanter the small, second segment of the leg, situated between the coxa and the femur.

tympanum the name for the hearing organ of many insects, variably located in different insects—on the front limbs, in mole crickets and katydids, for example; on the thorax between the hindlegs, in praying mantids; on the wings, in lacewings and many moths; ventrally, on the first abdominal segment, in cicadas.

vein a structural wing strut, often tubular, containing a trachea and haemolymph.

venation the branching arrangement of veins structuring insect wings (or plant leaves), often used to classify insects into families and species.

ventral the underside or lower surface of an insect's body.

viviparous where eggs hatch within the female and the female lays young larvae.

Bibliography

Beattie, A J, ed. 1995. *Living Wealth: Australia's Biodiversity*, Reed, Chatswood.

Bradstock, R A, 1995. *Conserving Biodiversity: threats and solutions*, Surrey Beatty & Sons in association with NSW NPWS, Sydney.

Canard, M, Semeria, Y and New, T R, 1984. *Biology of Chrysopidae*, W. Junk, The Hague, Boston.

Chadwick, C E, 1995. *Entomology in New South Wales 1770-1990: A brief account*, The Society for Insect Studies, Sydney.

Clyne, D, 1998. *Densey Clyne's wildlife of Australia*, Reed New Holland, Frenchs Forest.

Clyne, D, 1996. *How to attract butterflies to your garden*, Kangaroo Press, Kenthurst.

Common, I F B, 1993. *Moths of Australia*, Melbourne University Press, Melbourne.

Common, I F B, 1998. Waterhouse, D F, *Butterflies of Australia*, CSIRO.

CSIRO, Division of Entomology, 1996. *The Insects of Australia: A Textbook for Students and Research Workers*, Melbourne University Press, Melbourne.

Evans, H E, 1964. *Wasp Farm*, Harrap, London.

Ewin, T L, 1983. 'Beetles and other arthropods of the tropical rainforest canopies of Manuas, Brasil, sampled with insecticidal fogging techniques', in S.L. Sutton, T.C. Whitmore, and A.C. Chadwick (eds), *Tropical rainforests: Ecology and Management*, Blackwell Scientific, London.

Ewin, T L, 1988. 'The tropical forest canopy: the heart of biotic diversity', in E.O. Wilson, *Biodiversity*, National Academy of Science Washington DC.

Frazer, F C, 1960. *A Handbook of the dragonflies of Australasia: with keys for the identification of all species*, Royal Zoological Society of New South Wales, Sydney.

Gaston, K J. 'The magnitude of global insect species richness', *Conservation Biology*, vol. 5 (1991), pp. 283–96.

Hadlington, P W and Johnston, J A, 1998. *An introduction to Australian Insects* (rev. edn), NSW University Press, Sydney.

Hammer, P M, 1990. 'Insect abundance and diversity in the Dumoga-Bone National Park, N. Sulawesi', in W J Knight and J D Holloway (eds) *Insects and the Rainforests of Southeast Asia*, Royal Entomological Society, London.

Hardy, B, 1998. *The Australian market basket survey, 1996: a total diet survey of pesticides and contaminants*, Information Australia, Melbourne.

Harrington, R and Stork, N E, 1995. *Insects in a Changing Environment*, Academic Press, London.

Harris, A C, 1987. *Pompilidae (Insects: Hymenoptera)*, Science Information Publishing Centre, DSIR, Auckland.

Harvey, M and Yen, A L, 1997. *Worms to Wasps*, Oxford University Press, Melbourne.

Hawkeswood, T, 1987. *Beetles of Australia*, Angus and Robertson, Sydney.

Horne, P A and Crawford, D J, 1996. *Backyard insects*, Melbourne University Press, Victoria.

Korboot, K, 1961. *Observations of the life histories of the stick insects Acrophylla tessellata, Gray and Extatosoma tiaratum*, Macleay, University of Queensland Press, St Lucia.

Lawrence, J F and Briton, E B, 1994. *Australian Beetles*, Melbourne University Press, Melbourne.

McGavin, G C, 1993. *Bugs of the World*, Blandford, Press–Cassell, London.

May, R M. 'How many Species Inhabit the Earth?' *Scientific American* (1992) 267 (4): 18–24.

Moore, B P A, 1980–1992.*Guide to the Beetles of Southeastern Australia*, Australian Entomological Press, Sydney.

Moulds, M, 1990. *Australian Cicadas* NSW University Press, Sydney.

New, T R, 1997. *Butterfly Conservation*, Melbourne Oxford University Press, Melbourne.

New, T R, 1996. *Name that Insect: A Guide to the Insects of Southeastern Australia*. Melbourne Oxford University Press, Melbourne

New, T R, 1988. *Associations between Insects and Plants*, NSW University Press in association with the Australian Institute of Biology, Sydney.

New, T R, 1991. *Insects as Predators*, NSW University Press in association with the Australian Institute of Biology, Sydney.

O'Toole, C, 1995. *An Exploration of the Lives of Insects: Alien Empire*, BBC Worldwide Publishing, London.

Preston–Mafham, K, 1990. *Grasshoppers and Mantids of the World*, Blandford Press–Cassell, London.

Pyke, G H and Balzer, L, 1985. *The effects of the introduced honeybee (Apis mellifera) on Australian native bees*. NSW NPWS Occasional paper, report no. 7, Sydney.

Ramsay, G W, 1990.'Mantodea (Insecta), with a review of aspects of functional morphology and biology', *Fauna of New Zealand Series* no. 19, DSIR Publishing, Wellington.

Rentz, D C F, 1996. *Grasshopper Country*, UNSW Press Sydney.

Shattuck, S O, 1998. *Australian Ants: a guide to the genera*, CSIRO, Collingwood.

Short, K, 1994. *Quick poison slow poison: pesticide risk in the lucky country*, Envirobook, St Albans.

Smithers, C, 1988. *The Handbook of Insect collecting: Their collection, Preparation and Storage*, Angus & Robertson Publishers, United Kingdom.

Suzuki, D, 1998. *Earth Time*, Allen & Unwin, Sydney.

Suzuki, D, 1999. *Naked Ape to Superspecies*, Allen & Unwin, Sydney.

Upton, M S, 1997, A rich and diverse fauna: the history of the Australian National Insect Collection 1926-1991, CSIRO Publishing, Melbourne.

Valentine, P S; photography by C and D Frith, 1998. *Australian tropical butterflies*; Frith & Frith Books, Malanda.

Watson, J A L and Theischinger, H M, 1991. The Australian dragonflies: a guide to the identification, distribution and habits of Australian Odonata, CSIRO, East Melbourne.

Wheeler, Q D. 'Insect Diversity & Cladistic Constraints', *Annals of the Entomological Society, America* (1990), 83: 1031–1047.

Williams, C B, 1964. *Patterns in the Balance of Nature*, Academic, New York.

Williams, G A, 1996. *Hidden Rainforests: Subtropical Rainforests and their Invertebrate Diversity*, UNSW Press, Sydney.

Williams, J B, Harden, G J and McDonald, W J F, 1984. *Trees and shrubs in rainforest of NSW and southern Queensland*, Botany Dept, University of New England, Armidale.

Wooten, A, 1984. *Insects of the World*, Blandford Press, Poole.

Zimmerman, E C, 1994. *Australian Weevils*, CSIRO, Melbourne.

Zborowski, P and Storey, R, 1995. *A Field Guide to Insects in Australia*, Reed, Melbourne.

Index

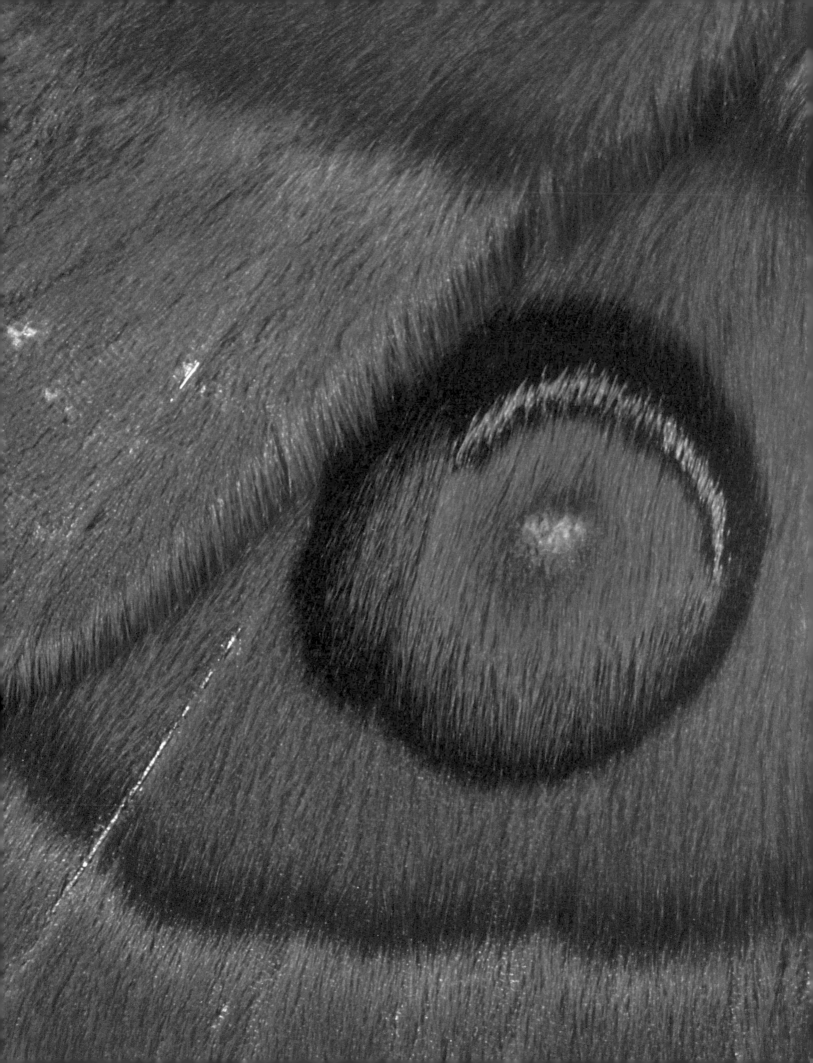